MW01070167

The Gift of the Nile?

The Gift of the Nile?

Ancient Egypt and the Environment

EDITED BY
THOMAS SCHNEIDER AND CHRISTINE L. JOHNSTON

THE EGYPTIAN EXPEDITION
Tucson, Arizona
2020

Cover Image

The Flooded Courtyard of Amenhotep III in the Luxor Temple, albumen photograph by Antonio Beato, c. 1875. Courtesy of the J. Paul Getty Museum, Los Angeles (acc. no. 84.XM.1382.9).

Designed & Typeset by NDpendent Press for The Egyptian Expedition

EgyptianExpedition.org

ISBN: 978-0-9649958-7-1

Copyright 2020 by The Egyptian Expedition and the Authors

All rights reserved. No part of this publication may be reproduced, stored in a retrieval system, or transmitted in any form or by any means, electronic, mechanical, photocopying, recording, or otherwise, without the prior written permission of the publisher.

For Manfred Bietak

ON THE OCCASION OF HIS EIGHTIETH BIRTHDAY

Contents

Authors

Judith Bunbury
St Edmund's College,
University of Cambridge
Mount Pleasant
Cambridge
CB3 OBN
United Kingdom
jmb21@cam.ac.uk

Leesha Cessna
Pacific Christian Academy
Federal Way, WA
United States
lcessna@pacificchristianwa.com

Pearce Paul Creasman
ACOR in Amman, Jordan
P.O. Box 2470
Amman 11181
Jordan
pcreasman@acorjordan.org

Angus Graham
Department of Archaeology and Ancient
    History
Uppsala University
Box 626, 751 26 Uppsala
Sweden
angus.graham@arkeologi.uu.se

Christine Johnston
Assistant Professor of Ancient
    Mediterranean History
Western Washington University
BH 336, 516 High Street
Bellingham, WA 98225
United States
christine.johnston@wwu.edu

Nadine Moeller
Professor of Near Eastern Languages and
    Civilizations
Yale University
320 York St, New Haven, CT 06511
United States
nadine.moeller@yale.edu

Juan Carlos Moreno García
Directeur de Recherche CNRS
UMR 8167 CNRS "Orient & Méditerranée"
Centre de Recherches Egyptologiques de la
    Sorbonne - CRES
Sorbonne Université
1 rue Victor Cousin
75230 Paris Cedex 05
France
jcmorenogarcia@hotmail.com

Joanne Rowland PhD, MA, BA (Hons),
    FSA Scot
Senior Lecturer in Archaeology
School of History, Classics and
    Archaeology
William Robertson Wing, Old Medical
    School, Teviot Place, Edinburgh
EH8 9AG
United Kingdom
Joanne.Rowland@ed.ac.uk

Thomas Schneider
Professor of Egyptology and Near Eastern
    Studies
University of British Columbia, Department
    of Classical, Near Eastern and Religious
    Studies
1866 Main Mall
Vancouver, BC
Canada
V6T 1Z1
thomas.schneider@ubc.ca

Leslie Anne Warden, PhD
Joanne Leonhardt Cassullo Associate
    Professor of Art History and
    Archaeology
Roanoke College, Dept. of Fine Arts
221 College Lane
Salem, VA 24153
United States
warden@roanoke.edu

Acknowledgments and Dedication

The editors are indebted to the Social Sciences and Humanities Research Council of Canada for providing the financial support of the conference *Gift of the Nile? A Symposium and Workshop on Ancient Egypt and the Environment* held at Quest University Canada on April 2, 2017, and at the University of British Columbia on April 3, 2017. Additional financial support was granted by the UBC Hampton Grant through its SPARC program (Support Programs to Advance Research Capacity; special thanks go to Helene Dragatsi for improving the grant proposal). We would like to thank UBC and the Institute of Asian Research for hosting the April 3 conference, Quest University Canada and its former president Peter Englert for hosting the April 2 workshop, the Egyptian Expedition (Pearce Paul Creasman) for publishing the proceedings and the UCLA Encyclopedia of Egyptology (Willeke Wendrich) for in-kind support and for providing a forum for ongoing open-access publications relating to the Egyptian environment. We are thankful to Leesha Cessna, who helped to organize the conference and who prepared an initial bibliographic database relating to the Nile and the environmental history of Egypt.

The editors and authors dedicate this volume to Prof. Dr. Dr. h.c. Manfred Bietak, on the occasion of his 80th birthday. With his 1975 monograph *Tell el-Dab'a II: Der Fundort im Rahmen einer archäologisch-geographischen Untersuchung über das ägyptische Ostdelta*, Manfred Bietak has established a new methodological standard in the reconstruction of historical landscapes in ancient Egypt, and paved the way for the further study of the interface of the Nile and human society in Egyptology. As a leading archaeologist of ancient Egypt and the Near East for the past 50 years, he has shaped and transformed the discipline in a lasting way. The dedication of this volume is a tribute to his lifetime achievements in the field and moreover, the interdisciplinary dialogue that he has fostered beyond the field between the humanities and the natural sciences.

Thomas Schneider and Christine Johnston

Chapter One

From Object to Subject: Towards a New Narrative for the Nile and Water in Ancient Egyptian Civilization

Thomas Schneider

Abstract[1]

According to a famous statement by Herodotos (*Histories*, 2.5.1), Egypt is the "gift of the Nile." Princeton historian Robert Tignor says about this statement in his 2010 *Short History of Egypt*, that it is not the least of the truisms of the Greek historian, understanding it as a reference to the abundance and fecundity of Egypt, and to the Nile as the ultimate cause for the emergence and blossom of Egypt's civilization. Not only is this understanding a misinterpretation of Herodotos, it is also part of an older scholarly narrative that sees the Nile as an object of human activity. This chapter will describe a paradigm shift which, in alignment with the recent "river turn" in historiography and the increased ascription of agency to rivers, sees the Nile as Egypt's "true despot" (to use a term coined by Joseph Manning) and the country as a social cage for its inhabitants. Recent archaeological work has shown to what extent a changing riverscape and variable Nile floods affected settlement and population patterns, agricultural productivity, the economy, and the distribution of power. The Nile must also be seen as the fundamental driver of Egyptian history in its role in the spread of diseases and the level of mortality. Other water events such as torrential rains and flooding have also become obvious in their impact on Egyptian civilization, and can be ascertained by archaeological and historical studies. They all contribute to the need to forge a new historiographical narrative that perceives the Nile and water as the subject and agent of Egyptian society and culture.

According to a famous statement made by Herodotos in his *Histories* (2.5.1), Egypt is a gift of the Nile. In his 2010 *Short History of Egypt*, Princeton historian Robert Tignor says that this statement is not the least of the truisms of the Greek historian.[2] Like myriads of authors, Tignor understands Herodotos' remark as a reference to the abundance and fecundity of Egypt, with the Nile as the ultimate cause for the emergence and blossom of Egypt's civilization. This purported truism, however, might be less true than commonly believed. A recently suggested paradigm shift perceives Egypt not so much as the gracious gift of the river but sees the Nile instead as Egypt's "true despot," and the country as a social cage for its inhabitants, to use an assessment made by Michael Mann in his "The

The Gift of the Nile? Ancient Egypt and the Environment
edited by Thomas Schneider and Christine L. Johnston
Tucson, Arizona: Egyptian Expedition, 2020

FIGURE 1. Inundation Floodplain at Dashur (image courtesy of
Dr. Edouard Lambelet, Lehnert and Landrock).

Sources of Social Power" and resumed more recently by Joseph Manning.[3] This position inverses Karl Wittfogel's 1957 claim about hydraulic civilizations whereby state power would have relied historically on massive irrigation works, a concept refuted conclusively for ancient Egypt as early as 1978 in a study by Wolfgang Schenkel.[4] Manning takes issue with the conventional idea of a centralized Egyptian state under an authoritarian ruler who controlled the economy. Rather, he perceives kingship primarily as a fiscal institution that coordinated local production centres and maintained a state equilibrium within the country's highly fractured topography and society. The variable annual inundation of the Nile affected settlement and population patterns, and created diffused irrigated landscapes with local and socially stratified power structures. In this volatile environmental context, the key to Egypt's economy was the solidarity of the local communities that co-operated for the harvest, with the state being present in the form of the local elites and temples that administered labor, agriculture, and taxes. Beyond the country's economy, the Nile must also be seen as the fundamental driver of Egyptian history in its contribution to the spread of diseases and the level of mortality, its active role in transport and communication, and even its facilitation of military defense and defeat.

While the annual flooding of the Nile (Fig. 1) was a crucial element of the interface of the river and humans from Egypt's prehistoric cultures to the last inundation in 1964, due to the modern damming of the river, other changes in the riverscape would require longer time spans to observe. Geoarchaeological surveys of the Nile valley and delta and select projects of augering in the flood plain have determined the migration of the Nile river within the river valley, and reveal dramatic changes to its riverscape. One example often evoked in the literature is the abandonment of the capital city of Piramses around 1050 BCE—when the Pelusiac branch of the Nile is supposed to have sedimented up—and

Figure 2. Wadi Garawi dam (Sadd al-Kafara) (courtesy of Jean-Luc Frérotte).

the reuse of much of Piramses' stone architecture in the new capital city of Tanis, 40 km to the north.[5]

In addition to the volatility of the river system, scholars have for some 20 years now become more aware of the impact on Egyptian civilization of other water events such as torrential rains and flash floods.[6] Massive rains that occurred in Upper Egyptian Luxor in late 1994 and early 1995 became an incentive for scholars to study the occurrence of such water events in ancient Egypt.[7] For example, the heavy rainfall on November 1–2, 1994, created a 2 m deep flash flood out of the Valley of the Kings that destroyed modern houses and caused damage to the funerary temple of Seti I at Qurna. With regard to ancient Egypt, a sequence of 30 rain events could be ascertained through layers of mud and debris washed into the tomb of Ramses X after its construction was discontinued.[8] Such events can be assumed for all of Egypt's history even though precise evidence for such events will often not exist.[9] Structures such as the Wadi Garawi dam from the late Third and early Fourth Dynasties southeast of modern day Helwan, fulfilled the purpose of flash flood control (Fig. 2).[10]

Events of this kind need to be acknowledged in a modern historiographical reconstruction not only as physical events but as social and cultural occurrences.[11] We would then have to reconstruct Egypt's civilization much more fundamentally as the complex human adaptation to a changing riverscape, the oscillation and systematic periodicities of the Nile flood (Said 1993, 155-169 with an analysis of the records of the Roda Nilometer), and the effects of rain and other environmental events—more so than as the free creation of the beneficiaries of a gift. Interestingly, the much-invoked "truism" of an abundant Egypt being a gift of the river is itself a misinterpretation of Herodotos by later historians and public imagination. The historian makes instead a scientific statement about the fact that the Nile delta and a part of the valley appear to have been sedimented up by the river; this added part of the country is the river's gift to Egypt, and not its fertility and abundance.[12] In his introduction to the recent volume on "Fluvial Landscapes in the Roman World,"[13] Tyler Franconi says that in past scholarship on ancient Rome:

> [t]he social context of rivers in the Roman world has been largely ignored ... Many studies view fluvial landscapes as backdrops to historical events, as passive landscapes controlled by Rome. Rarely are elements of the landscape appreciated as being directly connected to daily life.

Similarly, Egyptology used to situate human life in a static Nilotic landscape, allowing for a narrative in which the humans were the main agents of history. In this narrative, the river was the object of human attention and exploitation, not an active element to which the Egyptians would most often be subjected. I provide two examples. A 2005 conference volume on the topic of water in ancient Egypt[14] focused almost exclusively on the benefits that the Egyptians drew from its water, and how Egypt used water, or related to it, in literature, culture, religion, and ritual.

A recent three volume monograph by Holger Kockelmann[15] gives an exhaustive and — in its philological thoroughness — admirable treatment of the three millennia of religious history of the Egyptian crocodile god Sobek, "the lord of lakes, marshes and watercourses," worshipped mainly in the Fayyum depression with its major lake. However, the study does not systematically correlate the extensive textual sources with scientific evidence about the changing aquatic environment in the lake basin, or the related questions of the habitat, population, and distribution of crocodile species in the Nile Valley. It presents *Crocodylus niloticus Laurenti 1768* as "the animal of Sobek,"[16] despite recent evidence in favour of a different, much less aggressive crocodile species (*Crocodylus suchus*; West African crocodile) that seems to also have inhabited the Nile river in historical times (Fig. 3).[17] This would have been an exemplary case where a most intense interdependence between nature and culture could be studied, where the Egyptians could negotiate more freedom from the social cage than in the Nile Valley, given the lesser reliance of the Fayum on the Nile inundation.

In contrast with Egyptology, there has been an effective "river turn" in historiography within the last 20 years, as a consequence of the rise of environmental history and a new place-sensitive form of historical narrative.[18] Fundamental works that have reshaped the debate here include Richard White's *The Organic Machine: The Re-Making of the Columbia River (1995)*[19] and Mark Cioc's *The Rhine: An Eco-Biography* (2002).[20] In an introduction to a volume on river histories published in 2008, Christof Mauch and Thomas Zeller summarized the new perspective as follows:

> Most historians now discuss rivers in terms of permanent or dialectical interchanges between the dynamics of nature and human intervention ... At the same time, rivers are themselves agents, providers of energy and resources, and a driving force in history.[21]

Adopting for ancient Egypt a historiographical approach that sees the Nile as "Egypt's true despot," in alignment with Joseph Manning's idea, would reconceptualize Egyptian historiography from an environmental angle, and at the same time, reposition Egyptology as a truly interdisciplinary field. Bruce Trigger, the late Canadian anthropologist, Egyptologist, archaeological theorist, and ethnohistorian, once remarked (in the introduction to his

FIGURE 3. *Crocodylus suchus* (West African crocodile), Kom Ombo Crocodile Museum (Image Credit: Fanny Schertzer, CC BY–SA 3.0. https://upload.wikimedia.org/wikipedia/commons/0/0a/Mummified_crocodiles_-_Crocodile_Museum%2C_Kom_Ombo_%282%29.jpg)

Ancient Egypt: A Social History): "Ancient Egypt has proved remarkably resistant to the writing of history which is not traditional in character; which is not, in other words, concerned primarily with the ordering of kings and the chronicling of their deeds"; but he also conceded: "the difficulties of writing 'alternative' histories of Egypt are, however, enormous."[22] The reasons for these difficulties are complex, and are rooted in the history of the discipline, its academic training, and a tradition of academic isolationism. In a recent contribution, Juan-Carlos Moreno García has given a lucid diagnosis of contemporary Egyptology as a "cursed discipline" that makes it, within the disciplines studying ancient civilizations, the "Egyptological exception". Unlike Near Eastern Studies, it maintains, García argues, more interest in spectacular finds than historical or sociological understanding, in description more than analysis, pursuing, as he formulates, the "reactionary utopia" of an "eternal Egypt," an elitist agenda focused on pharaohs and the spiritual rather than society and the materialist.[23]

It is time to give Egyptology an alternative historiographical agenda.[24] I see particular promise in an agenda that places at its core the Nile river and assesses ancient Egyptian institutions as well as social, economic, and cultural phenomena in their dependence on this environment. A first step towards an integration of traditional (mostly textual) methods and scientific data is the volume of proceedings from a 2013 conference at Johannes Gutenberg-Universität Mainz, published in 2017, *The Nile: Natural and Cultural Landscape in Egypt*. It addresses the fact that, despite its obvious core role, "the river as an environmental and cultural factor has been less intensively studied by archaeologists and Egyptologists than might be expected."[25]

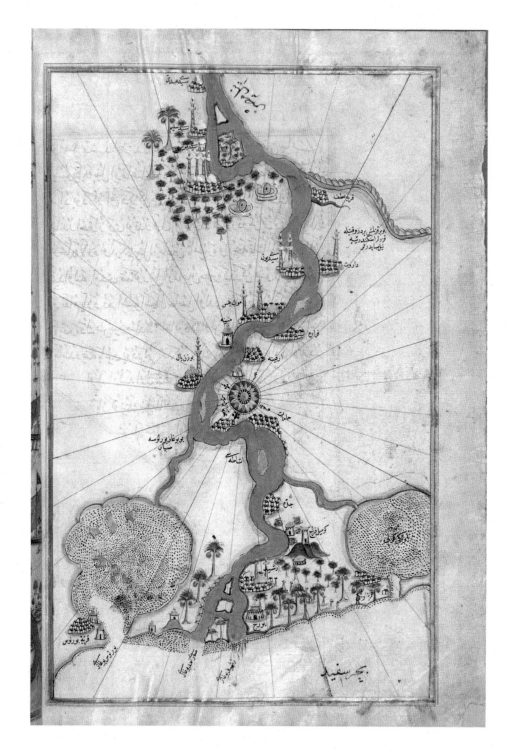

FIGURE 4. Map by Piri Reis of the Nile from the 16th century (Walters Art Museum W.658.304B; Image Credit: Google Art Project. https://upload.wikimedia.org/wikipedia/commons/c/c6/Piri_Reis_-_Map_of_the_River_Nile_From_Its_Estuary_South_-_Google_Art_Project.jpg)

The new historiographical agenda would come at a time when similar approaches have already been adopted for medieval and modern Egypt (Fig. 4). I mention here Alan Mikhail's two environmental histories of Ottoman Egypt (2011, 2017)[26] and Terje Tvedt's eco-political histories of the Nile under British rule and during the post-colonial period (2004, 2009).[27]

As far as antiquity is concerned, first steps to that goal have been taken, particularly for Roman Egypt. Walter Scheidel has produced a standard work *Death on the Nile: Disease and the Demography of Roman Egypt* (2001)[28] that focuses on the interface of the environment in the Nile river system and demography and health, producing a powerful counterbalance to the illusion of an "eternal Egypt." A new study by Katherine Blouin is the first attempt to reconstruct the interplay of society and state in the Nile delta in Roman times within the context of a changing riverscape (*Triangular Landscapes: Environment, Society, and the State in the Nile Delta under Roman Rule*, 2014).[29] In his new analysis of the economy of the Mediterranean basin between the first millennium BCE and the rise of Rome, including Egypt, Joseph Manning has more systematically integrated climate and environmental data.[30]

While the data pertinent to a Nile-centered history of ancient Egypt will only gradually become available, I mention here three examples for a "Nile history" of ancient Egypt from the site of ancient Thebes, where we have geoarchaeological, textual, and archaeological evidence.[31] Thebes rose to political and religious prominence in the early Middle Kingdom, when it was chosen as the cult center of the god Amun, a local god at that time who would become the state god of ancient Egypt throughout the second and first millennia BCE. His temple at Karnak would develop into the largest temple of Egypt, would control a significant part of the economy, own much of the land in Upper Egypt, and play a decisive political role. While earlier reconstructions of the early Middle Kingdom had assumed a topographical situation similar to later times when the entire temple complex was located on the Nile's east bank, recent work by the Karnak Land- and Waterscapes Survey, the Egypt Exploration Society Theban Harbours and Waterscapes Survey and the French Archaeological Institute at Cairo may show that this place goes back to a specific feature of the riverscape in the First Intermediate Period—an alluvial island.[32] In line with their cosmogonical views, the Egyptians could perceive this new island as the first mound that rose from the primeval ocean on the day of creation, and thus built a sanctuary on the island for their creator god Amun. An occurrence of the riverscape of Thebes around the start of the Middle Kingdom provides therefore a precise historical explanation for the origin of a cult and a sacred city that would determine Egypt's history until the end of its civilization.

For the New Kingdom, a secondary course of the Nile that ran very close to the western margin of the floodplain has been identified in recent years, a course that was most likely a natural event (through river avulsion upstream from Thebes).[33] It filled in and was abandoned in the late New Kingdom. The existence of this secondary course has considerable implications for our understanding of Western Thebes—the most important funerary landscape of New Kingdom Egypt with the royal funerary temples and tombs of the kings, queens, and the elite of state. It helps to explain the configuration of the diverse architectural structures, including the unusual fact that Amenophis III's funerary temple was the only one built into the flood plain, and reaching to the water course (Toonen et al. 2019), as well as features of the region's social and economic history during the New Kingdom (Fig. 5).

In this respect, it is significant to note that the proposed historiographical move from a human-centered approach to one that accords historiographical agency to changes of

Figure 5. Lithograph by Louis Haghe after a drawing by David Roberts, "Statues of Memnon at Thebes, during the inundation" (Image Credit: catalog.loc.gov/vwebv/search? searchCode=LCCN&searchArg=2--281869&searchType=1& permalink=y)

the Nile river, as well as other water and environmental events, is consistent with the ancient Egyptian distinction between human and divine agency. While the river Nile itself was never seen by the Egyptians as a deity, the unpredictable annual flooding of the Nile was as much considered divine (as the god Hapy) as were water events such as excessive inundations, heavy rainfall, the revelation of water sources in the desert, or the appearance of new features in the river system (such as the island for the Karnak temple), described in Egyptian as divine "miracles" or displays of divine power.[34]

The distribution of divine and human roles is obvious in the most explicit Egyptian description of a divine water event, the so-called Tempest Stele of the Theban king Ahmose from the early Eighteenth Dynasty, an unusual report about a disastrous torrential rain (Fig. 6).[35] This text describes the occurrence of a massive "tempest of rain" that caused darkness for an extended time period (the precise length is lost in the preserved text) so that the sun could no longer shine (lines 8–10). The text details that houses were destroyed, that bodies of people who had perished were floating in the Nile, and that the noise of the tempest was louder than the rapids of the Nile at Elephantine (lines 10–11). Very unusually for an Egyptian text, the text reports that cemeteries and the pyramid precincts (probably those of the Seventeenth Dynasty on the West Bank) were dramatically affected by the floods (line 17). Importantly, this rainstorm is described as "a manifestation of the power of a god" (line 14), and said to "surpass the power of the great god [Amun] and the wills

FIGURE 6. Recto and Verso of the Tempest Stele (Images courtesy of Sébastien Biston-Moulin)

FIGURE 7. Ramses III before Hapi in Medinet Habu (Image Credit: Janzig/Egypt/Alamy Stock Photo)

of the [other Egyptian] gods." On account of the classifier signs used in the text, it is clear that the god identified here by Ahmose as more powerful than the god Amun and all the Egyptian gods, was the Levantine storm god Seth-Baal, the principal god of Ahmose's opponents who controlled the north of the country—the Hyksos of the Fifteenth Dynasty. Thus, the rain storm was perceived by Ahmose as a massive and destructive sign of divine support of his political opponents, to which the Egyptian gods could not respond. The king sought accountability for this fact from Amun—"gold [the king in full armour] faced gold [the golden statue of the Amun]"—and, after receiving due supplies, set out to restore the Theban region from the inflicted damage.

In light of these and other texts, the motif of the king as a restorer of order may be more than the usually assumed topos: in Egypt's social cage with the Nile as Egypt's "true despot," and a volatile environment, the king's main function may indeed have been to facilitate cohesion and to coordinate resources and people (Fig. 7). Adopting a new historiographical agenda that sees the Nile and the environment as agents of Egypt's history, may thus be an important step to reconstruct the Egyptian past in a fundamentally new way—and also to reposition the discipline of Egyptology as a whole.

Works Cited

Amenta, Alessia, Maria Michela Luiselli, and Maria Novella Sordi, eds. 2005. *L'acqua nell'Antico Egitto: Vita, rigenerazione, incantesimo, medicamento. Proceedings of the First International Conference for Young Egyptologists - Italy, Chianciano Terme, October 15–18, 2003.* Rome: L'Erma du Bretschneider.

Baldi, Marina. 2015. "Exceptional Rainfall over Thebes in Ancient and Present Times: An Analysis of Possible Driving Mechanisms." In *Egyptian Curses.* Vol. 2, *A [sic] Research on Ancient Catastrophes,* edited by Giuseppina Capriotti Vittozzi, 255–264. Rome: CNR Edizioni.

Bietak, Manfred. 2017. "Harbours and Coastal Military Bases in Egypt in the Second Millennium B.C.: Avaris, Peru-nefer, Pi-Ramesse." In *The Nile: Natural and Cultural Landscape in Egypt. Proceedings of the International Symposium held at the Johannes Gutenberg-Universität Mainz, 22 & 23 February 2013,* edited by Harco Willems and Jan-Michael Dahms, 53–70. Bielefeld: Transcript-Verlag.

Blouin, Katherine. 2014. *Triangular Landscapes: Environment, Society, and the State in the Nile Delta under Roman Rule.* Oxford: Oxford University Press.

Boraik, Mansour, Luc Gabolde, and Angus Graham. 2017. "Karnak's Quaysides: Evolution of the Embankments from the Eighteenth Dynasty to the Graeco-Roman Period." In *The Nile: Natural and Cultural Landscape in Egypt. Proceedings of the International Symposium held at the, 22 & 23 February 2013,* edited by Harco Willems and Jan-Michael Dahms, 97–144. Bielefeld: Transcript-Verlag.

Biston-Moulin, Sébastien. 2015. "À propos de deux documents d'Ahmosis à Karnak: Karnak Varia." *Cahiers de Karnak* 15: 39–49.

Bunbury, J. M., Graham, A. and Hunter, M. A. 2008. "Stratigraphic Landscape Analysis: Charting the Movements of the Nile at Karnak through Ancient Egyptian Time." *Geoarchaeology* 23 (3), 351–373.

Butzer, Karl. 2016. "Landscapes and Environmental History of Ancient Egypt: Review and Prospectus." In *Gedenkschrift für Werner Kaiser,* edited by Daniel Polz and Stephan J. Seidlmayer, 59–80. *MDAIK* 70/71. Berlin and Boston: Walter de Gruyter.

Butzer, Karl, Elisabeth Butzer, and Serena Love. 2013. "Urban Geoarchaeology and

Environmental History at the Lost City of the Pyramids, Giza: Synthesis and Review." *Journal of Archaeological Science* 40: 3340–3366.

Cioc, Mark. 2002. *The Rhine: An Eco-Biography*, 1815-2000. Seattle: University of Washington Press.

Di Cosmo, Nicola. 2018. "The Scientist as Antiquarian: History, Climate, and the New Past. How Could the Constant Interaction between Humans and Nature Not Be Part of History?" *Historical Studies.* ias.edu/ideas/2018/di-cosmo-history-climate-and-new-past.

Dorn, Andreas. 2016. "The Hydrology of the Valley of the Kings: Weather, Rainfall, Drainage Patterns, and Flood Protection in Antiquity." In *The Oxford Handbook of the Valley of the Kings*, edited by Richard H. Wilkinson and Kent R. Weeks, 30–38. Oxford: Oxford University Press.

Dorn, Andreas, and Elina Paulin-Grothe. 2000. "Baugeschichte." In *Das Grab Ramses' X (KV 18)*, edited by Hanna Jenni, 21–34. Aegyptiaca Helvetica 16. Basel: Schwabe and Co.

Evenden, Matthew. 2018, 9 August. "Beyond the Organic Machine? New Approaches in River Historiography." *Environmental History.* doi.org/10.1093/envhis/emy054.

Feinman, Peter. 2015. "The Tempest in the Tempest: The Natural Historian. *Bulletin of the Egyptological Seminar* 19: 253–262.

Franconi, Tyler V. 2017. "Introduction: Studying Rivers in the Roman World." In *Fluvial Landscapes in the Roman World*, edited by Tyler V. Franconi, 7–22. Journal of Roman Archaeology Supplementary Series 104. Portsmouth, R.I.: Journal of Roman Archaeology.

Gabolde, Luc. 2018. *Karnak, Amon-Ré: la genèse d'un temple, la naissance d'un Dieu.* Bibliothèque d'étude 167. Cairo: Institut français d'archéologie orientale.

Gamer-Wallert, Ingrid. 1981. Review of Wolfgang Schenkel: *Die Bewässerungsrevolution im alten Ägypten. 1978. Welt des Orients* 12: 174–176.

Garbrecht, Günther. 1995. *Meisterwerke antiker Hydrotechnik: Einblicke in die Wissenschaft: Technik.* Leipzig: Teubner.

Graefe, Erhart. 1986. "Art. Wunder." In *Lexikon der Ägyptologie*. Vol. 6, *Stele-Zypresse*, edited by Wolfgang Helck and Eberhard Otto, 1298–1299. Wiesbaden: Verlag Otto Harrassowitz.

Graham, A. 2010. "Islands in the Nile: A Geoarchaeological Approach to Settlement Locations in the Egyptian Nile Valley and the Case of Karnak." In M. Bietak, E. Czerny and I. Forstner Müller (eds.), *Cities and Urbanism in Ancient Egypt*, 125–143. Papers from a workshop in November 2006 at the Austrian Academy of Sciences. Denkschriften der Gesamtakademie, LX. Untersuchungen der Zweigstelle Kairo des Österreichischen Archäologischen Instituts, XXXV. Vienna: Österreichischen Akademie der Wissenschaften.

Graham, A. and Bunbury, J. 2005. "The Ancient Landscapes and Waterscapes of Karnak." *Egyptian Archaeology* 27, 17–19.

Harper, Karl. 2017. *The Fate of Rome: Climate, Disease, and the End of an Empire.* Princeton: Princeton University Press.

Hekkala, Evon, Matthew H. Shirley, George Amato, James D. Austin, Suellen Charter, John Thorbjarnarson, Kent A. Vliet, Marlys L. Houck, Rob Desalle, Michael J. Blum. 2011. "An Ancient Icon Reveals New Mysteries: Mummy DNA Resurrects a Cryptic Species within the Nile Crocodile." *Molecular Ecology* 20: 4199–4215.

Ikram, Salima. 2010. "Crocodiles: Guardians of the Gateways." In *Thebes and Beyond: Studies in Honour of Kent R. Weeks*, edited by Z. Hawass and S. Ikram, 85–98. Cairo: SCA.

Kelly, Jason M., Philip Scarpino, Helen Berry, James Syvitski, and Michel Meybeck, eds. 2017. *Rivers of the Anthropocene.* Oakland, C.A.: University of California Press.

11

Kockelmann, Holger. 2018. *Der Herr der Seen, Sümpfe und Flussläufe: Untersuchungen zum Gott Sobek und den ägyptischen Krokodilgötter-Kulten von den Anfängen bis zur Römerzeit.* 3 vols. Ägyptologische Abhandlungen. Wiesbaden: Harrassowitz.

Manning, Joseph G. 2012. "Water, Irrigation and their Connection to State Power in Egypt." Paper read at "Resources: Endowment or Curse, Better or Worse?" Yale University, 24 February 2012, http://www.econ.yale.edu/~egcenter/manning2012.pdf, 18–2.

———. 2018. *The Open Sea. The Economic Life of the Ancient Mediterranean World from the Iron Age to the Rise of Rome.* Princeton: Princeton University Press.

Mauch, Christof. 2009. "Introduction." In *Natural Disasters, Cultural Responses: Case Studies toward a Global Environmental History,* edited by Christof Mauch and Christian Pfister, 1–16. Lanham: Lexington Books.

Mauch, Christof, and Thomas Zeller. 2008. "Rivers in History and Historiography: An Introduction." In *Rivers in History: Perspectives on Waterways in Europe and North America,* edited by Christof Mauch and Thomas Zeller, 1–10. Pittsburgh: University of Pittsburgh Press.

Mikhail, Alan. 2011. *Nature and Empire in Ottoman Egypt: An Environmental History.* Cambridge: Cambridge University Press.

———. 2017. *Under Osman's Tree: The Ottoman Empire, Egypt, and Environmental History.* Chicago: The University of Chicago Press.

Moreno García, Juan-Carlos. 2015. "The Cursed Discipline? The Peculiarities of Egyptology at the Turn of the Twenty-First Century." In *Histories of Egyptology: Interdisciplinary Measures,* edited by William Carruthers, 50–63. New York and London: Routledge.

Quack, Joachim Friedrich. 2013. "Gibt es in Ägypten schriftliche Quellen zum Thera-Ausbruch?" In *1600 — Kultureller Umbruch im Schatten des Thera-Ausbruchs? 4. Mitteldeutscher Archäologentag vom 14. bis 16. Oktober 2011 in Halle (Saale),* edited by H. Meller, F. Bertemes, H.-R. Bork, and R. Risch, 221–233. Tagungen des Landesmuseums für Vorgeschichte Halle 9. Halle: Landesmuseum für Vorgeschichte.

Ritner, Robert K., and Nadine Moeller. 2014. "The Ahmose Tempest Stela: An Ancient Egyptian Account of a Natural Catastrophe." In *Egyptian Curses 1: Proceedings of the Egyptological Day held at the National Research Council of Italy (CNR), Rome, 3rd December 2012, in the International Conference "Reading Catastrophes: Methodological Approaches and Historical Interpretation. Earthquakes, Floods, Famines, Epidemics between Egypt and Palestine, 3rd–1st millennium BC. Rome, 3rd–4th December 2012, CNR-Sapienza University of Rome,"* edited by Giuseppina Capriotti Vittozzi, 63–81. Roma: CNR Edizioni.

Said, Rushdi. 2013. *The River Nile: Geology, Hydrology and Utilization.* Oxford etc.: Pergamon Press.

Scheidel, Walter. 2001. *Death on the Nile: Disease and the Demography of Roman Egypt.* Leiden: Brill.

Schenkel, Wolfgang. 1978. *Die Bewässerungsrevolution im alten Ägypten.* Deutsches Archäologisches Institut, Sonderschriften 6. Mainz am Rhein: Philipp von Zabern.

Schneider, Thomas. 2010. "A Theophany of Seth-Baal in the Tempest Stele." *Egypt & the Levant* 20: 405–409.

Tignor, Robert L. 2010. *Egypt: A Short History.* Princeton: Princeton University Press.

Toonen, Willem H.J., Angus Graham, Benjamin T. Pennington, Morag A. Hunter, Kristian D. Strutt, Dominic S. Barker, Aurélia Masson-Berghoff, Virginia L. Emery. 2018. "Holocene Fluvial History of the Nile's West Bank at Ancient Thebes, Luxor, Egypt, and Its Relation with Cultural Dynamics and Basin-Wide Hydroclimatic Variability." *Geoarchaeology* 33: 273–290.

Toonen, W.H.J., Graham, A., Masson-Berghoff, A., Peeters, J., Winkels, T.G., Pennington, B.T., Hunter, M.A., Strutt, K.D., Barker, D.S., Emery, V.L., Sollars, L., Sourouzian,

H. 2019. "Amenhotep III's Mansion of Millions of Years in Thebes (Luxor, Egypt): Submergence of High Grounds by River Floods and Nile Sediments." *Journal of Archaeological Science: Reports* 25, 195–205.

Trigger, Bruce G. 2004. *Ancient Egypt: A Social History.* Cambridge: Cambridge University Press.

Tvedt, Terje. 2004. *The River Nile in the Age of the British: Political Ecology and the Quest for Economic Power,* London and New York: I.B. Tauris.

———, ed. 2009. *The River Nile in the Postcolonial Age: Conflict and Cooperation among the Nile Basin Countries,* London and New York: I.B. Tauris.

White, Richard. 1995. *The Organic Machine: The Re-Making of the Columbia River.* New York: Hill and Wang.

Willcocks, W. and Craig, J. I. 1913. *Egyptian Irrigation.* Third edition. London: E. & F. N. Spon.

Willems, Harco, and Jan-Michael Dahms, eds. 2017. *The Nile: Natural and Cultural Landscape in Egypt. Proceedings of the International Symposium held at the Johannes-Gutenberg Universität Mainz, 22 & 23 February 2013.* Bielefeld: Transcript-Verlag.

Notes

[1] Beyond the acknowledgments made on p. 1, I would like to thank the members of the 2017 River cluster working group from the University of British Columbia and Simon Fraser University for the conversations that have also influenced this paper; and in particular Matthew Evenden for sharing with us the manuscript of his article on the "river turn" in historiography (infra n. 18). I am grateful to Jing Zhichun for having invited me as a keynote speaker to the Third Shanghai Archaeology Forum in December 2017 where I presented a preliminary version of these remarks. Angus Graham has kindly commented on this paper and suggested some bibliographical additions.

[2] Tignor 2010, 5.

[3] Manning 2012; the idea now also developed in Manning 2018, 94–103.

[4] Schenkel 1978; Manning 2018, 139. Despite the affirmative title of Schenkel's monograph, the author actually denies that an irrigation revolution contributed to the establishment of the Egyptian state (cf. Gamer-Wallert 1981).

[5] Bietak 2017, 63.

[6] Baldi 2015.

[7] Dorn, 2016.

[8] Dorn and Paulin-Grothe 2000, 30–34, figs. 14–15.

[9] Some of the evidence has received controversial interpretations. For example, for the pyramid city of the Giza plateau, Karl Butzer has posited 10 destructive flash flood events documented within a period of 50 years at the end of the Fourth Dynasty (Butzer et al. 2013; Butzer 2016, 71–76, fig. 6). According to Mark Lehner (personal communication), this is a mistaken assessment of the archaeological evidence.

[10] Garbrecht 1995.

[11] Mauch 2009, 4.

[12] "And I think that their [the priests'] account of the country was true. For even if a man has not heard it before, he can readily see, if he has sense, that Egypt to which the Greeks sail is land deposited for the Egyptians, the river's gift—not only the lower

country, but even the land as far as three days' voyage above the lake [Lake Moeris, the Fayum], which is of the same nature as the other, although the priests did not say this, too" (cf. Manning 2018, 94). Cf. Willcocks and Craig (1913, 131) who state: "The Blue Nile is the true parent of the land of Egypt. The deposits of its muddy waters have made the land" (reference kindly provided by Angus Graham).

13 Franconi 2017, 7.
14 Amenta et al. 2005.
15 Kockelmann 2018.
16 Kockelmann 2018, 1:2–10.
17 Ikram 2010; Hekkala et al. 2011.
18 Evenden 2018. See also Kelly et al. 2017.
19 White 1995.
20 Cioc 2002.
21 Mauch and Zeller 2008, 7.
22 Trigger 2004, xi.
23 Moreno García 2015.
24 See more generally Di Cosmo 2018. For a recent reassessment of Roman history from a climate perspective, see Harper 2017.
25 Willems and Dahms 2017, 7.
26 Mikhail 2011, 2017.
27 Tvedt 2004, 2009.
28 Scheidel 2001.
29 Blouin 2014.
30 Manning 2018, 94–103, 158–172.
31 See, for example, the exemplary study by Boraik et al. 2017.
32 Graham and Bunbury 2005; Bunbury, Graham and Hunter 2008; Graham 2010; Gabolde 2018.
33 Toonen et al. 2018.
34 Graefe 1986.
35 From the last years, see Schneider 2010; Quack 2013; Ritner and Moeller 2014; Biston-Moulin 2015; Feinman 2015.

Chapter Two

A Compendium of Recent Evidence from Egypt and Sudan for Climate Change during the Pharaonic Period

Pearce Paul Creasman

Investigation of the impact that a changing climate might have had on ancient Egyptian civilization was essentially initiated about 50 years ago by Barbara Bell.[1] Written prior to the availability of palaeoenvironmental proxies, at least for the region under discussion, Bell's works were thorough, forward-thinking, and insightful. Accordingly, it has been to Bell that most accounts have until recently deferred.[2] Through three articles published in the early and mid-1970s, she presented an accumulation of textual, archaeological, and geoarchaeological evidence for a shifting environment in the Nile Valley that encompassed the Old Kingdom,[3] First Intermediate Period,[4] Middle Kingdom, and Second Intermediate Period.[5] Bell provided a compelling, interwoven narrative of climate and culture, the fate of the latter hinging on the former. Most notable is her argument that the Old Kingdom centralized state, an early apogee noted for the construction of colossal stone pyramids, devolved on account of famine and other stresses consequent to a devastating series of low Nile floods, causing Egyptian society to devolve into a drought-stricken state of political fragmentation, the First Intermediate Period.[6] Egypt, she argued, was not alone in descending into the world's "First Dark Age" at this time, ca. 2200–2000 BCE: there was a "drought—widespread, severe, and prolonged—lasting for several decades and occurring more or less simultaneously over the entire eastern Mediterranean and adjacent lands."[7] Furthermore, she cited arguments that such an event had also occurred later, resulting in a Second Dark Age (ca. 1200–900 BCE).[8]

Bell's scenario of fluctuating climate events and societal reactions throughout the pharaonic period, seemingly so relevant to the present-day Anthropocene, was widely embraced.[9] Her discussion of the Old Kingdom/First Intermediate Period transition in particular has been assimilated into interpretations of an abrupt drought known as the 4.2 ka BP event.[10] Although scientific evidence for the 4.2 ka BP event is usually derived from sources beyond Egypt[11] (particularly marine cores from the Gulf of Oman and the Indian Ocean, in the vicinity of the Indus River mouth[12]), the fate of the Egyptian Old Kingdom is central to the hypothesis that an abrupt climate change caused widespread societal

The Gift of the Nile? Ancient Egypt and the Environment
edited by Thomas Schneider and Christine L. Johnston
Tucson, Arizona: Egyptian Expedition, 2020

collapse in the late third millennium BCE. Evidence suggests that the climate anomaly occurred around 4,200 years ago, and hence it has become known as the "4.2 ka event." Old Kingdom Egypt is integral to the debate because of the state's preeminence in the region at the time, and also because its decline is so well attested in both the historical and archaeological records. Over recent times, the collapse of the Egyptian state has become a battleground between socio-political factors and the climate determinism.[13]

Acceptance of Bell's climate-driven hypothesis, although widespread, was not universal. Karl W. Butzer,[14] himself long a proponent of climate-influenced social change,[15] and Stephan Seidlmayer,[16] among others, have concluded that there is no evidence for a catastrophic drought coeval with, let alone causal of, the end of the Egyptian Old Kingdom. In 2005, Nadine Moeller critiqued in detail[17] the notion that rapid climate change contributed to the demise of the Old Kingdom in light of newer archaeological and environmental evidence from Egypt, as well as Near Eastern environmental proxy data for the 4.2 ka BP event.[18] Moeller pointed to studies that call into question the 4.2 ka BP megadrought/extensive societal collapse hypothesis: some environmental proxy data from the Near East fail to record a drought, and some archaeological data fail to record, or need not be interpreted as, cultural collapse.[19] Regarding Egypt, she concluded that "there is currently no evidence for a short term, abrupt [climate] anomaly, which would have led to the collapse of the Old Kingdom state in Egypt."[20]

Since Moeller's review, Felix Höflmayer,[21] Thomas Schneider,[22] and many others[23] have examined cultural/social/political transformations that took place from the Aegean to the Indus River Valley in the mid- to late third millennium BCE with the benefit of more refined chronological data.[24] They have come to conclusions that are analogous to, and even more assertive than, Moeller's for not only Egypt but also well beyond.[25] It has become evident that the 4.2 ka BP event and other climate episodes have origins and impacts that are "spatially complex"[26] (that is, are not the worldwide phenomena once thought, as Gatto and Zerboni demonstrate for North Africa[27]), they do not have the clear climate signals once accepted,[28] and, when these events did occur, they were not as abrupt as often portrayed[29] or they have been misunderstood entirely.[30]

While Bell-based scenarios for Egypt appear to have been invoked to help define a new age within the Holocene epoch called the Meghalayan,[31] broad-scale, long-term analyses of Holocene climates and environments tend to neglect Egyptian data.[32] Many scholars have perpetuated Moeller's call for more data from Egypt, Sudan, and adjacent seas in order to draw reliable conclusions and incorporate into both expansive and more localized regional discussions of climate and the relationship between climate and society.[33]

What role, if any, climate played in influencing past human societies cannot be properly assessed without a proper understanding of three types of relevant data: historical, environmental, and chronological. Although some, notably Harvey Weiss,[34] continue to advocate for the 4.2 ka BP event as the engine for social change in the late third millennium BCE,[35] the lack of temporal synchronicity between its data proxies and, for example, the radiocarbon-supplied dates of ca. 2500 BCE for the disappearance of urbanized settlements in the Levant at the end of the Early Bronze III (one of the purported archaeological hallmarks for the megadrought) is now recognized.[36] For Egypt, historical and chronological issues, both absolute and relative, are increasingly under scientific review.[37] Because Egypt, with its wealth of written records, has traditionally provided the framework for wider regional chronologies, chronological revisions have ripple effects beyond, or into, the Nile Valley.[38] As for elsewhere in the world, Egyptian radiocarbon dates are out of step with commonly accepted understandings of Egyptian history.[39] This discord is a problem that only the application of dating techniques more precise than radiocarbon can ultimately settle.

Likewise, fundamental interpretations of the historical record are being revisited: many now question, for example, the conclusions that the Old Kingdom "collapsed" abruptly and that the First Intermediate Period was a time of environmental and economic stress.[40] A variety of endogamous and exogamous human factors are now commonly viewed as primary motivators of cultural change throughout the region.[41] "Collapse" itself is disputed, increasingly discussed as "transformation," "transmutation," and "transition."[42]

With the recognition of the more complex and localized nature of past climate events, and heeding the call for additional data, the present literature review accumulates published data applicable to the fundamental question: What evidence has accumulated since 2005 regarding climate change in pharaonic and Ptolemaic Egypt and Sudan?[43] Scholars across many fields have been working on various largely isolated aspects of this temporally broad, regionally focused question. The relevant data are largely sedimentological, drawn from the greater Nile River system (including East African lakes) and the Red Sea, and further include analyses of faunal remains, human bones, settlement sites, iconography, and documentary texts. Alone, none can provide a full picture, but in the aggregate, presented here for the first time, they seem to present a critical mass that should not be ignored: the climate *was* changing, but at what scale, precisely when, and to what result remains unclear.

BROAD-SCALE AND LONG-TERM ANALYSES

A 2015 meta-analysis of Nile River system Holocene fluvial events with available ^{14}C and optically-stimulated luminescence (OSL) dates, undertaken by Mark G. Macklin et al., revealed that, throughout the epoch, the stability in seasonality of the annual inundation was accompanied by considerable fluctuations in the magnitude of the floods.[44] The data cover <11,700 BCE onward and include palaeochannels and the Fayum depression; 63% were taken from the floodplain, although floodplain units are absent from 700 BCE–300 CE.[45] Most data are derived from the desert Nile[46] and delta (83 and 20 fluvial units, respectively) rather than the Blue and White Nile headwaters (9 units), but all of these elements of the river system offer pharaonic-era data.[47] The data from the desert Nile and delta tend to be discrete from each other, coinciding in the pharaonic period only in 2600–2500 BCE.[48]

Three of the 10 "multi-centennial length periods characterised by high frequencies of fluvial units" detected by the meta-analysis fall within the pharaonic period (3400–2900, 2200–1100, and 1000–600 BCE), with a particularly large number clustered in the New Kingdom (1300–1100 BCE).[49] Meta-analysis revealed the Nile data to be "broadly synchronous" with other climate data from elsewhere in eastern Africa: Lake Victoria (in the White Nile catchment), Lake Tana (Blue Nile catchment), and the proxy temperatures from Mount Kilimanjaro ice cores.[50] Their specific contributions will be discussed in their respective historical periods below. Several recent studies that are neither included in the meta-analysis of Macklin et al. nor discussed in depth elsewhere in the present paper are discussed here.

Varying percentages of pollen during the pharaonic period in the eastern delta, from cores obtained from Avaris and Mendes, indicate changing environments. A prehistoric humid period (ca. 8500 BCE) is suggested by the (relatively) great abundance of *Lycopodium* spores.[51] These spores had markedly decreased (by roughly 30–50%) by the time of the Predynastic (ca. 3500–3100 BCE), but humid conditions persisted in the Predynastic, evidenced by the continued presence of *Typha* (cattails), suggesting reedy swamps. By the Early Dynastic (ca. 2920–2575 BCE), *Poaceae* (grasses) and *Asteraceae* peak. *Cyperaceae* (sedges), which can grow in either dry or wet locations, continue and even peak at Avaris. Neither the Old Kingdom nor the First Intermediate Period is represented in the published tables, but the Middle Kingdom evidences growth of water plants (*Nymphea, Jussiae*), which "suggest Nile water and tributaries, [and] also reflects Nile flooding at this period."[52] The Second Intermediate Period is absent; for the New Kingdom, *Chenopodiaceae* dominate at Mendes and *Poaceae* at Avaris.[53] Throughout the sequence, *Lycopodium* dwindles, having all but disappeared from Mendes during the New Kingdom[54] and being missing entirely at Avaris from the Middle Kingdom onward.[55]

Changes in the location of the apex of the Nile delta result "mostly [...] from climate changes," including changes in sea level.[56] Based on reviews of the location of the delta head recorded in literature and observations made by Sarah Parcak (who suggests that the delta head may have been at Lisht), Judith Bunbury et al.[57] conclude that the delta head seems to have corresponded to the ancient capital city of Memphis during the Old Kingdom. However, this has not been demonstrated with certainty via the sedimentological record, as the work has yet to be attempted. For the Middle Kingdom, "texts and models of delta development suggest that the palace and the delta head were further south [of Memphis], possibly at Itiy-Tawi (currently thought to be in the Lisht area)," but even so, "Memphis re-emerged as a regional centre."[58] The delta head moved back to Memphis, a process "completed by the beginning of the New Kingdom."[59] Part of this same phenomenon—an accumulation of sediment—"also contributed to the consolidation of the delta[,] reducing the area of marsh and increasing the agricultural potential."[60] The delta head has continued to move north, giving rise, ultimately, to Cairo.[61]

Alexandra Touzeau et al. sought climate data proxies in the mummies of ancient Egyptians who were living, presumably, in the Nile Valley and likely consuming exclusively, or at least primarily,[62] river water.[63] Phosphate in teeth and bones preserves changes in oxygen isotopes ratios ($\partial^{18}O_p$), which can be converted to oxygen isotope ratios of drinking water ($\partial^{18}O_w$).[64] The 53 mummies studied, which came mostly from Upper Egypt and particularly the Theban area, covered the broad range of ancient history, ca. 6.0–1.31 ka BP: Predynastic, Old Kingdom, Middle Kingdom, New Kingdom, Late Period, Ptolemaic Period, Greco-Roman period, and Coptic/Byzantine period.[65] Forty-eight of the mummies were human, the remaining five being hyena, cat, crocodile, and fish.[66]

The strontium isotopes of 12 (human) individuals were tested for evidence of migration from other regions. The results, which were consistent with those of the "Theban carbonate rocks," indicated that, most likely, almost all had lived in the Theban area throughout their lives.[67] Within each period, considerable variation in $\partial^{18}O_p$, was present, possibly resulting from variations in the Nile discharge, changes in diet throughout the lifetime of the individuals, or their movement within the Nile Valley.[68] Conversion of $\partial^{18}O_p$ values to $\partial^{18}O_w$ values revealed a decrease in rainfall of 3% (140 mm) and an increase of water temperature of 1.8° C from the Predynastic Period (ca. 5.5 ka BP) to the Late Period (ca. 2.5 ka BP), which then remained essentially steady from the Greco-Roman period until modern times.[69] The animal data, all of Greco-Roman date, confirmed the results for their period.[70] Compared to the differences between the mean $\partial^{18}O_p$ of other periods, the Eighteenth Dynasty and Late Period samples presented a "significant" jump in data derived from teeth and from bone[71] for which the authors do not offer an explanation. They conclude, overall, that these findings support the long-term aridification in the region.[72]

Justin D. Yeakel et al. modeled predator-prey ratios for large-bodied (> 4 kg) mammals through randomized, computer-aided extinction simulations (5 x 10^5 replicates) that were based on a variety of sources (faunal, iconographic, etc.) covering 6,000 years of

Egyptian history.[73] After conducting computer-aided simulations to evaluate if perceived "extinctions" (i.e., last attestation in the archaeological or iconographic record) of these herbivores (elephant, giraffe, antelopes, hippopotamus, equids, caprids, bovines, etc.) and their mammalian predators (canids, felids, hyenas, etc.) were random events,[74] the authors found that the ratio increased from the Late Pleistocene through the end of the New Kingdom. Besides the late Predynastic/Early Dynastic transition (ca. 5.0 ka BP), during the pharaonic period the "most dramatic shifts" took place ca. 4.14 ka BP, ca. 3.52 ka BP, and ca. 3.035 ka BP.[75] The authors do not assign causality to climate change for any of the specific resulting modeled extirpations,[76] although they do note that these changes were "contemporaneous with extreme environmental and historical events."[77] Although computer modeling might be a novel approach to these data, iconography in the form of hunting scenes with a vegetated, savanna-like landscape with associated animals has long been cited as reflecting a changing climate in this period: this motif, it is argued, disappeared with the flora and fauna that fell victim to much drier conditions.[78] Despite apparent parallels from the Levant,[79] as Linda Evans has pointed out,[80] the foundation of this model neglects to consider that the representation of animals in ancient Egyptian art need not accurately reflect their contemporary occurrence in the environment: either because of artistic archaizing (e.g., artists of later periods emulating Old Kingdom reliefs) or for symbolic purposes, taxa may be depicted long after their extirpation, or they might be present in the landscape but omitted due to the types of scenes being included in tombs. Furthermore, as Butzer et al. observed a short while before, the extent of such conditions suggests that, by the Old Kingdom, this type of environment might have existed only at aquifers that received Nile groundwater along the desert edge; the animals may have been maintained in enclosures.[81]

Mammalian microfaunal remains excavated from Old Kingdom and Roman period contexts at Abusir are interpreted by Petr Pokorný et al. as suggesting a long-term trend toward taxa that live in desert environments: the percentage of those adapted for damp areas (e.g., *Nesokia indica*, short-tailed bandicoot-rat; *Suncus etruscus*, pygmy white-toothed shrew) present in the Old Kingdom record had decreased dramatically in the Roman period,[82] although the only amphibian remains ("probably a species of desert toad") were present exclusively in the latter.[83] While enticing, the implications of this study (i.e., more desert animals means more desert environment) should be regarded with caution. In part, there is great temporal distance and not a complete record of data across it, but in all periods, there *should* be more desert animals represented at site such as Abusir (on the edge of the desert) than, for example, sites in the delta (e.g., Mendes, Tanis, etc.). Studies such as Pokorný et al.'s would be more valuable in discerning a larger understanding if they were conducted at multiple sites, for multiple eras, and then compared.

OLD KINGDOM, THE TRANSITION TO THE FIRST INTERMEDIATE PERIOD, AND THE "4.2 KA BP EVENT"

A monument created in the Fifth Dynasty preserves records of not only royal accomplishments but also heights of the Nile's annual inundation during the reigns of Egyptian kings from the Early Dynastic Period and part of the Old Kingdom.[84] The Palermo Stone and its associated fragments[85] have been a major springboard for discussion of climate change, although its records, accounting only for Egypt's earliest kings through the first half of Neferirkare's reign (Fifth Dynasty), fall well short of the 4.2 ka BP event commonly implicated in the "decline and fall" of the Sixth Dynasty.[86]

These Old Kingdom annals record that flood levels varied from year to year within ranges comparable to those noted historically,[87] with a general trend toward decline from the First through Fifth Dynasties, as has been noted since their initial publication.[88] The earliest flood data—records of eight years during the reign of Djer (First Dynasty)—average 2.78 m;[89] in the Second Dynasty, floods were markedly lower, and the last recorded floods—late Fourth and early Fifth Dynasties—were rather consistent,[90] averaging 1.83 m.[91]

Although suggestive, as Bell[92] noted and Moeller reemphasized,[93] these data present a number of difficulties. They are selective (not all reigns include flood levels[94]) and incomplete (there are no records for the late Old Kingdom). These (and similar records) were created for a religious rather than administrative context; some of the given figures have been questioned as "pure fiction."[95] Furthermore, the nature of the Nilometer(s) by which they were obtained is unknown. The early Nilometer is only *inferred* to have had a fixed point from which the measurements were taken, as did later examples in the form of a staircase.[96] With that in mind, the differences in flood levels are potentially even greater if one takes into account accumulating deposits of alluvium, the rate of which Bell conventionally presumed to be 10 cm per century, or 500 cm overall for these records.[97] If, however, the Nilometer was a portable device, the ancient figures might already account for the rising alluvium.[98]

The siting of structures at Elephantine Island at the first Nile cataract seems to corroborate a trend toward lower Nile floods. The First Dynasty fortress there was built at a notably higher level (ca. 96 m asl) compared to constructions of the Second Dynasty (94 m asl) and the Sixth Dynasty (92 m asl).[99] However, as Moeller points out, the purpose of the building must be taken into account. For a fortress, the primary choice of a location may be to create a statement of power, with the height of the inundation and the chance of flood damage only a secondary factor.[100] The Sixth Dynasty buildings do seem to have been flooded (to 93 m asl) at some later date.[101] Moeller concedes that this offers "firm evidence for relatively low flood levels during the 6th Dynasty," although these structures were not, apparently, intended to be permanent, and it is also possible that need for the space was great enough to run the risk of flooding.[102] The repeated destruction and rebuilding of the Fourth Dynasty pyramid town at Giza,[103] to be discussed below, demonstrates that the Egyptians willingly installed buildings in locations at great jeopardy, a trend that did not stop in the Old Kingdom and continued throughout pharaonic history.[104]

There was supportive sedimentary evidence of failing floods available to Bell, who pointed to observations from Lower Nubia that suggested a period of erosion (dissection) and lessened flood discharges during the Old Kingdom.[105] Such studies have proliferated particularly since the turn of the century;[106] one of the major periods of climate change revealed by the meta-analysis of Nile Valley fluvial data by Macklin et al. is evident at 2800–2450 cal. BCE.[107] They detect large-scale drying (contraction) of both floodplain and channels 2700–2550 BCE.[108]

The Nile River—which until dam construction in the 20th century CE overflowed its banks in an annual inundation—and lakes fed by its waters provide a variety of climate and environmental proxies. An exotic river, it flows through Egypt from two major headwaters farther south in Africa. The White Nile, fed by equatorial rainfall,[109] provides the year-round base flow of the Egyptian Nile.[110] From headwaters in the Ethiopian highlands, the Blue Nile and Atbara River together contribute more than half of the annual Nile water discharge,[111] but most of this input occurs when they are swollen by summer monsoon rains and deliver to Egypt the annual inundation, which rises quickly in June and tapers off from its peak in August.[112] The present-day Blue Nile and Atbara together account for at least 97% of the riverine-derived sediments deposited in modern Egypt.[113] Due to the differing natures of the rocks through which each headwater flows, isotopic and mineralogical analyses of ancient Nile sediments in Egypt have been used to determine their source. Sediments brought down by the Blue Nile/Atbara Rivers, which pass through the readily eroded volcanic rocks of the Ethiopian highlands, have low $^{87}Sr/^{86}Sr$ ratios,[114] high ratios of Fe/Al, Ti/Al, Mn/Al, Ni/Al, and Co/Al,[115] and a high percentage of pyroxene and iron oxide heavy minerals.[116] The much harder crystalline basement rocks through which the White Nile flows result in sedimentary deposits with amphiboles, epidotes, and metamorphic heavy minerals and high ratios of Ca/Al, Na/Al, K/Al[117], and $^{87}Sr/^{86}Sr$.[118]

Rushdi Said[119] and Moeller[120] expressed reservation regarding such isotopic and mineralogical studies, because, first, these analyses are predicated on the assumption that no contribution from now-inactive Nile tributaries changed the mineralogical composition of the sediments, and, second, the processes that influenced these varying mineral contributions are not entirely understood. That such concerns are warranted is suggested by recent advances in river sediment systems studies in general[121] and a reexamination of the sediment inputs from wadi outflow and aeolian processes in Sudan and Egypt (the "desert Nile catchment").[122]

Analyses of sediment cores from the delta have suggested changing proportional contributions from the White and Blue Niles through the period approximately corresponding to the Old Kingdom. Mollusk shells, fragments of echinoderms, and wood from sediment core S-21, from Lake Manzala in the northeastern delta,[123] yielded 11 accelerator mass spectrometry (AMS) ^{14}C dates between 6840 ±40 cal BP and present,[124] including dates of 5190 ±50 cal BP and 4170 ±30 cal BP.[125] The span of these latter two, which encompasses the late Predynastic and Old Kingdom, presents a rapid[126] decrease in $^{87}Sr/^{86}Sr$[127] and Ti/Al ratios,[128] and an apparent increasing proportion of sediment derived from the Blue Nile.[129] Jean-Daniel Stanley et al. interpreted these findings as reflecting a decrease in rainfall in the Ethiopian highlands, causing not merely a succession of low Nile floods but also a period of low Nile baseflow:[130] less rainfall in the highlands resulted in less vegetation there and, consequently, greater erosion; another consequence of the lessened rainfall was a lower Nile inundation, which, in turn, deposited a greater amount of sediment in the Nile Valley floodplain than a higher one would have.[131] However, Jamie Woodward et al. determined through isotopic analysis that during this same period, before 4.5 ka BP, the desert Nile tributaries supplied a significant amount to the river's sediment load.[132] Furthermore, due to the actions of the Blue Nile, which as it rises blocks the output of the White Nile, White Nile contribution of sediments laid on the floodplain may, in fact, be immeasurable.[133] They propose that the apparent "stronger 'White Nile signal'" in some Nile delta (e.g., S-21[134]) and Mediterranean marine cores may result from the fact that White Nile sediments travel in the river channel.[135] (Note that 63% of the fluvial units in Macklin et al.'s meta-study are from the floodplain.[136]) To the methodological caveats inherent in the findings of Woodward et al.[137] is added Moeller's observation that Stanley et al. modeled their interpretation on the existing hypothesis of low Niles rather than considering, for example, hypothetical anthropogenic causations in the Ethiopian highlands, such as livestock grazing.[138]

Pollen and microscopic charcoal obtained from the upper 10.5 m of sediment core S-53, taken from the Burullus Lagoon in the north-central area of the Nile delta, indicated two of its four major pollen zones (II–III) with subzones encompassing the pharaonic and Greco-Roman periods (IIb, 7.51–4.35 m, 5100–3500 cal B.P, through IIIb, 3.23–1.67 m, ca. 2000–490 cal BP).[139] Dates were determined through seven ^{14}C AMS dates, calibrated using the Intcal09 curve; age-model creation was undertaken by Clam 1.0.2, using linear interpolation (2012: 615). *Cyperaceae* pollen, carried by the river from marshes in Sudan, serves as a proxy for freshwater input (i.e., variances in Nile flow resulting from variations in precipitation in the region of the headwaters) in the delta.[140] Decreasing amounts of *Cyperaceae* pollen signal a decrease in vegetation, presumed to be caused by low rainfall in the Ethiopian plateau (itself a result of a more southerly mean position of the Intertropical Convergence Zone [ITCZ]), which results in increased erosion in the Blue Nile that manifests in the delta as an increase in heavy and light minerals in the deposited sediments.[141] This correspondence of decreasing *Cyperaceae* pollen and increasing minerals was observed in core S-53 for the period covering the Old Kingdom.[142] Concurrent with decreasing *Cyperaceae* pollen was an increase in microscopic charcoal, which Christopher E. Bernhadt et al., in their study of the eastern Mediterranean, have determined relates to increasingly frequent fires correlating with aridity.[143]

Connected to the main Nile channel via the Bahr Yusef, the lake (or lakes) of the Fayum basin has been responsive to Nile fluctuations.[144] In Macklin et al.'s meta-analysis, its record of high water levels ca. 2800–2450 cal. BCE is not synchronous with data from the Nile Valley.[145]

A high percentage of benthic diatoms in cores (for example, 82% from a core taken at Ain Seleen) reflects that, at some point before the Old Kingdom, the basin was occupied by a very shallow lake (about 8–10 m asl).[146] A First Dynasty seal (King Narmer) suggests a relative date for this shallow lake to Fekri Hassan and M. Hamdan.[147] Leszek Marks et al. found in their own examination of sediments from the southern shore of the present Qarun Lake (core FA-1[148]) that at about 5.0–4.8 cal ka BP (i.e., the late Predynastic/early Archaic period), the Fayum was a slightly shallow freshwater lake with an increasing sedimentation rate (ca. 17.0 mm a^{-1} to 37.7 mm a^{-1}) and a diatom assemblage (predominantly *Aulacoseira* sp. and *Stephanodiscus* sp.) demonstrating seasonal input from the Nile.[149] Rises in Ca^{2+}, Mg^{2+}, Na^+, K^+, SO_4^{2-}, NH^{4+}, NO^{3-}, and Cl^- indicate the occurrence of a "short and weak brackish episode" ca. 5.1 cal ka BP.[150]

Hassan and Hamdan report that the lake rebounded rapidly from 8–10 m asl to 18–22 m asl, evidenced as deep lacustrine sediments without fluvial or beach sediments.[151] The quay at Qasr El-Sagha, which served boats operating in conjunction with the nearby basalt quarries during the Fifth and Sixth Dynasties, furnishes historical estimates for the date and renewed height of lake, 18–20 m asl.[152]

Mollusk shells provide a proxy for water conditions through study of changes in their carbon and oxygen isotopes ($\partial^{13}C$, $\partial^{18}O$), which are affected by surface evaporation and changes in Nile inflow.[153] Greater evaporation (correlated with lower lake levels) results in higher $\partial^{18}O$ values; it is thought to be a consequence of low-Nile episodes.[154] Related to this is variation in $\partial^{13}C$ values, which also increase during periods of evaporation.[155] Correspondingly, lower $\partial^{18}O$ and $\partial^{13}C$ ratios indicate high lake levels.[156] Low $\partial^{18}O$ of *Melanoides* sp. (sample FM 9) and *Corbicula* sp. (FM 10) shells taken near Kom K, at the north edge of the Fayum lake,[157] indicate that the lake maintained a high level 6.0 to 5.0 cal ka BP, at which time an approximately 500-year decline began (5.0–4.5 cal ka BP).[158] *Corbicula* sp. samples (FM10, FM11), radiocarbon dated to the late Predynastic (5636–5835 cal BP) and Old Kingdom (4.4 cal ka BP), respectively,[159] demonstrate an increase in ^{18}O over this span,[160] signaling a period of transition to more arid conditions in which the lake may have dried out completely for a time.[161]

While the methodological caveats inherent in the findings of Woodward et al. (2015) must be kept in mind, the data of isotopic studies and petrological analyses of cores taken from the Nile delta likewise reveal, generally, a gradual decrease in river levels.[162] This was evidently the case as well with the large (estimated 1100 km²) so-called West Nubian Palaeolake of northwestern Sudan, which occupied a basin associated with the Wadi Howar.[163] Examination of its carbon and oxygen isotopes, with uncorrected radiocarbon dating of 9400 ±90 – 3805 ±65 cal BP, provides evidence that the wet phase that had begun ca. 9.5 ka BP ended ca. 4.0 ka BP, although deposits related to its termination were missing from the samples, having evidently eroded out.[164] However, extremes of the trend, as well as distinct episodes, are evident, with ^{14}C dates clustering generally in the second half of the fifth millennium BCE.

The minimal $^{87}Sr/^{86}Sr$ ratio of core S-21 from Lake Manzala occurred at a depth of 36 m, ^{14}C-AMS dated through mollusk shells to 4.6 cal. ka BP;[165] Jean-Daniel Stanley et al. corrected this date 4.2 cal ka BP on account of a 400-year marine reservoir effect calculated by studies of surface planktonic foraminifera from the Levantine basin.[166] (This figure has also been established for the Bay of Alexandria.[167]) In core S-53 (Burullus Lagoon), a peak in microscopic charcoal, an increase in light and heavy minerals, and a longer-term low-pollen event for *Cyperaceae* occurs ca. 4.2 cal ka BP, which "may indicate a sustained effect on the delta vegetation in response to a single drought event."[168] Each of two cores taken from the freshwater central Nile delta (S-86, Rosetta branch; S-97, near Tanta) features a unique, very thin (~5 cm) layer of reddish-brown silt; interpolated ^{14}C dates for these layers are 4250 and 4050 cal BP, respectively.[169] Their color is provided by the presence of iron/manganese hydroxide, which suggests sediment that dried and remained exposed to air "for a prolonged period."[170] Hassan and Hamden view this as "conclusive" evidence of a long-term desiccation of the floodplain.[171]

Marks et al. note a similar pattern in core FA-1.[172] Sand deposition begins ca. 4.4 cal ka BP, perhaps as a result of intense rains; winter winds mixing the water column could account for the continued very high abundance of *Stephanodiscus* sp. At some point during the period of 4.4–3.0 cal ka BP, "the lake was basically cut off from the Nile," although the river could occasionally still reach the lake, as indicated by clayey silt deposits and occurrences of *Aulacoseira* sp.[173] A drying lake is indicated by increasing amounts of Mg^{2+}, Ca^{2+}, and SO^{2-} and the presence of gypsum. The authors suggest that the "beginning of this phase may be related to the 4.2 ka event."[174]

Fayum core QURA9 yielded a single ^{14}C date: 4055–3797 cal BP at 8 m core depth, which falls within the span of the late Old Kingdom–First Intermediate Period.[175] This layer is distinguished by two iron-rich silt layers separated by a layer of minerals, including gypsum and anhydrite that form during evaporation.[176] These are taken to indicate that the Fayum Lake "almost dried up for a considerable period of time."[177] Mg, Al, Si, Ti, and Fe strikingly decrease in the First Intermediate Period level,[178] where, however, Si levels rebounded, evidently because of the introduction of desert sand.[179] Ratios of planktonic and benthic diatoms present in Old Kingdom and First Intermediate Period layers also change in a manner suggesting desiccation of the lake; the $\partial^{18}O$ of mollusk shells also differ between the layers with high values, indicating, again, a low water level during the later end of this timespan.[180] Because the lake is fed by the Nile, Mohamed Hamdan et al. conclude that this evident evaporation suggests that the river experienced extremely low floods at this time.[181] Cores taken at Ain Seleen in Fayum feature an "erosional hiatus" reflecting an episode in the decline of the Fayum lake, as do cores taken from the bottom sediments of the modern lake; Hassan and Hamdan associate the erosional hiatus with the First Intermediate Period.[182] The change at Fayum was, in their words, "swift and severe."[183] Once the Fayum depression was cut off from the Nile and thus receiving only groundwater seepage, the process of evaporation (170 cm annual evaporation rate) would have taken about 40 years.[184]

The Red Sea presents evidence of a severe event independent of Nile River flow only slightly less swift than that suggested for the Fayum region. A gravity core (GeoB 5836-2), obtained from the brine-filled Shaban Deep in the northern Red Sea (26.2250° N, 35.3500°

E; in latitude, this is slightly north of Luxor), at a depth of 1475 m, features partly laminated sediments that offer the potential of high-resolution data for climate studies because they may document annual deposition cycles.[185] *Globigerinoides sacculifer* foraminifera from the sediments were radiocarbon dated by accelerator mass spectrometry; the age model was based on a six ^{14}C-AMS dates (average spacing of 300 years) with linear interpolation and conversion to calendar years using Calib 4.2.[186] The section of core GeoB 5836-2 examined encompasses dates of about 5.9 to 3.9 cal ka BP, accounting for a regional deviation from the global reservoir effect of about 180 years.[187] A date of ca. 4.210 cal ka BP (4320 ±40 BP) was obtained from a core depth of 21 cm.[188] At this core depth is an indication of an anomaly that Helge W. Arz et al. described as "the most significant [...] in our middle Holocene records from the northern Red Sea."[189] Evidence from changes in planktonic formanifera and pteropods from three short multicores (MC98, MC93, MC91) extracted near Port Sudan revealed a similar anomaly—but of longer dated attribution, ca. 4.4–3.3 ka BP—described by Yael Edelman-Furstenberg et al. as indicative of "the most arid climate in the past ~6000 years."[190]

In GeoB 5836-2, below a core depth of 21 cm, laminae averaging 120 μm in thickness alternate between light (coccoliths, terrigenous material) and dark (diatoms, organic matter), representing summer and winter deposits, respectively.[191] Containing no benthic fossils, these sedimentary layers were evidently deposited during periods when the environment of the sub-basin from which the core was extracted contained an accumulation of brine and was low in oxygen.[192] Above this, sediments deposited in a more ventilated environment with a lower brine level are evident: they are homogenized, feature decreasing organic content, increasing manganese-oxide content, and sediment-dwelling foraminifera (*Bulimina marginata*).[193] Examination of the $\partial^{18}O_c$ of the planktonic formanifera (*Globiegerinoides ruber*), which reflect changes in sea-surface salinity, also revealed an anomalous increase in salinity of about 3 psu[194] occurred 4.2–4.0 cal. ka BP.[195] A similarly less stratified water column was detected through changes in relative abundance of planktonic formanifera and pteropods by Edelman-Furstenberg et al. in MC98, MC93, and MC 91, each of which displayed the greatest period of aeration at ca. 4.4–3.3 ka BP.[196]

Arz et al. postulate the change from laminated to homogenous sediment deposition in GeoB 5836-2 was brought about by a substantial increase in evaporation rates caused by an "anomalously strong air subsidence over the northern part of the Red Sea,"[197] and/or a decrease in water exchange with the Indian Ocean, perhaps brought about by changes in the monsoonal surface-wind field.[198] Possible explanations for such an event include anomalous latent heat release over the Indian subcontinent and an anomalous high-pressure system in the Mediterranean, perhaps related to Arctic Oscillation/North Atlantic Oscillation (i.e., changes in surface atmospheric pressure/wind patterns in these regions that go on to influence weather in the Mediterranean and elsewhere).[199] The change reflected by the sedimentation could hypothetically have been effected over the course of less than a century.[200] Factors affecting marine ventilation can include tectonic activity, but in the case of the Shaban Deep, this is considered unlikely.[201]

Changes in the North Atlantic Oscillation have been implicated in the Egyptian Old Kingdom wet phase, evidence for which exists concurrent with data interpreted as aridification: near the apex of the Nile delta, in the Memphite necropolis (which includes Giza, Saqqara, Dahshur, Abusir, and Meidum), numerous Old Kingdom structures built between the Third and Sixth Dynasties present distinctive evidence of damage or destruction resulting from strong episodes of rainfall.[202] These records may reflect localized weather events rather than broader climate, and it must be considered that robust temporal controls are currently lacking for this early period.[203]

An undisturbed five-series sequence of sedimentary layers (natural and anthropogenic, which included datable Old Kingdom ceramics) was found at a late Old Kingdom cemetery at Saqqara, west of the Step Pyramid of Djoser (Netjerykhet; Third Dynasty).[204] Ash from the lowest part of the sequence (Series 1) provided a ^{14}C date of 4.82–4.67 cal ka BP (confidence limit of 45.8%), indicating the Third Dynasty.[205] This series—comprising compacted limestone rubble, pebbles, and fragments of mud brick transported by water from a higher elevation during an intensive wet phase during the Third Dynasty—is the first of three resulting from sheet flows during the Old Kingdom.[206] Episodes of sheet flows were frequent in Series 1 but not in post-Third Dynasty Series 2.[207] (Series 3, of Sixth Dynasty date, will be addressed below.) The period of Series 1 evidently experienced a more varied climate. How long the wet phases persisted cannot be determined, but they presumably occurred during winter months (December–March), when rain occasionally falls even today in the area.[208]

At Abusir, dust storms produced series of thin (typically 1–2 mm) laminae of aeolian sand, each covered with a thin layer of dust and clay.[209] Two sequences of Third to early Fourth Dynasty date and each probably spanning "several decades," revealed 60 and 98 laminae, with 11 (of the 60) and nine (of the 98) formed by "more intensive events," which usually featured rain.[210]

Flooding from a wadi destroyed an occupation site at Giza dating to the mid-Fourth Dynasty reign of Khafre.[211] During the subsequent reign of Menkaure, a town for the workers building this king's pyramid was installed over the site. Commonly called Heit el-Ghurab (Arabic, "Wall of the Crow") after a distinctive Old Kingdom feature, the town and its occupation lasted into the reign of Userkaf, founder of the Fifth Dynasty, as attested by the presence of seals from his reign.[212] Khafre's and Userkaf's reigns bookended a roughly 40-year period during which desert flash floods spread alluvial fans from the wadi out onto the river floodplain[213] and devastated the settlement on average every four years, requiring repeated rebuilding.[214] One of these floods was especially destructive and seems to have prompted construction (never completed[215]) of the Wall of the Crow late in occupation of the town.[216] The degree of destruction and amount of movement of debris suggests that 200–300 mm of precipitation fell at Giza during each of these winter rain events.[217] Similar, if less extensive, damage of about the same date (late Fourth Dynasty) is reported as a layer of colluvial sand, 15 cm deep, that had washed over and partly destroyed an Old Kingdom pavement beside the seasonal, groundwater-fed lake at Abusir, probably during heavy rains.[218]

In the West Saqqara five-series sequence, Series 3 was similarly deposited during the Sixth Dynasty (4.2 cal ka BP), when winter rains were evidently of longer duration and more frequent than they had been in the Third Dynasty (Series 1).[219] Laminae of clays and silts gradually accumulated over a season in small reservoirs filled during episodes of rain of varying length and intensity.[220] Dated to 4.2 cal ka BP, these were temporary, lasting weeks or months and not seemingly conducive to the growth of vegetation requiring a permanent water source, as any evidence for such species was absent.[221] Within most of the tombs of West Saqqara (most of which are of Sixth Dynasty date), diluvial deposits (of limestone rubble, rock weathering waste, and degraded mud brick), clayey-silt laminae, and mud accumulations indicate rainfalls.[222] The intensity of these storms was "most unusual" in the late Sixth Dynasty, after the reign of Pepi II.[223] This extensive damage is thought to have been the major factor in the decline of the cemetery.[224]

Following a period in which a relatively shallow layer of mud collected in stagnant, seasonal pools (Series 4) at West Saqqara, stratified sands were deposited "from a desert area in the west."[225] This is Series 5, dated to 4.1–4.0 cal ka BP; the transition from Series

4 to the drier period of Series 5 was fairly swift.[226] Only a small percentage of these sands was aeolian in nature; the clearly dominant morphology of the quartz grains indicated short fluvial transport, a trend that persisted into the present.[227] Larger-scale material was also on occasion moved by heavy winds.[228] Elsewhere in the Memphite necropolis, the rate of deposition of aeolian sand at the Bent Pyramid valley temple at Dahshur (a process that had begun by the end of the Fourth Dynasty) reached its greatest rate late in the Sixth Dynasty.[229] At Abusir a rapid transition from deposition of diluvial gravel to aeolian sand is evident above the Third through Fifth Dynasty sequence.[230] Beetles recovered from later (Sixth Dynasty) tombs at Abusir also point to this trend: although rarely used in analyses of palaeoclimates, abundant and habitat-specialized insects can serve as environmental proxies.[231] From the discovery of species that inhabit arid and salty environments in contexts contemporary with the Sixth Dynasty burials (*Scarites* sp., *Prionetheca coronata*, *Sclerum orientale*, and *Poecius pharao*), Miroslav Bárta and A. Bezděk conclude that the area was a desert near a seasonal salt lake by the reign of Teti, early in the Sixth Dynasty.[232]

Although widespread (e.g., in the Fayum[233]), sand accumulations have not been universally recorded. Recent bore-hole investigations at the Memphis settlement site have yet to reveal corresponding deposits of aeolian sand except as brought by the river from upstream.[234] But core SAQA22, taken from the floodplain near Saqqara, features at core depth 10.5–11 m a sedimentation comprising sandy silt with a 5 cm layer of aeolian sand at a level ^{14}C dated (at core depth 10.84 m) to 4.15–4.4 cal ka BP.[235] The small amounts of Fe and Al present in the floodplain sediment suggest to Hamdan et al. that both the Blue and the White Niles were contributing little sediment.[236] There is also a peak in zirconium on account of the windblown desert sand.[237] This falls within the period of increased dune activity reported for the dunes of the Khor Abu Habl wadi alluvial fan in the White Nile Valley, dated very broadly by optically stimulated luminescence (OSL) to 4.8 ±0.9 ka BP.[238] Aridification was further corroborated in the Fayum lake by ^{18}O-isotope analysis of freshwater shells collected from the core, with an enrichment peak, which indicates the occurrence of a high rate of evaporation of Nile floodwater and higher temperatures in this period.[239]

Section Summary

In summary, aggregate evidence from the Old Kingdom and First Intermediate Period—environmental proxies and archaeological remains—clearly points to a changing climate. Macklin et al. (2015) reached this conclusion in their meta-analysis for the period of 2800–2450 cal. BCE.[240] Additional data not incorporated into their study only lends support to their deduction. Several sediment cores present evidence of significantly lowered water levels/drier environment in the delta through pollen,[241] mineral formation,[242] and aeolian sand deposition.[243] Such climate change is likewise attested by not only Fayum sediments[244] but also marine cores from the Red Sea.[245] These events are commonly noted as long term and/or severe,[246] but presently lack the temporal resolution and specificity to be applied in anything resembling a causal context. Approximate dates of the aridification event(s) are not entirely in accordance, but do generally overlap. Macklin et al.'s meta-analysis resulted in a 2800–2450 cal. BCE;[247] other evidence from the Nile delta have produced results of 4.4–3.0 cal ka BP,[248] ca. 4.2 cal ka. BP,[249] and 4250 and 4050 cal BP,[250] with the Red Sea marine cores contributing 4.4–3.3 ka BP[251] and 4.2–4.0 cal ka BP.[252] Similarly, the Fayum appears to have been largely severed from the Nile sometime between 4.4 and 3.0 cal ka BP,[253] but some data for the Fayum's aridification, at 4055–3797 cal BP,[254] are asynchronous with those of the Nile Valley, a phenomenon noted by Macklin et al.[255] From this arid period comes the seemingly paradoxical archaeological evidence reflecting heavy rainfall at the Memphis necropolis during the late Sixth Dynasty,[256] for which the Fayum offers additional, sedimentological evidence of storms starting ca. 4.4 cal ka BP.[257] With temporally imprecise, some seemingly conflicting records, and a lack of a framework to understand how a "normal" or "good" environment might present in these records today, considerably more data is needed to properly place this information in context.

Middle Kingdom and Second Intermediate Period

Discussion of Egyptian climatological evidence in recent decades has tended to focus on the period of the Old Kingdom/First Intermediate Period transition just surveyed here. Published data regarding what transpired after this phase—the Middle Kingdom—are addressed in less detail,[258] perhaps because their resolution is lower and the record offers only more general indications of long-term trends. This is the case, for example, in marine cores MC98, MC93, and MC91 from near Port Sudan, which indicate a millennium of severely arid climate ca. 4.4–3.3 ka BP,[259] encompassing the Middle Kingdom through New Kingdom, and the $^{87}Sr/^{86}Sr$ ratios in core S21, which have been interpreted as indicating a period of low sedimentation rate (i.e., high Nile flow) for 4.75–2.05 ka BP.[260] However, such methods and interpretations have been subject to critique[261] and cannot be solely relied upon. In some instances, proxies for the period are missing, such as aquatic mollusk shells of late Middle Kingdom date absent from core S21 (Manzala Lake).[262] As already mentioned, even the data of shell samples FM 14 and FM 15, associated with Twelfth Dynasty absolute and regnal dates (see below), may reflect an evaporative episode of the earlier period.[263]

While the royal annals and the locations of structures on Elephantine have been noted for suggesting a Nile that slowly failed through the Old Kingdom, dated flood records inscribed at installations along the second Nile cataract in Nubia have been used to argue quite the opposite for the Middle Kingdom.[264] Some of these remained in situ at the fortress of Semna into modern times, preserving the actual positions of high-water marks during the reigns of Amenemhat III and Amenemhat IV of the late Twelfth Dynasty and kings of the early Thirteenth Dynasty.[265] Beginning with the early years of Amenemhat III, these floods are, on average, 7.3 m higher than those recorded in modern times.[266] Explanations for this vast discrepancy have included erosion lowering the riverbed and a cliff collapse that widened the channel.[267] As with the Old Kingdom annals, the accuracy of these records has been questioned.[268] The documentation is incomplete and accounts for neither all Middle Kingdom reigns nor all years within a given reign. That only floods of "great and unusual height" were inscribed suggested to Bell that these floods were recorded for that very reason, "as wondrous curiosities."[269] These floods were, she postulates, likely atypical, 20 or 30 occurring over a span of less than a century.[270]

Analysis of the $^{87}Sr/^{86}Sr$ ratios in core S21 (Lake Manzala) suggests a period of low sedimentation rates, which would be indicative of high Nile flow, for 4.75–2.05 ka BP, the only one after the Predynastic Period;[271] however, for reasons already discussed, data from this core require review. Intrusive alluvium deposits occur at a number of sites of Middle Kingdom date, ranging from second cataract forts to delta settlements. On the island of Elephantine, alluvium filled a depression between Twelfth Dynasty Stratum IV(2) and New Kingdom Stratum V, above 96 m asl, in an episode that apparently destroyed Twelfth Dynasty walls here.[272] There is no evidence of occupation dating from the end of the Middle Kingdom through the Second Intermediate Period in this area.[273] Walls of the Middle Kingdom town at Abu Ghalib were in places covered with mud more than 2.5 m deep.[274] Zbigniew Szafrański suggests that the Second Intermediate Period appearance of casemate foundations, which supported a large platform on which a building was then constructed, was a response to the dramatic late Middle Kingdom floods that laid such deposits.[275]

Human effort, rather than high flood levels, is most often credited with reestablishing the Bahr Yussef as a connection between the Nile and the Fayum basin, where rulers of the Middle Kingdom are thought to have undertaken major building and agricultural projects.[276] However, extreme flood events could have yielded a similar result, washing out prior records. If resumption of Nile inflow at this time is recorded in Fayum core FA-1, Marks et al. do not note it; instead, they report that a "more regular seasonal water supply from the Nile returned presumably at the beginning of [the 3.0–1.5 cal ka BP] phase when the lake contained much silica and planktonic Aulacoseira were common in spring."[277] Indeed, they found complete lack of diatoms at ca. 3.2 cal ka. BP,[278] which would indicate that desiccation of the lake persisted throughout the Bronze Age.

Corbicula shells obtained from loose mud bricks from two pyramids in the Fayum area (FM 15, Senwosret II at Lahun, 3830–3824 cal BP; FM 14, Amenemhat III at Hawara, 3805–3758 cal BP) were examined by Hassan et al. with the presumption that they, and the mud in which they were found, were of local origin.[279] Their absolute temporal placement was provided by radiocarbon dating calibrated with OxCal 4.0;[280] regnal assignment was determined by archaeological context, with the caveat that, given their secondary context, their ^{14}C dates must be termini ante quem.[281] The ∂^{18}O values of FM 15 and FM 14 were "moderately positive" (+2.96%, +3.47%, respectively), and their ∂^{13}C "strongly negative" (-6.31%, -6.04%, respectively).[282] The authors relate these data to "a markedly reduced Nile flood discharge at ca. 3750 BP [...] during the building of the pyramids at Lahun and Hawara, a time when hydrological engineering in the Hawara channel [to rejoin the Fayum lake with the Nile] was beginning as Nile flood[s] were high."[283] An earthen dam with floodgates regulated water that entered the lake; this is now known to be of Middle Kingdom date.[284]

Judged by locations of a temple of Sobek and colossal statues of Amenemhet III, during this king's reign, the lake level was below 18 m asl, and likely 4 m lower in the event of particularly high inundations.[285] That the lake subsequently rose higher, to c. 20 m asl, is indicated by "a stratified section of lake shoreface deposits" noted by Hassan "above the ground-level of one of the [statue] pedestals, underlying a fallen block of stone from the pedestal."[286] Even later in the Middle Kingdom, the lake rose higher, above 22 m asl, perhaps on account of increased sedimentation.[287] At about this time, the dam seems to have been no longer able to withstand the river floodwaters, which may have destroyed it.[288]

All of these high-water events seem to lie outside the fourth "major period of hydroclimatic change" noted by Macklin et al. in their meta-analysis; in this, the second to take place during the pharaonic period, water levels in East African lakes dropped and a cooling trend began ca. 1600 BCE.[289]

New Kingdom to the Greco-Roman Period

Data from East African lakes (Victoria, Tana, Challa) and Kilimanjaro ice cores evidence a period of significant climate change marked by diminishing lake levels and cooler temperatures from 1600 cal BCE until 1100 cal BCE.[290] This could correspond with the end of a very lengthy period of shallowness in the Fayum lake reported by Marks et al. in core FA-1 for 4.4–3.0 cal ka BP,[291] but it contrasts with data from the Nile Valley in Macklin et al.'s meta-analysis, which indicates increased Nile flow and Fayum lake levels ca. 1450 cal

BCE and a series of notably high inundations starting about a century later (1350–1100 cal BCE).[292] It is in this period, at 3.0 cal. ka BP rather than the Middle Kingdom, that Marks et al. note a reconnection between the Nile River and the Fayum lake.[293] The lake had begun the 3.0–1.5 cal ka BP period as a brackish lake (with diatomic species favoring such conditions, following a period in which there had been no diatoms at all) and may have deepened (the presence of pyrite suggesting an anaerobic environment).[294] Over about 500 years, the lake desalinized, indicated by falling levels of Ca^{2+}, Mg^{2+}, Na^+, SO_4^{2-}, Cl^-, and NO_3^-.[295] That desalinization began 2.3 cal ka BP suggests to the investigators that this is a signature of freshwater brought in by Ptolemaic canal works.[296]

The stratigraphy of the so-called deep well drilled at Karnak,[297] suggests a period of "high Nile flow" in the Eighteenth Dynasty;[298] [14]C dating of a piece of acacia wood with evidence of having been worked by human hand found in this level returned a date of 3158 ±47 cal BP, interpreted (1σ) as 1494/1402 BCE[299] (calibrated with OxCal 4.1[300]).

Climate proxies from eastern Mediterranean sites beyond northeastern Africa have suggested a crisis-inducing drought at the transition between the Late Bronze Age and the Iron Age, ca. 1100 BCE (the so-called "3.2 ka event", or Bell's Second Dark Age[301]), thought to be related to increased levels of microscopic charcoal ca. 3.0 cal ka BP in Burullus Lagoon core S-53.[302] The Egyptian evidence cited most frequently for this event abroad is documentary. In the mid-Nineteenth Dynasty, Merenptah (conventionally mid-/late 13th century BCE) could spare large shipments of grain for the Hittite Empire in Anatolia, which was evidently suffering from a famine, although its cause is not known, drought being only one possibility; the availability of grain to send abroad would indicate that Nile inundations were good.[303] However, by the time of Ramesses III (conventionally 12th century BCE), strikes and riots of royal artisans, who were paid in food rations, suggest food shortages in Egypt.[304] This social unrest and bouts of grain-price inflation are evident from documents dating to the reign of Ramesses IV (mid-12th century BCE).[305] Non-climate factors, such as raids by Libyan tribes and government corruption, would have been at work[306] but Butzer offers that "the repeated waves of wild inflation strongly suggest that famines were triggered by Nile failures."[307]

To these often-cited data has been added statistical analysis of administrative records related to fish delivered as part of wages for the artisans responsible for creating the royal tombs in the Valley of the Kings at the very end of the Egyptian New Kingdom.[308] These papyri survive in some quantity for the Twentieth Dynasty (reigns of Ramesses III–XI, covering about a century and a quarter). Jean-Christophe Antoine's analysis uncovered an apparent correlation between "fish production" and the inundation.[309] Fish deliveries peaked during months when the inundation was receding. A "significant" reduction in fish deliveries to the workers during the reigns of Ramesses IX–X was also revealed by Jean-Christophe Antoine's analysis.[310] He argues that neither administrative factors, fishing methods, nor greater reliance on dried fish are likely to have produced the latter result.[311] Social unrest might have been a factor, but he concludes that the pattern of deliveries implies that climate was a significant, although not unique, influence.[312] That a "great inundation" in one of the documents is dated to late January, when the inundation should have already receded, "suggests a delayed or excessive and prolonged flood."[313] Furthermore, either during or following each year with very low fish deliveries was a "report of hunger or shortage of fish, grain, or vegetables."[314] An excessively high or prolonged inundation could account for poor harvests from both river and field, and early modern Egypt offers parallels for this.[315]

In Lake Manzala core S21, fluctuating [87]Sr/[86]Sr ratios (0.7080–0.7082) between ca. 4.0 and ca. 2.35 ka BP (that is, broadly the Middle Kingdom nearly to Ptolemaic times) is followed by a period, starting at 2.2 ka BP, of decrease to 0.07075, which remained relatively steady until 950 years BP, and Ti/Al ratios vary similarly.[316] A long period of low sedimentation (thought to correspond to low sediment input from the Blue Nile) was detected between 4.75 and 2.05 ka BP;[317] cautions have already been suggested for such data. Published Nile Valley data analyzed by Macklin et al. detected drought, ca. 1100–900 BCE, as well as high floods.[318]

In Sudan, at Amara West, sediment cores were taken from a palaeochannel that had formerly separated an island on which a Ramesside-era town of was built.[319] OSL dating of the channel fill showed that the fill had accumulated to a depth of 2.74 m over a span of a thousand years or so, from 3280 ±215 BP (by which time the channel had already failed to perennially fill with water) to 2215 ±180 BP,[320] when it was entirely silted up.[321] Excavators believe that the process cutting off the channel's perennial flow was swift, perhaps three decades.[322] It accords with a period of significant drying of palaeochannels upstream, in the Northern Dongola Reach.[323] Here, OSL dating of sands from a levee neighboring the Alfreda Nile palaeochannel demonstrates that floodwaters deposited sediment here until ca. 1320 (±270) BCE; desiccation of the Alfreda palaeochannel took place, according to OSL dating, not long before 1290 (±160) BCE.[324] The period of decline may not have been as swift as dates would seem to indicate, due to the OSL uncertainty factor, but Macklin et al. assess this as a "sudden failure of this system, perhaps in less than a century."[325]

Both the Alfreda and two palaeochannels in the vicinity of Amara West (the Amara West channel and the larger Northern channel 2 km downstream) preserve sedimentary evidence of exceptionally high floods after this dry period. Six such events deposited sediment in the Amara West channel;[326] OSL dating of aeolian sands to ca. 205 BCE suggest a date of about 200 BCE for the last flood to deposit there.[327] The Northern palaeochannel shows "major flood events between 910 (±350) and 520 (±255) B.C."[328] The Alfreda Nile palaeochannel flood events are dated (OSL) to between ca. 780 (±130 yr) BCE and 730 (±150 yr) BCE[329] This wet phase is evidenced much farther upstream, in the vicinity of Jebelein, on the White Nile in Sudan. Two samples (S2-1, S2-2) of a level of gravelly sandy clay from a trench excavated near the right bank of the river produced OSL dates of 3.1 ±0.6 ka BP and 3.0 ±0.9 ka BP at a depth of 60 cm;[330] at a depth of 75 cm, a late Neolithic or early Iron Age grindstone was found.[331] This unit is interpreted as sediment laid by the river on the floodplain during "a brief interval of slightly wetter climate."[332] On the other hand, at Khor Abu Habl on the White Nile, the dunes that had been restabilized by vegetation following the previously mentioned period of activity dated (by OSL) to 4.8 ±0.9 ka BP became active again at 2.9 ±0.5 ka BP.[333]

At the other end of the Nile River system, core Al 19 from the Eastern Harbor of Alexandria presented evidence of substantial anthropogenic contributions to changes present in late pharaonic/Ptolemaic-era sediments in the form of pollen assemblages—including the appearance of cultivated taxa (e.g., *Vitis* sp. [grapes])—and increased amounts of microscopic charcoal.[334] This core produced nine ^{14}C-AMS calibrated dates; three of its stratigraphic units are attributed in whole or in part to pharaonic (Middle Sand Unit III; 5.6–2.3 ka BP) and Ptolemaic (Upper Mud Unit IV, Upper Sand Unit V, ca. 2.3 ka BP–present) times.[335] The pollen assemblage of Middle Sand III changes in about the middle of the unit (3.6–2.9 ka BP, interpolated to ca. 3.25 ka BP) from one largely in common (P-MC Zone Ib) with the level below it (Lower Muddy Sand II, ca. 6.0–5.6 ka BP; predominantly *Amaranthaceae*, followed by *Cichorioideae*) to one with a significantly decreasing level of *Amaranthaceae* (P-MC Zone IIa) and the appearance of cultivated plants, including *Vitis* sp.[336] The wide span of dates in a section approximately 15 cm thick is thought to be the result of an erosional hiatus brought about by wave action (e.g., storm surge).[337] The change from Middle Sand III to Upper Mud IV is attributed to the construction of an immense causeway from the mainland to the island of Pharos in the late 4th century BCE.[338]

In the Red Sea, the aerated conditions that disrupted the water column (as indicated by species and abundance of foraminifera and pteropods in cores MC98, MC93, MC91) persisted until about 3.3 ka BP.[339] Until ca. 3.3 ka BP there was a "relatively high abundance" of *Globigerinoides sacculifer* and *G. siphoniphera*, and "very high abundance" of *Limacina bulimoides*. After this, "an almost total decrease in *L. bulimoides*," "slight increase *in Clio convexa*," and "high abundance of *G. ruber*" and other epipelagic (surface-zone) formanifera indicate more humid conditions that lasted until another period of water-column aeration, less severe than the previous, beginning ca. 2.0 ka BP (i.e., the Roman period) and ending ca. 700 BP, indicated by a rebound in the population of *G. sacculifer*.[340]

Conclusion

Bell's climate-change narrative for pharaonic Egypt relied largely, although not entirely, on archaeological and textual data, and was, thus, necessarily incomplete, written, as it was, before the availability of most environmental proxy data. By the early 2000s, looking specifically at the Old Kingdom/First Intermediate Period transition, Moeller could not find enough scientifically derived environmental data to substantiate Bell's hypothesis. The present review of diverse evidence developed since then—unavailable to (or overlooked by) Moeller at the time of her own writing—demonstrates that a critical mass of scientific data now supports something like Bell's environmental inferences.

Nonetheless, if the occurrence of climate change in ancient Egypt now seems unassailable, its proxies introduce equally undeniable ambiguities and imprecisions that must be addressed before the environmental data can be incorporated into the ancient Egyptian historical framework with sufficient precision to support accurate conclusions regarding any relationship between climate change and socio-political transformation during the pharaonic period. Even with the development of methods to refine radiocarbon dates,[341] environmental-cultural coincidences cannot yet be recognized with the temporal precision necessary[342] to even begin to suggest causation. Accurately synchronizing the myriad environmental and cultural data will require development of a precise chronological method and a timeline specific to Egypt.[343]

Until the temporal resolution for the socio-political events of Egypt and its neighbors is considerably improved, and more and better quality environmental proxy data for Egypt and Sudan are available, the climate of the Nile Valley should be discussed and considered unto itself, not as a complement to or within the framework of "North Africa and the Middle East," as often occurs.[344] There is not, for example, sufficient evidence to suggest that ancient Egypt was so inextricably intertwined with its outside world that societal "collapse" or climate shifts elsewhere necessarily produced socio-political change along the Nile: Egypt appears on the list of victims of severe events prominent in ancient Egypt's interconnected world (notably the 4.2 ka BP aridification event) through *circulus in probando*. Still, that the societies of the ancient Mediterranean, Near East, and North Africa had complex interactions and were, in some ways, interdependent—Butzer's "contentious complementarity"[345]—cannot be ignored.[346] Egypt's socio-political and environmental history will also have to be synchronized with that of the world beyond it.

Scholarship has approached the point at which the nuanced cultural and environmental records can be more fully understood, but applying those understandings with the required

31

exactitude still lies beyond the grasp of even collective effort. Scholars working in relevant fields are progressing, approaching the point at which historical, environmental, and cultural records can be directly linked, but precise proxy records and greater application of the broad range of analytical methods available to archaeological science are necessary in Egypt. Regulatory restrictions that limit these efforts are stifling the kinds of progress just discussed. Such efforts have been well rewarded in the regions neighboring Egypt, but, for now, the complementary human and environmental records for the pharaonic world remain untethered from one another.

ACKNOWLEDGMENTS

The author is grateful to several anonymous reviewers, Noreen Doyle, and Angus Graham for comments on this manuscript, which improved it considerably.

WORKS CITED

Alexanian, N., W. Bebermeier, and D. Blaschta. 2018 "The Discovery of the Lower Causeway of the Bent Pyramid and the Reconstruction of the Ancient Landscape at Dahshur (Egypt)." In *Landscape Archaeology: Egypt and the Mediterranean World*, edited by Y. Tristant and M. Ghilardi, 7–18. Cairo: Institut français d'archéologie orientale.

Antoine, J.-C. 2006. "Fluctuations of Fish Deliveries at Deir el-Medina in the Twentieth Dynasty: A Statistical Analysis." *Studien zur Altägyptischen Kultur* 35: 25–41.

———. 2009. "The Delay of the Grain Ration and Its Social Consequences at Deir el-Medîna in the Twentieth Dynasty: A Statistical Analysis." *Journal of Egyptian Archaeology* 95: 223–234.

Arz, H.W., F. Lamy, and J. Pätzold. 2006. "A Pronounced Dry Event Recorded Around 4.2 ka in Brine Sediments from the Northern Red Sea." *Quaternary Research* 66: 432–441.

Bar-Oz, G., E. Tsahar, I. Izhaki, and S. Lev-Yadun. 2015. "Mammalian Extinction in Ancient Egypt, Similarities with the Southern Levant." *Proceedings of the National Academy of Sciences of the United States of America* 112(3): E238.

Bárta, M. 2015. "Long Term or Short Term? Climate Change and the Demise of the Old Kingdom." In *Climate and Ancient Societies*, edited by S. Kerner, R.J. Dann, and P. Bangsgaard, 177–195. Copenhagen: Museum Tusculanum Press.

Bárta, M., and A. Bezděk. 2008 "Beetles and the Decline of the Old Kingdom: Climate Change in Ancient Egypt." In *Chronology and Archaeology in Ancient Egypt (the Third Millennium B.C.)*, edited by H. Vymazalová and M. Bárta, 214–224. Prague: Czech Institute of Egyptology, Faculty of Arts, Charles University in Prague.

Bell, B. 1970. "The Oldest Records of the Nile Floods." *The Geographical Journal* 136(4): 569–573.

———. 1971. "The Dark Ages in Ancient History. I. The First Dark Age in Egypt." *American Journal of Archaeology* 75(1): 1–26.

———. 1975 "Climate and the History of Egypt: The Middle Kingdom." *American Journal of Archaeology* 79(3): 223–269.

Bernhardt, C., B.P. Horton, and J.-D. Stanley. 2012. "Nile Delta Vegetation Response to Holocene Climate Variability." *Geology* 40(7): 615–618.

Bond, G., W. Showers, M. Cheseby, R. Lotti, P. Almasi, P. deMenocal, P. Priore, H. Cullen, I. Hajdas, and G. Bonani. 1997. "A Pervasive Millennial-Scale Cycle in North Atlantic Holocene and Glacial Climates." *Science* 278(5341): 1257–1266.

Bronk Ramsey, C., and A.J. Shortland, eds. 2013. *Radiocarbon and the Chronologies of Ancient Egypt*. Oxford: Oxbow.

Bronk Ramsey, C., M.W. Dee, J.M. Rowland, T.F.G. Higham, S.A. Harris, F. Brock, A. Quiles, E.M. Wild, E.S. Marcus, and A.J. Shortland. 2010. "Radiocarbon-Based Chronology for Dynastic Egypt." *Science* 328: 1554–1557.

Bunbury, J., A. Tavares, B. Pennington, and P. Gonçalves. 2017. "Development of the Memphite Floodplain: Landscape and Settlement Symbiosis in the Egyptian Capital Zone." In *The Nile: Natural and Cultural Landscape in Egypt*, edited by H. Willems and J.-M. Dahm, 71–96. Bielefeld: transcript Verlag.

Butzer, K.W. 1983. "Human Response to Environmental Change in the Perspective of Future, Global Climate." *Quaternary Research* 19: 279–292.

———. 1984. "Long-term Nile Flood Variation and Political Discontinuities in Pharaonic Egypt." In *From Hunters to Farmers: Causes and Consequences of Food Production in Africa*, edited by J.D. Clark and S.A. Brandt, 102–112. Berkeley: University of California Press.

———. 1997. "Sociopolitical Discontinuity in the Near East C. 2200 B.C.E.: Scenarios from Palestine and Egypt." In *Third Millennium B.C. Climate Change and Old World Collapse*, edited by H.N. Dalfes, G. Kukla, and H. Weiss, 245–296. NATO ASI Series (Series I: Global Environmental Change) 49. Berlin: Springer.

———. 2012. "Collapse, Environment, and Society." *Proceedings of the National Academy of Sciences of the United States of America* 109(10): 3632–3639.

Butzer, K.W., E. Butzer, and S. Love. 2013. "Urban Geoarchaeology and Environmental History at the Lost City of the Pyramids, Giza: Synthesis and Review." *Journal of Archaeological Science* 40: 3340–3366.

Cílek, V., L. Lisá, and M. Bárta, M. 2011. "The Holocene of the Abusir Area." In *Abusir and Saqqara in the Year 2010*, vol. 1, edited by M. Bárta, F. Coppens, and J. Kreči, 312–326. Prague: Czech Institute of Egyptology, Faculty of Arts, Charles University in Prague.

Cílek, V., M. Bárta, L. Lisá, A. Pokorná, L. Juříčková, V. Brůna, A.M.A. Mahmud, A. Bajer, and J. Beneš. 2012. "Diachronic Development of the Lake of Abusir During the Third Millennium B.C., Cairo, Egypt." *Quaternary International* 266: 14–24.

Clarke, J., N. Brooks, E.B. Banning, M. Bar-Matthews, S. Campbell, L. Clare, M. Cremaschi, S. di Lernia, N. Drake, M. Gallinaro, S. Manning, K. Nicoll, G. Philip, S. Rosen, U.-D. Schoop, M.A. Tafuri, B. Weninger, and A. Zerboni. 2016. "Climatic Changes and Social Transformations in the Near East and North Africa During the 'Long' 4th Millennium B.C.: A Comparative study of Environmental and Archaeological Evidence." *Quaternary Science Reviews* 136: 96–121.

Claussen, M. 2003. "Simulation of Holocene Climate Change Using Climate-System Models." In *Global Change in the Holocene*, edited by A. Mackay, R. Battarbee, J. Birks, and F. Oldfield, 422–434. London: Arnold.

Cline, E.H., A. Yasur-Landau, and A. Koh. 2017. "The Absolute Chronology of the Middle Bronze Age Palace at Tel Kabri: Implications for Aegean-Style Wall Paintings in the Eastern Mediterranean." In *Chronological Conundrums: Egypt and the Middle Bronze Age Southern Levant*, edited by F. Höflmayer and S.L. Cohen, 43–47. Journal of Ancient Egyptian Interconnections 13. Tucson: University of Arizona Egyptian Expedition.

Cohen, K.M., S.C. Finney, P.L. Gibbard, and J.-X. Fan. 2018. "International Chrono-stratigraphic Chart." *International Commission on Stratigraphy*, http://www.stratigraphy.org/ICSchart/ChronostratChart2018-08.pdf (accessed 29 May 2019).

Cohen, S.L. 2017. "Reevaluation of Connections between Egypt and the Southern Levant in the Middle Bronze Age in Light of the New Higher Chronology." In *Chronological Conundrums: Egypt and the Middle Bronze Age Southern Levant*, edited by F. Höflmayer and S. L., 34–42. Journal of Ancient Egyptian Interconnections 13. Tucson: University of Arizona Egyptian Expedition.

Creasman, P.P. 2014. "Tree Rings and the Chronology of Ancient Egypt." *Radiocarbon* 56(4): S85–S92.

Creasman, P.P., and R.H. Wilkinson, eds. 2017. *Pharaoh's Land and Beyond: Ancient Egypt and Its Neighbors.* Oxford: Oxford University Press.

Cullen, H.M., P.B. deMenocal, S. Hemming, G. Hemming, F.H. Brown, T. Guilderson, and F. Sirocko. 2000. "Climate Change and the Collapse of the Akkadian Empire: Evidence from the Deep Sea." *Geoarchaeology* 28(4): 379–382.

Dee, M.W. 2017. "Absolute Dating Climatic Evidence and the Decline of Old Kingdom Egypt." In *The Late Third Millennium in the Ancient Near East: Chronology, C14, and Climate Change,* edited by F. Höflmayer, 323–331. Chicago: The Oriental Institute of the University of Chicago.

Dee, M.W., J.M. Rowland, T.F.G. Higham, A.J. Shortland, F. Brock, S.A. Harris, and C. Bronk Ramsey. 2012. "Synchronising Radiocarbon Dating and the Egyptian Historical Chronology by Improved Sample Selection." *Antiquity* 86: 868–883.

Devecchi, E., and J.L. Miller. 2011. "Hittite-Egyptian Synchronisms and Their Consequences for Ancient Near Eastern Chronology." In *Egypt and the Near East—The Crossroads. Proceedings of an International Conference on the Relations of Egypt and the Near East in the Bronze Age, Prague, September 1–3, 2010,* edited by J. Mynářova, 139–176. Prague: Charles University in Prague.

Edel, E. 1994. *Die ägyptisch-hethitische Korrespondenz aus Boghazköi in babylonischer und hethitischer Sprache.* 2 vols. Abhandlungen der Rheinisch-Westfälischen Akademie der Wissenschaften 77. Opladen: Westdeutscher Verlag.

Edelman-Furstenberg, Y., A. Almogi-Labin, and C. Hemleben. 2009. "Palaeoceanographic Evolution of the Central Red Sea During the Holocene." *The Holocene* 19(1): 117–127.

Evans, L. 2015. "Ancient Egypt's Fluctuating Fauna: Ecological Events or Cultural Constructs?" *Proceedings of the National Academy of Sciences of the United States of America* 112(3): E239.

Falconer, S.E., and P.L. Fall. 2017. "Radiocarbon Evidence from Tell Abu en-Ni'aj and Tell el-Hayyat, Jordan, and Its Implications for Bronze Age Levantine and Egyptian Chronologies." In *Chronological Conundrums: Egypt and the Middle Bronze Age Southern Levant,* edited by F. Höflmayer and S.L. Cohen, 7–19. Journal of Ancient Egyptian Interconnections 13. Tucson: University of Arizona Egyptian Expedition.

Finné, M., K. Holmgren, H. Sundqvist, E. Weiberg, and M. Lindblom. 2011. "Climate in the Eastern Mediterranean, and Adjacent Regions, During the Past 6000 Years—A Review." *Journal of Archaeological Science* 38(12): 3153–3173.

Finné, M., K. Holmgren, C.-C. Shen, H.-M. Hu, M. Boyd, and S. Stocker. 2017. "Late Bronze Age Climate Change and the Destruction of the Mycenaean Palace of Nestor at Pylos." *PLoS ONE* 12(12): e0189447.

Flaux, C., C. Claude, N. Marriner, and C. Morhange. 2013. "A 7500-year Strontium Isotope Record from the Northwestern Nile Delta (Maryut Lagoon, Egypt)." *Quaternary Science Reviews* 78: 22–33.

Gatto, M.C., and A. Zerboni. 2015. "Holocene Supra-regional Environmental Changes as Trigger for Major Socio-Cultural Processes in Northeastern Africa and the Sahara." *African Archaeological Review* 32: 301–333.

Ghilardi, M., Y. Tristant, and M. Boraik. 2012. "Nile River Evolution in Upper Egypt during the Holocene: Palaeoenvironmental Implications for the Pharaonic sites of Karnak and Coptos." *Géomorphologie* 18(1): 7–22.

Giddy, L., and D. Jeffreys. 1992. "Memphis, 1991." *Journal of Egyptian Archaeology* 78: 1–11.

Goiran, J.-P. 2001. "Recherches géomorphologiques dans la région littorale d'Alexandrie en Egypte." Ph.D. dissertation, Université de Provence—Aix-Marseille I.

Greenberg, R. 2017. "No Collapse: Transmutations of Early Bronze Age Urbanism in the Southern Levant." In *The Late Third Millennium in the Ancient Near East: Chronology, C14, and Climate Change*, edited by F. Höflmayer, 31–58. Chicago: The Oriental Institute of the University of Chicago.

Hamdan, M.A., F.A. Hassan, R.J. Flower, and E.M. Ebrahim. 2016. "Climate and Collapse of Egyptian Old Kingdom: A Geoarchaeological Approach." In *Archaeology and Environment: Understanding the Past to Design the Future: A Multidisciplinary Approach: Proceedings of the International Workshop "Italian Days in Aswan," 15th–18th November 2013*, edited by G. Capriotti Vittozzi and F. Porcelli, 37–48. Rome: Consiglio Nazionale delle Ricerche Istituto di Studi sul Mediterraneo Antico.

Hamdan, M.A., S.M. Martinez, M.T. Garcia Vallès, J.M. Nogués, F.A. Hassan, R.J. Flower, M.H. Aly, A. Senussi, and E.S. Ebrahim. 2013. "Ancient Egyptian Pottery from the Subsurface Floodplain of the Saqqara-Memphis Area: Its Mineralogical and Geochemical Implications." *Archaeometry* 56(6): 987–1008.

Hassan, F.A. 1986. "Holocene Lakes and Prehistoric Settlements of the Western Faiyum, Egypt." *Journal of Archaeological Science* 13: 483–501.

Hassan, F.A., and M. Hamdan. 2008. "The Faiyum Oasis—Climate Change and Water Management in Ancient Egypt." In *Traditional Water Techniques: Cultural Heritage for a Sustainable Future: SHADUF Project*, edited by F.A. Hassan, 117–147. [Luxembourg]: European Commission, Sixth Framework Programme.

Hassan, F.A., and G. Tassie. 2006. "Modelling Environmental and Settlement Change in the Fayum." *Egyptian Archaeology* 29: 37–40.

Hassan, F.A., M.A. Hamdan, R.J. Flower, and K. Keatings. 2012. "The Oxygen and Carbon Isotopic records in Holocene Freshwater Mollusc Shells from the Faiyum Paleolakes, Egypt: Their Paleoenvironmental and Paleoclimatic Implications." *Quaternary International* 266: 175–187.

Hassan, F.A., M. Hamdan, R.J. Flower, and G. Tassie. 2011. "Holocene Geoarchaeology and Water History of the Fayoum, Egypt." In *Natural and Cultural Landscapes in the Fayoum: The Safeguarding and Management of Archaeological Sites and Natural Environments*, edited by R. Pirelli, 116–133. Cairo: UNESCO.

Hoelzmann, P., H.-J. Kruse, and F. Rottinger. 2000. "Precipitation Estimates for the Eastern Saharan Palaeomonsoon Based on a Water Balance Model of the West Nubian Palaeolake Basin." *Global and Planetary Change* 26: 105–120.

Höflmayer, F. 2014. "Dating Catastrophes and Collapses in the Ancient Near East: The End of the First Urbanization in the Southern Levant and the 4.2 ka B.P. Event." In *Overcoming Catastrophes: Essays on Disastrous Agents Characterization and Resilience Strategies in Pre-classical Southern Levant*, edited by L. Nigro, 117–140. La Sapienza Studies on the Archaeology of Palestine and Transjordan 11. Rome: La Sapienza.

———. 2015. "The Southern Levant, Egypt, and the 4.2 ka B.P. Event." In *2200 B.C.—A Climatic Breakdown as a Cause for the Collapse of the Old World?* edited by H. Meller, H.W. Arz, R. Jung, R. Risch, S. Hämmerle, I. Aitken, and D. Tucker, 113–130. Halle (Saale): Landesmuseum für Vorgeschichte.

———. 2017a. "The Late Third Millennium B.C. in the Ancient Near East and Eastern Mediterranean: A Time of Collapse and Transformation." In *The Late Third Millennium in the Ancient Near East: Chronology, C14, and Climate Change*, edited by F. Höflmayer, 1–28. Chicago: The Oriental Institute of the University of Chicago.

———, ed. 2017b. *The Late Third Millennium in the Ancient Near East: Chronology, C14, and Climate Change.* Chicago: The Oriental Institute of the University of Chicago.

Höflmayer, F., and S.L. Cohen. 2017a "Chronological Conundrums: Egypt and the Middle Bronze Age Southern Levant." In *Chronological Conundrums: Egypt and the Middle Bronze Age Southern Levant,* edited by F. Höflmayer and S.L. Cohen, 1–6. Journal of Ancient Egyptian Interconnections 13. Tucson: University of Arizona Egyptian Expedition.

Höflmayer, F., and S.L. Cohen, eds. 2017b. *Chronological Conundrums: Egypt and the Middle Bronze Age Southern Levant.* Journal of Ancient Egyptian Interconnections 13. Tucson: University of Arizona Egyptian Expedition.

Hornung, E., R. Krauss, and D.A. Warburton. 2006. *Ancient Egyptian Chronology.* Leiden: Brill.

Jesse, F. 2006. "Cattle, Sherds and Mighty Walls—The Wadi Howar from Neolithic to Kushite Times." *Sudan and Nubia* 10: 43–54, pls. XXV–XXXI.

Kaniewski, D., E. Paulissen, E. Van Campo, H. Weiss, T. Otto, J. Bretschneider, and K. Van Lergerghe. 2010. "Late Second–Early First Millennium B.C. Abrupt Climate Changes in Coastal Syria and Their Possible Significance for the History of the Eastern Mediterranean." *Quaternary Research* 74: 207–215.

Kaniewski, D., E. Van Campo, J. Guiot, S. Le Burel, T. Otto, and C. Baeteman. 2013. "Environmental Roots of the Late Bronze Age Crisis." *PLoS ONE* 8(8): 1–10.

Kenoyer, J. 2015. "The Archaeological Heritage of Pakistan: From the Palaeolithic to the Indus Civilization." In *A History of Pakistan,* edited by R.D. Long, 1–90. Karachi: Oxford University Press.

Kraemer, B. 2010. "The Meandering Identity of a Fayum Canal: The Henet of Moeris / Dioryx Kleonos / Bahr Wardan / Abdul Wahbi." In *Proceedings of the Twenty-Fifth International Congress of Papyrology, Ann Arbor 2007,* edited by T. Gagos and A. Hyatt, 365–376. Ann Arbor: Scholarly Publishing Office, The University of Michigan Library.

Krom, M.D., J.D. Stanley, R.A. Cliff, and J.C. Woodward. 2002. "Nile River Sediment Fluctuations over the Past 7000 Yr and Their Key Role in Sapropel Development." *Geology* 20(1): 71–74.

Kuraszkiewicz, K.O. 2016. "Architectural Innovations Influenced by Climatic Phenomena (4.2 KA Event) in the Late Old Kingdom (Saqqara, Egypt)." *Studia Quaternaria* 33(1): 27–34.

Kuzucuoğlu, C., and C. Marro. 2007. "Northern Syria and Upper Mesopotamia at the End of the Third Millennium B.C.: Did a Crisis Take Place?" In *Sociétés humaines et changement climatique à la fin du troisième millénaire: une crise a-t-elle eu lieu en Haute Mésopotamie? Actes du Colloque de Lyon (5–8 décembre 2005),* edited by C. Kuzucuoğlu and C. Marro, 583–590. Istanbul: Institut français d'études anatoliennes.

Liu, F., and Z. Feng. 2012. "A Dramatic Climatic Transition at ~4000 cal. yr. B.P. and Its Cultural Responses in Chinese Cultural Domains." *The Holocene* 22(10): 1181–1197.

Mackay, A., R. Battarbee, J. Birks, and F. Oldfield, eds. 2003. *Global Change in the Holocene.* London: Arnold.

Macklin, M.G., and J. Lewin. 2015. "The Rivers of Civilization." *Quaternary Science Reviews* 114: 228–244.

Macklin, M.G., W.H.J. Toonen, J.C. Woodward, M.A.J. Williams, C. Flaux, N. Marriner, K. Nicoll, G. Verstraeten, N. Spencer, and D. Welsby. 2015. "A New Model of River Dynamics, Hydroclimatic Change and Human Settlement in the Nile Valley Derived from Meta-analysis of the Holocene Fluvial Archive." *Quaternary Science Reviews* 130: 109–123.

Macklin, M.G., J.C. Woodward, D.A. Welsby, G.A.T. Duller, F.M. Williams, and M.A.J. Williams. 2013. "Reach-Scale River Dynamics Moderate the Impact of Rapid Holocene

Climate Change on Floodwater Farming in the Desert Nile." *Geology* 41(6): 695–698.

Manning, S., M.W. Dee, E.M. Wild, C. Bronk Ramsey, K. Bandy, P.P. Creasman, C.B. Griggs, C.L. Pearson, A.J. Shortland, and P. Steier. 2014. "High-Precision Dendro-14C Dating of Two Cedar Wood Sequences from First Intermediate Period and Middle Kingdom Egypt and a Small Regional Climate-Related 14C Divergence." *Journal of Archaeological Science* 46: 401–416.

Marks, L., A. Salem, F. Welc, J. Nitychoruk, Z. Chen, M. Blaauw, A. Zalat, A. Majecka, M. Szymanek, M. Chodyka, A. Toloczko-Pasek, Q. Sun, X. Zhao, and J. Jiang. 2017. "Holocene Lake Sediments from the Faiyum Oasis in Egypt: A Record of Environmental and Climate Change." *Boreas* 47(1): 62–79.

Marshall, M.H., H.F. Lamb, D. Huws, S.J. Davies, R. Bates, J. Bloemendal, J. Boyle, M.J. Leng, M. Umer, and C. Bryant. 2011. "Late Pleistocene and Holocene Drought Events at Lake Tana, the Source of the Blue Nile." *Global and Planetary Change* 78: 147–161.

Mayewskia, P.A., E.E. Rohling, J.C. Stager, W. Karlen, K.A. Maasch, L.D. Meeker, E.A. Meyerson, F. Gasse, S. van Kreveld, K. Holmgren, J. Lee-Thorp, G. Rosqvist, F. Rack, M. Staubwasser, R.R. Schneider, and E.J. Steig. 2004. "Holocene Climate Variability." *Quaternary Research* 62: 243–255.

Middleton, G.D. 2017. *Understanding Collapse: Ancient History and Modern Myths.* Cambridge: Cambridge University Press.

Moeller, N. 2005. "The First Intermediate Period: A Time of Famine and Climate Change?" *Ägypten und Levant* 15: 153–167.

Moreno García, J.C. 2015. "Climatic Change or Sociopolitical Transformation? Reassessing Late 3rd Millennium B.C. in Egypt." *Tagungen des Landesmuseums Vorgeschichte für Halle* 13: 1–16.

Morris, E. 2006. "'Lo, Nobles Lament, the Poor Rejoice'": State Formation in the Wake of Social Flux." In *After Collapse: The Regeneration of Complex Societies*, edited by G.M. Schwartz and J.J. Nichols, 58–71. Tucson: University of Arizona Press.

Obrochta, S.P., H. Miyahara, Y. Yokoyama, and T.J. Crowley. 2012. "A Re-examination of Evidence for the North Atlantic '1500-Year Cycle' at Site 609." *Quaternary Science Reviews* 55: 23–33.

O'Mara, P.F. 1996 "Was There an Old Kingdom Historiography? Is It Datable?" *Orientalia* Nova Series 65(3): 197–208.

Pachur, H.-J., and S. Kröpelin. 1993. "Wadi Howar: Paleoclimatic Evidence from an Extinct River System in the Southeastern Sahara." *Science* 237: 238–300.

Pokorný, P., P. Kočár, Z. Sůvová, and A. Bezděk. 2009. "Palaeoecology of Abusir South According to Plant and Animal Remains." In *Abusir South.* Vol. 2, *Tomb Complex of the Vizier Qar, His Sons Qar Junior and Senedjemib, and Iykai*, edited by M. Bárta, 27–48. Abusir 13. Prague: Czech Institute of Egyptology, Faculty of Arts, Charles University in Prague.

Revel, M., E. Ducassou, F.E. Grousset, S.M. Bernasconi, S. Migeon, S. Revillon, J. Mascle, A. Murat, S. Saragosi, and D. Bosch. 2010. "100,000 Years of African Monsoon Variability Recorded in Sediments of the Nile Margin." *Quaternary Science Reviews* 29: 1342–1362.

Roland, T.P., C.J. Caseldine, D.J. Charman, C.S.M. Turney, and M.J. Amesbury. 2014. "Was There a '4.2 ka Event' in Great Britain and Ireland? Evidence from the Peatland Record." *Quaternary Science Reviews* 83: 11–27.

Römer, C. 2017. "The Nile in the Fayum: Strategies of Dominating and Using the Water Resources of the River in the Oasis in the Middle Kingdom and Graeco-Roman Period." In *The Nile: Natural and Cultural Landscape in Egypt*, edited by H. Willems and J.-M. Dahms, 171–191. Bielefeld: transcript Verlag.

Said, R. 1993. *The River Nile: Geology, Hydrology and Utilization.* Oxford: Pergamon.

Schloen, J.D. 2017. "Economic and Political Implications of Raising the Date for the Disappearance of Walled Towns in the Early Bronze Age Southern Levant." In *The Late Third Millennium in the Ancient Near East: Chronology, C14, and Climate Change,* edited by F. Höflmayer, 59–71. Chicago: The Oriental Institute of the University of Chicago.

Schneider, T. 2010. "Contributions to the Chronology of the New Kingdom and the Third Intermediate Period." Ägypten *und Levant* 20: 373–403.

———. 2012. "Le casse-tête de la chronologie égyptienne." *Pour la science* 413: 28–33.

———. 2017. "'What is the Past but a Once Material Existence Now Silenced?' The First Intermediate Period from an Epistemological Perspective." In *The Late Third Millennium in the Ancient Near East: Chronology, C14, and Climate Change,* edited by F. Höflmayer, 311–322. Chicago: The Oriental Institute of the University of Chicago.

Seidlmayer, S. 2000. "The First Intermediate Period (c.2686–2125 B.C.)." In *The Oxford History of Ancient Egypt,* edited by I. Shaw, 108–136. Oxford: Oxford University Press.

Shaltout, M., and M. Azzazi. 2014. "Climate Change in the Nile Delta from Prehistoric to the Modern Era and Their Impact on Soil and Vegetation in Some Archaeological Sites." *Journal of Earth Science and Engineering* 4: 632–642.

Sheffield, J., and E.F. Wood. 2011. *Drought: Past Problems and Future Scenarios.* London: Earthscan.

Spencer, N., M. Macklin, and J. Woodward. 2012. "Re-assessing the Abandonment of Amara West: The Impact of a Changing Nile?" *Sudan and Nubia* 16: 37–43.

Stanley, D.J., and C.E. Bernhardt. 2010. "Alexandria's Eastern Harbor, Egypt: Pollen, Microscopic Charcoal, and the Transition from Natural to Human-Modified Basin." *Journal of Coastal Research* 26(1): 67–79.

Stanley, D.J., and G.A. Goodfriend. 1997. "Recent Subsidence of the Northern Suez Canal." *Nature* 388: 335–336.

Stanley, D.J., J.E. McRea, Jr, and J.C. Wilson. 1996. *Nile Delta Drill Core and Sample Database for 1985–1994: Mediterranean Basin (MEDIBA) Program.* Washington, D.C.: Smithsonian Institution Press.

Stanley, D.J., M.D. Krom, R.A. Cliff, and J.C. Woodward. 2003. "Nile Flow Failure at the End of the Old Kingdom, Egypt: Strontium Isotopic and Petrologic Evidence." *Geoarchaeology* 18(3): 395–402.

Szafrański, Z.E. 2003. "The Impact of Very High Floods on Platform Constructions in the Nile Basin of the Mid-Second Millennium B.C." In *The Synchronisation of Civilisations in the Eastern Mediterranean in the Second Millennium B.C. II. Proceedings of the SCIEM 2000-EuroConference, Haindorf, 2nd of May–7th of May 2001,* edited by M. Bietak, 205–281. Vienna: Verlag der Österreichischen Akademie der Wissenschaften.

Taylor, R., and O. Bar-Yosef. 2014. *Radiocarbon Dating.* New York: Routledge.

Touzeau, A., J. Blichert-Toft, R. Amiot, F. Fourel, F. Martineau, J. Cockitt, K. Hall, J.-P. Flandrois, and C. Lécuyer. 2013. "Egyptian Mummies Record Increasing Aridity in the Nile Valley from 5500 to 1500 yr Before Present." *Earth and Planetary Science Letters* 375: 92–100.

Trzciński, J., K.O. Kuraszkiewicz, and F. Welc. 2010. "Preliminary Report on Geoarchaeological Research in West Saqqara." *Polish Archaeology in the Mediterranean* 19: 194–206.

Weiberg, E. 2017. "Early Helladic III: A Non-monumental but Revitalized Social Arena?" In *Social Change in Aegean Prehistory,* edited by C. Wiersma and S. Voutsaki, 32–48. Oxford: Oxbow.

Weiss, H. 2000. "Beyond the Younger Dryas: Collapse as Adaptation to Abrupt Climate Change in Ancient West Asia and the Eastern Mediterranean." In *Environmental Disaster and the Archaeology of Human Response*, edited by G. Bawden and R.M. Reycraft, 75–98. Albuquerque: Maxwell Museum of Anthropology.

———. 2015. "Megadrought, Collapse, and Resilience in Late 3rd Millennium B.C. Mesopotamia." In *2200 B.C.—A Climatic Breakdown as Cause for the Collapse of the Old World?*, edited by H. Meller, H.W. Arz, R. Jung, R. Risch, S. Hämmerle, I. Aitken, and D. Tucker, 35–57. Halle (Saale): Landesmuseum fur Vorgeschichte.

———. 2017. "4.2 ka B.P. Megadrought and the Akkadian Collapse." In *Megadrought and Collapse: From Early Agriculture to Angkor*, edited by H. Weiss, 93–160. New York: Oxford University Press.

Welc, F. 2011. "The Third Dynasty Open Quarry West of the Netjerykhet Pyramid Complex (Saqqara)." Études et Travaux 24: 271–304.

Welc, F., and L. Marks. 2014. "Climate Change at the End of the Old Kingdom in Egypt Around 4200 B.P: New Geoarchaeological Evidence." *Quaternary International* 324: 124–33.

Wilkinson, T.A.H. 2000. *Royal Annals of Ancient Egypt: The Palermo Stone and Its Associated Fragments*. London: Kegan Paul International.

Williams, M.A.J. 2009. "Late Pleistocene and Holocene Environments in the Nile Basin." *Global and Planetary Change* 69: 1–15.

Williams, M.A.J., F.M. Williams, G.A.T. Duller, R.N. Munro, O.A.M. El Tom, T.T. Barrows, M. Macklin, J. Woodward, M.R. Talbot, D. Haberlah, and J. Fluin. 2010. "Late Quaternary Floods and Droughts in the Nile Valley, Sudan: New Evidence from Optically Stimulated Luminescence and AMS Radiocarbon Dating." *Quaternary Science Reviews* 29: 1116–1137.

Woodward, J., M. Macklin, L. Fielding, I. Miller, N. Spencer, D. Welsby, and M. Williams. 2015. "Shifting Sediment Sources in the World's Longest River: A Strontium Isotope Record for the Holocene Nile." *Quaternary Science Reviews* 130: 124–140.

Woodward, J., M. Macklin, N. Spencer, M. Binder, M. Dalton, S. Hay, and A. Hardy. 2017. "Living with a Changing River and Desert Landscape at Amara West." In *Nubia in the New Kingdom: Lived Experience, Pharaonic Control and Indigenous Traditions*, edited by N. Spencer, A. Stevens, and M. Binder, 227–257. Leuven: Peeters.

Yeakel, J.D., M.M. Pires, L. Rudolf, N.J. Dominy, P.L. Koch, P.R. Guimarães, Jr., and T. Gross. 2014. "Collapse of an Ecological Network in Ancient Egypt." *Proceedings of the National Academy of Sciences of the United States of America* 111(40): 14472–14477.

NOTES

[1]   Bell 1970, 1971, 1975.
[2]   Among hundreds of citations are, e.g., Said 1993, 142; Taylor and Bar-Yosef 2014.
[3]   Bell 1970.
[4]   Bell 197a1.
[5]   Bell 1975.
[6]   Bell 1970, 1971.
[7]   Bell 1971, 2.
[8]   Bell 1971, 1–3.
[9]   For citations for those who question Bell's thesis, see Moeller 2005, especially note 4 (page 153).
[10]   E.g., Weiss 2000; as compared to Finné et al. 2011.

11   For evidence from Egyptian archaeological contexts but relating directly to the 4.2 ka B.P event in the Levant rather than Egypt, see Manning et al. 2014.

12   Cullen et al. 2000.

13   Dee 2017, 323.

14   Butzer 1997.

15   Butzer 1983, 1984, 2012.

16   Seidlmayer 2000, 129.

17   Moeller 2005.

18   Cullen et al. 2000; Weiss 2000.

19   Moeller 2005, 163–165; cf., e.g., Greenberg 2017; Höflmayer 2017a; Schneider 2017.

20   Moeller 2005, 167; affirming Butzer 1997.

21   Höflmayer 2017b.

22   Schneider 2017.

23   See, for example, the papers in Höflmayer 2017b.

24   Regarding which, notably for Egypt, see Hornung et al. 2006; Bronk Ramsey et al. 2010; Höflmayer and Cohen 2017b.

25   Morris 2006, 58–71; Moreno García 2015; Höflmayer 2017a; Middleton 2017.

26   Roland et al. 2014, 11.

27   Gatto and Zerboni 2015.

28   I.e., the "Bond events" (Bond et al. 1997), countered by Obrochta et al. (2012) as "artifact(s) of averaging with minimal statistical justification" (Obrochta et al. 2012, 31).

29   Cf. Hoflmayer 2015; Kenoyer 2015; Weiberg 2017; Middleton 2017.

30   Liu and Feng 2012.

31   Cohen et al. 2018.

32   E.g., Mayewskia et al. 2004; in Mackay et al. (2003), there appears to be no references to Egypt or the Nile Valley, although one paper does discuss the pre-pharaonic "green Sahara" (Claussen 2003, 426–429).

33   Creasman 2014; Manning et al. 2014; Gatto and Zerboni 2015; Macklin et al. 2015, 109–110.

34   Weiss 2015, 2017.

35   Cf. Butzer 2012.

36   E.g., Höflmayer 2014, 2017a, 3–12; Schloen 2017.

37   E.g., Bronk Ramsey et al. 2010; Devecchi and Miller 2011; Dee et al. 2012; Bronk Ramsey and Shortland 2013; Dee 2017; Höflmayer and Cohen 2017b.

38   E.g., Devecchi and Miller 2011; Cline et al. 2017; Cohen 2017; Falconer and Fall 2017.

39   Bronk Ramsey et al. 2010, 1556 Table 1; Höflmayer 2017a, 14; Höflmayer and Cohen 2017a, 2.

40   Moeller 2005; Schneider 2017.

41   Höflmayer 2017a; Kuzucuoğlu and Marro 2007.

42   Weiss 2000; Moreno García 2015; Clarke et al. 2016; Greenberg 2017; Höflmayer 2017a; Höflmayer and Cohen 2017b; Schloen 2017; Schneider 2017.

43   For two recent surveys of evidence for pre-pharaonic times, specifically as related to societal change, see Gatto and Zerboni 2015; Clarke et al. 2016, 115–116.

44   Macklin et al. 2015, 113–117, 119–120.

45   Macklin et al. 2015, 113.

46   The portion of the Nile River that is bound primarily by the deserts, as opposed to the Nile delta region.

47   Macklin et al. 2015, 113.

48 Macklin et al. 2015, 113, 115 fig. 5.
49 Macklin et al. 2015, 113, 115 fig. 5.
50 Macklin et al. 2015, 116.
51 Shaltout and Azzazi 2014, 637 Table 3, 638 Table 4, 641.
52 Shaltout and Azzazi 2014, 637 Table 3, 638 Table 4, 640–641.
53 Shaltout and Azzazi 2014, 637 Table 3, 638 Table 4, 640.
54 Shaltout and Azzazi 2014, 638 Table 4.
55 Shaltout and Azzazi 2014, 637 Table 3.
56 Bunbury et al. 2017, 73.
57 Bunbury et al. 2017, 77.
58 Bunbury et al. 2017, 90.
59 Bunbury et al. 2017, 91.
60 Bunbury et al. 2017, 91.
61 Bunbury et al. 2017, 91.
62 Relative to other sources, e.g., wells (Touzeau et al. 2013, 97–98).
63 Touzeau et al. 2013, 93.
64 Touzeau et al. 2013, 98.
65 Touzeau et al. 2013, 93.
66 Touzeau et al. 2013, 95.
67 Touzeau et al. 2013, 97 fig. 4.
68 Touzeau et al. 2013, 97, 98.
69 Touzeau et al. 2013, 98.
70 Touzeau et al. 2013, 95, 98.
71 Touzeau et al. 2013, 95, 96 Tables 1–2.
72 Touzeau et al. 2013, 98.
73 Yeakel et al. 2014.
74 Yeakel et al. 2014, 14473.
75 Yeakel et al. 2014, 14473.
76 Yeakel et al. 2014, 14476.
77 Yeakel et al. 2014, 14473.
78 E.g., Bell 1970, 572; Stanley et al. 2003, 395–396; Welc and Marks 2014, 130.
79 Bar-Oz et al. 2015, E238.
80 Evans 2015, E239.
81 Butzer et al. 2013, 3364–3365.
82 Pokorný et al. 2009, 39–41.
83 Pokorný et al. 2009, 38–39.
84 Bell 1970, 569.
85 Wilkinson 2000.
86 E.g., Bell 1970, 1971; Stanley et al. 2003; Welc and Marks 2014; Bárta 2015.
87 Bell 1970, 572.
88 Bell 1970, 569.
89 Bell 1970, 571 Table 1.
90 Höflmayer 2014, 123.
91 Bell 1970, 571 Table 1.
92 Bell 1970.
93 Moeller 2005.
94 Bell 1970, 572.
95 Moeller 2005, 156–157; cf. O'Mara 1996, 201–203.
96 Bell 1970, 571–572.

97   Bell 1970, 571.
98   Bell 1970, 572.
99   Moeller 2005, 155–156; Höflmayer 2014, 123; Bárta 2015, 181–182.
100   Moeller 2005, 155–156.
101   Moeller 2005, 156; Höflmayer 2014, 123.
102   Moeller 2005, 156.
103   Butzer et al. 2013.
104   For example, the construction of temples and pylons during the New Kingdom in the
      Theban floodplain (Wilkinson 2000, 172–200).
105   Bell 1970, 572–573.
106   Besides those discussed in this survey, see Moeller 2005, 157–58 and Macklin et al.
      2015.
107   Macklin et al. 2015, 116.
108   Macklin et al. 2015, 116.
109   Stanley et al. 2003, 400.
110   Woodward et al. 2015, 125–126.
111   Revel et al. 2010, 1343.
112   Woodward et al. 2015, 126 fig. 1.
113   Revel et al. 2010, 1345; Woodward et al. 2015, 125.
114   Stanley et al. 2003, 398.
115   Hamdan et al. 2016, 41.
116   Hamdan et al. 2016, 41.
117   Hamdan et al. 2016, 41.
118   Stanley et al. 2003, 398.
119   Said 1993, 58.
120   Moeller 2005, 158.
121   Macklin and Lewin 2015; Woodward et al. 2015.
122   Woodward et al. 2015. It is worth noting that there is disagreement regarding whether
      some of these tributaries were permanent. The now extinct Yellow Nile occupied the
      Wadi Howar, which has a Nile outlet at Old Dongola (Sudan). Fed by local rains
      from mountains in eastern Chad (Pachur and Kröpelin 1993, 298–300), this ancient
      watercourse has been described as "flow[ing] throughout the year" during the Early
      Holocene as one of the Nile's "important tributaries" (Woodward et al. 2015, 126;
      see also Williams 2009), but Friederike Jesse (2006, 44) maintains that it should be
      understood as a "chain of lakes and water pools" in the Early and Middle Holocene
      rather than a flowing river.
123   Stanley et al. 2003, 398.
124   Stanley and Goodfriend 1997, 335; Stanley et al. 2003, 398, 399 fig. 2.
125   Stanley et al. 2003, 399 fig. 2.
126   Krom et al. 2002, 72.
127   Krom et al. 2002, 72; Stanley et al. 2003, 398.
128   Krom et al. 2002, 72.
129   Stanley et al. 2003, 398.
130   Stanley et al. 2003, 401; cf. Hamdan et al. 2016, 41–42.
131   Stanley et al. 2003, 398.
132   Woodward et al. 2015, 134–135, 138.
133   Woodward et al. 2015, 135.
134   Krom et al. 2002; Stanley et al. 2003, 399 fig. 2.
135   Woodward et al. 2015, 135–136.

136 Macklin et al. 2015, 113.
137 Woodward et al. 2015.
138 Moeller 2005, 158 with n. 50. For comparison, an anthropogenic effect is evident for a much later period at Lake Tana, which contributes 8% of the Blue Nile flow (Marshall et al. 2011, 148) and evidences a long-term aridification leading up to 4.2 cal. ka BP (Marshall et al. 2011, 157–159). Human activity has "compromis[ed] the palaeoclimate record" of the lake from 1.7 cal. ka BP onward (Marshall et al. 2011, 159). Cf., as well, the effects at Alexandria from c. 3.0 cal. ka BP onward (Stanley and Bernhardt 2010, 76–77). See also Macklin and Lewin (2015, 236) for a comparative example (the Yellow River in China).
139 Bernhardt et al. 2012, 616.
140 Bernhardt et al. 2012, 616.
141 Bernhardt et al. 2012, 617.
142 Bernhardt et al. 2012, 617.
143 Bernhardt et al. 2012, 617.
144 Hassan and Hemdan 2008, 122.
145 Macklin et al. 2015, 116.
146 Hassan and Hamdan 2008, 128–129; cf. Marks et al. 2017, 75.
147 Hassan and Hamdan 2008, 128.
148 Marks et al. 2017, 64. Marks et al. (2017, 65–66) describe this 26 m deep core as "probably the longest, best-dated and most complete succession of Holocene lake sediments in northeastern Africa." Dating was by ^{14}C AMS of organics within the mud, corrected isotopic fractionation corrections and calibrated with OxCal v. 4.2 and IntCal13; Bayesian age modeling was done using Bacon.
149 Marks et al. 2017, 75.
150 Marks et al. 2017, 75.
151 Hassan and Hamdan 2008, 128.
152 Hassan and Hamdan 2008, 129.
153 Hassan et al. 2012, 181–182, 185.
154 Hassan et al. 2012, 182–183.
155 Hassan et al. 2012, 182.
156 Hassan et al. 2012, 182, 185.
157 Hassan et al. 2012, 178.
158 Hassan et al. 2012, 184.
159 Hassan et al. 2012, 178 Table 1.
160 Hassan et al. 2012, 184 fig. 9, 184–185.
161 Hassan et al. 2012, 185.
162 Höflmayer 2014, 123.
163 Hoelzmann et al. 2000, 115.
164 Hoelzmann et al. 2000, 115, 117.
165 Stanley et al. 2003, 398.
166 Stanley et al. 2003, 398.
167 Goiron 2001, 54–57; cf. Flaux et al. 2013, 26.
168 Bernhardt et al. 2012, 617.
169 Stanley et al. 2003, 400–401; see Stanley et al. 1996, 17,198–203.
170 Stanley et al. 2003, 400.
171 Hassan and Hamden 2008, 129.
172 Marks et al. 2017, 76.
173 Marks et al. 2017, 76.

[174]   Marks et al. 2017, 76.

[175]   Hamdan et al. 2016, 42.

[176]   Hamdan et al. 2016, 42 with fig. 5.

[177]   Hamdan et al. 2016, 42.

[178]   Hamdan et al. 2016, 43 fig. 7.

[179]   Hamdan et al. 2016, 43–44.

[180]   Hamdan et al. 2016, 43.

[181]   Hamdan et al. 2016, 42.

[182]   Hassan and Hamdan 2008, 129. No ^{14}C date is given.

[183]   Hassan and Hamdan 2008, 131.

[184]   Hassan and Hamdan 2008, 137.

[185]   Arz et al. 2006, 433.

[186]   Arz et al. 2006, 435.

[187]   Arz et al. 2006, 436.

[188]   Arz et al. 2006, 435 and Table 1.

[189]   Arz et al. 2006, 436, 438.

[190]   Edelman-Furstenberg et al. 2009, 124. The age model used for the analysis of MC98, MC93, and MC 91 was ^{14}C AMS of *Globigerinoides sacculifer*, calibrated with Calib 5.02, accounting for a regional deviation from the global reservoir effect of about 180 years (Edelman-Furstenberg et al. 2009, 120).

[191]   Arz et al. 2006, 436.

[192]   Arz et al. 2006, 436, 438 fig. 5.

[193]   Arz et al. 2006, 436.

[194]   PSU refers to "practical salinity units," the common method of determining salt concentration is seawater based on its conductive properties. In the past decade, there have been efforts to replace this system of measurement (and others related to it) with the thermodynamic equation of seawater (see http://www.teos-10.org/).

[195]   Arz et al. 2006, 437.

[196]   Edelman-Furstenberg et al. 2009, 124.

[197]   Arz et al. 2006, 438.

[198]   Arz et al. 2006, 437, 438.

[199]   Arz et al. 2006, 436.

[200]   Arz et al. 2006, 437.

[201]   Arz et al. 2006, 436.

[202]   Welc and Marks 2014, 131.

[203]   Creasman 2014, S85–S87.

[204]   Welc and Marks 2014, 126–127; cf. Trzciński et al. 2010, 195–202.

[205]   Welc and Marks 2014, 127.

[206]   Trzciński et al. 2010, 195–202; Welc 2011, 283–286, 299; Welc and Marks 2014, 127–129.

[207]   Welc and Marks 2014, 128–129; cf. Trzciński et al. 2010, 195–202, 203–205; Welc 2011, 286, 299.

[208]   Butzer et al. 2013, 3363–365; Welc and Marks 2014, 129–130; cf. Marks et al. 2017, 76.

[209]   Cílek et al. 2011, 323.

[210]   Cílek et al. 2011, 323, 325.

[211]   Butzer et al. 2013, 3342, 3363.

[212]   Butzer et al. 2013, 3343.

[213]   Butzer et al. 2013, 3365.

[214]   Butzer et al. 2013, 3353–3355, 3362, 3363.

[215]   Butzer et al. 2013, 3353–3354, 3363, 3364.

[216] Butzer et al. 2013, 3341, 3364.

[217] Butzer et al. 2013, 3362–3363.

[218] Cílek et al. 2012, 19, 21, 22 fig. 8.

[219] Welc 2011, 299; Welc and Marks 2014, 129.

[220] Welc and Marks 2014, 129–130.

[221] Welc and Marks 2014, 129–130.

[222] Welc and Marks 2014, 130.

[223] Welc 2011; Welc and Marks 2014, 130.

[224] Welc and Marks 2014, 130. For architectural adaptations to these rainstorms during the second half of Pepi II's reign, see Kuraszkiewicz 2016.

[225] Welc and Marks 2014, 129; cf. Trzciński et al. 2010, 205.

[226] Trzciński et al. 2010, 205; Welc and Marks 2014, 129, 130.

[227] Welc and Marks 2014, 129, fig. 6. Cf. remarks regarding fluvial vs. aeolian transport by Butzer et al. 2013, 3343.

[228] Trzciński et al. 2010, 205; Welc and Marks 2014, 130.

[229] Bunbury et al. 2017, 81; Alexanian 2018, 10.

[230] Cílek et al. 2011, 316–317, 326.

[231] Bárta and Bezděk 2008, 214, 218.

[232] Bárta and Bezděk 2008, 223.

[233] Marks et al. 2017, 76.

[234] Bunbury et al. 2017, 81; cf. Giddy and Jeffreys 1992, 2.

[235] Hamdan et al. 2016, 40.

[236] Hamdan et al. 2016, 41–42.

[237] Hamdan et al. 2016, 40–42.

[238] Williams et al. 2010, 1126–1128, 1134.

[239] Hamdan et al. 2016, 40–41.

[240] Macklin et al. 2015.

[241] Bernhardt et al. 2012.

[242] Stanley et al. 2003; Marks et al. 2017.

[243] Trzciński et al. 2010, 205; Cílek et al. 2011; Welc and Marks 2014; Bunbury et al. 2017; Alexanian et al. 2018.

[244] Hamdan et al. 2016.

[245] Arz et al. 2006; Edelman-Furstenberg et al. 2009.

[246] E.g., Stanley et al. 2003, 400; Arz et al. 2006, 438; Edelman-Furstenberg et al. 2009, 124; Hamdan et al. 2016, 42.

[247] Macklin et al. 2015, 116.

[248] Marks et al. 2017, 76.

[249] Bernhardt et al. 2012.

[250] Stanley et al. 2003, 400–401.

[251] Edelman-Furstenberg et al. 2009, 124.

[252] Arz et al. 2006, 437.

[253] Marks et al. 2017, 76.

[254] Hamdan et al. 2016, 42.

[255] Macklin et al. 2015, 116.

[256] Welc 2011; Welc and Marks 2014.

[257] Marks et al. 2017, 76.

[258] Core SAQA22, for example, presents not only the previously discussed level corresponding to the Old Kingdom (11–12 m), but also the Middle Kingdom (9–10.1 m), Late Period (6.50–9 m; with ^{14}C date of 2470 cal. BP at 7.75 m), and Ptolemaic Period

(5–5.7 m) (Hamdan et al. 2016, 40). For detailed discussion of the pottery throughout the sequence, however, see Hamdan et al. 2013.

[259] Edelman-Furstenberg et al. 2009, 124.

[260] Krom et al. 2002, 72–73.

[261] Woodward et al. 2015.

[262] Hassan et al. 2012, 178 Table 1, 184 fig. 9.

[263] Hassan et al. 2012, 185.

[264] Bell 1975, 229–230.

[265] Bell 1975, 229, 230 ill. 2.

[266] Bell 1975, 229, 234.

[267] Bell 1975, 230–231.

[268] See Moeller (2005, 156–157) for a discussion of this and other disputed flood-height records from the period, including those from the reign of Senwosret I that very likely copy an Old Kingdom original.

[269] Bell 1975, 235.

[270] Bell 1975, 235–237.

[271] Krom et al. 2002, 72–73. The other is 6.55–5.65 ka BP.

[272] Szafranski 2003, 211.

[273] Szafranski 2003, 211.

[274] Szafranski 2003, 211.

[275] Szafranski 2003, 215–217.

[276] Bell 1975, 249–252, 254–255; Hassan and Hemdan 2008, 134–139; Hassan et al. 2011, 123–126. At present, there does not appear to be a strong data-driven basis for this explanation, which seems to be overly reliant on written records (e.g., Herodotus).

[277] Marks et al. 2017, 76.

[278] Marks et al. 2017, 76.

[279] Hassan et al. 2012, 178 Table 1.

[280] Hassan et al. 2012, 180.

[281] Hassan et al. 2012, 179.

[282] Hassan et al. 2012, 181.

[283] Hassan et al. 2012, 185.

[284] Hassan and Tassie 2006, 40; Hassan and Hemdan 2008, 137, 141–143; Hassan et al. 2011, 123, 125; Römer 2017, 177.

[285] Hassan and Hemdan 2008, 139; cf. Hassan 1986, 491; Hassan et al. 2011, 126.

[286] Hassan 1986, 491.

[287] Hassan and Hemdan 2008, 145; Hassan et al. 2011, 128.

[288] Hassan and Hemdan 2008, 145; Hassan et al. 2011, 128.

[289] Macklin et al. 2015, 116.

[290] Macklin et al. 2015, 116.

[291] Marks et al. 2017, 76.

[292] Macklin et al. 2015, 116.

[293] Marks et al. 2017, 76.

[294] Marks et al. 2017, 76.

[295] Marks et al. 2017, 77.

[296] Marks et al. 2017, 77. On the canals, see, for example, Kraemer 2010; Römer 2017, 179–189.

[297] Ghilardi et al. 2012, §13, fig. 6.

[298] Ghilardi et al. 2012, §125.

[299] Ghilardi et al. 2012, Table 1.

[300] Ghilardi et al. 2012, §19.

[301] E.g., Kaniewski et al. 2010; Kaniewski et al. 2013; Finné et al. 2017. Finné et al. (2017) took a less deterministic approach, considering that eastern Mediterranean agricultural cycles may have been negatively influenced by a brief period of dry conditions.

[302] Bernhardt et al. 2012, 617.

[303] Butzer 2012, 3634. As N. Doyle (pers. comm.) has pointed out, Ramesses II had previously sent irrigation specialists to Hatte (KUB III 34: Edel 1994, 1:84–85, 2:274–282).

[304] Antoine 2006; 2009, 232; Butzer 2012, 3634.

[305] Butzer 2012, 3634.

[306] Butzer 2012, 3634–3635.

[307] Butzer 2012, 3635.

[308] Antoine 2006.

[309] Antoine 2006, 32.

[310] Antoine 2006, 32.

[311] Antoine 2006, 32–33.

[312] Antoine 2006, 33–35.

[313] Antoine 2006, 33–34.

[314] Antoine 2006, 34.

[315] Antoine 2006, 34.

[316] Krom et al. 2002, 72.

[317] Krom et al. 2002, 72–73.

[318] Macklin et al. 2015, 116.

[319] Woodward et al. 2017, 239–40.

[320] Spencer et al. 2012, 39; Woodward et al. 2017, 237.

[321] Spencer et al. 2012, 39, 41; Woodward et al. 2017, 238.

[322] Woodward et al. 2017, 240.

[323] Macklin et al. 2013, 697; Woodward et al. 2017, 238–239, 240.

[324] Macklin et al. 2013, 697.

[325] Macklin et al. 2013, 697.

[326] Spencer et al. 2012, 39; Woodward et al. 2017, 237–238.

[327] Woodward et al. 2017, 237–238.

[328] Woodward et al. 2017, 240.

[329] Macklin et al. 2013, 697.

[330] Williams et al. 2010, 1123 Tables 2–3, 1128.

[331] Williams et al. 2010, 1128.

[332] Williams et al. 2010, 1128, 1134.

[333] Williams et al. 2010, 1126, 1128.

[334] Stanley and Bernhardt 2010, 74–77; cf. Goiran 2001, 208–228; Flaux et al. 2013, 30–31.

[335] Stanley and Bernhardt 2010, 74.

[336] Stanley and Bernhardt 2010, 75, 76.

[337] Stanley and Bernhardt 2010, 76.

[338] Stanley and Bernhardt 2010, 77.

[339] Edelman-Furstenberg et al. 2009, 124.

[340] Edelman-Furstenberg et al. 2009, 124.

[341] E.g., Bronk Ramsey et al. 2010; Dee 2017.

[342] Schneider 2010; 2012. Annual resolution in ancient Egypt extends to 664 BCE with confidence; recent efforts *may* have reached into the 8th century BCE (summarized in Creasman 2014, S85).

343   Creasman 2014.
344   Sheffield and Wood 2011, 78.
345   Butzer 1997.
346   E.g., Creasman and Wilkinson 2017; Höflmayer 2017a; Höflmayer and Cohen 2017b.

Chapter Three

Nile Management: The Evolving Dialogue Between Egyptians and Their Mighty, Migrating River

Judith Bunbury

E very archaeological site in Egypt has been affected by landscape and climate change; whether by the convulsions of the Nile or the pulsation of the deserts.[1] Geo-archaeology, although a relatively infant subject, is already contributing to our understanding of many sites in Egypt by elucidating these effects. Archaeologists learn how changes in landscape have left sites without water, transport, or food and thus lead to adaptation or abandonment. If these issues are of interest in our own time, they were of primary concern to those living at the sites in antiquity who, in many cases, had to manage landscape change or simply leave in search of more suitable habitats.

Climate and Landscape Change in Egypt

Cycles of global climate through ice ages and warm periods also encompass shorter cycles of cooling and warming. The Holocene (that started around 11,000 years ago) is characterised by a rapid warming followed by cycles that result in a general slow cooling (Fig. 1) until the recent rapid rise in temperature since the industrial revolution of the mid-eighteenth century.[2]

Global warming affects Egyptian landscapes in two important ways; through sea-level rise and through an expanded equatorial rain belt with an enhanced Ethiopian Monsoon. The first results in an inundation of the coastal delta areas which in turn holds water back in the Nile Valley making it marshier. The second results in a movement of climatic zones northwards and the increase of seasonal rains in the Saharan area, that also add to the marshiness of the Nile Valley. The combination of these two factors can cause very high water-levels in the Nile Valley with the river impinging upon the marginal desert and into the mouths of the wadis and, at times, even overflowing into the desert to form lakes.[3] In the Early Holocene, these lakes and other rain-fed lakes produced by winter and summer rains were extensive and provided rich habitat.[4]

The Gift of the Nile? Ancient Egypt and the Environment
edited by Thomas Schneider and Christine L. Johnston
Tucson, Arizona: Egyptian Expedition, 2020

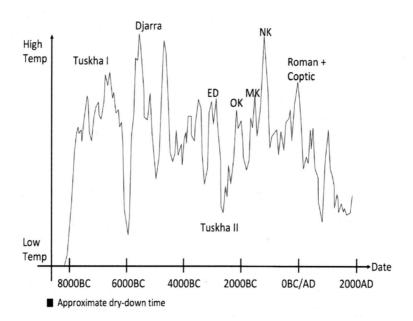

GISP2 Temp Proxy Curve

FIGURE 1. Greenland ice core data for Holocene showing the GISP2 temperature proxy curve and the main periods of occupation of the Kharga Oasis. Tuskha I–contemporary with sites in the Wadi Tuskha; Djarra–Contemporary with Djarra Cave; ED–Early Dynastic; OK–Old Kingdom; MK–Middle Kingdom; NK–New Kingdom.

Conversely, global cooling produces a falling sea-level as water is locked-up in the polar ice caps and a contraction of the equatorial rain belt with attendant recession of the other climatic belts. Under these conditions, the Nile flow is low and the river channel becomes tightly focussed and erosive, cutting down through its earlier sediments to form a canyon. At the same time, a reduction or cessation of the Ethiopian Monsoon reduces summer flooding making the Nile "tamer" and the Nile floodplain easier to cultivate. Meanwhile, in the deserts, the same retreat of climate belts southwards reduces rainfall and desert lakes, and makes wells dry up (Fig. 2).

Throughout the Holocene, residents of Egypt and the surrounding deserts have found themselves on a see-saw between habitable deserts with a "wild Nile"[5] on the one hand and a habitable Nile with an uninhabitable desert hinterland on the other. The distribution and use of sites in space and time reflects their responses to these changes (Fig. 3).

After each of these climate changes, the Nile and its surroundings start the process of re-equilibrating. If the delta is swamped by rising sea-level, then sediment dropped into the coastal waters starts to re-build the delta. If wind-blown sand produced by desertification pours into the Nile, the river system flushes it towards the sea in a series of islands and sand-bars. As the floodplain approaches equilibrium, the river starts to meander and migrate across it. These sideways migrations of the river channel typically average around 2 km per thousand years and present an additional challenge to those living on the river banks.[6] Luckily, the more stable meandering channels also have distinct levees, banks that

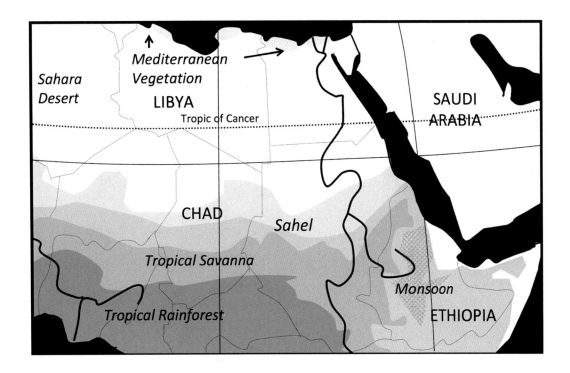

Figure 2. Map of Saharan Climate belts.

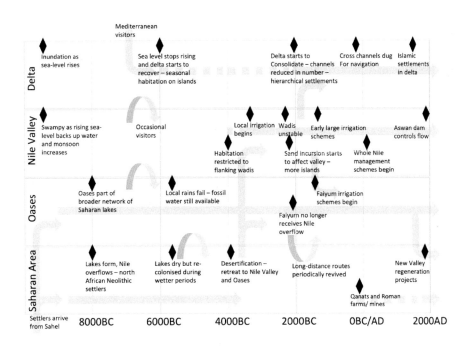

Figure 3. The four main habitats of Egypt with migrations from one environment to another indicated with arrows. Diamonds indicate timing of known events.

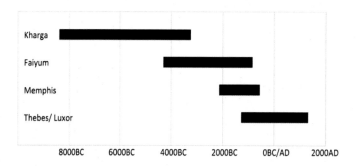

FIGURE 4. The four sites discussed in this paper and their relative time ranges.

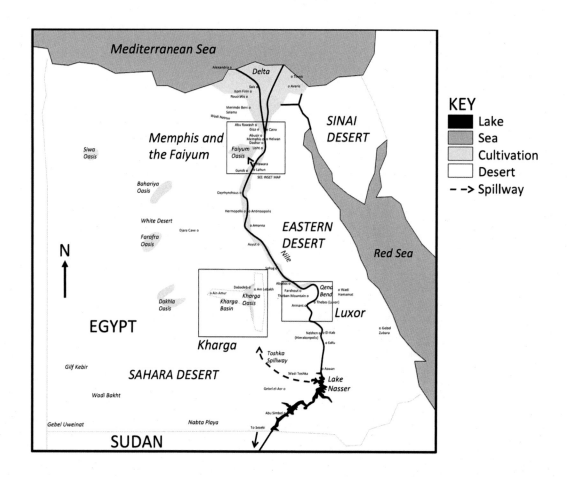

FIGURE 5. Location map to show the location of the areas discussed in this paper and the location of the Nile and principle oases.

are up to 2 m above the surrounding floodplain that may extend 200–300 m along its flanks; these sites are habitable even during the annual flood.

Understanding these factors and how they affect any given site in Egypt is an important part of exploring its history. Through dissemination of the early work of Butzer[7] and Jeffreys[8] many students of archaeology have been trained to consider the geo-archaeological aspects of sites. In an ideal world, all archaeologists would have sufficient training in geo-archaeology to include this aspect in their investigations and would also have access to geo-archaeologists to join their teams. Many digs in Egypt already host geo-archaeological teams and some projects are led by geo-archaeologists who can expertly decipher and reveal the landscape history of a site. Excellent examples of these latter projects include the work of two teams on the Memphite floodplain; those of David Jeffreys and Fekri Hassan and Mohammed Hamdan at Cairo University[9] and work on the Theban floodplain led by Angus Graham of Uppsala University.[10]

In the hope of making geo-archaeology accessible to all, I have recently compiled a book for Cambridge University Press, "Understanding the Nile in Ancient Egypt", that draws together evidence from more than twenty sites in order to develop a landscape history of Egypt. In this paper I will explore the processes that have steered the landscape history of four areas in Egypt by way of a thumbnail sketch of this inferred landscape history. These areas are Kharga, The Faiyum, Memphis, and Karnak (Fig. 4; location map 5). Archaeological evidence is now revealing that the inhabitants of Egypt were not passive subjects of landscape change but observed it, predicted it, anticipated it, and, with time, managed it. Egypt's history is a dialogue between its people and its landscape.

KHARGA — RAIN IN THE DESERT AND AN OVERFLOWING NILE

Kharga, now one of Egypt's largest oases, was even more expansive during the global warming of the Early Holocene and was home to many scattered populations living the settled hunter-gatherer life of the North African Neolithic.[11] As climate warmed the sub-tropical climate belt extended further to the north, forming many lakes that collected in the abandoned lakebed of an earlier, Pleistocene lake. Tumultuous floods in the Nile Valley also overtopped a gap in the Wadi Toshka forming a chain of lakes and expanding them. The Khargan lake grew until it had a maximum extent of around 3000 km2 (Fig. 6).[12]

Bone deposits and fish remains are reflected in the rock art that was inscribed around this highest high-stand shoreline.[13] A local aquifer, a later and smaller unit of sandstone much like the larger Nubian Aquifer below it, was filled with this water and in times of low rainfall helped the lake to persist and leaving wells and waterholes during dryer periods. Similar lake-shore sites in the Farafra area to the north also formed and here analysis of plant remains reveals that there were both winter and summer rains.[14]

At this time, Kharga was also well-connected to the Nile Valley since the chain of lakes in the Toshka spillway provided access to the south while the flourishing of numerous small oases and the patchwork of lakes provided discontinuous but reachable habitats. In practise, our observations of settlement areas in the Kharga basin suggest that populations were low and therefore settlements were only formed in "ideal" habitats. Preferred sites from this period tend to be on a promontory close to the shore line, for example Aa Rock, Fish Rock, Split Rock, and Tree Water (Fig. 7). The selection of a promontory site may suggest a defensive element and, considering the low density of habitation and the appearance of elephant, crocodile, and lions in the rock-art scenes, the anxiety may have been occasioned by animal as much as human threats.

FIGURE 6. Sediments at the Seth Pass reveal the level of ancient lakes. The pale sediments close to the skyline formed on the beaches of the erstwhile lake.

A period of cooling (around 8,200 years ago) led to the recession of the lakes and a condensation of people into the remaining oases but another episode of warmer climate and increased rainfall produced new lakes in the basins during the sixth millennium BCE (5800–5300 BCE).[15] Some of these lakes, like those at Nabta Playa to the south,[16] persisted for sufficient time to accumulate some metres of sediment and for their shores to be well-populated, for example at Pot Playa (see Fig. 7). However, by this time, the Nile levees around the Wadi Toshka had risen and the Nile was no longer full enough during the summer flood to overtop them leaving the rain-fed lakes without augmentation from the Nile.

Increasing numbers of dry periods led to the desiccation of the lakes but, in the case of Pot Playa, sufficient rain still fell to nourish a forest. At this location, the fossilised remains of trees up to 2 m in girth attest to the stable climate. Flint debitage is common in these areas and, being associated with the penumbra of the tree remains, suggests that they are contemporary. As the population moved into the lake beds it relied during the dry season on wells and were able to garner grain from the lake beds as well as hunt game in the thickets. Evidence for a reliance on grain as well as relative stability of location comes from large grinders (up to 50 cm long) that remain in situ. No pottery survives from this period although contemporary cultures elsewhere in Egypt were already using pottery. However, abundant ostrich egg-shell scatters may be the remains of a lighter and stronger source of

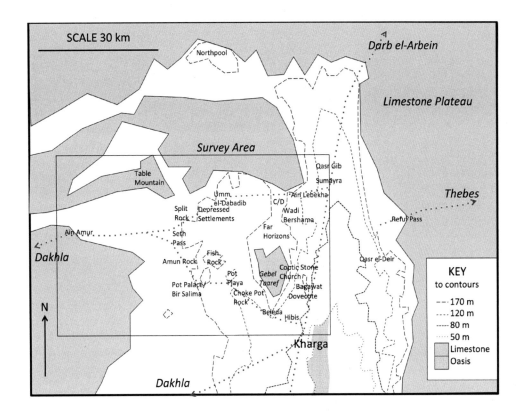

FIGURE 7. Map of the North Kharga Oasis showing successive lake-shore high stands and the archaeological sites associated with them.

containers and may reflect a similar culture found at Farafra.[17] At Pot Playa the remains of a bead workshop are also associated with this period. Unfortunately for the ancient inhabitants, the excellent preservation of these units, including the tree stump, is the result of an influx of an additional 40 cm of sediment during a flood that seemed to mark the end of the occupation of the lake bed and environs.

By the Pre-dynastic, visitors to the area were rare; the transient seeming to confine their transits to springs, wells, waterholes, and hunting redoubts. We infer that the surviving population moved away into the core of the oasis and perhaps into the Nile Valley for, at Hierakonpolis around this time, there seems to be an increase of population and a flourishing of culture. David Dufton showed that Badarian (around 4,000–5,000 BCE) and contemporary cultures were particularly anchored to the areas where wadi systems debouched into the Nile while suggesting that a combination of wadi pastoralism and Nile visits for hunting and fishing comprised their annual round.[18] The Badarian seems to have been at the tipping point between the life of the Saharan lakes and a condensation of population into the Nile. After this, brief periods of global warming led to a temporary increase in rainfall and the replenishment of the local aquifer and therefore renewed visits to the outlying parts of the Khargan basin. The addition of inscriptions, for example during the New Kingdom, to outcrops of the water-bearing sandstone and scatters of pottery are the chief residue from these visitors.

In the main, aridification pushed people away from the Saharan area towards the Nile Valley and finally, during the Early Dynastic, into the Nile Floodplain where they started to develop strategies for irrigation and agriculture. Occasional periods of increased Saharan rainfall led to ephemeral re-occupations of which the most notable and persistent was during the Ptolemaic and Roman Periods when the implementation of *qanat* (or *manwir*) technology saw multiple long tunnels up to 5 km long used to collect water from the area around settlements.[19] In the Kharga area, settlements supported by qanats were established at Ain Lebakh and Debadeb among others and were associated with the exploitation of local alum deposits. Earlier wells were re-opened at sites like Bir Salima and a temple was built close to the well at Ain Amur. However, climate cooling, even with modern pumps that draw water from the deep Nubian Aquifer more than 1 km below the surface, has now reduced the current habitable area of the Kharga Oasis to less than 1% of the early Holocene lake.

The Faiyum — From Oasis to Irrigation

In the same way as our earlier example, Kharga, The Faiyum was also the recipient of over-spill water from the Nile. As the channel through the Hawara gap required a lower flood to overtop it, The Faiyum continued periodically to receive floodwater until the end of the Old Kingdom turning it into a lake. Early Pre-dynastic settlements occupied beach-ridges along the shores of this lake but it was by no means permanent.[20] Fekri Hassan has documented the history of the Nile flood and the way in which the Faiyum lake sometimes diminished and became saline while at other times it was expansive and filled the whole of the Faiyum depression save a small sedimentary fan where the incoming floodwaters debouched into the basin.[21] This fan became the site of permanent settlement and eventually the Graeco-Roman city of Crocodopolis, modern Faiyum City. During the FIP (First Intermediate Period), the Hawara gap ceased to be overtopped and The Faiyum lake rapidly dried to leave only a small lake, Birket Qarun, at the north-western side of the oasis (Fig. 8).

Opposite the entrance to The Faiyum, two channels of the Nile flowed northwards: to the east of the Nile Valley, the main Nile, and to the west a smaller channel known in its southern portion as the Bahr Yusuf and further north as the Bahr Libeini. Studies of the Giza-Memphis area by Goncalves reveal that the western channel flowed past the foot of the pyramids at Giza during the Old Kingdom while the eastern channel flowed towards the eastern side of the Nile Canyon at that latitude as it does today.[22] Goncalves also posits a further channel towards the centre of the valley at Memphis (Fig. 9).[23] During the Middle Kingdom, Amenemhat III took the initiative to divert the Bahr Yusuf from its course towards Memphis into The Faiyum basin to replenish the lake and provide water for irrigation. We can only speculate on the benefits and losses of this diversion on Memphis. On the one hand, there was a loss of water from the Bahr Yusuf with an attendant loss of a defensive channel but, on the other, the irrigation system allowed additional grain to be produced by irrigation in The Faiyum adding wealth to the area. Ying Qin suggests that at Memphis, during the Ptolemaic Period, there may have been a deliberate renewal of the defensive channel by diverting water from the main Nile, which had now approached the site from the east, into the defunct waterway.[24]

The Faiyum continued to be irrigated and managed during the New Kingdom with the development of a Palace at Gurob, at the entrance to The Faiyum, and the diversion of water via a number of channels and regulators in the Lahun area. These systems continued

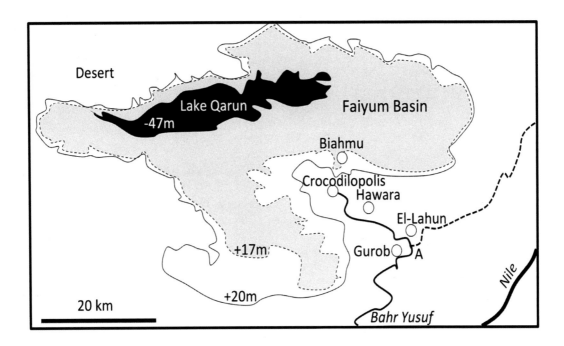

FIGURE 8. Map to show how the Faiyum lake dried down to
the current Lake Qarun (after Gasperini 2010).

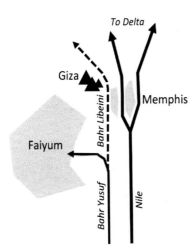

FIGURE 9. Schematic diagram to show the diversion of the Bahr
Yusuf from its original course into the Faiyum basin.

to be revised and developed during the New Kingdom and later until by the Roman
Period; the Bahr Yusuf, the lesser channel of the Nile, was thoroughly under human
control. The fourth century BCE re-foundation of the town of Oxyrhynchus,[25] to the south
of The Faiyum, demonstrates that town planning at this time included management of
the Bahr Yusuf. Oxyrhynchus relied on a diversion of the Bahr Yusuf to the desert edge

where a system of channels and cisterns provided water to the town. Clean water flowed in at the top of the town and the dirty water flowed downhill returning to the Bahr Yusuf at the bottom of the town.[26] This mastery of the Bahr Yusuf set the scene for the control of the main Nile for which the earliest evidence is further south again at Antinoupolis,[27] where Hadrian's foundation in 130 CE sought to retain the main channel at the desert edge serving the town. So strong were the river defences built at that time that the Nile has been unable to migrate away from the site since.

Memphis—Delta Development and Early Landscape Management

As mentioned above, sand flux into the Nile Valley from the by then arid Saharan region affected the site of Memphis. Early Dynastic settlements at the base of the western scarp of the Nile Valley were drowned in wind-blown sand as sand flux intensified during the FIP.[28] The islands in the then marshy area of Memphis were added to by aeolian sand transported a short distance in the Nile as demonstrated from scanning electron microscope (SEM) analysis of sand grains collected at Memphis by Qin.[29] To the north of Memphis the marshes extended through the Delta, the sand influx had an additional dramatic effect of filling in marshes, consolidating its many unstable channels into fewer meandering channels, and pushing the estuarine and coastal areas northwards into the Mediterranean Sea. The Delta, that had been drowned by Early Holocene sea-level rise and had started to recover when sea-level rise slowed 6000 years ago, now began to stabilise rapidly.

In the Old Kingdom, the Delta was still relatively marshy and studies of Kom el-Hisn[30] suggest that islands in the Delta were used for cattle-ranching at that time. Modelling of the waterways and habitat of the Nile Delta,[31] based on other well-known deltas, suggests that during this period, all parts of the Delta had access to a range of foodstuffs and that travel by water was easy in every direction. However, a process of consolidation that had begun around 4000 BCE became more rapid around 2000 BCE, in the FIP, and the waterways became more hierarchical in structure as the channels stabilised. Moreover, the distribution of food-producing habitats became more inequitable, with rich estuarine habitats towards the coast, where there was a shortage of fresh water and sparser habitats inland where marshes and pools had filled in (Fig. 10).[32] These landscape changes seem to have increased the importance of Memphis as an entrepot since, being at the "head" of the Delta, it had privileged access to foodstuffs downstream in the Delta distributary network. The consolidation of the Delta also created a landscape suitable for large-scale irrigation and agriculture.

Up to this point, we have seen evidence of human response to climate change and the resultant landscape change in the digging of wells and the creation of irrigation schemes as well as through habitat tracking. From the Middle Kingdom onwards, human interventions in the landscape seem increasingly ambitious, starting with the diversion of a channel into The Faiyum in the Middle Kingdom and culminating in the 1960s with the construction of the Aswan High Dam that allowed complete management of the Nile flood. Although we will consider the management of water in The Faiyum above, Memphis also saw the effects of large-scale landscape interventions from the Middle Kingdom onwards, first as a result of being downstream of The Faiyum interventions and from the New Kingdom through direct landscape management.

Close observation and correlation of a large corpus of borehole data from the Memphite floodplain shows that, in order to lay out the foundations of the New Kingdom Ptah Temple, east-west dykes were constructed that segmented the central channel of

Large-Scale Crevassing   Meandering

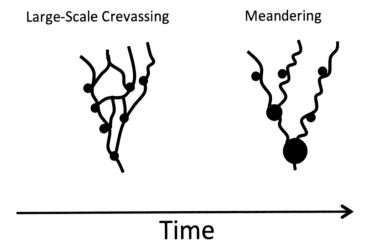

Time

FIGURE 10. Changing delta distributary networks. As the delta consolidates the early well-connected network is simplified and results in a more hierarchical river system (after Pennington et al 2016).

Memphis leaving an area of low but dry ground for the development.[33] The Ptah Temple had access to harbours in the basins of residual water to the north and to the south at the same time as having an eastern waterfront on the main Nile channel. Later, this ambitious project was exceeded by the work during the sixth century to construct Kom Tuman, the mound for the well-defended Palace of Apries. Pedro Goncalves shows how a large quantity of "missing" material was removed from the upper parts of the, by then, decayed western part of Memphis and placed to the north of the northern harbour bay to construct Kom Tuman.[34]

KARNAK—ISLANDS AND SAND-BARS; RIVER MIGRATION

During the Old Kingdom, habitation of the Nile levees and reliance on grain agriculture became common. Hunting and mining expeditions, vividly depicted in Old Kingdom tomb scenes, continued to be common but, to a great extent, Egyptians had turned their back on the Sahara. An extended period of progressive desertification beginning in the Old Kingdom and sweeping southwards during the following millennium destabilised Saharan grasslands and released fossil sand dunes that moved south south-eastwards across the region.[35] Where these dunes impinged on the western scarp of the Nile Valley or other sheltered spots, large quantities of sand accumulated and, in some places, for example Dahshur, overlaid monuments and the fringe of the Nile floodplain, narrowing it. The additional sand helped to stabilise the Nile channels and produced sandy levees onto which populations moved from their previously preferred sites in the mouths of the wadis.[36] At Memphis, windblown sand also accumulated against natural features and existing settlement sites and helped to stabilise the land upon which later parts of the city were constructed.

Incursion of sand and loss of habitat in the deserts fringing the northern Nile Valley, the first part to be affected, eventually led to the establishment of a new capital further south at Thebes (modern Luxor). In this area, small settlements started to be formed on sand-banks and levees in the Luxor area during the late First Intermediate Period (FIP). The temple of Karnak is thought, from auger exploration, to have been initially founded at this time on an island in the Nile.[37] A second island to the south was the site of a Middle Kingdom settlement and later became the site of the Temple of Mut. During the Middle Kingdom and New Kingdom, these islands were joined to other horned bars[38] until the whole site fused with the East Bank of the Nile during the late Eighteenth Dynasty of the New Kingdom and the Aten Temple of Akhenaten was laid out in the infilled channel.[39]

Taryn Duckworth, studying the area around Luxor, showed that islands in the Nile form and bond to the bank of the Nile in a relatively predictable way.[40] First a horned bar forms with an elevated sand-bank at the upstream end and thin banks of sediment trailing downstream (Fig. 11) surround a marshy core. In modern day Luxor, cattle are driven through the water to these islands to browse where they churn and manure the soil until it is suitable for crops to be planted. These soils are rich and well-watered so the additional effort of travelling to the island to farm is rewarded. Fish spawn in and water-birds visit the central marsh, which is correspondingly popular with fishermen. Vegetation on the flanks of the island baffles further sediment so that the island grows and stabilises further. Eventually buildings start to appear on the highest part of the island, the central marsh gradually fills in, and eventually the minor channel is also filled and the island becomes joined to the mainland over the period of around 60–100 years.

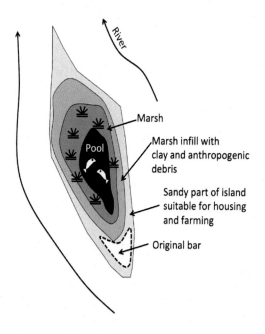

FIGURE 11. A diagram to show the generalised development of islands in the Nile (after Duckworth 2009).

The process of island formation and bonding is part of a broader process of Nile channel migration. Katy Lutley, by observing abandoned levees and islands, showed that, on average, the Nile channel migrates sideways by around 2 km per millennium.[41] This rate exceeds the average rate of floodplain rise of about 2 m per millennium by a factor of about a thousand and demonstrates that, for settlements adjacent to the Nile, channel migration is one of the most important factors. The patterns of channel migration, like those of island formation, are relatively predictable with bends migrating outwards and downstream until the river impinges upon the rocky and difficult-to-erode edge of the Nile Canyon. Thus, structures built on the outside of a bend are subject to almost immediate erosion while those on the inside of a bend will soon be isolated from the river by deposition. It follows from this that the most practical place to build is on the islands that form near bends in the channel. In the case of an island, whichever way the channel moves access to the Nile is maintained for the maximum possible time.

Although no texts are known that describe this pattern of erosion and deposition, the surviving monuments suggest that their architects were aware of these movements of the Nile, if only by a process of trial and error. For archaeologists today, the challenge is to determine the ancient environment in which a monument or settlement was founded and to assess how it changed during the lifetime of the site. Fortunately, conservatism in the delineation of agricultural plots in the Nile Valley means that the locations and sometimes even the names of historic islands are preserved. Roadways and canals also tend to follow the field-group (*hôd*) boundaries which in turn are often linked to topographic features such as old levees and so also reveal the history of the floodplain. Thus, assessment of cadastral maps and field patterns or topography from satellite imagery can assist the archaeologist in determining the direction and approximate timescale of historic movements of the Nile around a site.

Recent examples of island formation and channel migration in the Karnak area demonstrate how the process occurs and is recorded (Fig. 12) while the auger studies of the area beneath the Karnak temple suggest that these processes have been active during

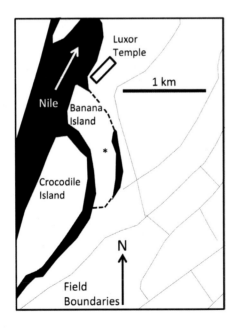

FIGURE 12. Map of Banana 'Island' that shows how the former island is attaching itself to the Nile bank.

61

the foundation and development of the temple between the First Intermediate Period and Roman Periods (Fig. 13). Moreover, the pattern of usage of the ancient islands suggests that the way that islands developed was familiar to the temple builders and that they were able to predict how they would form and develop. However, the most ambitious projects were still to come with the construction in the late nineteenth century of the Aswan Dam and in the late twentieth century of the Aswan High Dam. With the completion of these projects the technology to control the Nile's meanders as well as its flood was in place, at least for the time being.

In conclusion, landscape studies of many sites in Egypt are revealing an increasingly nuanced understanding of how we might expect landscape change to have affected any given site. We are also developing a greater understanding of how ancient people responded to and sought to manipulate landscape change to their advantage. We also begin to understand how the development of technology including wells, dams, irrigation networks, and qanats allowed the inhabitants of Egypt to make the best of the resources available at different times. The outline given here is intended to provide a broad overview and to encourage archaeologists exploring a new site to consider the landscape hinterland and how ancient peoples might have viewed and interacted with it during its history.

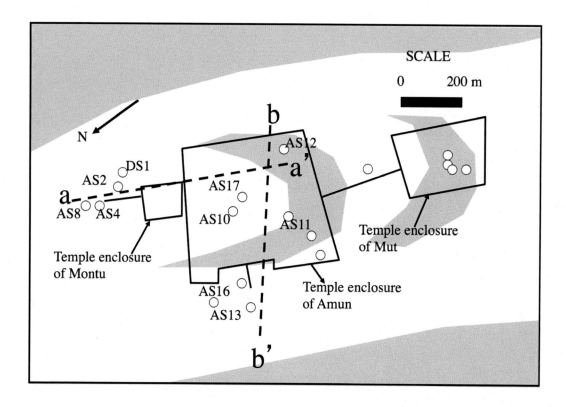

FIGURE 13. Map of Karnak temple showing what is interpreted to have been the original island core of the site.

WORKS CITED

Barich, B.E., G. Lucarini, M.A. Hamdan, and F.A. Hassan, eds. 2014. *From Lake to Sand. The Archaeology of Farafra Oasis (Egypt)*. Florence: All'Insegna del Giglio.

Bunbury, J.M., and S. Ikram. 2014. "Kharga Oasis: a Saharan patchwork of lakes." *Egyptian Archaeology* 45: 10–12.

Bunbury, J.M., A. Graham, and M.A. Hunter. 2008. "Stratigraphic Landscape Analysis: Charting the Holocene movements of the Nile at Karnak through Ancient Egyptian Time." *Geoarchaeology* 23: 351–373.

Bunbury, J.M., A. Graham, and K.D. Strutt. 2009. "Kom el-Farahy: A New Kingdom island in an evolving Edfu floodplain." *British Museum Studies in Ancient Egypt and Sudan* 14: 1–23.

Butzer, K. 1976. *Early Hydraulic Civilization in Egypt: A Study in Cultural Ecology*. Chicago: University of Chicago.

Duckworth, T., 2009. "The Development of Islands in the Theban Floodplain." Unpublished diss., Cambridge University.

Dufton, D. 2008. "Meander Bends of the Nile in the Abydos Region." Unpublished diss., Cambridge University.

El-Sanussi, A., and M. Jones. 1997. "A Site of the Maadi Culture near the Giza Pyramids." *Mitteilungen des Deutschen Archaologischen Instituts, Abt. Kairo* 53: 241–253.

Garcea, E.A.A. 2006. "Semi-Permanent Foragers in Semi-Arid Environments of North Africa." *World Archaeology* 38(2): 197–219.

Gasperini, V. 2010. "Archaeology and History of the Faiyum in the New Kingdom." Ph.D. diss., University of Bologna.

Goncalvez, P.M. 2018. "Landscape and Environmental Changes at Memphis during the Dynastic Period Egypt." Ph.D Diss., University of Cambridge.

Graham, A., M.A. Hunter, S. Jones, A. Masson, M. Millet, and B. T. Pennington. 2012. "Theban Harbours and Waterscapes Survey 2012." *Journal of Egyptian Archaeology* 98: 27–42.

Hassan, F.A. 1996. "Nile Floods and Political Disorder in Early Egypt." In *Third Millennium BC Climate Change and Old World Collapse*, edited by H.N. Dalfes, G. Kukla, and H. Weiss, 1–23. Berlin: Springer.

Hassan, F.A., R.J. Hamdan, R.A. Flower, N.A. Shallaly, and E. Ebrahem. 2017. "Holocene alluvial history and archaeological significance of the Nile floodplain in the Saqqara Memphis region, Egypt." *Quaternary Science Reviews* 176: 51–70.

Haynes, C.V. 1980. "Geochronology of Wadi Tushka: Lost Tributary of the Nile." *Science* 210: 68–71.

Haynes, C.V., P.J Mehringer, and S.A. Zaghloul. 1979. "Pluvial Lakes of North-Western Sudan." *The Geographical Journal* 145: 437–445.

Heidel, J.B. 2012–2013. "Antinoupolis, A Hadrianic Reinterpretation of the Abydos Sacred Landscape." *KMT, A Modern Journal of Ancient Egypt* 23: 60–67.

Holdaway, S., and W. Wendrich. 2017. *The Desert Fayum Reinvestigated*. Monumenta Archaeologica 39. Los Angeles: Cotsen Insitute of Archaeology Press.

Ikram, S., and C. Rossi. 2007. With contributions by A.J. Clapham, A. Dunsmore, A. Gascoigne, and N. Warner. "North Kharga Oasis Survey 2004 Preliminary Report: Ain el-Tarakwa, Ain el-Dabashiya and Darb Ain Amur." *MDAIK* 63: 167–184.

Jeffreys, D.G. 1985. *The Survey of Memphis*. Vol. 1, *The Archaeological Report*. London: Egypt Exploration Society.

———. 2010. *The Survey of Memphis*. Vol. 7, *the Hekekyan Papers and Other Sources for the Survey of Memphis*. London: Egypt Exploration Society.

Jeffreys, D., and A. Tavares. 1994. "The Historic Landscape of Early Dynastic Memphis." *MDAIK* 50: 143–173.

Kröpelin, S., D. Verschuren, A.M. Lézine, H. Eggermont, C. Cocquyt, P. Francus, J-P. Cazet, M. Fagot, B. Rumes, J.M. Russell, F. Darius, D.J. Conley, M. Schuster, H. von Suchodoletz, and D.R. Engstrom. 2008. "Climate-Driven Ecosystem Succession in the Sahara: The Past 6000 Years." *Science* 320(5877): 765–768.

Kuper, R., and S. Kröpelin. 2006. "Climate-controlled Holocene Occupation in the Sahara: Motor of Africa's Evolution." *Science 313*: 803–807.

Lutley, C.J., and J.M. Bunbury. 2008. "The Nile on the Move." *Egyptian Archaeology* 32: 3–5.

Marcott, S.A., J.D. Shakun, P.U. Clark, and A.C. Mix. 2013. "Supplementary Materials for A Reconstruction of Regional and Global Temperature for the Past 11,300 Years." *Science* 339(6124): 1198–1201.

Maxwell, T.A., B. Issawi, C.V. Haynes Jr. 2001. "Evidence for Pleistocene Lakes in the Tushka Region, Southern Egypt." *Geoarchaeology* 16: 7–28.

Parsons, P. 2007. *City of the Sharp-Nosed Fish: Greek Lives in Roman Egypt.* London: Weidenfeld and Nicolson.

Pennington, B., J.M. Bunbury, and N. Hovius. 2016. "Emergence of Civilisation Changes in Fluvio-Deltaic Styles and Nutrient Redistribution Forced by Holocene Sea-Level Rise." *Geoarchaeology* 130(1): 17–28.

Qin, Y. 2009. "Landscape change in the Saqqara/Memphis area of Egypt from 3000 BC to the present." M.Sci. diss., University of Cambridge.

Rodrigues, D., P.I. Abell, S. Kropelin. 2000. "Seasonality in the Early Holocene Climate of Northwest Sudan: Interpretation of Etheria Elliptica Shell Isotopic Data." *Global and Planetary Change* 26: 181–187.

Said, R. 1981. *The Geological evolution of the River Nile.* New York: Springer-Verlag.

———. 1993. *The River Nile: Geology, Hydrology and Utilization.* Oxford: Pergamon Press.

Subias, E., J.I. Fiz Fernandez, and R. Cuesta. 2013. "The Middle Nile Valley: Elements in an approach to the structuring of the landscape from the Greco-Roman era to the nineteenth century." *Quaternary International* 312: 27–44.

Wendorf, F., and R. Schild. 1998. "Nabta Playa and its role in Northeastern African Prehistory." *Journal of anthropological archaeology* 17: 97–123.

Notes

[1] The work summarised here is the product of work with Salima Ikram of the North Kharga Oasis Survey, Ian Shaw of the Gurob Harem Palace Project, Marine Yoyotte of the Gourob Archaeological Excavation of IFAO, Joanne Rowland at Merimde, David Jeffreys and Mark Lehner at Memphis, Angus Graham and the Karnak Land and Waterscape Survey, and Piers Litherland of the Theban Mountain Expedition. My postgraduate students, in particular Taryn Duckworth, Katy Lutley, and Pedro Goncalves, have also been generous in discussing their ideas. Thanks must also go to the many inspectors of antiquities in Egypt who have assisted our work as well as to the Ministers and Secretaries of the Ministry of Antiquities/Supreme Council of Antiquities under whose aegis permission was granted. Particular supporters include Mr Mansour Boraik and Mr Suleyman Ibrahim in Luxor. Our work has continued through the generosity of The Egypt Exploration Society, The British Academy, The British Museum, The Gurob Harem Palace Project, Ancient Egypt Research Associates, New Kingdom Research Foundation, Centre National des Récherces Scientifiques, Metropolitan Museum, American University in Cairo, and Cambridge University.

2   Marcott et al. 2013.
3   Haynes 1980.
4   Rodrigues et al. 2000; Barich et al. 2014.
5   Said 1981, 1993.
6   Bunbury et al. 2009.
7   Butzer 1976.
8   Jeffreys 1985, 2010; Jeffreys and Tavares 1994.
9   Hassan et al. 2017.
10   Bunbury et al. 2008.
11   Garcea 2006.
12   Haynes et al. 1979; Maxwell et al. 2001.
13   Ikram and Rossi 2007; Bunbury and Ikram 2014.
14   Barich et al. 2014.
15   Karin Kindermann personal communication.
16   Wendorf and Schild 1998.
17   Barich et al. 2014.
18   Dufton 2008.
19   Ikram and Rossi 2007.
20   Holdaway and Wendrich 2017.
21   Hassan 1996.
22   Bunbury et al. 2009; Goncalves 2018.
23   Goncalves 2018.
24   Qin 2009.
25   Subias et al. 2013.
26   Parsons 2007.
27   Heidel 2012–2013.
28   Jeffreys and Tavares 1994.
29   Qin 2009.
30   Wenke et al. 1998.
31   Pennington et al. 2016.
32   Pennington et al. 2016.
33   Goncalves 2018.
34   Goncalves 2018.
35   Kuper and Kropelin 2006; Kröpelin et al. 2008.
36   Jeffreys and Tavares 1994; El-Sanussi and Jones 1997.
37   Bunbury et al. 2008.
38   Graham et al. 2012.
39   Redford personal communication.
40   Duckworth 2009.
41   Lutley and Bunbury 2008.

Chapter Four

Human-Environmental Relationships within Neolithic Adaptations

JOANNE ROWLAND

ABSTRACT

Our understanding of the origins of sedentary life in Egypt and the motivation for the first human groups to adopt more settled ways of life, lies in part in the sites of the later sixth and fifth millennium BCE, together with earlier Epipalaeolithic evidence, where available. An examination of the various transitions and adaptations that human groups passed through has often been lacking in the literature, and many publications give the impression of the Neolithic being a rather "known" period (e.g., as discussed in Barker 2013); this is far from the case. Sometimes settled life is presented as a necessarily positive transition,[1] which is not an assumption to be made lightly. A recent conference in Berlin ("Revolutions", October 2015[2]) helped to highlight just how variable the adoption and adaptation of aspects associated with the Neolithic are when looking across North Africa and the Levant, and that aspects, or processes, of Neolithisation (for want of a better term) encompass a wide range of possible outcomes. It also flagged up how crucial the relationship between humans and their environment is (implying interaction rather than determinism) and how there is a profound need for more chronologically robust climatic models and availability of raw data.

Merimde Beni Salama was the second "Neolithic" settlement to be discovered in the Nile Delta in the 1920s,[3] and is one of only four known today in any detail, alongside el-Omari and Sa el-Hagar, with the recent addition of Tell es-Samara (see Figs. 1 and 2).[4] It has long been acknowledged that the settlement shows variation over time—with scholars suggesting this to be a reflection of "foreign" influences[5]—but a relationship much closer to home, that between humans and their environment, has been embedded in fewer investigations.[6] The complexity of the landscape chosen for settlement at Merimde has not been satisfactorily addressed, given that the area is suitable for a great many different and complementary reasons. Human-environmental relationships are central to the first part of this contribution, aimed at re-assessing issues of environmental reconstruction, achieving chronological refinement within this reconstruction, and human

The Gift of the Nile? Ancient Egypt and the Environment
edited by Thomas Schneider and Christine L. Johnston
Tucson, Arizona: Egyptian Expedition, 2020

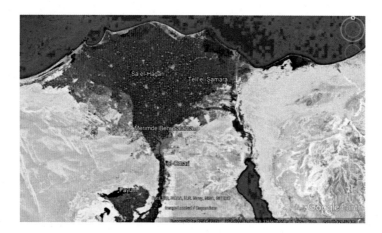

Figure 1. Neolithic sites of Lower Egypt (Google Earth).

exploitation of this landscape. Results of new analyses from Merimde Beni Salama will be discussed alongside outstanding research aims, together with the goals and challenges in moving forward. The second part of the contribution focusses upon aspects of the Neolithic often assumed to be givens, looking from the perspective of Merimde Beni Salama, within wider chronological and regional contexts, notably the nature of the introduction of Neolithic subsistence strategies. Finally, there is a discussion of future research challenges that need to be addressed to move our knowledge in this area forward.

Introduction

The paper presented in Vancouver consisted of two key parts: the first looking at themes related to Human-Environmental Relationships that are examined within the section below on "Environmental Investigations at Merimde Beni Salama," including current and former environmentally-concerned research; with the second part, considering the variable ways in which human groups do or do not adopt settled lifeways. This included thoughts on these issues at Merimde Beni Salama, notably the timing of change, and the use of space for certain activities over time. The spatial distribution of activities has been addressed in part in a recent paper by Rowland,[7] and therefore, is only briefly referred to here. The second part includes the discussion of broader climatic change as well as interactions between pre-existing and non-local groups across the landscape, which is under discussion within "Wadi el-Gamal—a new perspective on Merimde Beni Salama," and "Putting Merimde Back into the Wider World" in this contribution.

Returning to investigate Merimde Beni Salama in 2013, 30 years after the end of the last major project at the site, one of the key questions remaining is that of the motivating factors for settlement in that specific location within the western Nile Delta, within the context of the wider appearance of Neolithic settlements in the northern Egyptian Nile Valley and the Delta after c. 5500 BCE.[8] Why were groups starting to take up sedentary ways of life and why at this relatively late date, when compared to other Near Eastern sites.[9] Looking to this question in the first decades of the 21st century, the impact of the environment automatically features, being today an obvious factor within the discussion of what might have encouraged, or necessitated, the laying down of roots in a particular place. The importance of the ancient environment within archaeological research, broadly speaking, has been increasingly apparent over the past four decades, and ever more so in recent years, with climate change being such a prevalent theme within our daily lives. Today, it is increasingly commonplace to integrate environmental surveys (to a greater or lesser extent) within archaeological fieldwork, whether led by geologists, geoarchaeologists, geomorphologists, or by archaeologists. Within archaeology in Egypt, figures including Manfred Bietak made great bounds towards re-discovering the placement of the Nile branches running through the eastern Delta with geoarchaeological investigation in the 1970s.[10] At the same time, Karl Butzer's slim, yet game-changing volume emphasised the specifics of the "Hydraulic Civilization" of Egypt, addressing questions about the density of settlement patterning, the origins of agriculture, and ecology and settlement.[11] Fekri Hassan[12] deeply embedded the environment within his research, including discussion of demographic factors within his publications,[13] and the cores taken by Jean-Daniel Stanley within his research into the evolution of the Nile Delta has been a major contribution, with the data being used widely by colleagues working in the region.[14] Today, a variety of research agendas target climatically and environmentally specific aspects, from fluctuating locations of river branches over time within the Delta (see Fig. 2),[15] to ancient and religious waterscapes,[16] to fluctuating, greening, and increasingly arid environments within the Eastern Sahara,[17] and the impact on, and of, human activity. The timescales under discussion range from the Palaeolithic until historical times. Research in the Eastern Sahara is notably of great importance for our understanding of changing modes of subsistence and lifeways, including that in Farafra Oasis.[18] Here the decline in settlement density by c. 5300 BCE,[19] as will be referred to again below, occurs at a time when activity regarded as Neolithic in the Fayum is recognised already, and shortly thereafter at Merimde Beni Salama and Sa el-Hagar.

Environmental investigations are not new to Merimde Beni Salama (hereafter "Merimde"). Merimde was one of the sites included within a key article by Karl Butzer that examined the environment within which the first human groups began to move towards sedentary lifestyles in Egypt, including the fringes of the Nile Delta (in the case of Merimde; see Fig. 2).[20] Human-environmental relationships within these Neolithic adaptations have been a key element of the author's field project since its inception in 2013, with the promotion of environmental investigation deeply embedded within the design of the pilot project.[21] Prior to this in the late 1970s, Hawass, Hassan, and Gautier's work was concerned with the environment into which groups settled and began subsisting through a mixture of domesticated plant and animals species, supplemented with hunting and fishing.[22] One of the key aims of the current project has been to look again to Merimde within its wider hinterland, and within the context of other Neolithic settlements, to bring new evidence and understanding as to what encouraged settlement in this particular area by c. 5000 BCE, as well as considering from where people were coming.

A central issue that remains as a huge lacunae lies in the preceding Epipalaeolithic. As yet it remains questionable as to whether Junker encountered Epipalaeolithic finds at nearby Merimde Abu Ghalib,[23] and there is nothing convincing within the finds from and immediately around Merimde to suggest groups were present in the area directly prior to the first settlement evidence. However, the lack of sickle blade inserts from the earliest layer (I or *Urschicht*) at Merimde[24] and the ephemeral nature of the (possible) dwellings of this layer already indicate the gradual introduction of aspects associated with Neolithic settlement, albeit domesticated animals are in evidence.[25] The substantial quarrying and disturbance through cultivation along the desert edge close to Merimde, particularly

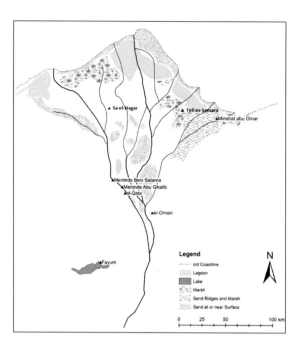

FIGURE 2. Reconstruction of the ancient Delta including the Neolithic sites of Merimde Beni Salama, Tell es-Samara, Sa el-Hagar, and el-Omari. Map by S. Schmidt and G. Cyrus, after Butzer (2002).

during the past 30 years, may play a part in distorting the evidence however. At Sa el-Hagar, sickle blades are absent from the earliest Neolithic layers found to date, Sais Ia, and it is thought that this layer might represent an Epipalaeolithic rather than Neolithic phase;[26] this discussion will be returned to below ("Putting Merimde back into the wider world").

ENVIRONMENTAL INVESTIGATION AT MERIMDE BENI SALAMA

Investigations in the Western Delta from the 1930s Onwards

The 1970s and early 1980s marked a period of increased interest in Egyptian prehistory,[27] following on from the upsurge in activity into prehistory as part of the UNESCO Nubian Campaign during the building of the Aswan High Dam.[28] This came hand-in-hand with the increasing concern with the ancient environment noted above, which had already been integral to some of the early investigations into Egyptian prehistory, particularly in the research of Caton-Thompson and Gardner in the Fayum.[29] Sandford and Arkell worked in close proximity to Merimde and northwards to Khatatbah, and although their research was more focused on the Palaeolithic, they include valuable commentary on the environment during the Neolithic.[30] Research which can be said to have an integral environmental component has looked at reconstructing the broader palaeoenvironment in the region over a long time span (notably in the work of Sandford and Arkell[31]), at tightening the chronological, environmental and cultural record, which was the focus of the fieldwork of Hawass et al.[32] The latter looked to the dynamics of new sedentary farming strategies at Merimde, and most recently the current author is investigating the wider human exploitation of the landscape,[33] as well as a reconstruction of the natural environment. Hawass et al.'s work,[34] just a year before the commencement of the German Archaeological Institute's (DAI) reinvestigation of the site led by Josef Eiwanger,[35] focussed on test trenches within areas of the Neolithic settlement, trenches that were located to the north of those excavated by Junker in the 1930s.[36] During the excavations, sediments were collected which showed that gravels had moved down from the Pleistocene terraces to the west of the settlement, which they noted were caused due to pebbles being "dislocated" from those gravels (pebbles now detected *in situ* within the Pleistocene contexts during our investigations in 2016).[37] The sediments also consisted of silt, which they noted as the result of human activities, hypothesising also that the settlement was made on slope wash from the Pleistocene terraces to the west, an area (the Wadi el-Gamal[38]) that will be returned to below.[39] Both the work of Hawass et al. and Eiwanger contributed to the understanding of Merimde's chronology—both in relative and absolute terms. Both missions contributed new conventional radiocarbon measurements to improve our knowledge on the absolute dating of the site—which suggested settlement by c. 5000 BCE, with a 900–1000 year duration of settlement activity (for the Neolithic), with a possible hiatus after the first phase of occupation.[40]

New Environmental Data from Merimde

Following their fieldwork in 1976, Hawass et al. noted that they did not consider cultural layers to exist below the gravels under the Neolithic settlement.[41] Recent work in 2015 and 2016 on the Wadi el-Gamal, to the southwest of the better known settlement area of Merimde, yielded such evidence, however, with varied lithic assemblages dating also to the Middle Palaeolithic.[42] In addition, at higher sub-surface levels on the Wadi el-Gamal, fresh evidence dating to the Neolithic was found, which will be discussed below. During the first season of the new project at Merimde in spring 2013, a geophysical survey[43] highlighted additional settlement remains that were subsequently proven, through test trenches, to be Neolithic.[44] Simultaneously, an environmental survey was carried out in collaboration with Mohamed Hamdan (Cairo University) and Judith Bunbury (University of Cambridge). The initial season in 2013 was focussed on establishing the extent of the site, given the dramatic changes in the recent local landscape, as well as integrating what is planned as a long-term research goal of establishing the local palaeoenvironment. This is one of the key ways in which it will be possible to better comprehend the dynamics surrounding the earliest settlement at Merimde towards the end of the sixth millennium BCE. This will bring information to local changes along the western fringes of the Delta, as well as considering broader fluctuations that could have affected the individual Neolithic sites across the Delta; crucially, a means of chronological control beyond typological proxies needs to be approached, the latter being insufficient as a re-assessment of the typical Merimde I–V is attempted.

This initial environmental survey carried out in 2013 was aimed at establishing an environmental and topographical profile of the area through and either side of the settlement.[45] The purpose of this cross section through the landscape was to better think about what type of features might have constituted a suitable and inhabitable or indeed inhabited landscape before and during the time when Merimde was in use. The intention was to better inform future investigations for prehistoric sites along the desert edge, especially given that the landscape has altered so much even in recent years as a result of

FIGURE 3. The current location of the Rosetta branch of the Nile.
The curved pattern of fields in the loop to the west highlights
the movement of the branch over time. Merimde shown to the
south (Google Earth).

modern development and cultivation. Additionally, during the rescue season of winter–
spring 2016,[46] it was possible to examine valuable sections in the excavation trenches on
the Wadi el-Gamal, as well as larger exposed sections running north–south, which were
cleaned and sketched/photographed before this area was taken down as part of the site
development. *In situ* visual examination by M. Hamdan could clarify that the landscape
and environment on the Wadi el-Gamal is very different to the arid landscape which was
present until recent reclamation of the land for cultivation on either side of the wadi.
M. Hamdan's initial observations suggest that during the Middle Palaeolithic, and also
probably later in the Neolithic, that this would have been a landscape with some braided
channels and vegetation.[47] The Delta existed but probably began further to the north in
the Middle Palaeolithic, meaning that the region around Merimde was not part of this
system.[48] The surface level would have been more consistent with that of the highest levels
on the Wadi el-Gamal today; the Wadi had not been cut into the landscape during the
Middle Palaeolithic. The highest extents of the Pleistocene terraces however are still visible
today, although with the quantity of local quarrying, this may not be the case for very
much longer. Much of the work on the changing environment in the Delta that has been
carried out in recent decades is related to the Predynastic period (fourth millennium BCE)
and later, but the increasing aridification ultimately draws more and more groups into the
Delta and the Nile Valley more than a millennium earlier. Marriner et al. imply that the
Delta plain comes under increasing use from c. 5000 years ago,[49] with decreasing floods
and "seasonally receding flood zones." They note the inferred higher levels of Nile floods
prior to this, and the importance of higher ground for shelter from the inundation.[50] This is
an interesting issue when considering not only the bigger picture, but the more immediate
situation around Merimde; how close was the local Nile branch at c. 5000 BCE for example

(see Fig. 3 for the current location of the Rosetta branch)? Although settlers would need more permanent water sources *if* they are moving from more arid areas—and this is only one scenario—they would also need safe higher land for their dwellings and animals, and later their domesticated crops. In these respects, the area of this earliest settlement in the Delta was highly suitable, sitting on top of the Late Pleistocene dune sands.[51]

WADI EL-GAMAL—A NEW PERSPECTIVE ON MERIMDE BENI SALAMA

The contexts excavated on the Wadi el-Gamal highlight, if anything, the necessity in 2019 of reconsidering the way in which we think about the settlement at Merimde Beni Salama. Although former research has succeeded in bringing structure to our understanding of the settlement, through creation and refinement of the types associated with layers I–V, the activity on the Wadi el-Gamal begs the question of who was there, when, and what activities they were undertaking. The preliminary observations regarding the environment since 2015 have provided new possibilities for thinking about these activities and interactions with wild fauna, and also grazing of domesticated animals, and considering the wider hinterland being used by the groups subsisting from Merimde, and beforehand. A crucial factor within this is how these activities varied over time.[52] It can be hypothesised that the annual Nile inundation already by c. 5000 BCE could have required movement of herds, and that yearly fluctuations in temperature would also impact upon the ways in which the elevated land of the wadi, and other surrounding lands could be used. Such issues as the quantity of water flowing across the wadi and shade available in particular seasons would have been important factors. It has been long known from the analysis of the faunal remains from the excavations of the German Archaeological Institute, that there is a mixture (albeit varied in proportions) of the presence of wild as well as domesticated animals through the layers I–V at Merimde.[53] There is likewise discussion of the cultivated land and its variability over time,[54] but the new evidence from the Wadi el-Gamal, both archaeological and environmental, allows for the presentation of scenarios hitherto not considered. The artefactual evidence includes that for grinding, with the presence of a lower grinder of red quartzite, as well as work requiring bone awls, bladelets, cooking as evidenced through coarse ceramics with burning marks (in some instances), as well as dozens of simple and probably short-lived hearths.[55] These activities may have been undertaken over prolonged periods, as may be suggested by the remains of shelters, in the form of substantial stone-lined postholes of c. 0.30 m diameter, within which posts and roofing could have been erected and taken down as required.[56] This could be the case particularly during the earlier periods of settlement by varied groups—potentially—at Merimde, notably if they are only remaining there for part of the year as has been suggested.[57] It may be more likely, that temporary occupation of Merimde was the case during the earlier periods of settlement, notably when it might have been occupied by a number of disparate groups. During later periods, if the settlement was consolidated into a more cohesive community, then some of the community presumably must have remained at the site to secure stored foodstuffs, as well as cultivated fields. Animals may variably have been taken to pastures over a much wider area, potentially providing one of the means of contact between different groups and communities during the fifth millennium BCE, and the Wadi el-Gamal (see Fig. 4) may have played a part within this at certain times of year. It is also possible that it might rather have been a location when wild animals were hunted as they came in search of water, away from the more precarious main Nile branch, which also had denser human occupation in closer proximity.

Putting Merimde Back into the Wider World: The Chronological and Regional
Perspectives

The way in which human groups of various origins interacted and exchanged knowledge
as new species were being introduced into the Delta remains poorly understood. However,
challenging preconceived and unsubstantiated ideas, as well as re-examining chronology,
environment, human relationships, and artefactual transitions, is proving rewarding for
Neolithic contexts in northern Egypt. When interpreting the results of recent fieldwork, as
well as re-examining the archival records and materials from former investigations, new
perspectives have led to the revision of older theories, in the Fayum, for example, the recent
work of scholars including Shirai[58] and Wendrich, Phillipps, and colleagues.[59] Through
the 1990s, research continued both on and off already known sites in connection with
Neolithic contexts in the Delta.[60] It was not until the 21st century, however, that previously
unknown Neolithic evidence was uncovered at Sa el-Hagar (ancient Sais) by P. Wilson,[61]
and at Tell es-Samara by F. Guyot,[62] where an Egyptian mission had been investigating the
Predynastic and Early Dynastic cemetery since the 1990s.[63] Before the discovery of these
sites deeper inside the Delta floodplain, site preservation at el-Omari and Merimde seemed
to suggest that the ideal environmental conditions that may have encouraged settlement
by the end of the sixth millennium BCE might have been found specifically on the fringes
of the Delta. However, given the close chronological proximity between the earliest (thus
far) known occupation at Sa el-Hagar and that at Merimde, the inner Delta was also clearly
suitable, although only future investigations will be able to assess the date of the earliest
Neolithic layers at Tell es-Samara. At Sa el-Hagar, as at Merimde, the earliest settlement
was on the west of the local Nile branch,[64] and although the two sites have very different
environmental surroundings, both have crucial access to immediate higher ground, in the
case of Sa el-Hagar a *gezira* and for Merimde, the immediately adjacent higher land to the
southwest (Wadi el-Gamal terraces, see Fig. 4), representing a much more extensive area
than at Sa el-Hagar. At the latter, however, it is thought that the earliest subsistence strategy
was heavily reliant on fish, with dense deposits from fish processing on the river bank of
an ancient channel (Sais Ia), whereas the farmers (later Sais Ib) were within the floodplain,
quite a distance away from the river.[65] El-Omari areas A and B are both located up on
wadi terraces, albeit not at an elevation as high as the Wadi el-Gamal, but also in a location
quite distant from the Nile.[66] El-Omari is in the area of the Wadi Hof which is unlike the
case at Merimde, where the Wadi el-Gamal is only a very minor wadi; el-Omari is in close
proximity to the limestone plateau.[67] In addition, it seems that in the area of Gebel Hof by
el-Omari, that rainwater would have had the opportunity to collect, providing another
attractive source of water.[68] The new evidence from the Wadi el-Gamal at Merimde does,
however, stress that the inhabitants were probably trying to take advantage of a wider
range of species and the benefits of using the high elevations along the desert edge.[69] Tell
es-Samara, similarly to Sa el-Hagar, has its earliest finds (Neolithic) within close proximity
to a *gezira*.[70] The investigations so far have uncovered artefacts typologically similar to the
later phases at Merimde, el-Omari and Sa el-Hagar,[71] however, much more data should be
forthcoming following future seasons of fieldwork.

Little is known about the Delta during the period directly preceding the settlement
at these sites, however, by the time of the first settlers, and then throughout the fifth
millennium BCE, it would seem reasonable to suppose a fluidity in the relationship between
mobile and less mobile groups, animals and their landscape. Hassan noted already in 1997
that he believed the area around Merimde to have been suitable for farming (or at least

Figure 3. The Wadi el-Gamal, looking southeast towards the high ground of the Pleistocene terraces'. The centre of the wadi is roughly aligned with the cultivation in this image. The Neolithic settlement lies to the left of the picture (to the northeast). Photo by J. Rowland.

for pastoralism) by c. 8000 BCE,[72] and this is supported by the new environmental survey evidence from Merimde,[73] with the existence of the sheltered fan already by the end of the Epipalaeolithic. The research of colleagues working further west, for example in Farafra Oasis,[74] has shown that following the desert re-occupation and stable phases that came to a sudden end by 5300 BCE,[75] favourable conditions for settlement might have existed c. 300 years earlier than settlement at Merimde is currently believed to date to.[76] Likewise Djara in the western Desert seems to have been abandoned by c. 5300 BCE.[77] It may be that there was no need to adopt new modes of subsistence before then (even if people had been exposed to them), and there is no reason why there must have been a considerable population in the Delta region until towards the end of the sixth millennium BCE. The model of Kuper and Kröpelin[78] is supported by the climatic fluctuations detected at Farafra in the lake, and a brief arid period by c. 7000 cal BP.[79] Barich and Lucarini's research has shown a sharp decrease in settlement evidence by 5300 BCE which includes the Hidden Valley at the Wadi el-Obeyid.[80] Although the Epipalaeolithic data is very apparent in some regions, for example the Fayum and the area around Helwan, there are a great many places where it is not, such as Merimde, and this begs the question of the extent of prior population in this region, as well as Sa e-Hagar, in the latter part of the sixth millennium BCE.[81] It may be that the first groups are also those who are settling for shorter periods, seasonally perhaps, and that the distinct differences in the evidence from the earlier and later levels at Merimde are in fact the closest evidence that we will find.[82] Ongoing investigation into the environment at Merimde will help to establish reasons for the gap between the *Urschicht* and layer II.[83] At Sa el-Hagar, already, a shift in the local river channel has been observed from the east to the west in between Sais Ia and Sais Ib, with very different subsistence strategies apparent through the evidence thus far.[84] As noted above, Sais Ia has dense and potentially very extensive fish middens, yet in Ib more evidence for domesticated plants and animals, as well as wild species; this suggests a gradual settling/seasonal settling of groups, with a later (Ib) introduction of farming in the area.[85] The evidence from Sa el-Hagar likewise suggests a gap between Ia and Ib, which maybe be due to environmental and climatic change.[86] Wilson considers that this may relate to the Middle Holocene Moist Phase and suggests that the onset of this phase could have been a key moment at which the Delta environment could be exploited to the full.[87] At Merimde there is a noticeable increase in hunting of wild animals (notably antelope and gazelles), particularly in II and in IV.[88] Fishing seems to increase considerably over time at Merimde within the overall proportions of species in the record.[89] El-Omari has a high proportion of fish remains in proportion to other animal protein subsistence strategies, but the element of change over time cannot be seen with the lack of finer chronological control.[90]

Researchers have pointed to different regional similarities associated with the evidence from the Merimde I–V layers. The earliest layer at Merimde (the *Urschicht*—layer I) shows no evidence that specific tools have been introduced for harvesting, although both wild and domestic plants and animals are in evidence from this lowest level. When the area is first settled, it is probable that a number of (possibly) unconnected small groups have their temporary shelters spread across the space and they might function quite separately. If at least some of the groups are inhabiting the area only seasonally, then this is maybe why we are not seeing the remains of intensive cropping and tools for harvesting. These are visible from layer II onwards. The material cultural remains of layer I have been suggested by Eiwanger and others to have evidence that suggests similarities to Levantine material culture in the *Urschicht*, which is also discussed by Wilson et al. in reference to Sa el-Hagar.[91] Hassan suggests changing climatic conditions (drought) in the Levant as a reason for movement of groups towards the Delta,[92] and future research at and around Merimde will hopefully add more precise data as to the nature of the climate there at the time of the earliest settlement, which could be as early as c. 5000 BCE, although the earliest reliable radiocarbon date is 4912–4608 BCE.[93] It will then be possible to better assess the nature of this change and how it may have impacted upon the community or communities living there and more widely within the Delta throughout the fifth millennium BCE. For the middle Merimde culture (c. 4775–4600 BCE), which does not seem to be represented at Sa el-Hagar, Eiwanger cites Saharo-Sudanese similarities.[94] Butzer comments that agriculture in the Delta has similarities to "recessional agriculture" systems south of the Sahara.[95] For Kuper and Kröpelin's Regionalization Phase,[96] they suggest that the evidence points to "seasonal or episodic transhumance" by populations seeking suitable environmental conditions, and migration into the Sudanese Sahara.[97]

At el-Omari (c. 4600–4400 BCE), the settlement evidence appears to correspond with the II–IV phases at Merimde[98] and with Sais Ib (the later Neolithic, c. 4500–4300 BCE).[99] For Merimde, the material culture associated with the youngest layers of the settlement is compared to that of the later Fayum Neolithic.[100] Given the reasonably close geographical proximity between the sites, communication is to be expected, but a finer-tuned absolute chronology is really needed in order not to rely so predominantly on typological comparisons to link the sites. J. Emmitt,[101] writing on the variation in ceramic fabrics at Neolithic sites, notes that Merimde displayed a high degree of variation.

Future Challenges for Environmental Research into the Earliest Settlements at Merimde and Further Afield

Some of the key outstanding questions regarding the earliest settlements in the Delta, and in Egypt more broadly, can only be addressed by developing new opportunities for scientific sample analysis. Although the author and colleagues have been able to revisit the evidence from the Junker investigations[102] and apply methods not available during previous excavations (e.g., new AMS radiocarbon measurements),[103] possibilities for analyses on well-contexted, recently excavated material are extremely limited. AMS measurements, for example, cannot be conducted within Egypt as there is currently no AMS facility up and running in the country, and the conventional method of liquid scintillation can only be carried out if there are sufficient quantities of organic remains, which is nearly always *not* the case. As such, the possibility of gaining the necessary degree of chronological refinement is currently unlikely. Other methods needed to take the debate forward as to the origins of domesticated species include stable isotope analysis and aDNA on animal remains in particular, both currently not available within Egypt, and hence not possible on any freshly excavated material. There are, nonetheless, possibilities for material from earlier excavations at Merimde. Other important analyses, particularly relating to environmental reconstruction are closer to becoming a reality, and in some cases already are, notably the possibilities for thin sections for petrographic analysis (ceramics) and for micromorphology (sediments). The debate over such issues relating to sample analysis must remain high on the agenda, and applications pursued and possibilities investigated into suitable equipment in-country that could be used,[104] that meets international standards.[105]

DISCUSSION

More and more data resources are becoming widely available, environmental and other,[106] which is enabling more multi-disciplinary work to be carried out. Databases of dates of Nile flow levels become available,[107] with publications bringing together data generated by various projects running in Egypt.[108] Colleagues including Angus Graham and Judith Bunbury, and others, are amassing huge amounts of environmental core data, and working within varied projects to bring a fuller environmental picture, as well as adding specific details to the research questions of certain projects. We do not necessarily always need to be working on big projects together all of the time, but by discussing what we are doing, sharing data, at least once it is published, if not before, this will enable colleagues in different disciplines working apart as well as together, to achieve more holistic approaches. This can come from and contribute to work at single sites in detail, across sites within and between regions, and within larger survey areas. If we can make published data available more widely, either via the internet, or through our research links, then it lessens the spending of valuable resources on generating the same data, and will allow colleagues to work towards deeper levels of understanding. As archaeologists working to forward our collective knowledge of the first human settlements, as has been seen even in this contribution, there are a myriad of approaches that can help to clarify issues such as gradual, as well as sudden, climate change, in detail at Merimde, for example, and to look at the timing of this change, which will hopefully be possible in the coming years. Depositories of data from satellite images, to environmental core data, to pollen data will help research efforts as we move forward, and help move beyond broader, more general links to major climate change, for example the 8.2 ka cal BP sudden arid events, to understanding how this played out at individual sites. Individually, we cannot all generate all of the data we would like to have, however, if we collaborate on each other's projects, enabling more work between provinces within Egypt, then we stand to push research forward with robust datasets and new (as well as tried and trusted) methodologies. Historical data constantly needs to be revisited, we work with historical maps and photographs, as well as earlier publications, which reveal an environment very different to the Egypt of today. We have also a responsibility to train the generations of scholars of all countries who follow us, including colleagues who may not have regular access to specific equipment that may help to achieve certain results. A sharing of knowledge and the possibilities of certain analyses will hopefully pave the way for more change, although much change has already happened in very recent years. Living through times when climate change is a daily discussion through the vast networks of communication, notably through the internet, reminds us of the ways in which climatic change is having a different impact on different regions in extreme as well as more subtle ways, and the reaction is hugely varied, dependent on infrastructure, resources, and cultural differences. As we look, comparatively, at regions which had exposure to

"Neolithic" ways of life, it is therefore unsurprising that looking between regions (e.g., from the Levant across North Africa, and in the southern Mediterranean) we see little consistency in terms of which aspects are taken up, which not, and which have greater longevity.[109]

Works Cited

Abbo, S., and Gopher, A. 2017. "Near Eastern Plant Domestication: A History of Thought." *Trends in Plant Science* 22 (6): 491–511.

Bagh, T. 2002. "Abu Ghâlib, an Early Middle Kingdom Town in the Western Nile Delta: Renewed Work on Material Excavated in the 1930s." *MDAIK* 58: 29–61.

Baghdadi, S. G. el-. 2008. "The Protodynastic and Early Dynastic Necropolis of Tell el-Daba'a (El-Qanan) and Tell el-Samara (El-Dakahlia province, northeast Delta)." In *Egypt at Its Origins 2: Proceedings of the International Conference "Origin of the State. Predynastic and Early Dynastic Egypt," Toulouse (France), 5th–8th September 2005*, edited by B. Midant-Reynes Y. and Tristant, 1151–1155. Leuven: Peeters; Departement Oosterse Studies.

Barich, B. 2019. "Eastern Borders of the Sahara and the Relations with the Nile Valley and Beyond." In *Climate Changes in the Holocene: Impacts and Human Adaptation*, edited by E, Chiotis, 201–220. Boca Raton/London/New York: CRC Press.

Barich, B., and G. Lucarini. 2014. "Social Dynamics in Northern Farafra from the Middle to Late Holocene: Changing Life under Uncertainty." In *From Lake to Sand: The Archaeology of Farafra Oasis, Western Desert, Egypt*, edited by B. Barich, G. Lucarini, M.A. Hamdan, and F.A. Hassan, 467–484. Florence: All'Insegna del Giglio.

Barich, B., G. Lucarini, M.A. Hamdan, and F.A. Hassan. 2014. *From Lake to Sand: The Archaeology of Farafra Oasis, Western Desert, Egypt*. Florence: All'Insegna del Giglio.

Barker, G. 2013. "The Neolithisation of Northeastern Africa: Reflections on Knowns, Unknowns, and Unknown Unknowns." In *Neolithisation of Northeastern Africa*, edited by N. Shirai, 249–256. Berlin: Ex oriente.

Bernhardt, C., B.P. Horton, and J.-D. Stanley. 2012. "Nile Delta Response to Holocene Climate Variability." *Geology* 40(7): 615–618. DOI:10.1130/G33012.1.

Bietak, M. 1975. *Tell el-Dab'a II*. Vienna: Österreichische Akademie der Wissenschaften.

Butzer, K.W. 1960. "Archaeology and Geology in Ancient Egypt." *Science* 132 (3440): 1617–1624.

———. 1976. *Early Hydraulic Civilization*. Chicago: University of Chicago Press.

———. 2002. "Geoarchaeological Implications of Recent Research in the Nile Delta." In *Egypt and the Levant: Interrelations from the 4th through the Early 3rd Millennium BCE*, edited by E.C.M. van den Brink, T.E. Levy, 83–97. Leicester University Press: London and New York.

Caton-Thompson, G., and E. Gardner. 1934. *The Desert Fayum*. London: Royal Anthropological Institute.

Debono, F., and B. Mortenson. 1990. *El Omari: a Neolithic Settlement and Other Sites in the Vicinity of Wadi Hof Helwan*. Mainz am Rhein: Philipp von Zabern.

Emmitt, J.J. 2017. "The Neolithic Pottery of Egypt: Investigating settlement pattern in middle Holocene northeast Africa with ceramics." Unpublished Ph.D. diss., University of Auckland.

Eiwanger, J. 1980. "Dritter Vorbericht über die Wiederaufnahme der Grabungen in der neolithischen Siedlung Merimde-Benisalâme." *MDAIK* 36: 61–76.

———. 1984. *Merimde-Benisalâme*. Vol. 1, *Die Funde der Urschicht*. Mainz am Rhein: Philipp von Zabern.

————. 1988. *Merimde-Benisalâme*. Vol. 2, *Die Funde der mittleren Merimdekultur*. Archäologische Veröffentlichungen 51. Deutsches Archäologisches Institut, Abteilung Kairo. Mainz am Rhein: Philipp von Zabern.

————. 1992. *Merimde-Benisalâme*. Vol. 3, *Die Funde der jüngeren Merimdekultur*. Mainz am Rhein: Philipp von Zabern.

Fahmy, A. 2014. "Plant Food Resources at Hidden Valey, Farafra Oasis." In *From Lake to Sand: The Archaeology of Farafra Oasis, Western Desert, Egypt*, edited by B. Barich, G. Lucarini, M.A. Hamdan, and F.A. Hassan, 333–344. Florence: All'Insegna del Giglio.

Ginau, A., R. Schiestl, F. Kern, and J. Wunderlich. 2017. "Identification of Historic Landscape Features and Settlement Mounds in the Western Nile Delta by Means of Remote Sensing Time Series Analysis and the Evaluation of Vegetation Characteristics." *Journal of Archaeological Science: Reports* 16: 170–184.

Ginter, B., and J. Kozłowski, J. 1983. "Investigations on Neolithic Settlement." In *Qasr el-Sagha 1980*, edited by J. Kozłowski, 37–67. Warszawa-Kraków: Państwowe Wydawnictwo Naukowe.

Graham, A., K.D. Strutt, W.H.J. Toonen, B.T. Pennington, D. Löwenborg, A. Masson-Berghoff, V.L. Emery, D.S. Barker, M.A. Hunter, K.-J. Lindholm, and C. Johansson. 2016. "Theban Harbours and Waterscapes Survey, 2015." *Journal of Egyptian Archaeology* 101: 37–49.

Guyot, F. 2016. *Excavations at the Neolithic Site of Tell el-Samara (Daqahliya Governorate, Nile Delta): Preliminary Report of the First Season, 2015*. Unpublished Report.

Hamdan, M.A. 2014. "Sedimentological Characteristics and Geomorphic Evolution of the Holocene Playa of Wadi el-Obeiyid." In *From Lake to Sand: The Archaeology of Farafra Oasis, Western Desert, Egypt*, edited by B. Barich, G. Lucarini, M.A. Hamdan, and F.A. Hassan , 81–128. Florence: All'Insegna del Giglio, 81–128.

Hassan, F.A. 1981. *Demographic Archaeology*. London and New York: Academic Press.

————. 1985. "Radiocarbon Chronology of Neolithic and Predynastic Sites in Upper Egypt and the Delta." *African Archaeological Review* 3: 95–116.

————. 1988. "The Predynastic of Egypt." *Journal of World Prehistory* 2(2): 135–185.

————. 1997. "The Dynamics of a Riverine Civilization." *World Archaeology* 29: 51–74.

Hawass, Z., F.A. Hassan, and A. Gautier. 1988. "Chronology, Sediments, and Subsistence at Merimda Beni Salama." *Journal of Egyptian Archaeology* 74: 31–38.

Hendrickx, S. 1999. "La chronologie de la préhistoire tardive et des débuts de l'histoire de l'Egypte." *Archéo-Nil* 9: 13–81.

Hillier, J.K., J. Bunbury, and A. Graham. 2007. "Monuments on a Migrating Nile." *Journal of Archaeological Science* 34: 1011–1015.

Hoffman, M.A. 1980. *Egypt Before the Pharaohs*. London: Ark.

Holdaway, S.J., R.S. Phillipps, J.J. Emmitt, and W. Wendrich. 2016. "The Fayum Revisited: Reconsidering the Role of the Neolithic Package, Fayum North Shore, Egypt." *Quaternary International* 410 (A):173–180. doi: 10.1016/j.quaint.2015.11.072.

Junker, H. 1928. *Bericht über die von der Akademie der Wissenschaften in Wien nach dem Westdelta entsendete Expedition (20. Dezember 1927 bis 25. Februar 1928). Denkschriften der Kaiserlichen Akademie der Wissenschaften in Wien, Philosophisch-Historische Klasse* 68(3). Vienna: Hölder-Pichler-Tempsky A.-G.

————. 1929. "Vorläufer Bericht über die Grabung der Akademie der Wissenschaften in Wien auf der neolithischen Siedlung von Merimde Benisalame (Westdelta)." *Anzeiger der Akademie der Wissenschaften in Wien, Philosophischhistorische Klasse* XVI–XVIII: 156–250.

————. 1930. "Vorläufer Bericht über die Grabung der Akademie der Wissenschaften in Wien auf der neolithischen Siedlung von Merimde Benisalame (Westdelta)." *Anzeiger der Akademie der Wissenschaften in Wien, Philosophisch-historische Klasse* V–XIII: 21–83.

———. 1932. "Vorläufer Bericht über die Grabung der Akademie der Wissenschaften in Wien auf der neolithischen Siedlung von Merimde Benisalame (Westdelta)." *Anzeiger der Akademie der Wissenschaften in Wien, Philosophisch-historische Klasse* I–IV: 36–97.

———. 1933. "Vorläufer Bericht über die Grabung der Akademie der Wissenschaften in Wien auf der neolithischen Siedlung von Merimde Benisalame (Westdelta)." *Anzeiger der Akademie der Wissenschaften in Wien, Philosophisch-historische Klasse* XVI–XXVII: 54–97.

———. 1934. "Vorläufer Bericht über die Grabung der Akademie der Wissenschaften in Wien auf der neolithischen Siedlung von Merimde Benisalame (Westdelta)." *Anzeiger der Akademie der Wissenschaften in Wien, Philosophisch-historische Klasse* X: 118–132.

———. 1940. "Vorläufer Bericht über die Grabung der Akademie der Wissenschaften in Wien auf der neolithischen Siedlung von Merimde Benisalame (Westdelta)." *Anzeiger der Akademie der Wissenschaften in Wien, Philosophisch-historische Klasse* I–IV: 3–25.

Kindermann, K., O. Bubenzer, S. Nussbaum, H. Riemer, F. Darius, N. Pöllath, and U. Smettan. 2006. "Palaeoenvironment and Holocene Land Usse of Djara, Western Desert of Egypt." *Quarternary Science Reviews* 25: 1619–1637.

Krzyżaniak, L. 1993. "New Data on the Late Prehistoric Settlement at Minshat Abu Omar, Eastern Nile Delta." In *Environmental Change and Human Culture in the Nile Basin and Northern Africa until the Second Millennium B.C.*, edited by L.Krzyżaniak, L. Kobusiewicz, and J. Alexander, 321–325. Poznań: Poznań Archaeological Museum.

Kuper, R., and S. Kröpelin. 2006, 11 August. "Climate Controlled Holocene Occupation in the Sahara: Motor of African's Evolution." *Science* 313(5788): 803–807. DOI: 10.1126/science.1130989.

Macklin, M., W.H.J.Toonen, J.C. Woodward, M.A.J. Williams, C. Flaux, N. Marriner, K. Nicoll, G. Verstraeten, N. Spencer, and D. Welsby. 2015. "A New Model of River Dynamics, Hydroclimatic Change and Human Settlement in the Nile Valley Derived from Meta-Analysis of the Holocene Fluvial Archive." *Quaternary Science Reviews* 130: 109–123. https://doi.org/10.1016/j.quascirev.2015.09.024.

Marriner, N., C. Flaux, C. Morhange, and J.-D. Stanley. 2013. "Tracking Nile Delta Vulnerability to Holocene Change." *PLoS ONE* 8(7; e69195): 1–9. https://doi.org/10.1371/journal.pone.0069195.

Menghin, O. 1932. "Die Primitivtypen des Neolithikums von Merimde-Benisalâme." In *Vorbericht über die dritte, von der Akademie der Wissenschaften in Wien in Verbindung mit dem Egyptiska Museet in Stockholm, unternommene Grabung auf der neolithischen Siedlung von Merimde-Benisalâme vom 6. November 1931 bis 20. Jänner 1932*, edited by H. Junker, 83–88. Wien; Leipzig: Hölder-Pichler-Tempsky.

Midant-Reynes, B. 2000. *The Prehistory of Egypt*. Oxford: Blackwell.

Miller, N.F., and W. Wetterstrom. 2000. "The Beginnings of Agriculture: The Ancient Near East and North Africa." In *The Cambridge World History of Food*, edited by K.F. Kiple, and K.C. Ornelas, 1123–1239. Cambridge: University of Cambridge Press.

Olsson, I. 1959. "Uppsala Natural Radiocarbon Measurements I." *American Journal of Science Radiocarbon Supplement* 1: 89–102.

Pennington, B.T., F. Sturt, P. Wilson, J. Rowland, and A.G. Brown. 2017. "The Fluvial Evolution of the Holocene Nile Delta." *Quaternary Science Reviews* 170: 212–231.

Phillipps, R., S. Holdaway, W. Wendrich, and R. Cappers. 2012. "Mid-Holocene occupation of Egypt and Global Climatic Change." *Quaternary International* 251: 64–76.

Robb, J. 2013. "Material Culture, Landscapes of Action, and Emergent Causation: A Nsew Model for the Origins of the European Neolithic." *Current Anthropology* 54(6): 657–683.

Rowland, J.M. Forthcoming a. "New Perspectives on Activity Areas within the Village and

Wider Landscape at Merimde Beni Salama." In *Origins 6: International Conference on Predynastic and Early Dynastic Egypt*, edited by E.C. Köhler, F. Junge, N. Kuch, and A.-K. Jeske. Leuven: Peeters.

————. Forthcoming b. "New Perspectives and Methods Applied to the 'Known' Settlement of Merimde Beni Salama, Western Nile Delta." In *Revolutions: The Neolithisation of the Mediterranean Basin: The Transition to Food Producing Economies in North Africa and Southern Europe. Proceedings of the Workshop 29ᵗʰ–31ˢᵗ October 2016, TOPOI, Freie Universität, Berlin*, edited by J.M. Rowland, G.J. Tassie, and G. Lucarini. Berlin: Edition Topoi.

Rowland, J.M., and L. Bertini. 2016. "New Results and Perspectives from Fieldwork at Merimde Beni Salama." *Quaternary International* 410(2016): 160–172.

Rowland, J.M., and G.J. Tassie. 2017. "The Neolithic in the Nile Delta: Topoi Research Project A-2-4." *Edition Topoi*. DOI: 10.17171/1-9.

Rowland, J.M., G.J. Tassie, and G. Lucarini. Forthcoming. *Revolutions: The Neolithisation of the Mediterranean Basin: The Transition to Food Producing Economies in North Africa and Southern Europe. Proceedings of the Workshop 29ᵗʰ–31ˢᵗ October 2016, TOPOI, Freie Universität, Berlin*. Berlin: Edition Topoi.

Sandford, K.S., W.J. and Arkell. 1939. *Paleolithic Man and the Nile Valley in Lower Egypt*. Chicago: University of Chicago Press.

Schmidt, K. 1980. "Paläolithische Funde aus Merimde-Benisalâme." *MDAIK* 36: 411–435.

Shirai, N. 2010. *The Archaeology of the First Farmer-Herders in Egypt*. Leiden: Leiden University Press.

————. 2013. "Was Neolithisation a Struggle for Existence and the Survival of the Fittest, or Merely the Survival of the Luckiest? A Case Study of Socioeconomic and Cultural Changes in Egypt in the Early–Middle Holocene." In *Neolithisation of Northeastern Africa*, edited by N. Shirai, 213–235. Studies in Early Near Eastern Production, Subsistence, and Environment 16. Berlin: Ex oriente.

Stanley, J-D., A.G. Warne, and G. Schnepp. 2004. "Geoarchaeological Interpretation of the Canopic, Largest of the Relict Nile Delta Distributaries, Egypt." *Journal of Coastal Research* 203: 920–930. DOI: 10.2112/1551-5036(2004)20[920:GIOTCL]2.0.CO;2.

Tassie, G.J. 2014. *Prehistoric Egypt: Socioeconomic Transformations in East Africa from the Last Glacial Maximum to the Neolithic, 24,000 to 4,000 BC*. London: Golden House.

Tristant, Y. 2006. *L'occupation humaine dans le delta du Nil aux 5e et 4e millénaires*. Toulouse: École des hautes études en sciences sociales.

von den Driesch, A., and J. Boessneck. 1985. *Die Tierknochenfunde aus der neolithischen Siedlung von Merimde-Benisalâme am westlichen Nildelta*. Munich: Staatliche Sammlung Ägyptischer Kunst.

Wendrich, W., R.E. Taylot, and J. Southon. 2010. "Dating Stratified Settlement Sites at Kom K and Kom W: Fifth Millennium BCE Radiocarbon Ages for the Fayum Neolithic." *Nuclear Instruments and Methods in Physics Research B* 268: 999–1002.

Wilson, P. 2006. "Prehistoric Settlement in the Western Delta: A Regional and Local View from Sais (Sa el-Hagar)." *Journal of Egyptian Archaeology* 92: 75–126.

————. 2014. "The Prehistoric Sequence at Sais: Temporal and Regional Connections." In *The Nile Delta as a Centre of Cultural Interactions between Upper Egypt and the Southern Levant in the 4th Millennium BC*, edited by A. Mączyńska, 299–318. Studies in African Archaeology 13. Poznan, Poland: Poznań Archaeological Museum.

————. 2017. Landscapes of the Bashmur—Settlements and Monasteries in the Northern Egyptian Delta from the Seventh to the Ninth Century. In *The Nile: Natural and Cultural*

Landscapes, edited by H. Willems and J.-M. Dahms, 345–368. Mainzer Historische Kulturwissenschaften 36. Mainz: Bielefeld.

Wilson, P., and G. Gilbert. 2002. "Pigs, Pots and Postholes." *Egyptian Archaeology* 21: 12–13.

———. 2003. "The Prehistoric Period at Saïs." *Archéo-Nil* 13: 65–72.

———. 2012. "Prehistoric Saïs: Results from the Western Delta Floodplain." In *Prehistory of Northeastern Africa: New Ideas and Discoveries,* edited by J. Kabaciński, M. Chłodnicki, and M. Kobusiewicz, 25–40. Studies in African Archaeology 11. Poznań: Poznań Archaeological Museum.

Wilson, P., G. Gilbert, and G.J. Tassie. 2014. *Sais.* Vol. 2, *The Prehistoric Period.* London: Egypt Exploration Society.

Zeder, M.A. 2008. "Domestication and Early Agriculture in the Mediterranean Basin: Origins, Diffusion, and Impact." *Proceedings of the National Academy of Sciences* 105 (33): 11597–11604.

Notes

[1]   For discussion, see Robb 2013.

[2]   Rowland et al. forthcoming.

[3]   Junker 1928.

[4]   Debono and Mortensen 1990; Wilson et al. 2014; Guyot 2016. Ceramic sherds were found in a drill core at Minshat Abu Omar which Krzyżaniak (1993, 323–325; Guyot 2016, 12) noted had similarities in terms of technology to Neolithic wares.

[5]   Eiwanger 1980, 69; 1988; Midant-Reynes 2000; Tristant 2006.

[6]   Butzer 1960; Hawass et al. 1988; Wilson 2006, 2014; Wilson et al. 2014; Rowland and Bertini 2016.

[7]   Rowland forthcoming a.

[8]   The Delta evidence is currently only confirmed as falling in the fifth millennium BCE in so far as the reliable radiocarbon measurements are concerned (Olsson 1959, 96–97; Hassan 1985, 104–105; discussed in Rowland forthcoming a). The Fayum evidence for domesticated species and storage facilities, if not substantial evidence for settlement structures, dates earlier, from the middle of the sixth millennium BCE (including Phillipps et al. 2012). Hassan (1988, 147–148) discusses the evidence for postholes found by the Polish Mission in the Fayum, as published by Ginter and Kozłowski (1983, 40–42), but other than that hearths and storage pits.

[9]   Zeder (2008) provides a review of research into animal domestication in the Near East, and Abbo and Gopher (2017) discuss the history of thought on Near Eastern plant domestication.

[10] Bietak 1975.

[11] Butzer 1976.

[12] Notably Hassan 1988, 1997.

[13] Hassan 1981.

[14] Some recent examples of collaborations include Stanley et al. 2004; Bernhardt et al. 2012; Marriner et al. 2013.

[15] This includes research into settlement placement (e.g., Wilson 2017; Ginau et al. 2017).

[16] The work of Graham (including in this volume; Hillier et al. 2007; Graham et al. 2016).

[17] Including the "Peopling the Green Sahara" project https://www.greensahara-leverhulme.com/, and decades of research into the western desert by sub-projects of the wider ACACIA project of the University of Cologne http://www.uni-koeln.de/sfb389/.

[18] Barich et al. 2014.

[19]   Barich and Lucarini 2014.

[20]   Butzer 1960.

[21]   The project is now the "Imbaba Governorate Prehistoric Survey," which is part of the Egypt Exploration Society's Delta Survey.

[22]   Hawass et al. 1988. Other scholars, notably including Hoffman (1980), integrated environmental hypotheses within their work, stressing the importance of climatic change and increasing aridification on the earliest settlements within Egypt.

[23]   Bagh (2002, 42) raises the question of the uncertain dating of the Abu Ghâlib microdrills, and she considers it possible that they may be Predynastic or Protodynastic, rather than Epipalaeolithic. This material has not yet been re-examined (pers comm. Bagh), but is part of the upcoming research of the author and colleagues.

[24]   Eiwanger 1988, Abb. 15.

[25]   Von den Driesch and Boessneck 1985.

[26]   Wilson et al. 2014, 73.

[27]   The preceding period had been in the 1920s, with the discovery of Merimde by Junker and the team of the Austrian WestDelta Expedition (1928), where Junker subsequently directed excavations into and throughout the 1930s (Junker 1929, 1930, 1932, 1933, 1934, 1940), together with a separate concession of the then Egyptian Museum in Stockholm. The 1920s were also witness to the work on the Fayum Lake Shores by Caton-Thompson and Gardner (1934), and the discovery of the settlement at el-Omari in 1924 (Debono and Mortensen 1990).

[28]   Notably the instigation of the Combined Prehistoric Expedition.

[29]   Caton-Thompson and Gardner 1934, 10–19.

[30]   Sandford and Arkell 1939, 42–44, 51, 52, 53, 55, 84, 90, and 96.

[31]   See supra n. 12.

[32]   Hawass et al. 1988.

[33]   Rowland and Bertini 2016 (especially 169–170); in Rowland forthcoming a.

[34]   Hawass et al. 1988.

[35]   The DAI's focus was to re-assess and refine the chronology of Merimde Beni Salama, published to date, in over three main volumes of settlement data in Eiwanger (1984, 1988, and 1992), with aspects under re-analysis at the present time by Eiwanger and the current author.

[36]   Junker 1929, 1930, 1932, 1933, 1934, and 1940.

[37]   Hawass et al. 1988, 33–35.

[38]   Schmidt (1980, 411) actually refers to the area as the Wadi el-Gamal, whereas, e.g., Menghin (1932, 83) refers rather to the Nile Terrace to the west of the Neolithic settlement.

[39]   Hawass et al. 1988, 35, 38. These activities were noted as including the use of mud-brick, although this probably rather refers to the construction of mud slabs for the structures known (at least to date) from Merimde.

[40]   Hawass et al. 1988, 38. Von den Driesch and Boessneck (1985, 1) note occupation throughout the fifth millennium BCE. The various radiocarbon dates for Merimde are discussed in Olsson 1959, 96–97; Hassan 1985, 105–106; Eiwanger 1992, 75; Phillipps et al. 2012, 69; Rowland forthcoming a.

[41]   Hawass et al. 1988, 35.

[42]   As yet it has only been possible to date the assemblages on the basis of comparative typology.

[43]   See Rowland and Bertini (2016, 165–167 and Fig. 5) for details of the results of the geophysical survey. The survey was carried out by Eastern Atlas, Berlin.

44   Rowland and Bertini 2016.
45   The environmental survey will be the subject of a forthcoming publication.
46   The season was funded by the National Geographic Society Exploration Europe GEFNE165-16 and the American Research Center in Egypt Antiquities' Endowment Fund.
47   M. Hamdan pers. comm.
48   M. Hamdan pers. comm.
49   Marriner et al. 2013, 7.
50   Marriner at al. 2013, 7. The higher ground in these cases has been formed during the Pleistocene.
51   Based on Hamdan's interpretations of the continuous cores extracted from the site of Merimde down to the modern Nasiry canal to the east. Hawass et al. (1988, 38) suggest that the Merimde settlement was above the "effective level" of the Nile floods.
52   More detailed information will be available after analysis in upcoming seasons.
53   Von den Driesch and Boessneck 1985.
54   Von den Driesch and Boessneck 1985, 24.
55   Rowland forthcoming a.
56   Eiwanger (pers comm.) has recently suggested to the author that this could be the case in other instances at Merimde.
57   Miller and Wetterstrom (2000, 1129) have suggested this throughout the use of the settlement. Emmitt (2017, 251) also refers to the possibility that despite the structures at Merimde, its occupants might not have spent the whole year there, however, the presence of substantial basket-lined storage pits suggests large quantities of commodities being stored, rendering this suggestion slightly problematic.
58   Shirai has re-opened discussions on the hiatus between the Epipalaeolithic and the Neolithic in the Fayum; see supra n. 57 (Shirai 2010, 2013).
59   Wendrich et al. 2010; Phillipps et al. 2012. The UCLA and University of Auckland teams have provided new archaeological evidence using new theoretical perspectives, as well as new technologies, to issues of the environment, chronology and use of resources across wider areas.
60   M. Boraik conducted fieldwork at Merimde in the early 1990s and the volume on the earlier work at el-Omari was published by Debono and Mortensen (1990).
61   Wilson and Gilbert 2003, Gilbert 2012; Wilson 2006, 2014; Wilson et al. 2014.
62   Guyot 2016.
63   Baghdadi 2008.
64   A palaeo-channel was identified through geophysical survey and auger samples, as were the now buried *gezira* sands (Wilson et al. 2014, 4, Figs. 3 and 4). Wilson et al. (2014, 5) consider that the shifting of this branch further east was at the roof of a fundamental shift from the site's relationship with the regions west in the fifth millennium and its subsequent relations with areas to the north and east in the fourth millennium BCE.
65   Wilson et al. 2014, 50.
66   Debono and Mortensen 1990, 90.
67   Debono and Mortensen 1990, 88.
68   Debono and Mortensen 1990, 90.
69   Debono and Mortensen (1990, 91) discuss their opinions as to the similar climatic environments between Merimde and el-Omari, noting that the key difference appears to be the additional water sources in the Wadi Hof area.
70   Guyot 2016, 11.

71 Guyot 2016, 11–12.

72 Hassan 1997, 64. Butzer (2002, 93–96) does not believe that the geomorphology of the floodplain was necessarily a key factor in the question of when the first farming groups appear and start to settle.

73 Evidence from the environmental coring survey carried out by M. Hamdan and J. Bunbury in 2013.

74 Hamdan 2014, 90–91. Hamdan refers here in particular to the "arid episode" between 8200–8000 bp (in his description of Unit II at the El-Bahr Basin at the Wadi el-Obeiyid) which is associated with Epipalaeolithic finds, followed by a humid middle Holocene described in Unit III and associated with Early Neolithic material. Fahmy's (2014, 343) discussion of the macro botanical assemblage, relates to the fluctuating wet and arid phases of the middle Hololcene and the wetter conditions at 7600–6100 bp—this latter date is approximately the time at which Merimde is first settled.

75 Kuper and Kröpelin 2006; Barich 2019, 205.

76 Hassan 1985, 104–105; Hendrickx 1999, 18–19; Rowland forthcoming a, b.

77 Kindermann et al. 2006, 1626; as discussed also in Wilson et al. 2014, 156.

78 Kuper and Kröpelin 2006.

79 Barich 2019, 205.

80 Barich and Lucarini 2014, 480–481.

81 Sandford and Arkell (1939, 70, 76) considered the later-Palaeolithic and pre-Neolithic evidence to be deeply buried under the Delta silts, with probably later Palaeolithic "habitation sites and refuges" having been on high land on top of the turtlebacks. They commented that this evidence would be located only through boring, which of course turned out to be the case at Sa el-Hagar (Wilson and Gilbert 2002).

82 Wilson et al. (2014, 160) refer back to Midant-Reynes (2000, 111) and the discussion of whether the Merimde *Urschicht* (Eiwanger 1984), and possibly the earliest layers at Sa el-Hagar, have more in common with the Epipalaeolithic than the Neolithic. Certainly the issue of the absence of sickle blade inserts is observed by Eiwanger for the *Urschicht* (Eiwanger 1984, Abb. 15), who believes that an earlier date for the *Urschicht* is likely reaching back into the sixth millennium BCE (Eiwanger 1988, 54 FN 312; Hendrickx 1999, 18; Midant-Reynes 2000, 111). Wilson et al. (2014, 160) refer back to Midant-Reynes' (2000, 111) comment that the *Urschicht* might indeed fall within the Fayum hiatus between the Epipalaeolithic and the Neolithic, however, in more recent years, comments by Shirai (2010, 52–53) suggest that this gap in the Fayum is shorter than originally thought (perhaps around 200 years), and reflects the hiatus shown at other sites, including Nabta Platya, Dakhleh Oasis, and Djara at c. 6000 BCE.

83 Eiwanger 1984, 59.

84 Wilson 2014, 300–304, including environmental detail in Fig. 1 (300), also in Wilson et al. 2014, 153 (Fig. 130).

85 Wilson 2014, 302–304.

86 Wilson 2014, 300, Fig. 1.

87 Wilson (2014, 306), with reference to Tassie's (2014, 191–194) review of the impact of changing environmental conditions on groups from the Early through Middle Holocene, notably changes to the level of mobility and subsistence patterns.

88 Von den Driesch and Boessneck 1985, 111.

89 Von den Dreisch and Boessneck 1985, 107–108.

90 Wilson et al. 2014, 137, Table 34; Debono and Mortensen 1990, 99–107.

91 Eiwanger 1984; Wilson et al. 2014, 122.

92 Hassan 1997, 65.

[93] Hassan 1985, 98, Table1.

[94] Eiwanger 1988, 41, 53; also discussed by Midant-Reynes (2000) and Tristant (2006).

[95] Butzer 2002, 95.

[96] Kuper and Kröpelin 2006, Fig. 1.

[97] Kuper and Kröpelin 2006, Fig. 2.

[98] Hendrickx (1999, 19) refers to this correspondence. It is difficult to assign specific absolute dates for II–IV given that the most reliable radiocarbon measurements from the DAI excavations relate to I and V (Hassan 1985, 98).

[99] Debono and Mortensen (1990, 80–81) suggest comparison with Merimde II–IV; the date range is c. 4600–4400 BCE from the radiocarbon measurements available, but they concur with Hassan (1985, 105) that el-Omari might be better regarded as comparable with the latest phases Merimde III–V. Wilson et al. 2014, 122.

[100] Eiwanger (1992), including remarks on similarities and connections (49–52, 61, 63, 64, 73, and 74).

[101] Emmitt 2017, 247.

[102] Topoi A-2-4 database.

[103] Rowland forthcoming a, b. Further measurements have just been realised on plant remains, including wood charcoal, from the excavations of J. Eiwanger (DAI) from the 1970s.

[104] In some cases equipment may be available in Egypt, being used for non-archaeological purposes. Such discussions were raised at the first International Science and Ancient Egyptian Materials Technology (SAEMT) conference in Cairo in November 2017, and it is hoped that such a list of equipment may be forthcoming and the wider scientific community can work together to enable the types of analyses on Egyptian material so that Egyptian archaeology can function at the same level of scientific rigour as archaeology in other regions does as a matter of routine.

[105] As raised in the discussion of the SAEMT conference, November 2017.

[106] For example the database of finds from the Junker excavations at Merimde (Rowland and Tassie 2017), with environmental data including the huge corpus of cores of Jean-Daniel Stanley referred to above; databases of radiocarbon dates, for example that collated by the Egyptian Chronology Project of the University of Oxford: https://c14.arch.ox.ac.uk/egyptdb/db.php.

[107] Macklin et al. 2015. This paper includes Supplementary Material comprising the dated (OSL or 14C) fluvial units in the Nile Delta and Nile catchment for the Holocene.

[108] For example recently for the Delta, Pennington et al. (2017), where environmental core data from a number of projects has been brought together to enable bigger questions to be examined.

[109] Emmitt (unpublished) refers to the work of Holdaway et al. (2016) who question not when and how the Neolithic arrived in Egypt, but rather *whether* it arrived at all. Rowland et al. in press will present varied case studies that highlight these points in contributions from the archaeologists working across this area who came together to discuss these issues at the Revolutions' Workshop in winter 2015 as part of the Topoi A-2-4 research group's activities.

Chapter Five

The Role of Settlements and Urban Society for the History of Ancient Egypt: The Case Study of Tell Edfu During the Late Old Kingdom

Nadine Moeller

Settlement systems in ancient Egypt are intrinsically linked to the specific characteristics of the local environment and the dynamic river floodplain that kept changing over time. The choice of founding a new settlement of any kind was typically governed by considerations as to it being protected by the annual floodwaters of the Nile which would assure safety and stability for the existence and growth of the site. Other important considerations included certain strategic concerns, for example a convenient access to trade routes and the proximity to a major water source, such as the river or canal, that would provide a steady supply of water for the inhabitants in addition to serving as the main artery for travel in order to be able to connect via boat with different parts of the region and country.[1] Although many settlement sites in Egypt are marked by a long continuity of occupation with nuanced phases of contractions and expansions, it is also evident that sites could change locations based on the changes in the meandering river which is particularly noticeable in the Nile Delta and the fluctuating delta head of the Nile in the Memphite region.[2] Urban sites could vary conspicuously in density and size depending on the particular parameters of the local environment, such as trends in the annual flood height and whether a site was situated along the desert edge or in the middle of the floodplain. Upper Egypt is one of the more stable regions with regard to changes in the river since the floodplain is relatively narrow to start with but even here recent geomorphological research was able to detect significant changes in the location of the main river channel during the past millennia.[3] The following article will use the case study of Tell Edfu's development during the late Old Kingdom with the aim to illustrate how the local history of provincial towns in Upper Egypt and their inhabitants very much evolved within the parameters of this dynamic river floodplain environment in addition to constantly (re-) negotiating the relationship between center and periphery. It is also important to note that geomorphological work in Egypt is still pretty limited and the investigation of geomorphological processes of larger stretches of land within the Nile Valley and the Delta would be a desirable research project in the future.

The Gift of the Nile? Ancient Egypt and the Environment
edited by Thomas Schneider and Christine L. Johnston
Tucson, Arizona: Egyptian Expedition, 2020

Preliminary Results Concerning the Geomorphology at Tell Edfu

The ongoing fieldwork at the ancient city of Tell Edfu has revealed numerous new insights into its long-term evolution throughout the Pharaonic period, in particular through the excellent preservation of the stratified settlement layers that form a massive tell which is currently preserved up to an elevation of 15 m above the natural bedrock (Figs. 1a and b).[4] The tell of Edfu contains an almost uninterrupted sequence of habitation phases starting in the late Old Kingdom until the early Islamic Period (10th century CE).[5] Of course, the pharaonic periods are mostly defined in our minds by the powerful ancient Egyptians kings and the political history more generally. However, when investigating a provincial center with relatively few remains and finds that provide clear links to these kings and their political achievements described in most textbooks on ancient Egyptian history, reconstructing the story of a particular town site becomes more challenging and one very quickly enters the sphere of microhistories, which are strongly site-specific. When looking at the longue-durée trends in the town development at Edfu which can be traced over 1000 years, it is also noticeable that a number of those are also common elsewhere indicating broader regional phenomena. In this article, I will focus on the archaeological evidence discovered during our recent fieldwork at the site dating to the late 5th and early 6th Dynasties which offers an important addition to the detailed textual data about the administration in Upper Egypt and in particular the relationship between local officials and the central government based at Memphis in the north.

The precise origins of Edfu's foundations are still unclear but indirect evidence has hinted at a possible first settlement dating as early as the 3rd millennium BCE.[6] The fact that not far from the town of Edfu remnants of a small step-pyramid were located at the edge of the western desert near the modern village of el-Ghonameya, which has recently been the objective of larger cleaning and restoration campaign led by the Tell Edfu Project team in order to preserve the site that had been in danger of disappearing, indicates that already the late 3rd/early 4th Dynasty kings (Huni and/or Snofru) recognized the importance of Edfu within this region.[7] Moreno García suggested in a recent study on the development of the provincial administration during the 3rd millennium BCE that in Dynasty 3 there might have existed a kind of "ideal landscape" in Upper Egypt, which included the small step pyramids and local sanctuaries as "markers of the frontiers of the kingdom and as memorials to the power of the king."[8] Those regions and their towns located in the vicinity of the small step-pyramids would have been the main focal points of attention by the king and his highest officials with regard to obtaining various kinds of resources by making best use of the existing infrastructure in the provinces. The step-pyramid at el-Ghonameya is situated on the desert edge and probably marks the access point for an important route towards the oases in the Western Desert which would explain its location in some distance to the town of Edfu.[9]

A sanctuary dedicated to Horus of Edfu is mentioned on one of the reliefs from the underground chambers in the South Tomb of the Djoser pyramid complex (also Dynasty 3), which is another significant indication that the town of Edfu was already established as a regional center and possessed its own local sanctuary.[10] In contrast to such local cult installations, the small step-pyramids seem to have been specifically dedicated to the royal cult while the local temples, however small they were at that time, can be considered as one of the main institutional links between the inhabitants of these provincial towns and the central government based at Memphis during the Old Kingdom.[11] In addition to the local temples, the kings also founded on a regular basis and in large numbers new royal foundations (ḥwt-ꜥt, ḥwt, grgt, swnw) that were destined to obtain the necessary revenue from the provinces.[12]

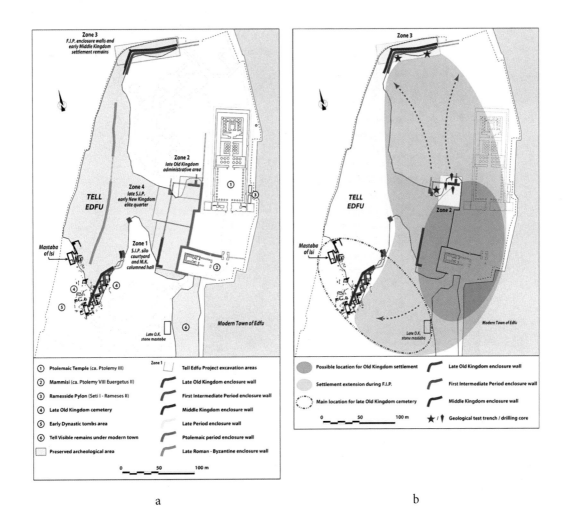

a   b

FIGURE 1a. General plan of Tell Edfu showing the various
excavations zones of the Tell Edfu Project. © Tell Edfu Project.

FIGURE 1b. Plan indicating the long-term evolution of Tell Edfu
and showing the location of the geological test trenches. © Tell
Edfu Project.

Before we delve into further details about the long-term changes of the town of Edfu
during the Old Kingdom, it is important to clarify why the location of Edfu was chosen
for settlement in the first place because this has significant implications on the general
history of occupation of the site. Geological data from Edfu—which is still quite sparse and
only at the very beginning of a larger investigation of the geomorphology of the site and
its surroundings—has offered some new insights into its history of occupation. Between
2014 and 2018, several test trenches and drill cores were dug into different parts of the tell

Figure 2a. Test trench in Zone 2 showing the natural sandstone bedrock marked by water erosion. © Tell Edfu Project.

Figure 2b. Test trench in Zone 3, north-western corner, underneath the enclosure walls. © Tell Edfu Project.

which revealed underneath multiple layers of coarse fluvial sand deposits a thick sandstone formation (for a general location of the test trenches and drill cores see Fig. 1b). This sandstone bedrock was reached in all three test trenches, two of which were excavated along the northern limit of the tell, from west to east, and one in the Zone 2 excavation area next to several phases of late Old Kingdom enclosure walls (Figs. 2a and b). Marks of erosion caused by the quickly moving waters from the Nile river on the sandstone leaving incised grooves on the stone surface were only observed in the test trench in Zone 2, which also had the thickest accumulation of fluvial sands covering the bedrock (Fig. 2a). More generally, it was also possible to note that the layers of alluvial sand deposits were generally thicker towards the east than in the west of the site, which is relative to the proximity of the riverbed, and a gentle slope of the bedrock could be observed from west towards the east and the river.[13] These results also indicate that the area of Zone 2 had once been exposed to the flooding by the river had which caused the erosion of the stone surface and the deposition of the thick and often coarse sand layers but the precise date when this happened is unclear (Fig. 2a). It has also not yet been possible to determine the overall thickness of the sandstone formation in all parts of the site, except for some earlier observations in the Old and Middle Kingdom cemetery area at Edfu, which is located along the southwestern edge, below and partially still covered by the tell (Fig. 1a). Here the sandstone formation was identified as a distinct layer with a thickness of around 0.20–0.40 m, which the ancient inhabitants used to their advantage to cut into in order to take out the underlying softer marl layer (1.5–2.0 m thick, before reaching a second layer of sandstone) for building the underground tomb chambers.[14] Since the cemetery is located on the outer margins of the tell, the thickness of the sandstone is expected to be much more prominent closer to the river and temple, which has been confirmed during the recent investigations by the groundwater lowering project around the Ptolemaic temple. Additional observations as to Edfu's bedrock formation have been obtained during several geological investigations carried out under the auspices of CDM Smith for the recently completed groundwater lowering project around the temple. During this work it was reported to us by the chief engineer of the project, Thomas Nichols, that the eastern side of the temple sits on a relatively steep sandstone cliff, which was recorded during an investigation using ground-penetrating radar. This is further confirmed by the deep level of foundations of the eastern tower of the pylon, which has its foundations reaching down to 10 m below the current surface level while the western pylon tower's foundation is only 3 m deep.[15] Given these indications, it is very likely that the city was originally founded on a sandstone island formation that directly bordered the Nile river in antiquity. This is important for understanding the foundation of the ancient settlement in this area, which can now be linked to the favorable environmental conditions provided by this natural island formation. Today the Nile has moved more than a mile further to the east, which in the long run has permitted the ancient and more recently the modern town of Edfu to expand into this direction.[16]

As the evidence stands now, the ancient city was founded in this rather advantageous location of a sandstone island allowing its inhabitants to remain close to the river, which was ideal for being well connected to the main waterway of the country and offering additional food sources through its fish and a constant water supply. The site was also situated high enough in order to be protected from the annual floodwaters, a major concern for the inhabitants and their mudbrick houses. We suspect that the earliest traces of settlement were most likely located in the area of the Ptolemaic temple but they were probably removed when the latter was built above any earlier settlement and temple structures that once would have stood there.[17] As a result, the current temple of Horus can be considered the largest and most extensive temple phase at Edfu, which saw the removal of a significant portion of the ancient tell for the construction of the new mudbrick temenos wall whose foundation trench cuts vertically through the entire tell. During our excavations in Zone 1 on top of the tell, it was possible to see this foundation trench particularly clearly for the section of the mammisi (started under Ptolemy VIII, 170–116 BCE) which was cutting earlier Ptolemaic house walls (ca. late 3rd to mid–2nd century BCE).[18]

The Town of Edfu During the Late Old Kingdom

The so-far earliest settlement remains excavated at Edfu are located in Zone 2, to the north of Zone 1, and close to the Ptolemaic temenos wall (Fig. 1a). A large excavation area measuring 25 x 50 m was opened here in 2012 and revealed an important ex-nihilo foundation of a new town quarter dating to the late 5th Dynasty which constitutes a phase of expansion from the original core of the town most likely located further to the east. These mudbrick installations, which are built directly on the natural sand in this area, constitute the first phase of settlement here and can be identified as a phase of expansion from the earlier settlement core that we assume was situated further to the east. Based on the evidence from numerous discarded clay sealings that can be associated with the first phase of occupation in this area, it is possible to assign the chronological timeframe for this new foundation to the second half of the 5th Dynasty. The most frequently mentioned royal name in this context is Djedkare-Isesi whose Horus name has appeared on a large number of broken clay sealings discovered during the excavations. Several sealings also mention the names of Niuserre and Menkauhor, and those sealings were also found in occupation layers of the first phases of use, but their number is significantly smaller than those of Djedkare. Based on this evidence, it is obvious that the late 5th Dynasty marks the beginning of a new urban dynamic for Edfu. The archaeological remains in Zone 2 are also significant in this regard, they consist of two monumental structures, one with extremely thick and sloping walls (Northern Building 1) and a second large building south of it (Southern Building 2) (Fig. 3).[19] Both structures were fronted by a large open courtyard area in which archaeological evidence for various activities have been found—for example, many traces for metallurgical activities linked to copper smelting were discovered, in addition to more than 200 inscribed broken clay sealings with traces of cylinder seal impressions which attest to official administrative activities having taken place here. Numerous fireplaces and ash deposits related to the cooking of bread were excavated as well as a significant number of beer jars and globular storage jars, some of which were found concentrated in a small room to the east of Southern Building 2 (Fig. 4).[20] Also significant for establishing the function of these ex-nihilo structures are their perimeter walls dividing the two monumental buildings into two discrete areas and limiting their large courtyards to the east (see walls W1210, W1170, and W1258 in Fig. 3). It can be observed that the perimeter wall not only separates these two structures from one another, but there are no walls or additional structures that lean against this perimeter wall leaving deliberately an empty space between the two monumental buildings and this enclosure. This organization is quite conspicuous and very different in comparison to the usual domestic installations where mudbrick walls frequently abut one another, and buildings are constructed and expanded in an agglutinated fashion.[21]

The associated finds and traces for the different activity areas that can be related mainly to official and administrative tasks in addition to the peculiar architecture and size of the buildings excludes any regular domestic function, but it has been a real challenge to identify their exact purpose since there are so far no known parallels from any other site in Egypt that might be used for comparison. Nevertheless, there is increasing evidence in conjunction with the current understanding of the administrative system in the provinces during the

FIGURE 3. Overview of the two monumental buildings and their associated courtyards in Zone 2. © Tell Edfu Project.

FIGURE 4. Room with globular storage jars east of Southern Building 2. © Tell Edfu Project.

Figure 5. Details of the entrance area of Northern Building 1.
© Tell Edfu Project.

Old Kingdom, particularly in Upper Egypt, that puts these archaeological results in a better perspective to what we know about the role of provincial towns and their elites at that time. In the following paragraphs I will highlight the most pertinent pieces of evidence that suggest that this newly founded town quarter has a lot to offer in terms of complementing our textual records of this period. As mentioned above, the unusual architectural features of Northern Building 1 are particularly noteworthy, such as the extremely thick walls (more than 2.5 m wide at their base) and their distinct slope. Only the entrance area of this building is preserved because the *sebbakhin* destroyed most of the remains immediately to the west where the interior would have been (Fig. 5).[22] The impressive thickness of the external walls might be an indication for creating a certain level of security but this might also be sign for an important elevation of this building because its strong foundations could have certainly supported the weight of an additional level on top, maybe in the form of some kind of tower, but this remains entirely speculative at this point. As far as the material culture is concerned that can be associated with the use of this structure, we can almost entirely exclude a mortuary or cultic function—none of the characteristic finds were present during the excavation (i.e., the typical ceramics used for offerings and cultic activities, inscribed stone elements, libation basins and drains, etc.). In its courtyard, the first phase of occupation contained many clay sealing fragments and a thick black layer with much copper slag and crucible fragments from copper smelting activities.

The interior of Southern Building 2 has not yet been excavated, but its walls are generally thinner and do not show a slope. Similar to the Northern Building 1, its interior seems to be largely destroyed due to *sebakh* digging, and most traces for any associated activities were

94

FIGURE 6. Clay sealings with the Horus name and cartouche
of Djedkare – Isesi and the title "overseer of the *sementiu*."
© Hilary McDonald, Tell Edfu Project.

discovered in the courtyard area on its eastern side. The precise chronological relationship between these two structures is still being investigated, and there is a slight possibility that the Southern Building 2 is somewhat later than Northern Building 1.[23]

As mentioned above, it has been a difficult task to find out more about the precise purpose of this settlement quarter for which a domestic function can be excluded based on the architectural features and associated material culture. One of the most significant results is that this part of the town is a new, ex-nihilo foundation on a previously unoccupied area at Edfu. In addition to this important observation, most of the clues as to the precise purpose of this newly founded town quarter come from the occupation layers and activity areas excavated in the two courtyards to the east of the two monumental buildings in addition to a workshop installation that was excavated on the northern limit of Zone 2. On the associated floor levels in all of these courtyards, a large number of broken clay sealings were recovered, which bear fragmentary signs and inscriptions left by high-quality cylinder seals that were finely engraved with hieroglyphs. The preliminary study of these provided some unexpected links to royal expeditions for the extraction of copper and precious raw materials in the Eastern Desert. Most significant is the mention of an "overseer of the *sementiu* (prospectors)" (*jmj-r smntjw*) which are closely linked to the extraction of these resources in the Eastern Desert and the Sinai peninsula (Fig. 6).[24] Traces of copper ore and copper smelting together with the presence of crucible fragments were found in the entire area and those activities can now be directly linked to royal expeditions that were sent from Edfu into the Eastern Desert to obtain this important resource.[25] Additional titles found on the sealings also attest to officials that participated in these expeditions such as the nautical title of "overseer of the steersmen of the king" (*jmj-r sb³tjw njswt*)²⁶ which appears on the same sealing as the mention of the *sementiu* prospectors. Another link to expeditions into the Eastern Desert can be inferred from the peculiar occurrence of numerous Nubian pottery sherds that are difficult to classify as they are neither A-Group nor C-group but more likely a kind of "desert ware" indicating the regular interactions with nomadic peoples living in the Eastern Desert regions the expeditions went to.²⁷ This evidence can be further complemented by several graffiti recorded in the various wadis accessible from the Edfu region, which confirm the mining activity in this area during the late Old Kingdom.²⁸ Edfu's location, as mentioned above, was strategically chosen to be close to important routes into both the Eastern Desert through Wadi Baramiya and an access to the Western desert route near el-Ghonameya.²⁹ Additional activities that were carried out in these open courtyards are less specific, such as numerous fire places and bread moulds as well as beer jars (in equal proportions) that were frequently discarded in larger trash pits dug into the ground. Noteworthy however, is a room with several globular storage jars (Fig. 4) located to the southeastern side of the courtyard that can be associated with Southern Building 2, which also seems to belong to the administrative sphere.

The chronological information that can be obtained from our preliminary analysis of the sealing fragments dates this installation to the late 5th Dynasty, the name of Djedkare Isesi is the most frequently royal name attested on the sealings (Fig. 6), but last season we also found a small number of sealings that name Niuserre and Menkauhor, the two predecessors of Djedkare.³⁰ Thus, we are well anchored chronologically in the second half of Dynasty 5. Now that we have established the official/administrative function of this settlement quarter in Zone 2 at Edfu based on the archaeological evidence, it is worth taking a closer look at the relationship between the royal court and the central administration based in the Memphite region and the regional centers and their local elites in the south. A couple of important points can be made here which shed more light on the overall context of these archaeological discoveries.

By the 5th Dynasty it is possible to see the first emergence of local but high-level administrators who were in charge of various provincial centers representing the interest of the central state. Those administrators were still closely bound to the king and its circle, but they remain relatively invisible in their personal identities in the provinces until the end of this dynasty simply because they did not engage in any particular activities associated with the display of the so-called high culture that leaves the most visible traces for their presence, such as decorated mastaba tombs and associated grave goods.³¹ However, this does not make them less important for the activities conducted in the provincial towns where they were in charge of the agricultural production and carrying out specific missions for the king, as a kind of "royal agent". Those officials are precisely those attested in the various titles on the clay sealings found at Edfu, without ever mentioning a personal name.³² Their personal identities were not included on their cylinder seals in contrast to their most important titles. In addition to various titles mentioned in connection with royal expeditions (see above), one sealing fragment mentions an "acquaintance of the king" (*rḫ - njswt*), which is common for the latter part of the Old Kingdom and designates an official with close ties to the palace. This official was also "overseer of commissions" (*jmj-r wpt*) and would have been in charge of carrying out various orders given to him by the king (Fig. 7).³³ During the 5th Dynasty there does not yet seem to be a formalized office and title of "governor" or "overseer of the nome," which becomes common during the 6th Dynasty but we are dealing with a system of officials, probably with close ties to local elites, who are being ordered by the king to fulfill certain tasks in the interest of the crown at important provincial centers like Edfu.³⁴ The titles we see on the various sealing fragments probably belonged to the officials in charge of Edfu one generation *prior* to the much more visible

Figure 7. Clay sealing showing the titles of *rḫ-njswt* and *jmj-r wpt*. © Hilary McDonald, Tell Edfu Project.

governors of the early 6th Dynasty, like Izi and his son Qar.[35] Izi, the famous nomarch who was later deified and worshipped as a local saint until the late Middle Kingdom, is most likely the first high-ranking official who received the privilege to choose a burial at Edfu, and his tomb, which was excavated in the 1930's, included some highly decorated elements such as the large inscribed stele (Louvre EA 14329) and a complete false door (Warsaw National Museum, N° 139944 MNW), which provide a wealth of information about the career and family of this personage. Interestingly, Izi's career starts under king Djedkare Isesi, when he receives the title of "eldest of the doorway" (*sr rwt*) and then moves up the ranks under king Unas to "governor of the *ḥwt*" (*ḥq3 ḥwt*). The latter title is also interesting since it implies the existence of such an institution at Edfu.[36] Much ink has been spilled on the precise definition and function of *ḥwt*, which based on the careful analysis of the available textual records can be identified as a royal estate that functioned as a processing and administrative center in the provinces. It could also be associated with a warehouse facility to store commodities that would be sent to the capital in regular intervals as part of tax payments, in addition to marking a building of defensive nature.[37]

Based on the current archaeological evidence, I would like to propose to tentatively identify the two monumental buildings in Zone 2 (Northern Building 1 and Southern Building 2) as the first archaeological examples ever identified for a royal *ḥwt* foundation.[38] All the uncovered elements in addition to the fact that they comprise entirely new foundations in this part of the town, would fit well to the definition of what such a royal foundation was used for, namely as a production and administrative center in addition to serving as a supply and logistical support base for royal expeditions. Excavations are still continuing in Zone 2 and hopefully more information confirming this identification will be possible in the near future.

From the end of the 5th Dynasty / early 6th Dynasty onwards we can observe a more rapid development of the city of Edfu in tandem with the more permanent installation of a now much more visible local elite whose mudbrick mastabas were excavated in the nearby cemetery. This elite was still closely tied to the Memphite region based on the biographies of Izi and his son Qar. The latter was educated at the royal court, a common phenomenon for members of the provincial elites while the former held titles that are closely associated with the palace, such as *ḥry-tp nswt* and *smr-wˁty*.[39]

Izi's biography as well as titles also hint directly to his duties as overseer of the king's work in the province. He is "master builder and scribe of the king" (*mḏḥ sš nswt*)[40] and he also mentions in his biography that he was "controlling the works of the king in the nome."[41] Izi was holding these titles under the reign of Teti in addition to having received the official title of "nomarch" (*ḥrj-tp ˁ3 n zp3t*) which starts to make its appearance amongst local elite families in the south at the beginning of Dynasty 6. From this time onwards, the members of these elite families were buried in mudbrick mastaba tombs in the local cemetery and through these tombs and associated inscriptions, the inhabitants of Edfu were gaining more visibility and status locally. Unfortunately, there is not yet any archaeological data available that could shed light on the location and specifics of the particular town quarter with its corresponding domestic structures that would have been inhabited by this newly emerging elite. As far the evolution of the structures in Zone 2 are concerned, they did not seem to remain in use for a long time and were abandoned some time during the first half of Dynasty 6 when they were filled in and small, informal, courtyards with few built structures entirely of domestic character were erected above those earlier levels.[42] The reason for this radical change in function of this particular town quarter is not clear but it is most likely linked to administrative changes which would have terminated the use of these particular *ḥwt* installation of the late 5th Dynasty in addition to a possible relocation of the administrative buildings probably further to the south. Another hypothesis could be that each ruler founded a new *ḥwt* building under his name. This would explain the relatively short period of use of these two structures in Zone 2, which were abandoned by the early 6th Dynasty and replaced by new *ḥwt* foundations whose precise locations are currently unknown. As far the evidence for royal expeditions being launched from Edfu are concerned, this activity seems to have continued until the reign of Pepi II at the end of the 6th Dynasty.[43]

The further evolution of the settlement in Zone 2 is marked by three phases of enclosure walls that were built partially above the earlier workshop area and the open courtyard space on the eastern and northern sides of Northern Building 1 during the early 6th Dynasty.[44] Those enclosures follow a distinct course with a marked right angle that deliberately seems to avoid Northern Building 1 even though it was no longer actively functioning by that time as can be seen from the thick fill layers covering its exterior spaces, especially the courtyard and workshop areas that had been completely filled in by that time. Similarly, the entrance of this monumental building, which was found almost intact during the recent excavations, was rapidly filled in up to the limit of the lintel by a thick layer of settlement debris and mudbrick demolition fill. It is noteworthy that the building itself was not dismantled, and its foundations up to the height of the door lintel of the main entrance in addition to the complete wooden door were found well-preserved during our fieldwork.[45] It is therefore evident that this structure, even after its abandonment, remained a known and possibly well-respected, monument in the memory of its inhabitants, which would make a lot of sense if it was a royal foundation. Zone 2 later continues to be occupied by domestic buildings well into the First Intermediate Period, which also suggests that the administrative core of Edfu (with additional *ḥwt* foundations by the 6th Dynasty kings?) shifted its location further south. First indications for such a southward shift were made during the excavations in Zone 1, on top of the tell, where we unearthed the governor's residence of the late Middle Kingdom consisting of two large columned halls. The remains of the governor's residence were built directly above earlier Middle Kingdom layers, which we were only able to reach in a few areas but they revealed significant amounts of the clay sealings with impressions made by button seals and tiny scarabs with decorative motifs that date to the late First Intermediate Period/early Middle Kingdom.[46] This might indicate a relocation of the official / administrative structures from Zone 2 to about 50 m further to the south. What factors prompted this shift and the abandonment of the two official buildings in Zone 2 is unclear so far, but it is possible to observe that the administrative core of the town remained within the limits of the late Old Kingdom inner enclosure walls. By the end of Dynasty 6, the town had spread further to the north and also to the west, which necessitated an entirely new system of town walls that can be seen by the particularly well-preserved enclosure walls stretching along the northern side of the tell (Zone 3, see Figs. 1a and b, 8). Interestingly, the northern limit of the settlement attained by the end of the 3rd millennium BCE, remained the maximum extension until the end of the occupation of Tell Edfu during the early Islamic Period in the 10th century CE.[47] The seems to be also the case for the western boundary of the site, which is marked by multiple phases of enclosure walls, starting from the early First Intermediate Period onwards partially covering the ancient cemetery area. These maximum limits of the ancient town were most likely dictated by the height of the annual flood waters since it is possible, even

FIGURE 8. The sequence of enclosure walls situated along the northwestern side of the tell (Zone 3). © Tell Edfu Project.

99

today, to see a marked drop in elevation further west and north in the areas bordering the exterior of the ancient city limits which are now occupied by agricultural fields and a large modern cemetery.[48] The reasons for this considerable expansion at the end of the Old Kingdom could be multifold, from a general growth of the population during this time, to a trend of nucleation with more people being attracted by these regional urban centers (for economic/security reasons?) who were moving to these important towns while at the same time abandoning their lives in scattered villages and hamlets. If this was indeed the case, such a population shift would have required an adjustment of the agricultural exploitation in this area with a significant hinterland being worked by city dwellers. Again there is little data available that could help to confirm this particular point and it is impossible to verify such a development on the ground since we do not possess any data about the larger Edfu region and its settlement patterns dating during the 3rd millennium BCE.

However, it is striking that similar trends of growth at provincial towns in Upper Egypt can be observed at several other sites (Elephantine, Kom Ombo, Elkab, Dendara, Abydos) which indicates that this was a wider phenomenon in Upper Egypt and not an isolated case at Edfu.[49] It is quite likely that such a trend can be related to a number of causes which include political and economic changes that offered favorable conditions in the southern provinces for a period of prosperity and growth in addition to environmental conditions that saw a gradual lowering of the flood levels. This would have allowed an expansion of these regional centers into areas that were previously prone to occasionally flooding (which is particularly visible at Elephantine) and which had become dry enough to settle on. Another important factor in the Edfu region that needs to be considered is the gradual shift of the main river channel eastwards, which might have also contributed as a favorable factor for the expansion of the town to the west and north. It remains to be seen whether we can obtain additional environmental data to support this hypothesis in the future. Another avenue of inquiry is currently under way with regard to a more general study of the faunal and archaeobotanical remains from different phases of occupation at Edfu covering the Old Kingdom and First Intermediate Period. It would be important to find out whether we can see a change in subsistence patterns that could be linked to an increase in marshy areas close to the river which might be one of the consequences of lower water levels.[50]

The long-term evolution on the eastern and southern sides of the ancient city are more difficult to evaluate since we do not possess much information about the archaeological stratigraphy in these areas that are still being occupied on top by houses of the modern town in the area east of the temple, where part of the ancient tell can be seen underneath the modern town forming a significant elevation of up to 20 m above the level of the temple threshold.[51] Most of the southern area of the tell was destroyed by *sebakh* digging a long time ago and is now occupied by the visitor center, offices of the antiquities service, tourist shops, and the ticket office. Little remains here that can be of any use for establishing the different phases of settlement since most of those were cleared down to the natural bedrock, which is already visible on the photographs of the site taken in the 1930s.

Conclusions

With regard to the evolution of Edfu as an important regional urban center, it is clear that its advantageous position within the local landscape, in addition to being strategically situated along the crossroads of important desert routes, attracted the attention from the central government during the Old Kingdom. Prior to 5th Dynasty and before the ex-nihilo foundation in Zone 2, Edfu was probably still quite a small town with a local shrine, no doubt the focal point of the local community, situated on a sandstone island formation that is now mostly covered by the Ptolemaic temple. By the second half of the 5th Dynasty, two monumental buildings were founded in Zone 2, directly on the natural bedrock surface, and whose functions can be linked via the various traces for administrative and metallurgical activities, such as the large number of clay sealings and the important traces for the processing of copper ore, to a royal building project. Also significant in this respect is the link to royal expeditions for the extraction of raw materials in the Eastern Desert as attested by the titles of high officials mentioned on the clay sealings. It is therefore very plausible that our structures in Zone 2 constitute the first archaeological evidence for a royal *ḥwt* installation, which is also the first direct link based on the archaeological evidence that exists between the provincial town of Edfu located in southern Egypt and the national capital at Memphis in the north

This particular case study of Edfu is a good example for the intertwined factors that impacted these provincial communities, such as the importance of suitable geographical parameters, favorable environmental conditions with the long-term trend of lower floodwaters that were taken advantage of by the central state and then gradually taken over by a newly established local elite that was expanding its sphere of influence and attracting more settlers. As far as the evidence stands right now, it is possible to demonstrate that the town of Edfu had grown into an important regional urban center at the end of the 3rd millennium BCE.

WORKS CITED

Alliot, M. 1935. *Rapport sur les fouilles de Tell Edfou (1933)*. FIFAO 10(2). Cairo: Institut français d'archéologie orientale.

Bietak, M., and I. Forstner-Müller. 2011. "The Topography of New Kingdom Avaris and Per-Ramesses." In *Ramesside Studies in Honour of K.A. Kitchen*, edited by M. Collier and S. Snape, 23–50. Bolton: Rutherford Press.

Bruyère, B., J. Manteuffel, J.S.F. Garnot, and K. Michalowski. 1937. *Tell Edfou 1937*. Fouilles franco-polonaises rapports. Cairo: Institut français d'archéologie orientale.

Bunbury, J. 2013. "Geomorphological Development of the Memphite Floodplain over the Past 6000 Years." *Studia Quaternaria* 30(2): 61–67.

Bunbury, J., A. Graham, and K.D. Strutt. 2009. "Kom El-Farahy: A New Kingdom Island in an Evolving Edfu Floodplain." *British Museum Studies in Ancient Egypt and the Sudan* 14: 1–23.

Dreyer, G., and W. Kaiser. 1980. "Zu den kleinen Stufenpyramiden Ober- und Mittel-ägyptens." *Mitteilungen des Deutschen Archäologischen Instituts Kairo* 36: 43–60.

Edel, E. 1954. "Inschriften des Alten Reichs." *Zeitschrift für Ägyptische Sprache* 79: 11–17.

Espinel, A.D. 2000. "Edfu and the Eastern Desert: Žába's Rock Inscriptions, No. A22 Reconsidered." *Archiv Orientální* 68(4): 579–586.

———. 2014. "Surveyors, Guides and Other Officials in the Egyptian and Nubian Deserts." *Revue d'égyptologie* 65: 29–48.

Fischer, H.G. 1976. *Varia*. New York: Metropolitan Museum of Art.

———. 1985. "More About the Smntjw." *Göttinger Miszellen* 84: 25–32.

Gardiner, A.H. 1944. "Horus the Behdetite." *Journal of Egyptian Archaeology* 30: 23–60.

Gascoigne, A.L. 2005. "Dislocation and Continuity in Early Islamic Provincial Urban Centres: The Example of Tell Edfu." *Mitteilungen des Deutschen Archäologischen Instituts*

Kairo 61: 153–190.

Henne, H. 1924. *Rapport sur les Fouilles de Tell Edfou (1921–1922)*. FIFAO 1(2). Cairo: Institut français d'archéologie orientale.

Jones, D. 2000. *An Index of Ancient Egyptian Titles, Epithets and Phrases of the Old Kingdom. Bar International Series*. 2 vols. Oxford: Hadrian Books.

Lutley, K., and J. Bunbury. 2008. "The Nile on the Move." *Egyptian Archaeology* 32: 3–5.

Marouard, G., and H. Papazian. 2012. "The Edfu Pyramid Project: Recent Investigation at the Last Provincial Step Pyramid." *Oriental Institute News & Notes* 213: 3–9.

Moeller, N. 2009. "Tell Edfu." In *The Oriental Institute 2008–2009 Annual Report*, edited by G. Stein, 117–125. Chicago: The Oriental Institute.

———. 2011. "Tell Edfu." In *The Oriental Institute 2010–2011 Annual Report*, edited by G. Stein, 111–120. Chicago: The Oriental Institute.

———. 2013, 1 August. "Edfu." *UCLA Encyclopedia of Egyptology*. http://digital2.library. ucla.edu/viewItem.do?ark=21198/zz002gw1kt

———. 2016. *The Archaeology of Urbanism in Ancient Egypt: From the Predynastic Period to the End of the Middle Kingdom*. Cambridge: Cambridge University Press.

Moeller, N., and G. Marouard. 2013. "Tell Edfu." *The Oriental Institute Annual Report 2012– 2013*: 113–125.

———. 2018. "The Development of Two Early Urban Centers in Upper Egypt During the 3rd Millennium BCE: The Examples of Edfu and Dendara." In *From Microcosm to Macrocosm: Individual Households and Cities in Ancient Egypt and Nubia*, edited by J. Budka and J. Auenmüller, 29–58. Munich: LMU.

Moreno García, J.C. 1998. "De l'ancien empire à la première période intermédiaire: L'autobiographie de Qꜣr d'Edfou, entre tradition et innovation." *Revue d'égyptologie* 49: 151–160.

———. 1999. *Ḥwt et le milieu rural égyptien du IIIe millénaire: Economie, administration et organisation territoriale*. Paris: Librarie Honore Champion.

———. 2007. "The State and the Organisation of the Rural Landscape in the 3rd Millennium BC Pharaonic State." In *Aridity, Change and Conflict in Africa*, edited by M. Bollig, O. Bubenzer, R. Vogelsang, and H.-P. Wotzka, 313–330. Colloquium Africanum. Köln: Heinrich-Barth-Institut.

———. 2013. "The Territorial Administration of the Kingdom in the 3rd Millennium." In *Ancient Egyptian Administration*, edited by J.C. Moreno García, 85–151. Handbook of Oriental Studies. Leiden, Boston: Brill.

Piacentini, P. 1989. *Gli "Amministratori di Proprieta" nell'Egitto del III millennio a.C. Studi di Egittologia e di antichità puniche*. Pisa: Giardini.

———. 1994. "On the Titles of the *Ḥqꜣw Ḥwt*." In *Grund und Boden in Altägypten (rechtliche und sozioökonomische Verhältnisse). Akten des internationalen Symposions, Tübingen 18.–20. Juni 1990*, edited by S. Allam, 235–249. Tübingen: Im Selbstverlag des Herausgebers.

Seidlmayer, S.J. 1996. "Die staatliche Anlage der 3. Dynastie in der Nordweststadt von Elephantine. Archäologische und historische Probleme." In *Haus und Palast im alten Ägypten*, edited by M. Bietak, 195–214. Wien: Verlag der Österreichischen Akademie der Wissenschaften.

Seyfried, K. 1976. "Nachträge zu Yoyotte: 'Les Sementiou…' BSFE 73, P. 44–55." *Göttinger Miszellen* 20: 44–47.

Yoyotte, J. 1975. "Les sementiou et l'exploitation des regions minières à l'ancien empire." *Bulletin de la Société française d'égyptologie* 73: 44–55.

Notes

¹   For a more detailed outline about environmental factors impacting ancient Egyptian settlements, see also Moeller 2016, 51–53.

²   The eastern Nile delta with the cities of Tell el-Dab'a and Pi-Ramesses (Qantir) is a particularly good example demonstrating such a long-term change in settlement location based on the changes of the Pelusiac Nile branch; see Bietak and Forstner-Müller 2011. For the long-term evolution of the delta head of the river in the Memphite region, see Lutley and Bunbury 2008; Bunbury 2013.

³   Bunbury et al. 2009.

⁴   Before the beginning of the archaeological fieldwork at the site, photos from the 1920s show the original, untouched surface of the tell at almost double its height (Henne 1924, pl. I, fig.1).

⁵   Moeller 2013, 6; Moeller and Marouard 2018, 31. It is very likely that a first phase of settlement existed at Edfu dating back to the late Predynastic/Early Dynastic periods based on the evidence from several burials excavated in the southern part of the tell close to the ticket office by the Edfu inspectorate (unpublished) in addition to some objects of these periods found by the Franco-Polish excavations in the cemetery area situated on the southwestern side of the tell.

⁶   Moeller and Marouard 2018, 31.

⁷   For more details on these step pyramids which have been located at several sites in Upper and Middle Egypt, see Dreyer and Kaiser 1980; Seidlmayer 1996; Marouard and Papazian 2012. For additional information about the cleaning/restoration campaign by the Tell Edfu Project team, see Moeller 2011, 118–119; Moeller and Marouard 2013, 122–125.

⁸   Moreno García 2013, 92.

⁹   Even today the location of the pyramid marks a main access point towards the western desert road from the Nile Valley.

¹⁰   Gardiner 1944, 32.

¹¹   Moreno García 2013, 92.

¹²   Moreno García 2013, 99.

¹³   In the test trench located in Zone 2 close to the late Old Kingdom enclosure walls, the fluvial sand deposits had a thickness of almost 1.5 m, while in the test trench along the northwestern corner of the site in Zone 3 these deposits were only about 0.4 m thick, which demonstrates that the thickest layers of fluvial deposits are in the eastern part of the tell, in closer proximity to the river.

¹⁴   Bruyère et al. 1937, 2. The excavator identifies the stone layer as "calcaire" (limestone) which is not correct since all the naturally occurring stone in the Edfu region is sandstone.

¹⁵   Thomas Nichols, personal communication.

¹⁶   It is possible to identify the current limits of the ancient tell, parts of which are still covered by the modern town, on satellite images. The parts of the site located to the east of the temple are inaccessible for excavations up to now and therefore it is impossible to determine the exact chronological phasing here.

¹⁷   The pylon of the Ramesside period which is located on the eastern side of the Ptolemaic peristyle courtyard is the oldest structure still preserved from earlier temple phases. It was entirely rebuilt during the time of the Ptolemies; its stone blocks do not possess any constructed foundation but are simply placed directly on the sand surface and lean against the eastern pylon. Its orientation probably had been originally north–south but was changed to east–west offering another gateway to the river, which is

perpendicular to the main temple axis. I would like to thank T. Nichols for verifying the condition of the Ramesside foundations during the groundwater lowering project and sharing the information with us.

[18] Moeller 2009, 121, fig. 5.

[19] For a detailed description of these remains, see Moeller and Marouard 2018, 35–38.

[20] Moeller and Marouard 2018, 35–38.

[21] See Moeller 2016, 68.

[22] In 1933, Maurice Alliot noted on his general plan of the site traces of two 'mastabas' in our Zone 2 which correspond exactly to the walls of the two monumental buildings (Alliot 1935, pl. XX). They must have already been partially been exposed at this time, and the sloping walls of Northern Building 1 led Alliot to misidentify this structure as an Old Kingdom tomb. Interestingly, the outline he marks on his plan indicates the presence of a square structure and it is entirely possible that more of its interior was still preserved at this point.

[23] This will be one of the main aims for the next fieldwork season at Edfu. The names of Niuserre and Menkauhor on clay sealings were found solely in connection with Northern Building 1 which might be a first indication for a slightly earlier foundation of this structure in comparison to the Southern Building 2.

[24] For more details see Moeller and Marouard 2018, 36–40. For the title *"smntjw"* (prospectors), see the studies by Yoyotte 1975; Fischer 1985; with additions by Seyfried 1976.

[25] We are planning an analysis of the copper ore for our next season at Edfu with the help of Jeff Newman, who will investigate the chemical markers of the copper that might provide further information as to its origin.

[26] For further information about this title, see Jones 2000, 225, no. 834.

[27] I would like to thank Aaron de Souza, who is in charge of the Nubian ceramics from Edfu, for this very valuable information.

[28] Espinel 2000; 2014, 37–39.

[29] Moreno García 1998, 152–153.

[30] A detailed archaeological report of the results in Zone 2 is currently in preparation. The fieldwork has not been fully completed yet and will be pursued over the next two seasons.

[31] Moreno García 2013, 108–115.

[32] It seems that the personal identity of the official using a particular seal was not a major concern. This changes drastically during the Middle Kingdom where private name sealings are ubiquitous.

[33] Moreno García 2013, 108–111.

[34] Moreno García 2013, 112–115.

[35] For the full translation of the biographies of Izi and Qar, see Edel (1954) and Moreno García (1998), respectively.

[36] Piacentini mentions at least three additional officials with this title at Edfu who succeeded Izi (Piacentini 1989, 174–175).

[37] For additional details, see Moreno García 2007, 317–322; and more comprehensively, the seminal study by Moreno García 1999.

[38] It is possible that these two buildings comprise two different *ḥwt* foundations under different rulers.

[39] Piacentini 1994, 246–247.

[40] This title has been translated both as 'overseer of the royal scribes' and 'master of the architects of the king', for further information see Fischer 1976, 30, no. 9; Jones 2000, 467–468.

41 Edel 1954, 14.

42 The precise chronological framework for the various phases of occupation in Zone 2 and in particular the abandonment of the two monumental buildings is still under investigation and will be a priority for the next two seasons.

43 The rock inscriptions in the Eastern Desert still provide evidence for the continuation of royal expeditions during the 6th Dynasty (see Espinel 2000, 2014). However, caution should be used for the precise dating of these rock inscriptions since the name of the king is not present.

44 For more details on these installations, see Moeller and Marouard 2018, 33–34, figs. 4–5.

45 See Moeller and Marouard 2018, 37, fig. 8.

46 Moeller 2009, 124, figs. 9–11.

47 Henne 1924, 10.

48 Bunbury et al. 2009.

49 Moeller 2016, 214–241. For Dendara, see Moeller and Marouard 2018, 50–52.

50 This study is currently in progress by Sasha Rohret (University of Chicago) for her PhD dissertation.

51 For the results of a brief survey and cleaning operation along the exposed slope of the tell in this area, see Gascoigne 2005.

Chapter Six

Interpreting Ramesside Landing Places Along the Egyptian Nile Valley: Landscape and Geomorphological Features of the Floodplain

ANGUS GRAHAM

The paper addresses how an understanding of geomorphological features found in the Nile valley and the timing of activities related to the annual cycle of the Nile can aid interpretations of landscape features in the textual sources. The discussion centres on the terms used for landing places of boats found in the Ramesside texts documenting the collection of grain.

LANDSCAPE TERMINOLOGY AND NILE VALLEY GEOMORPHOLOGICAL FEATURES

Applying an understanding of the geomorphology and the interpretation of landscape change in the Nile Valley has been used in order to attempt to understand the context of literary works, for example Sinuhe's journey out of Egypt[1] and also terms referring to parts of the Valley landscape.[2] Here I will address some of the locations of Ramesside Landing Places and see how we might tease out suggestions of their landscape features in the floodplain. This will be done by first looking at the annual cycle of the Nile as well as some of the geomorphological features of the Egyptian Nile valley and then by understanding when these activities took place within the annual cycle of the river and what landforms would have and would have not been available and suitable as landing places.

THE NILE BASIN AND TWENTIETH CENTURY DISCHARGE

A key part of Nile basin regime is the different drainage basins. The White Nile has its catchment basins in Rwanda, Tanzania, Kenya and Uganda, which flows into Lake Victoria, The water then flows through Lake Kyoga and Lake Albert into the Bahr el-Jebel in southern Sudan. Using data from the first half of the 20th century, Hurst[3] calculated a mean annual discharge of 21 cubic km. The Bahr el Ghazal, the main tributary, supplies a further 15 cubic

The Gift of the Nile? Ancient Egypt and the Environment
edited by Thomas Schneider and Christine L. Johnston
Tucson, Arizona: Egyptian Expedition, 2020

km. Thus approximately 36 cubic km enters the great swamps of southern Sudan known as the Sudd, where almost 50% of the water is lost through evapotranspiration and seepage. Downstream of the Sudd the Sobat adds a further 14 cubic km of water into the White Nile so that in Khartoum at its confluence with the Blue Nile, the White Nile discharge is c. 27.5 cubic km and it carries 2 million tonnes of fine sediment in suspension (<4% of the total sediment load).[4] The early summer and autumn rains in Uganda and Tanzania are held temporarily in the equatorial lakes and then slowed down further by their movement through the Sudd helping to even out the discharge. Hurst calculated that the White Nile only contributes 10% of the maximum discharge of the main Nile at Aswan (occurring early September).[5] Critically, however, it provides 83% of the minimum discharge (May and early June in the Egyptian Nile Valley and Delta).

The Blue Nile and Atbara River with their headwaters in the Ethiopian Highlands, on the other hand, are highly seasonal. About 70% of the annual rainfall in these headwaters falls between June and September.[6] The Blue Nile, with its origins in Lake Tana, had a mean annual discharge of about 51 cubic km in the early part of the 20th century with an annual mean sediment load of 41 million tons; 72% of the total annual load.[7] The Blue Nile's mean contribution to the maximum discharge was 68%, but only 17% during the period of minimun monthly discharge. The Atbara is even more seasonal. Whilst dry for eight months of the year, it provides 22% of the maximum monthly flow to the main Nile above the 5th cataract and almost 25% of the total sediment load.[8]

Annual Cycle — Timing and Rate of Rise / Decline of the River Levels

Prior to any barrage constructions across the Nile, Joseph Hekekyan[9] working at Memphis recorded a rise in the river of 187.5 inches (4.76 m) at Bedrahsein Sahil from 10th July[10] to 10th August 1852, a mean rise of approximately 15 cm/day. The river reached its maximum on 5th October having risen a further 64.75 inches (1.64 m), equal to a mean rise of 2.9 cm/day.

William Willocks provides records of river levels from numerous gauges from the White Nile and Blue Nile through to the Delta.[11] The most useful for this discussion of the annual cycle of the river are the five-day mean levels from Aswan and those from Asyut, which is closest to the stretches of the Nile visited by boats in the Ramesside texts discussed below. The five-day records from Roda, Cairo are not used in this study as they are more distant and all the records Willcocks presents post-date the completion of the Damietta and Rosetta barrages in 1861.[12]

Aswan 1892 and 1873–1902 Mean River Levels

Willcocks and Craig[13] present the five-day mean levels at Aswan throughout 1892, 1907, 1908, and 1912, and the mean for 1873–1902. They also provide less regular readings from 1874, 1877, 1878, 1879, and 1892.[14] As the Aswan Dam was completed in 1902 those records post-dating it are less useful for understanding the timing and annual cycle of Nile.[15] Willcocks and Craig describe 1892 as a "very high year".[16] However, by comparing the 1892 records with the mean for 1873–1902 and four other years with irregular readings we can more clearly assess the usefulness of the1892 data, given that a 30-year mean is not provided for Asyut (see Table 1 and Figs. 1 and 2). This is also a consideration of how meaningful this information is with respect to the timing of the annual regime, which of course varies from year to year (see discussion below).

TABLE 1. Five–day mean river levels taken at Aswan in 1892 (from Willcocks and Craig 1913, Table 84) and the 30-year mean at Aswan between 1873 and 1902 (from Willcocks and Craig 1913, Table 85). The mean daily rate of change in river level are calculated by this author. Bold marks the minima and maxima that year. *(Continued on next page.)*

Date	Day	1892 River level m a.s.l.	1892 Mean Daily Rate of Rise (+) / Fall (-) cm	Mean 1873–1902 River level m a.s.l.	Mean 1873–1902 Daily Rate of Rise (+) / Fall (-) cm
January	1–5	87.72	-	87.59	
	6–10	87.56	-3.2s	87.48	-2.2
	11–15	87.42	-2.8	87.37	-2.2
	16–20	87.35	-1.4	87.25	-2.4
	21–25	87.25	-2.0	87.14	-2.2
	26–31	87.07	-3.0	87.02	-2.0
February	1–5	86.95	-2.4	86.91	-2.2
	6–10	86.77	-3.6	86.80	-2.2
	11–15	86.63	-2.8	86.68	-2.4
	16–20	86.45	-3.6	86.56	-2.4
	21–25	86.29	-3.2	86.46	-2.0
	26–end*	86.11	-3.6	86.37	-1.8
March	1–5	85.95	-3.2	86.27	-2.0
	6–10	85.82	-2.6	86.17	-2.0
	11–15	85.72	-2.0	86.07	-2.0
	16–20	85.56	-3.2	85.96	-2.2
	21–25	85.40	-3.2	85.86	-2.0
	26–31	85.31	-1.5	85.74	-2.0
April	1–5	85.21	-2.0	85.64	-2.0
	6–10	85.07	-2.8	85.55	-1.8
	11–15	84.99	-1.6	85.48	-1.4
	16–20	84.90	-1.8	85.41	-1.4
	21–25	84.84	-1.2	85.35	-1.2
	26–30	84.73	-2.2	85.27	-1.6
May	1–5	84.67	-1.2	85.22	-1.0
	6–10	84.66	-0.2	85.16	-1.2
	11–15	84.63	-0.6	85.13	-0.6
	16–20	84.55	-1.6	85.09	-0.8
	21–25	84.57	0.4	**85.08**	-0.2
	26–31	84.48	-1.5	85.09	0.2

* All dates and heights of the river are as given in Willcocks and Craig (1913, Table 94). 1892 was a leap year. Thus, the fall of 0.18 m from the previous mean to the last record in February has been divided by four days giving daily mean fall of 4.5 cm. Note that this is against the trend and thus maybe incorrect and a divisor of five is more accurate. The last five-day mean for those months with 31 days in them have used a divisor of six.

Table 1, *continued*. Five–day mean river levels taken at Aswan in 1892 (from Willcocks and Craig 1913, Table 84) and the 30-year mean at Aswan between 1873 and 1902 (from Willcocks and Craig 1913, Table 85). The mean daily rate of change in river level are calculated by this author. Bold marks the minima and maxima that year. *(Continued on next page.)*

Date	Day	1892 River level m a.s.l.	1892 Mean Daily Rate of Rise (+) / Fall (-) cm	Mean 1873– 1902 River level m a.s.l.	Mean 1873– 1902 Daily Rate of Rise (+) / Fall (-) cm
June	**1–5**	**84.38**	-2.0	85.11	0.4
	6–10	84.42	0.8	85.15	0.8
	11–15	84.51	1.8	85.24	1.8
	16–20	84.56	1.0	85.37	2.6
	21–25	84.74	3.6	85.53	3.2
	26–30	85.04	6.0	85.86	6.6
July	1–5	85.43	7.8	86.15	5.8
	6–10	85.76	6.6	86.49	6.8
	11–15	86.46	14.0	86.90	8.2
	16–20	87.00	10.8	87.51	12.2
	21–25	88.33	26.6	88.28	15.4
	26–31	89.64	21.8	89.25	16.2
August	1–5	91.17	30.6	90.16	18.2
	6–10	91.57	8.0	91.14	19.6
	11–15	91.67	2.0	91.80	13.2
	16–20	92.06	7.8	92.18	7.6
	21–25	93.00	18.8	92.46	5.6
	26–31	93.34	5.7	92.69	3.8
September	1–5	93.48	2.8	**92.82**	2.6
	6–10	93.72	4.8	92.81	-0.2
	11–15	**93.79**	1.4	92.78	-0.6
	16–20	93.78	-0.2	92.70	-1.6
	21–25	93.74	-2.8**	92.60	-2.0
	26–30	93.49	-5.0	92.38	-4.4
October	1–5	93.27	-4.4	92.04	-6.8
	6–10	92.93	-6.8	91.72	-6.4
	11–15	92.53	-8.0	91.40	-6.4
	16–20	92.26	-5.4	91.03	-7.4
	21–25	91.95	-6.2	90.69	-6.8
	26–31	91.50	-7.5	90.26	-7.2

** This calculation is based upon the maximum of 93.88 m on 20 September (Willcocks and Craig 1913, Table 90). If the previous five-day mean height of the river 93.78m is used, then the mean daily decrease in the water level would have been 0.8 cm but this does not accurately reflect the fall in the water level.

TABLE 1, *continued*. Five–day mean river levels taken at Aswan in 1892 (from Willcocks and Craig 1913, Table 84) and the 30-year mean at Aswan between 1873 and 1902 (from Willcocks and Craig 1913, Table 85). The mean daily rate of change in river level are calculated by this author.

Date	Day	1892 River level m a.s.l.	1892 Mean Daily Rate of Rise (+) / Fall (-) cm	Mean 1873–1902 River level m a.s.l.	Mean 1873–1902 Daily Rate of Rise (+) / Fall (-) cm
November	1–5	90.95	-11.0	89.35	-18.2
	6–10	90.49	-9.2	89.48	2.6
	11–15	90.06	-8.6	89.16	-6.4
	16–20	89.76	-6.0	88.91	-5.0
	21–25	89.49	-5.4	88.71	-4.0
	26–30	89.21	-5.6	88.53	-3.6
December	1–5	88.98	-4.6	88.36	-3.4
	6–10	88.81	-3.4	88.21	-3.0
	11–15	88.66	-3.0	88.07	-2.8
	16–20	88.54	-2.4	87.93	-2.8
	21–25	88.43	-2.2	87.80	-2.6
	26–31	88.32	-1.8	87.64	-2.7

From the figures in Table 1 of the 1892 five-day mean river levels we can see that the minimum level of the Nile was recorded at 84.38 m a.s.l. during 1–5 June 1892[17] and the maximum level between 11–15 September 1892 at 93.79 m a.s.l. However, when we look at the irregular records for 1892 we see that the minimum is given as 84.40 m on 1 June and the maximum was 93.88 m on 20 June.[18] The individual maximum record suggest that there may have been a fall in the river level before a short resurgence of discharge taking it to its maximum on 20 June, which is masked by the five-day mean records. The 1892 inundation shows a rise of 9.50 m that year from its minimum.

Both the minimum and maximum levels occur c. 10 days before in the 1873–1902 mean. The minimum in 1892 is 0.7 m lower than the 30-year mean while the maximum is 1.06 m higher.[19] The mean rise between 1873–1902 is 7.74 m. Comparing the 1892 minimum and maximum to the 1874, 1877, 1878, and 1879 records reveals that in both instances the 1892 heights are the median of the five years. The mean minimum of the five years was 85.00 m and the mean maximum is 93.39 m.[20] Whilst 1 m higher than the 30-year mean, the 1892 inundation height is clearly not so abnormal within that period.

During June 1892 the river starts to rise slowly from the minimum level until the first days of July, with a rise of 1.05 m equating to a mean daily rise of 3.5 cm over that 30-day period. The next 10 days see a mean daily rise increase to >10 cm/day. From this point there is a rapid rise in levels with 16 days (21 July–5 August) where it rises c. 4.2 m (a mean daily rise of >0.26 m). The rate of rise then falls significantly to <10 cm/day through August and to the maximum level on 20 September with the exception of a short further impulse of water (21–25 August). In comparison, the 30-year mean of 1873–1902 shows a slower mean daily rise of c. 2.7 cm over a 40-day period to 1–5 July. The timing of the mean daily rise reaching >10 cm/day is five days later (16–20 July) and the period above 10 cm daily rise is

111

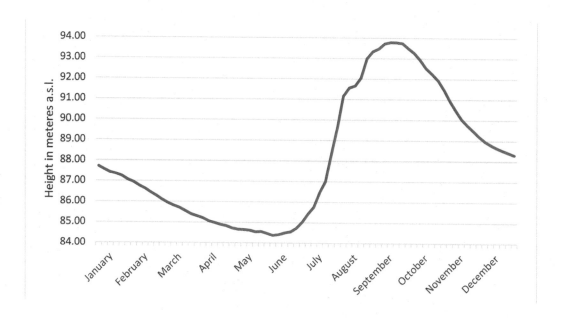

Figure 1. Diagram showing river levels throughout 1892 at Aswan produced from the five-day mean river levels in Willcocks and Craig (1913, Table 84) using Microsoft Excel.

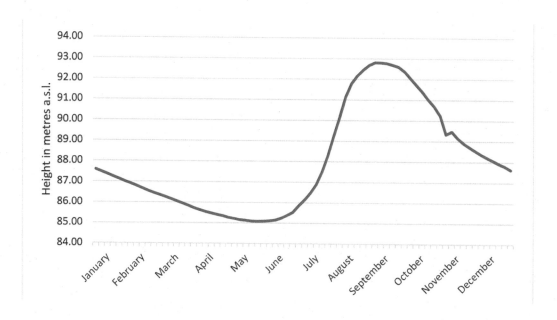

Figure 2. Diagram showing the mean 1873–1902 river levels at Aswan produced from the five-day mean river levels in Willcocks and Craig (1913, Table 84) using Microsoft Excel.

slightly longer than the 1892 water levels, but less rapid at >20 cm/day with the period of decreasing rise in the water level much shorter than the 1892 records.

As we have seen above in 1892 there seems to be a brief fall in the water level before the maximum is reached (20 September). It is during these days (11–15 and 16–20 Sept) that watermarks and measurements recorded on the Nilometers and the inscriptions of the water level would have been made. Such an oscillation in the water level could explain instances such as year 6 of Taharka's reign where we have two Nile markings, one at 74.39 m a.s.l. and another at 74.40 m on the western tribune at Karnak, where presumably the higher one came after a brief fall in the level after the lower level.[21]

Following the maximum in 1892, the rate of reduction in river levels increases up to a maximum of 11 cm/day in the first days of November with an overall mean daily rate of decrease of c. 6.8 cm over the 43 days,[22] by which time the river had fallen by 2.93 m. Throughout November and December there is an overall trend towards a slowing daily rate of reduction in the river level to c. 2 cm/day and by the end of the year the river has fallen a total of 5.5 m since its maximum. The mean river levels for 1873–1902 show an almost still period of c. 10 days where the river only falls 4 cm in total up to 11–15 September from its five-day mean maximum. From that time until the beginning of November we observe an increase in the rate of reduction in river levels up to a maximum of >18 cm/day. The river falls 3.43 m during this 50-day period with an overall mean daily rate of decrease of c. 6.9 cm, an almost identical rate of decrease as that in 1892. After the sharp period of decrease 1–5 November, as with the 1892 levels, the 30-year mean has a trend of a slowing daily rate of reduction to the end of the year. From mid-November this rate of decrease is almost identical in both the 1892 and 1873–1902 mean levels.[23]

Turning to the records for the first 5 months of 1892, we see that the river is within 3 m of its minima by mid-January. Over the following five weeks (to about 20 February) the levels fall by a further 1 m, and then a further 1 m over the next 30 days until about 22 March when the river is within 1 m of its minimum. It is almost 10 weeks before it reaches that point. It is within 0.5 m of the minimum by 21 April, 6 weeks before its minimum is reached. Looking at the mean levels for 1873–1902 we can see that the river is already within 3 m of its minimum by mid-December, a month earlier than in 1892. It is within 2 m of its minimum by about 26 January, about 25 days earlier than in 1892. As in 1892, the 30-year mean reaches within 1 m of its minimum 10 weeks before the minimum and within 0.5 m with just over 6 weeks before this point. This rate of decrease in the river levels is very similar, it is just the timing is about 10 days earlier in the case of 30-year mean.

When we compare 1892 to the 30-year mean river levels from 1873–1902 we have already noted that there is difference in the timing of both the minimum and maximum of about 10 days and the timing of the rate of fall of the river levels in the 3-4 months prior to the minimum. The rate of rise in 1892 is notably greater for a short period in July and early August than the 30-year mean and of course the maximum is c. 1 m higher in 1892 than in the 30-year mean, but there are other years with very similar maximum levels. Bearing in mind the differences we have seen, we can now turn our attention to the 1892 five-day mean water levels recorded at Asyut.

Asyut 1892 River Levels

Willcocks and Craig[24] present the five-day mean levels at Asyut throughout 1892 as well as after the completion of the Aswan Dam and the Asyut barrage, which will not be considered here (see Table 2 and Fig. 3). They do not provide a 30-year mean for Asyut for comparison. It is important to note that the Ibrahimiyah (Ibrahimia) Canal, an irrigation canal built in 1873, had its head on the west bank of the Nile at Asyut.[25] It is not clear from

TABLE 2. Five–day mean river levels taken at Asyut in 1892 with the mean daily rate of change in river level. Bold mark the minima and maxima that year (from Willcocks and Craig 1913, Table 85).

Date	Day	River level m a.s.l.	Mean Daily Rate of Rise (+) / Fall (-) cm	Date	Day	River level m a.s.l.	Mean Daily Rate of Rise (+) / Fall (-) cm
January	1–5	47.76	–	July	1–5	44.78	+2.8
	6–10	47.62	-2.8		6–10	45.10	+6.4
	11–15	47.48	-2.8		11–15	45.36	+5.2
	16–20	47.38	-2.0		16–20	46.00	+12.8
	21–25	47.31	-1.4		21–25	46.62	+12.4
	26–31 (see n. 11)	47.22	-1.5		26–31	47.98	+22.7
February	1–5	47.10	-2.4	August	1–5	49.47	+31.8
	6–10	46.99	-4.2		6–10	50.64	+23.4
	11–15	46.86	-2.6		11–15	50.97	+6.6
	16–20	46.70	-3.2		16–20	50.65	-6.4
	21–25	46.55	-3.0		21–25	51.25	+12.0
	26–end	46.41	-3.5		**26–31**	**51.97**	+14.4
March	1–5	46.26	-3.0	September	1–5	52.13	+3.2
	6–10	46.12	-2.8		6–10	52.40	+5.4
	11–15	45.99	-2.6		11–15	52.84	+8.8
	16–20	45.87	-2.4		16–20	44.56	+0.4
	21–25	45.73	-2.8		21–25	44.60	+0.8
	26–31	45.59	-3.5		26–30	44.64	+0.8
April	1–5	45.50	-1.8	October	1–5	53.11	-2.4
	6–10	45.40	-2.0		6–10	52.91	-4.0
	11–15	45.30	-2.0		11–15	52.70	-4.2
	16–20	45.18	-2.4		16–20	52.49	-4.2
	21–25	45.07	-2.2		21–25	52.31	-3.6
	26–30	45.00	-1.4		26–31	51.86	-9.0
May	1–5	44.92	-1.6	November	1–5	51.19	-13.4
	6–10	44.85	-1.4		6–10	50.66	-10.6
	11–15	44.80	-1.0		11–15	50.14	-10.4
	16–20	44.73	-1.4		16–20	49.81	-6.6
	21–25	44.67	-1.2		21–25	49.50	-6.2
	26–31	44.65	-0.3		26–30	49.24	-5.2
June	1–5	44.62	-0.6	December	1–5	48.97	-5.4
	6–10	44.55	-1.4		6–10	48.77	-4.0
	11–15	**44.54**	-0.2		11–15	48.58	-3.8
	16–20	44.56	+0.4		16–20	48.42	-3.2
	21–25	44.60	+0.8		21–25	48.29	-2.6
	26–30	44.64	+0.8		26–31	48.16	-2.6

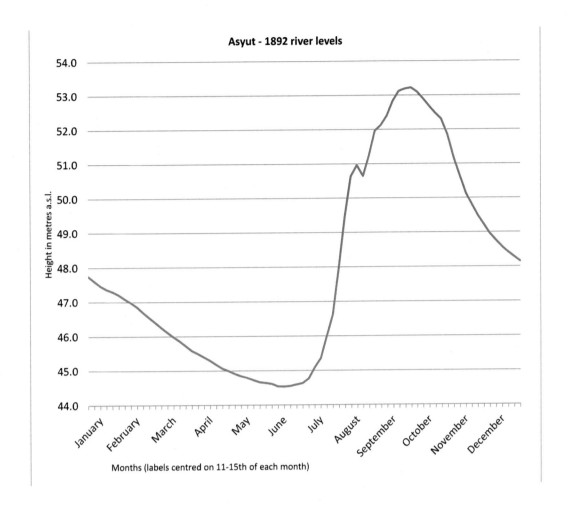

Figure 3. Diagram showing river levels throughout 1892 at Asyut produced from the five-day mean river levels in Willcocks and Craig (1913, Table 85) using Microsoft Excel.

where in Asyut that Willcocks took his readings, but there would have been some effect due to the additional carrying capacity afforded by the canal.

The minimum level of the Nile was recorded at 44.54 m a.s.l. during 11–15 June and the maximum level between 26–30 September at 53.23 m a.s.l. showing an annual rise and fall of 8.69 m. As we know from the Aswan 30-year mean data this maximum would have been higher than the mean, but not so abnormal. The timing of both the maximum and minimum are similarly probably about 10 days later than the 30-year mean.

From the end of May to the end of June we have c. 30 days (15 days before and after the minimum level) when the water level is within 0.1 m of its minima, which accords well with the 30-year mean data from Aswan. The first half of July sees a mean daily rise of almost 5 cm (the river rising 0.72 m in 15 days). From mid-July the rate of rise increases to >10 cm/day. The most rapid rise is in the last six days of July and the first 10 days of August. In those 16 days the river rises from 46.62 m a.s.l (21–25 July) to 50.64 m a.s.l. (6–10 August). This 4 m rise in the river equates to a mean daily rise of c. 25 cm. As we have seen from the Aswan data, the 30-year mean rate of rise may be more like 20 cm/day for this period. Taking the same dates as Hekekyan's records from 10 July to 10 August, Willcocks measurements show a daily rate of rise of c. 17.9 cm, which is very similar to Hekekyan's measurements given that his were taken in Bedrashein and the flood is lower as you move further downstream (see discussion below).

There is a small and brief decrease in the river levels of 0.32 m during 16–20 August. It seems unlikely that the Damietta and Rosetta barrages would have been the cause as they were usually opened in July each year as the water started to rise in the area of the barrages.[26] The Asyut barrage was not built until the late 1890s so had no effect on Willcocks' measurements.[27] The Ibrahimiyah Canal could have been a factor in this fall. However, the data from Aswan (Table 1) suggests that the brief fall in the river level in Asyut was due to a reduction of the discharge from the monsoonal rains in the Ethiopian Highlands followed by a secondary pulse of discharge. There occurred a rapid fall in the rate of river level increase in Awan from >30 cm/day (1–5 August) to 8.0 cm/day (5–10 August) and then to just 2.0 cm/day rise in Aswan during 11–15 August, just 5 days earlier than the fall in river level in Asyut. This was followed by a rise of 1.33 m over the next 10 days at the Aswan gauge, which is seen with a 5–10 day lag in the records from Asyut, which show a 1.32 m increase over the 11 days (21–31 August). As the monsoonal rains waned this can be seen in the slower rate of river rise during September at Asyut, which slows to a mean daily rate of c. 4 cm over the month[28] until the flood maximum.

Following the flood maximum there is a steady recession of river levels of c. 4 cm/day during October. Willcocks then recorded an increased rate in the fall of the Nile levels of >10 cm/day over 20 days (52.31 m during 21–25 October had gone down to 50.14 m by 11–15 November). From mid-November the rate of decrease of the Nile level reduces over the coming months to c. 4 cm/day in December. By the end of December the river has reduced in level by c. 5 m.

Looking at the data from the first half of 1892, we can see that this rate of decrease falls to < 2 cm/day in April, May, and the first half of June. The measurements show that the river was within 3.0 m of its minimum before mid-January, five months before it reached it. Given the data from 30-year mean at Aswan, we can propose that the river would be within 3 m of its minimum at Asyut more often by mid- to late-December. It was within 2.0 m of the lowest river level by 24 February almost 16 weeks in advance of the minima and by the beginning of April it was only 1.0 m above its minima occuring 11 weeks later. During April the river level fell a further 0.5 m taking it to within 0.5 m of its minima in 1892 and requiring a further 7 weeks to drop finally reaching its minimum level in mid-June.

These records only represent a single year of readings in two locations, Aswan and Asyut, which have been compared with the 30-year mean from 1873–1902 at Aswan. They provide us with a representation of the rise and fall of the Nile in these two locations over the annual cycle, but the discharge and the timing of it had both a range and difference according to the location along the course of the Nile valley and Delta. These aspects are briefly further unpacked in the following sections.

Lag Along the Course of the Nile

As we have seen from the 1892 records there is a lag in time along the course of the Nile in occurrence of the maximum and minimum. Willcocks' measurements discussed above show the maximum at Asyut occurs c. 8 days after the maximum in Aswan and the delay is c. 10 days for the minimum.[29] Said argues that in an "average year in the latter part of the nineteenth century" the flood minimum at Aswan was the end of May with the minimum occuring c. 12 days later in Cairo (10 June) and a further 5 days in Sais (15 June).[30] The time lag for the maximum was c. 6 days from Aswan (28–30 August) to Cairo (5–10 Sept) and an additional 3 days to Sais (7–10 Sept).[31]

The Regularity of the Annual Inundation

According to Said,[32] the flood is rarely sudden or abrupt and rises and falls with a fair degree of regularity. However, there is a time range for when the inundation reaches the Egyptian Nile valley, for the length of the flood and the timing of the minimum and maximum of the annual cycle. The average duration of the 46 floods between 1890 and 1935 was 110 days with a maximum length of 162 days occurred in 1894. In that period four floods (8.7%) lasted less than 75 days and 12 floods (26%) lasted more than 125 days.[33] During the peak flood the river would over top its banks and spill out across the floodplain covering a large area of the valley. Records from five years from 1874–1892 show that the time from minimum to maximum ranged from 100–114 days (see Table 3) and that there was a difference of only 13 days when the minimum was reached and 26 days between the earliest maximum (5 Sept) and the latest (1 October).

According to Said,[34] from the 820 floods recorded between the 7th and 15th centuries on the Roda Nilometer, 73% were "normal" floods, which reached a height sufficient to inundate all basins and subside at the proper time for sowing. Twenty-two percent of the floods were low, of which 15% only inundated part of the cultivable land and the other 7% never reached or had a late plenitude. The remaining 5% of floods were destructively high. Out of the 207 years in which both minimum and maximum levels were recorded at Roda the rise of the Nile began in May in 10% of cases, in June in 75%, and in 15% of cases in early July. In all 207 years it occurred between 17th May and 6th July.[35] So whilst we can see that for three in four years the Nile started to rise in Cairo in June, there is a range of 50 days from the earliest to the latest date. The maximum level was reached in the "latter

TABLE 3. Date and height of the minimum and maximum river levels in metres above mean sea level for five years (data taken from Willcocks and Craig 1913, 179, Table 90).

	Date	1874	1877	1878	1879	1892
Minimum	May 27		85.10		86.88	
	May 29	84.34				
	June 1					84.40
	June 9			84.29		
Maximum	Sept 5		91.27			
	Sept 6	93.97				
	Sept 13				93.70	
	Sept 20					93.88
	Oct 1			94.15		
Difference in river level between minimum and maximum (m)		9.63	6.17	9.86	6.82	9.48
No. of days from minimum to maximum		100	101	114	109	111

part of September and the early part of October"[36] in c. 87% of records.[37] In 5% of years the maxima occurred in November. Of all these records the earliest rise was 7 August and the latest 27 November.[38]

The previous two sections have at least provided some parameters for the annual cycle of the river, which we can then apply to understand further where in the Nile valley boats could have been loading their grain at different times of the year. In order to understand the past land- and waterscapes of the Egyptian Nile valley, we must address the characteristics of the Nile and geomorphology of the Nile valley.

Characteristics of the Nile and Geomorphology of the Nile Valley

An important and relatively easily understood characteristic of a river is the grain size of its bedload, which forms the bars and bedforms of the channel floor,[39] which in turn aid our understanding of the geomorphological elements that make up the river and its flood-plain. In general the Nile within the Egyptian Nile Valley has a sandy bedload.[40] However, Attia[41] concluded from his many boreholes throughout the Nile Valley that the upper surface of the Pleistocene ("diluvial") gravels is both uneven and irregular. It was as little as 8.4 m below the surface. Many of the sources of these are the wadis feeding in the eastern and western deserts, such as Wadi Qena. Schumm[42] suggests that at numerous locations the bed of the Nile within the Egyptian Nile valley could be in contact with sediment coarser than sand and thus affect its planform (see discussion below).

A river becomes braided (has more than a single channel) when sediment accumulates in the form of islands or bars. When the bars form mid-channel or a lateral bar becomes isolated from the channel bank, then the channel may split into two or more channels and form a braided pattern.[43]

Repetitive bedforms, ripples, and dunes are the principal features

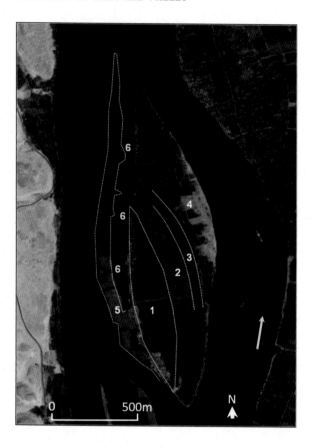

Figure 4. Development of the island west of Nag' el-Saiyid Sa'id el-Gedid. The field boundaries provide evidence of the development of the island. The white dotted polygon numbered 1 represents the "core" bar. There is evidence of two extensions of the field systems as lateral accretions on the eastern side have added to the island (numbered 2 and 3). This is followed be a further downstream extension (4). An emerging bar on the west flank of the island (5) creates a backwater or slough (6) between the bar and "core" of the island (Image background © Google Earth). The yellow arrow shows the direction of river flow.

of sandy bedload rivers. Falling discharge can lead to the partial emergence of the riverbed. The high areas that emerge first split the flow at a variety of scales from large compound bars to individual bedforms.[44] The largest morphological features (macroforms) of sandy bed streams are sand flats or sand bars. They occur in both marginal and mid-channel positions and have been variously called "side, lateral or alternate bars" and "mid-channel or braid bars" respectively.[45] The sand flats or bars form from the accretion of smaller mesoforms, for example dunes. Erosion from one bank and local scour of the bed are deposited in the "crossover" zone where flow diverges as the main current (talweg) moves from one bank to another.[46] Once a sand bar has developed it can persist for a considerable time and grow by the vertical accretion of fine-grained sediment held in suspension in the river. Baffling effects caused by the growth of vegetation on the bar aid deposition and add to its stability.[47]

With the lateral migration of the main curved channel, islands also expand laterally as well as extending downstream. Islands may also accrete upstream (see Fig. 4).[48] Although the channels on both sides of an island may co-exist for decades, in some bends the minor (chute) channel may be sealed off as the bend migration progresses and thus a slough or backwater is formed (see Fig. 5).[49] The slough fills in with fine-grained (silt and clay-sized) deposits and the island becomes attached to the floodplain (see Fig. 6). Augering in the former minor channel at Gezirat Bedrashein suggests that this can be a rapid process taking only tens of years.[50]

Studies of rivers from around the world as well as flume tests have shown that the planform of a river changes according to factors such as discharge, valley slope, and grain

FIGURE 5. Slough east of Edfu. The white arrow shows a slough formed by an island accreting to the point bar on the east side of the river. The yellow arrows show the talweg of the river. NB two Nile cruise vessels can be seen upstream of the lower arrow (Image background © Google Earth).

Figure 6. Island history upstream of el-Wasta. A number of islands situated close to the west bank of the river characterise the stretch of the Nile immediately upstream of el-Wasta (left). A close-up (right) reveals that field boundaries provide evidence of a former island (1) marked in yellow dash lines. Field boundaries to the west suggest lateral accretions on the western side (numbered 2 and 3 marked by light white dashed lines). The island has become attached to the floodplain as the silting up of the minor channel (c - with riverbanks marked in heavier dashed white lines) takes place. As the river flows around the concave east side of the island further lateral accretion has occurred (4) causing the river to migrate further eastwards (Image background © Google Earth).

size, for example increase in discharge can lead to an increase in sinuosity of a river with further increase in discharge causing a decrease in sinuosity and an increase in braiding.[51] Channel-forming discharge (i.e., annual floods) in the Nile has varied over the last five millennia[52] suggesting the general river planform would have been different in different periods. The planform of the river would also be affected in the areas of the Nile valley where the bed of the Nile is in contact with the coarser-grained sediments (gravel).[53] Schumm notes a distinct change in both river slope and valley slope downstream of Qena,[54] where coarse sediments that have been introduced by Wadi Qena resist erosion by the Nile, and argues that these have affected the planform of the river.

Another essential characteristic to recognise is that channel patterns look different at different flow stages (during the annual cycle of the Nile) and that channel geometry changes through time.[55] Channel patterns are dynamic in both space and time.[56] The degree of braiding observed is stage-dependent.[57] At lower flow stages many more sand flats and bars would have been exposed in the Nile making navigation more problematic during this period.[58]

CHANNEL MIGRATION

Channel migration occurs through a number of processes. We have already seen that the silting up of a minor (chute) channel of an island leads to a slough and the switching of all

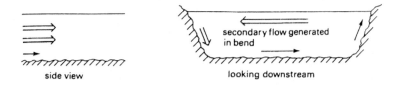

FIGURE 7. Vorticity vectors in a stream bend. The left image shows the velocity profile in a river (heavier arrows represent higher velocity). The right figure shows the secondary circulatory motion generated in a bend to the right. The outer (left) bank is eroded and the inner bank is the depositional side (after Scorer 1997, 83 Figs. 3.4.i and 3.4.ii).

the flow of the river to one side of the river. The "Classic Point Bar Model" describes how migration of a meandering alluvial channel occurs. The flow in meander bends is known to be helicoidal with the surface flowing towards the outer bank and bottom flow moving towards the inner bank.[59] Within a river the water close to the bed is slowed down by the frictional drag of the bed and drag due to particles carried in the stream that are either slowed down or brought to rest on the bed. Therefore, rivers can have slow-moving fluid at the bottom with the main body of water above moving faster.[60] At a bend centrifugal force (vorticity vector) causes the fast-moving water to move to the outside bank and the slow-moving fluid to rise on the inside bank (see Fig. 7).[61] The line of maximum depth in the channel, the *talweg*, corresponds approximately to the zone of maximum water velocity and this lies towards the outer concave bank of the bend and swings back and forth across the channel from one concave bank to the next with the helicoidal flow changing its sense of rotation.[62] The helicoidal flow pattern results in the erosion of the outer concave bank and the deposition of the inner convex bank with the channel as a whole migrating laterally and the

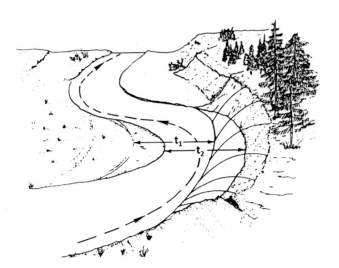

FIGURE 8. Deposition and meandering on a meandering river. This shows the former position of the river channel at t1 and its present position at t2 as a result of lateral shift by deposition on the point bar and erosion of the concave bank. The hatched area shows the erosion of the concave bank between t1 and t2. The dashed line with arrows shows the path of the talweg (after Waters 1992, Fig. 3.9).

121

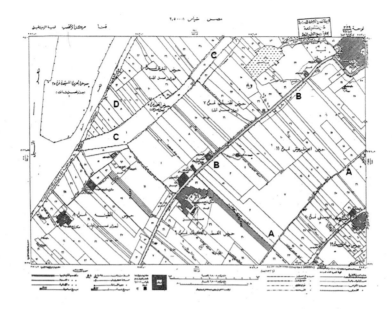

FIGURE 9. Hod boundaries on a cadastral map c. 3 km north of Karnak (A-A and B-B) represent the former east bank of the river. C marks a silted up channel between the east bank and a former island marked D (Survey of Egypt 1940, sheet 339/781,5).

bend migrating downstream (see Fig. 8). The erosion of the concave bank is influenced by the composition of the bank material.[63] The point bar is argued to have a top surface roughly horizontal at about the level of the surrounding floodplain that slopes down to the *talweg* of the channel. A steep concave bank provides the characteristic asymmetrical cross-section.[64]

Channel migration due to this point bar model appears to be seen just downstream of Karnak. Aerial photographs and the hod boundaries and field numbering and orientation found on cadastral maps in the area of al-Zaniyah show how the east bank of the river c. 3 km downstream of Karnak has migrated north and westwards (see Fig. 9). However, the only way to be certain of an interpretation using remote sensing is to ground-truth it through geoarchaeological (and if possible combined with geophysical) survey. While the point bar migration has yet to be confirmed by a borehole programme, the narrow channel (c. 50 m wide) was confirmed by a transect of augers.[65]

AVULSION

The process of avulsion as a way of forcing the diversion of the river flow has been observed in the West Bank floodplain of Thebes/Luxor through the borehole programme of the Theban Harbours and Waterscapes Survey. A channel flowing during the New Kingdom ran past the Colossi of Memnon and within c. 160 m of the pylon of the Ramesseum. It was separated from the main channel belt of the Nile by a floodbasin and thus could not have been formed by a gradual lateral migration of the river bed, but by a partial avulsion.[66]

Topographic maps of the Survey of Egypt and observations show that the natural levees rise 1–3 m above the lowest alluvial basin.[67] Because the banks of the channel are slightly higher than the surrounding floodplain this landform complex is known as a convex floodplain.[68] The levee development can result in low-lying backswamp areas.[69] Toonen et al.[70] argue that large flood events could have breached the levees and this channel route could have exploited low-lying floodplain depressions.[71]

IRREGULAR POINT BAR FORMATIONS

Numerous "irregular" point bar formations can be observed in the Nile today. They may be as a result of the process by which an envelope of slightly circulatory water develops adjacent to the convex (inner) bank (see Fig. 10).[72] Based upon his research of the Beatton River in British Columbia, Nanson argues that this zone of separation is not completely isolated from the main flow and that sediment loaded eddies move across the boundary depositing sediment principally across the outer edge of the zone where supply would be greatest.[73] As the inundation recedes a ridge of alluvium is left marking the position of this

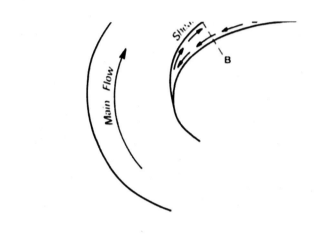

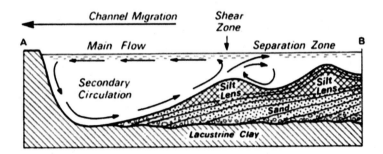

FIGURE 10. Formation of a separation zone adjacent to the convex bank also shows deposition of sediment (in this case silt) along the outer margin of this zone. These longitudinal ridges generate Langmuir circulation (after Nanson 1980, Fig. 22).

123

Figure 11. River bend east of At-Tiwayrat. A view looking downstream with Qena in the background shows the irregularity of the point bar. The water filled area between the inner bank is the zone of separation shown in Fig. 10, which had almost formed a slough at the time of observation (photo: A Graham, February 2009).

boundary flow. In the Beatton River these ridges are formed of silt. Although a study of the grain size of the point bar ridges on the Nile has yet to be done, given the nature of the suspended sediment in the river it seems most likely that its composition would be fine sand-sized or smaller particles (Φ <2.5). The result is a slough.

Field observations of point bar morphology in the stretch of the Nile between Qena and Luxor in November 2008 and February 2009 reveal the irregularity of the bar with an outer raised bar concentric with the convex bank being separated from the riverbank by a low-lying water filled area (see Fig. 11).

I have briefly explored the annual cycle and some of the geomorphological characteristics and processes within the Egyptian Nile valley. We now turn to understanding the timing of activities translating them from the Egyptian calendar to the Gregorian calendar so we can then assess when in the annual cycle of the river these events took place and what the river may have looked like at that time within its annual discharge cycle.

Converting the Timing of Activities to the Gregorian Calendar

Egyptian Civil Calendar dates used in administrative texts of the state have been converted into Gregorian calendrical dates so that the time of year when the activity took place can be understood with reference to the level of the river.

The Civil Calendar is 365 days long,[74] thus the Egyptian calendar shifts by one day every four years away from the Julian calendar (which includes a leap year every four years). The Gregorian year is fractionally shorter than the Julian year and was introduced in the late 16th century C.E. by Pope Gregory XIII. I have used Jürgen von Beckerath's conversion tables,[75] firstly by converting the dates to a Julian one using Table C and then subtracting the requisite number of days from that date using Table B to convert it to a Gregorian calendrical date.

I have used the dates in the chronology given in Hornung et al.[76] Scholars will have their views on the chronology dependent upon interpretations of co-regency, issues of reign length, et cetera. For every four years difference earlier you need to add one day to the Julian date and thus the Gregorian date. For forty years earlier you add 10 days and forty years later you subtract 10 days from the converted dates I present in this paper.

RAMESSIDE LANDING PLACES – MRYT, Pᶜт, IW, MȝWT AND NḤB

A particularly important text in understanding a number of lexical terms for landing places for the collection and loading of grain in the Ramesside Period is P. Amiens / Baldwin,[77] which can be dated to the Twentieth Dynasty.[78] On the *verso* we find only mention of *mryt* as the place of mooring whereas on the recto the boats moor and load grain at places labelled by a variety of topographical terms. I will look at this text together with a number of other Ramesside texts in an attempt to shed further light on the *mryt* and the other mooring places.[79]

Mryt *landing places*

P. Amiens / Baldwin *verso* gives eight dates, some only partial, that relate to the receipt and loading of small quantities of grain at the *mryt* between early December and late January with three toponymns including the divine name of Khnum (Hermopolite area) (see Table 4).[80] As we have seen this is at a time when the Nile inundation had receded from the floodplain, but was still receding within its riverbed and would be perhaps c. 3–4 m from its minimum level.[81] The upper part of the river bank would have been accessible by boat during this period of the annual cycle of the river.

P. Turin 2008 + 2016 and P. Brooklyn 35.1453A support the view that the *mryt* was readily accessible during the high levels of the river. P. Turin 2008 + 2016 has been dated to a Ramesside ruler after Ramesses V.[82] The activities of the boat over 17 days recorded in P. Turin 2008 + 2016 rt. took place in October perhaps just as or only a few days after the Nile had reached its maximum in the Memphite area (see Table 5).[83] The dating of the text begins in "[Regnal year 7, the first month] of winter, day 17" (I *prt* 17) when the boat departs the *mryt* of Heliopolis and travels to the *mryt* of Memphis, which is two months to the day since the departure from Thebes that was on III ȝḥt 17.[84] If we place year 7 in Ramesses VI's reign at 1139 B.C.E.,[85] then the boat departed Thebes on 8th August (Gregorian) during the height of the inundation. Two months later it left Heliopolis on 6th October arriving at Memphis on the same day. If the papyrus were dated to as late as year 7 of Ramesses XI's reign in 1099 B.C.E.,[86] this would shift the dates back by 10 days, placing the activity in late September to early October. Whatever the precise date was according to the reign in which these activities took place, it was most likely only the very uppermost part of the riverbank that was available for mooring.[87]

The transactions recorded in P. Brooklyn 35.1453A occur from the fourth month of the inundation, day 25 to day 29 and take place in the area of Iunet (Dendara) at a number of *mryt* and islands (*iw*) or former islands that retain this term in the toponym.[88] The date of

Table 4. Dates of Grain collection in P. Amiens/Baldwin verso.

Date (Egyptian)	Date (Gregorian)*	What given and to whom	Where given	Source**
Year 1, III *prt* …	December 1130	61/4 [1/8] sacks of grain	[on] the *mryt* of Khnum	P. Amiens vs. II, 4 (Janssen 2004, 47)
Year 1, III (?) *prt* 17	2 December 1130 (2 January 1129 if IV prt 17)	42/4 1/8 sacks of grain	[on] this *mryt* – which is the *mryt* of Khnum	P. Amiens vs. II, 5 (Janssen 2004, 47)
Year 1, IV *prt* 23	7 January 1129	12 sacks of grain are given to the ship of the captain Smen of the House of Amun	[on] the mryt of *mryt*	P. Baldwin vs. II, 8 (Janssen 2004, 44)
Year 1, IV *prt* 29	13 January 1129	3 sacks of grain are given to the ship of the captain Smen of the House of Amun	[on] the *mryt* of the Island of Meges	P. Baldwin vs. II, 11 (Janssen 2004, 45)
Year 1, IV *prt* 29	13 January 1129	3 sacks of grain	[on] the *mryt* of the Island [of Meges]	P. Amiens vs. II, 8 (Janssen 2004, 48)
Year 2, I *šmw* 7	23 January 1129	42/4 sacks of barley and 2/4 sack of emmer	[on the mr]yt of the village (*dmi*) of [Takes]bu	P. Amiens vs. II, 9 (Janssen 2004, 48)
Year 2, I *šmw* 12	28 January 1129	63/4 sacks of grain are given to the ship of the captain Smen of the House of Amun	[on] the *mryt* of this place – "this place" being "the *mryt* of Takesbu"	P. Baldwin vs. II, 13 (Janssen 2004, 45)
Year 2, I *šmw* 12	28 January 1129	6 sacks of grain	[on] the *mryt* of this place – "this place" being "the *mryt* of Takesbu"	P. Amiens vs. II, 10 (Janssen 2004, 48)

* The date is calculated based upon year 1 of Ramesses VIII reign as beginning in 1130 B.C.E. To cover the 20 years either side the reader needs to add 5 days to get to 1150 B.C.E. and conversely subtract 5 days to reach 1110 B.C.E.

** The entries have been ordered according to the correspondences between P. Amiens and P. Baldwin (Janssen 2004, 70).

the text is uncertain, but a "late Amarna Period" or early Nineteenth Dynasty date is most likely.[89] Using a date of 1300 B.C.E. just before the beginning of the Nineteenth Dynasty, we arrive at a Gregorian date of 25–29 October (± 10 days covers the period 1340–1260 B.C.E.). The river would have receded by approximately 2 m by this time, but would have still been as much as 5–7 m above its minimum. This text further fits with the argument that the *mryt*, being the upper part of the riverbank that was accessible during the higher river levels, together with islands, were the most suitable mooring locations during the periods of higher river levels.

A further ship's log (Papyrus Turin 2098 + 2100/306 verso) dated to the reign of Ramesses XI records the departure from Western Thebes arriving in Thebes the same day and then on

TABLE 5. Some dates and movements in "Ship's Log" P. Turin 2008 + 2016 (Janssen 1961).

Date of activity (Egyptian)	Date (Gregorian)* 1139 B.C.E.	Activity	Source
(Year 7, III *ȝḥt* 17)	(8 August)	Departure from Thebes	= rt. I, 1
[Year 7, I *prt*] 17	7 October	Departure from the *mryt* of Heliopolis	rt. I, 1
(Year 7, I *prt* 17)	(7 October)	[Mooring at] the *mryt* of Memphis	rt. I, 5
[Year 7, I *prt*] 18	8 October	[second day at] the *mryt* of Memphis	rt. I, 7
[Year 7, I *prt*] 24	14 October	.... the *mryt* of Memphis (eighth day at Memphis)	rt. I, 16
Year 7, I *prt* 25	15 October	the ninth day at the *mryt* of Memphis	rt. II, 2
Year 7, I *prt* [26]	16 October	the tenth day at the *mryt* of Memphis	rt. II, 19
Year 7, I *prt* 27	17 October	the eleventh day at the *mryt* of Memphis	rt. II, 21
Year 7, I *prt* 28	18 October	Departure from the *mryt* of Memphis	rt. II, 22
Year 7, I *prt* 28	18 October	Mooring (*mniw*) at the *mryt* of "The Pylons of the House of Osiris"	rt. II, 23
Year [7, I *prt*] 30	20 October	the third day at the *mryt* of "The Pylons of the House of Osiris"	rt. III, 2
Year 7, II *prt* 1	21 October	"the fourth day at the *mryt* of 'The Pylons of the House of Osiris.'" Departure from this place.	rt. III, 8
Year 7, II *prt* 1	21 October	Mooring at the *mryt* of "The New Land of the Pylons of the House of Osiris"	rt. III, 9
Year 7, II *prt* 2	22 October	"the fifth day in this place"**	rt. III, 11
Year 7, II *prt* 3	23 October	"the sixth day in this place"	rt. III, 13–14

* The Gregorian date is based upon year 7 of Ramesses VI's reign at 1139 B.C.E. (Hornung et al. 2006, 493).

** It seems from the text in P. Turin 2008 + 2016 rt, III,11–14 that the scribe recording the movements and activities of cargo boat regarded "The Pylons of the House of Osiris" and "The New Land of the Pylons of the House of Osiris" as one stay that is essentially the same place (Janssen 1961, 79). Why did the ship move on move from its initial mooring at the *mryt* to the *mryt* of the new land (*tȝ mȝwt*)? Was it in response to the falling river levels? The data from the 1892 Asyut records would suggest that this may be a time when the river level was falling rather slowly. However, given the range of the timing of the maximum it opens up the possibility that it was during the time when the river level was lowering far more rapidly (>10 cm/day in early November, see Table 2). Perhaps the *mryt* of the new land had been assessed after initial mooring and had dried out sufficiently with the falling river level to make it a more convenient mooring place.

the following day heading as far northwards as the area around modern day Asyut after six days of travelling. The remainder of the fragmentary text records the journey back towards Thebes possibly arriving on day 14 of the journey.[90] The text at least in part concerns the collection of grain.[91] Departure from Thebes is IV *ȝḥt* 1, which is suggested to be year 10 of Ramesses XI based upon palaeographical and internal evidence.[92] On day 3 they arrive at the *mryt* of the *nḥb* of Tjebu (*mryt pȝ nḥb n ṯbw*) where they most likely loaded grain from the chief of records. The *mryt* is subsequently recorded as their destination in days 4–9 with "mooring" (*mniw*) mentioned on days 10 and 14. Taking year 10 of Ramesses XI's reign as 1096 BCE,[93] the journey began north from Thebes on 12 August (Gregorian) with the 14th day of the Ship's Log occuring on 25 August.[94] Using the timing of the annual cycle from

127

1892 at Asyut (see Table 2), the journey would be starting around the time the river was rising most rapidly and would be >6 m above its minimum and still more than 2 m below its maximum at the time the boat passed through the area of modern day Asyut before returning southwards. This ship's log also appears to support the notion that the *mryt* may have referred to the upper part of the riverbank in these records, with of course the caveat that we cannot know the precise timing of the annual cycle for these individual years.

The dates of the activities on P. Amiens / Baldwin *verso* are significant when we compare them to the activities on the *recto* of the same papyrus. The *recto* of P. Amiens and P. Baldwin record the transport of grain by a flotilla of 21 boats, all engaged in a single expedition to locations in the Ninth and Tenth Upper Egyptian nomes.[95] The largest load of these boats is 1000¾ sacks of grain followed by another at 980 sacks with one vessel carrying only 300 sacks.[96] The text does not specify whether emmer or barley is meant by the term "grain."[97] However, the largest of the vessels would have a cargo of 40–50 tonnes depending on the ratio of emmer to barley in its cargo.[98] The draught of a vessels loaded with a cargo of 40–50 tonnes would have been only about 1.2–1.5 m, but possibly as little as 0.7 m.[99]

Although no dates are given on the *recto*, it seems clear from the quantities of grain that this is occurring some time after the harvest and before the land is inundated. "Gurob" Fragment L provides evidence of the timing of the collection of the harvest. Receipt of the harvest-tax occurs on day 18 of the first month of the Inundation (*ꜣḥt*) season, year 67, which clearly refers to the reign of Ramesses II.[100] This equates to 29th June 1213 B.C.E. (Gregorian). A month later a boat is loaded with what we have to assume to be grain on day 19 of the second month of the Inundation season, year 1, referring to the reign of Merenptah or 30th July 1213 B.C.E. (Gregorian). This is at a time when the river has most likely been at its minima in June and is starting to rise (see discussion in section: *The Regularity of the Annual Inundation*) so that many of the low-lying geomorphological features of the Nile valley could be exploited as landing places. By the end of July the river could be c. 3 m above its minima and starting to rise rapidly. Although there would still be sufficient time to collect grain before the flood maximum, the higher discharge would have affected upstream travel due to the increased velocity of the current.[101]

It is significant that when the Nile is considerably lower, far more terms for parts of the landscape, for example *mryt*, *pꜥt*-land, *nḥb*-land, *iw*, and *m tꜣ mꜣwt pꜣ iw*, are used to describe the mooring places for the cargo vessels loading the grain. *Pꜥt*-land, *nḥb*-land, *iw*, *iw n mꜣwt* and *mꜣwt* are all recorded in P. Wilbour dated to year 4 of Ramesses V. The land records in Text A were made from 7/8 July to 23/24 July (Gregorian),[102] a time when the river is rising, but perhaps only 2 m above its minima.

Pꜥt-*land*

Papyrus Amiens/Baldwin records 375 (200 + 175) sacks of grain[103] being loaded onto the ship of Neb'an at the *pꜥt*-land of He-nute (P. Amiens, rt. IV, 10–11) and 200 (100 + 100) sacks loaded onto the ship of captain (*ḥry wsḫ*) Amenhotep at the *pꜥt*-land of He-nute (P. Baldwin, rt. IV, 8–9).[104] Janssen[105] argues that *pꜥt*-land lay on the riverbank as "wet land". Erman and Grapow[106] translate it as "*Ufer*". Whilst Gardiner[107] believes that *pꜥt* may have come from the term *pꜣꜥy* found in the Pyramid Text, which in one passage means "flooded with water", meanings change over time and thus should be focussed on texts from the period in question. Gardiner[108] suggests that the two terms *idb* and *pꜥt* are to be seen as antithetical to each other. However, Katary[109] does not believe that such an antithesis can be seen in either the Onomasticon of Amenopě or in P. Wilbour and furthermore suggests that it could be identified with the arabic term *gezirah*.[110] Gasse[111] argues that it is certainly

Figure 12. View of the Nile c. 3 km downstream of Karnak
shows islands in the river and the point bar formation on the
inner (convex) bend of the riverbank (photo: A. Graham).

not part of the riverbank itself. From her analysis of P. Wilbour, Katary[112] argues that p^ct were relatively small plots of land measured in land-cubits as opposed to the larger aroura-measured land. Other parts of the text point to plots of land measured in cubits being used to grow horticultural crops such as fruits and vegetables and flax. Katary,[113] therefore, suggests that the p^ct-land may have been particularly suited to the cultivation of garden produce or flax, which require plenty of moisture and a temperate climate. Flax requires an abundance of phosphorus and potassium in the soil, which they would get if a plot was located on the river bank or lay alongside a major canal.[114] Furthermore, flax is suitable to grow in small plots of land as it is densely sown to prevent branching and gathered prior to maturity.[115] Flax (*Linum usitatissimum*) was sown in mid-November to December and takes about three months to mature.[116] The Twelfth Dynasty tomb of Djehutinakht at el-Bersheh (Tomb no. 1) shows the gathering of flax and dates this to the fourth month of the inundation, day 23,[117] which is equivalent to 26 March (Gregorian) in 1940 B.C.E. (16 March (Gregorian) in 1900 B.C.E.).[118] This would place the river levels within c. 1–2 m of its minima in Middle Egypt. Flax is therefore generally harvested before the emmer and barley crops, which are harvested as early as February and as late as May.[119] Given the understanding of p^ct-land as "wet land" and the time in the annual cycle when the fleet of boats was collecting grain, it would seem that these cultivable areas of land are low-lying. Such land would therefore only be used as a landing (and loading) place for a specific time outside the period of inundation.

P. Wilbour records 58 plots of p^ct-land in the total of 2157 plots recorded (2.7%).[120] Katary[121] argues that the term has a very limited use in the area of Middle Egypt documented

Figure 13. Close-up of the point bar formation showing possible pat-land. Note that this low-lying land is cultivated as soon as it becomes stable (photo: A. Graham).

in P. Wilbour appearing in only 11 measurement areas from a total of 185. Forty-five plots are found in only 4 measurement areas.[122] Antoine argues that they frequently occur near human occupation (temples, villages, other toponymns) and are "especially numerous near riversides."[123] *Pꜥt*-land was mostly said to be "at the front" (*ḫnty*).[124] As *pꜥt*-land was used as a mooring place for the loading of grain cargo, it has to be accessible to boats, it cannot therefore be located at the distal part of the floodplain as has been suggested.[125] If this were a consistent designation, we might consider that it refers to the "bar head" (the upstream part) of an island.[126] I would suggest that the term may well refer to a side bar that has become attached to the riverbank in the low water stage of the Nile or a lower exposed part of a point bar on the inner bend of the river (Figs. 12 and 13). Mooring here would enable the grain to be brought down from the high ground of the riverbank to be loaded on to the boats when the river levels were close to the minima.

Nḫb-*land*

P. Baldwin (rt. IV 13) records 60 sacks of grain given to the ship of the captain Amenhotep, son of Tjehennefer "in the fresh land of Tjanat" (*m pꜣ nḫb n tꜣnꜣt*)[127] and P. Baldwin (rt. IV, 11) records 50 sacks of grain being given by the cultivator Nakht-Nemtywy on "the riverbank of the fresh land of Tjunat" (*mryt n pꜣ nḫbw n twnꜣt*).[128]

Gardiner[129] argues that *nḫb* has the sense of "virgin soil" and therefore translates it as "fresh land" and is in contrast to *qꜣyt* ("ordinary" or "high land") and *tni* land ("tired land"; perhaps it has the sense of "older" land than *nḫb*). In the order of terms in the Onomasticon of Amenopĕ *nḫb* follows *iw* and precedes *tni* and *qꜣyt*.[130] If the order is significant, then I would argue we can place it in or adjacent to the river. However, in the Nauri decree it is listed first and followed by *iw* and then *qꜣyt*.[131] Assessment of yield from P. Wilbour suggests it is the most productive land at 10 sacks of grain per aroura compared to 7½ for *tni*-land and 5 sacks per aroura for *qꜣyt*-land.[132] Katary renders the term as "newly cultivated land."[133] However, given that it is known as a landing place

FIGURE 14. A lateral bar in the Nile showing possible *nḥb*-land.
This clearly shows the river bank (marked by white arrows)
with a low-lying side / lateral bar attached to the river bank.
This may be the *nḥb*-land and the modern-day landing place
(marked by yellow arrow) may be analagous to the *mryt n pꜣ
nḥbw n ṯwnꜣt* (photo: A. Graham, February 2005).

(in P. Amiens and Baldwin) which is connected to water that must be navigable by boat,
Katary's more recent suggestion that *nḥb*-land could well be restored basin-irrigated
qꜣyt-land does not fit with this criterion.[134] *Nḥb*-land is usually recorded in small plots
and in P. Wilbour has a high fiscal assessment.[135] Eyre suggests that it may be used for
high value crops such as fruit and vegetables and therefore may be "cultivable lower
land, or even *gezira* land."[136] I would suggest that the *nḥb*-land may refer to lateral bars
in the river, which are exposed during the falling river levels and become attached to
the riverbank (see Fig. 14). This land newly formed in the river would initally be highly
productive and during the period of grain collection would both prevent boats from
mooring at the actual riverbank and provide a good mooring location where grain from
the surrounding agricultural land could be loaded. In the case of the landing place *mryt
n pꜣ nḥbw* ("riverbank of the fresh" land) are recorded both in this text and Papyrus Turin
2098 + 2100/306 verso l. 5, and it may be a well-defined upper part of the bank of the
lateral bar that warrants the concept of *mryt*. The scene today (see Fig. 14) of the mooring
place on the lateral bar with the track running from it to the house on the riverbank
may well be a possible analogy for an ancient landscape with a track between the estate
owner's house and the mooring place.

Island (iw) and "New Land" (mꜣwt) Landing Places

Nine different Islands of Amun are mentioned in the recto of P. Amiens/Baldwin.[137] A further
seven islands are mentioned with reference to their direction from a named place in the

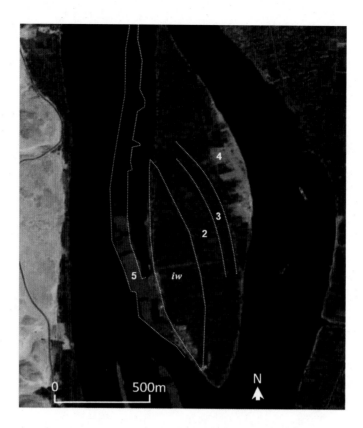

Figure 15. History of island enlargement through lateral accretion. This island is located in the stretch of the Nile Valley north of Kom Ombo (see Fig. 2.25) The initial island (marked iw) is c. 220 wide and 1080 m long with approximately 60 arouras of cultivable land. The first tranche of laterally accreted land (*tꜣ mꜣwt pꜣ iw*) (marked 2) amounts to about 40 arouras of additional land on the island in area. A further 20 arouras of new land (marked 3) is followed by 60–70 more arouras of new land (marked 4) producing an island c. 520 m wide and 1950 m long. The lateral bar (5) attached to the bar head (the upstream end of the initial island) is still forming (Image background © Google Earth).

floodplain, three to the west, two to the east, one to the south, and a further island found north of the *pꜥt*-land of a place called Pshay.[138] Two of these seven islands are referred to as "new" (*mꜣwt*), "the new island west of Khenemti" (*pꜣ iw n mꜣwt imntt ẖnmty*) and "the new island west of Inmut" (*pꜣ iw n mꜣwt mntt in-mwt*). I believe that Janssen[139] is mistaken in his belief that the numerous examples of *iw* found on the *recto* refer to pieces of land along the river and not necessarily within the river. Given our understanding of the geomorphology of the Nile and the range in size of islands in the river,[140] many could easily have supported cultivation of several hundred sacks of grain and seasonal if not permanent places to live (see Figs. 4–6).

Antoine states islands (*iw / iw n mꜣwt*) in P. Wilbour have a proper name referring to Amun in 16.7% of cases and suggests that those islands that are nameless may be recently formed.[141] He further suggests that they are near villages or other localities and that they may refer to "true islands" or pieces of land attached to a riverbank by one of its sides (see Figs. 13 and 14 and discussions above).

M3wt "new land" first occurs during the reign of Thutmose III and is argued to replace *ḥrw*.[142] Eyre argues that *m3wt* includes genuine islands in the Nile,[143] but that these are the exception. He does not believe that it is possible to see a direct equivalent between the term *m3wt* and the Arabic term *gezira*, a "quasi-technical term for riverside land between high and low water."[144] That said, Eyre[145] believes that it may be right to understand these "islands" generally as low land that emerged from the receding inundation typically along the river, seasonal watercourses or around swamps. He states that the Arabic term *gezira* does "focus on the 'island' as a category of land that stands above water."[146] Moreno García notes that in P. Harris I there is a clear indication that fields are created in the "new islands" (*jww m3wt*) and that such land was often granted to individuals or institutions.[147]

I suggest that the ancient Egyptians may be distinguishing between perennial islands (*iw*) and islands that become submerged during the inundation, which they may regard as *m3wt*. The *m3wt*-land is preceded by *šꜥy* in the Onomasticon of Amenope (P. Golenischeff I, 12 and P. Hood I, 11).[148] This may be recognising the formation processes of an island with the initial emergence of a sand flat or bar (*šꜥy*) from the river followed by its development such that it supports some cultivation (the so-called "new land" *m3wt*). This may or may not evolve into a higher and stable island (*iw*) over time.

T3 m3wt p3 iw

In P. Baldwin (rt. III, 7–8) the ship of the captain Iunakhtef is given a total of $587^1/_4$ sacks of grain ($101^3/_4 + 485^2/_4$) "in the new land of The Island" (*m t3 m3wt p3 iw*).[149] Janssen argues that in this case *p3 iw* is a toponym as *iw* is written with its phonetic complement.[150] It would thus appear that this place, which may still have been or was once an island has new land attached to it most likely formed by lateral accretion. "The new land of the island" (*t3 m3wt p3 iw*) may be simply what it says, in this case new land formed by lateral, downstream, or even upstream accretion to an island. Numerous examples of accretion can be seen in the Nile today (see Figs. 6 and 15).

Gardiner[151] raises a very important point concerning the difficulty of deciding whether an expression such as *t3 m3wt* is part of the composite place name or whether it is simply a descriptive term. In the case of "the New land of Samě" (P. Wilbour B 10, 5), Gardiner[152] argues that there is no certainty that the "new land" was actually new at the time of Ramesses V and it appears that this was an established local name. The process of an island becoming attached to the main floodplain is a common occurrence.

The evidence and discussion suggests that the grain collection is taking place within 4–5 weeks after the minima when the river is still within c. 2 m of its minima but not yet at its most rapid daily rate of rise when many of these low-lying geomorphological features remain exposed and can be used as landing places for the loading of grain. An important advantage of loading some of these large cargoes of up to 50 tonnes is that if the boat becomes grounded by the cargo it will soon be lifted clear by the rising river level.

SUMMARY/CONCLUSIONS

The paper has attempted to provide some suggestions for the physical attributes and proposes geomorphological features in the Egyptian Nile valley floodplain for lexical terms for landing places for boats in a number of instances for the loading of grain in the Ramesside Period.

This has been carried out by contextualising the use of these landing places within the annual cycle of the Nile, the timing of activities, and the geomorphological characteristics of the Nile and the floodplain it has fashioned. The suggestions for p^ct and $n\hbar b$ as point bar land and lateral bars respectively could be interchanged. Both appear attached to the main riverbank during the lower periods of discharge when these grain collections are taking place in P. Amiens and Baldwin and when the land register of P. Wilbour is being recorded. The timing of the use of the *mryt* as a landing place within these Ramesside texts points to it being associated with the upper part of the riverbank when the river was either rising towards its maximum or in the early period of its decline. Further statiscal analysis[153] and other analyses of these textual sources along with their geomorophological contextualisation will hopefully lead to further insights into the lexical terms referring to the various types of land that the Egyptians were using. There remains the issue of consistency of use of lexical terms, but further progress can surely be made.

The timing of these activities shows an intimate knowledge of and relationship by the Egyptians with the Nile. Despite the fact that the data that we have available has parameters in the timing of the maxima and minima of the annual cycle and the discharge volumes of the Nile have a considerable range, the agency of the river (see Schneider, this volume) in organising many aspects of the lives of the Egyptians can clearly be seen.

I agree with Thomas Schneider (this volume) and other colleagues present at the workshop in Vancouver that by applying the agency of the Nile and the environment to our rich datasets we can reposition Egyptology and construct new Egyptian pasts.

Acknowledgements

I commend Thomas Schneider's initiative in organising the workshop hosted by the University of British Columbia. I am also very grateful for his valuable comments on a draft of my paper. Andreas Dorn also provided invaluable comments and insights on a draft of this paper. Whilst their contributions have made for a much improved paper, any errors or misunderstandings remain mine alone. My sincerest thanks to Christine Johnson for her superb editing of my paper and her extreme patience.

Works Cited

Adamson, D.A., F. Gasse, F.A. Street, and M.A.J. Williams. 1980. "Late Quaternary History of the Nile" *Nature* 288: 50–55.

Antoine, J.-C. 2011. "The Wilbour Papyrus revisited: The Land and Its Localisation. An Analysis of the Places of Measurement." *Studien zur Altägyptischen Kultur* 40: 9–27.

———. 2017. "The Geographical and Administrative Landscape of Lower Middle Egypt in Text B of the Wilbour Papyrus." *Zeitschrift für ägyptische Sprache und Altertumskunde* 142(2): 104–119.

Ashmore, P. 1982. Discussion in "Channel Bars in Gravel-Bed Rivers," by M. Church and D. Jones. In *Gravel-Bed Rivers: Fluvial Processes, Engineering and Management*, edited by R.D. Hey, J.C. Bathurst, and C.R. Thorne, 291–338. Proceedings of the International Workshop on Engineering Problems in the Management of Gravel-Bed Rivers held at Gregynog, Newtown, UK, between 23 and 27 June 1980. Chichester and New York: John Wiley & Sons.

Attia, M.I. 1954. *Deposits in the Nile Valley and the Delta.* Cairo: Geological Survey of Egypt, Government Press.

Baer, K. 1962. "The Low Price of Land in Ancient Egypt." *Journal of the American Research Center in Egypt* 1: 25–45.

Bonneau, D. 1964. *La crue du Nil, divinité égyptienne, à travers mille ans d'histoire (332 av.-641 ap. J.-C.) d'après les auteurs grecs et latins, et les documents des époques ptolémaïque, romaine et byzantine.* Études et commentaires. Paris: Librairie C. Klincksieck.

Bridge, J.S. 2003. *Rivers and Floodplains: Forms, Processes and Sedimentary Record.* Oxford: Blackwell Publishing.

Bridge, J.S., N.D. Smith, F. Trent, S.L. Gabel, and P. Bernstein. 1986. "Sedimentology and Morphology of a Low-Sinuosity River: Calamus River, Nebraska Sand Hills." *Sedimentology* 33(6): 851–870.

Brown, A.G. 1997. *Alluvial Geoarchaeology: Floodplain Archaeology and Environmental Change.* Cambridge: Cambridge University Press

Bunbury, J. M. 2019. *The Nile and Ancient Egypt: Changing Land- and Waterscapes, from the Neolithic to the Roman Era.* Cambridge: Cambridge University Press.

Bunbury, J.M., and D.G. Jeffreys. 2011. "Real and Literary Landscapes in Ancient Egypt." *Cambridge Archaeological Journal* 21(1): 65–75.

Butzer, K.W. 1976. *Early Hydraulic Civilization in Egypt: A Study in Cultural Ecology.* Chicago and London: University of Chicago Press.

———. 1982. "Nil." In *Lexikon der Ägyptologie, IV. Megiddo-Pyramiden,* edited by W. Helck and E. Otto, 480–483. Wiesbaden: Otto Harrassowitz.

———. 1999. "Nile, Modern Hydrology." In *Encyclopedia of the Archaeology of Ancient Egypt,* edited by K.A. Bard and S.B. Shubert, 570–571. London: Routledge.

———. 2001. "Nile." In *The Oxford Encyclopedia of Ancient Egypt,* edited by D.B. Redford, 543–551. Oxford: Oxford University Press.

Carey, W.C. 1969. "Formation of Flood Plain Lands." *Journal of the Hydraulics Division, Proceedings of the American Society of Civil Engineers* 95: 981–994.

Church, M., and D. Jones. 1982. "Channel Bars in Gravel-Bed Rivers." In *Gravel-Bed Rivers: Fluvial Processes, Engineering and Management,* edited by R.D. Hey, J.C. Bathurst, and C.R. Thorne, 291–338. Proceedings of the International Workshop on Engineering Problems in the Management of Gravel-Bed Rivers held at Gregynog, Newtown, UK, between 23 and 27 June 1980. Chichester and New York: John Wiley & Sons.

Clagett, M. 1995. *Ancient Egyptian Science: A Source Book.* Vol. 2, *Calendars, Clocks and Astronomy.* Memoirs of the American Philosophical Society 214. Philadelphia: American Philosophical Society.

Collinson, J.D. 1970. "Bedforms of the Tana River, Norway." *Geografiska Annaler* 1: 31–56.

———. 1986. "Alluvial Sediments." In *Sedimentary Environments and Facies,* 2nd ed., edited by H.G. Reading, 20–62. Oxford: Blackwell Scientific Publications.

———. 1996. "Alluvial Sediments." In *Sedimentary Environments: Processes, Facies and Stratigraphy,* 3rd ed., edited by H.G. Reading, 37–82. Oxford: Blackwell Science.

Condon, V. 1984. "Two Account Papyri of the Late Eighteenth Dynasty (Brooklyn 35.1453 A and B)." *Revue d'égyptologie* 35: 57–82.

———. 1986. "'Two Variant Accounts?' by Janssen? (*VA* I, 3, 109–112)." *Varia Aegyptiaca* 2: 23–29.

Demarée, R.J. 2018. "A Late Ramesside Ship's Log (Papyrus Turin 2098 + 2100/306 verso)." In *Outside the Box: Selected Papers from the Conference "Deir el-Medina and the Theban Necropolis in Contact" Liège, 27–29 October 2014,* edited by A. Dorn and S. Polis, 131–140. Aegyptiaca Leodiensia 11. Liège: Presses Universitaires de Liège.

Dorn, A. 2011. "The Provenance and Context of the Accession-Ostracon of Ramesses VI: O. KV 18/6.924: Another Fragment Matching O. BM EA 50722 + O. Cairo CG 25726 (= *KRI* VI, 364)." In *Ramesside Studies in Honour of K.A. Kitchen*, edited by M. Collier and S. Snape, 159–168. Bolton: Rutherford.

Erman, A., and H. Grapow. 1926. *Wörterbuch der aegyptischen Sprache im Auftrage der Deutschen Akademien. Erster Band.* Leipzig: J.C. Hinrichs'sche Buchhandlung.

Eyre, C.J. 1994. "The Water Regime for Orchards and Plantations in Pharaonic Egypt." *Journal of Egyptian Archaeology* 80: 57–80.

Ezzamel, M. 2012. *Accounting and order.* Routledge Studies in Accounting 12. New York and London: Routledge.

Fourtau, R. 1915. "Contribution à l'étude des dépôts nilotiques." *Mémoires présentés à l'Institut égyptien* 8: 57–94.

Gardiner, A.H. 1941. "Ramesside texts relating to the taxation and transport of corn." *Journal of Egyptian Archaeology* 27: 19–73.

———. 1947. *Ancient Egyptian Onomastica. Text, Volume I.* Oxford: Oxford University Press.

———. 1948a. *Ramesside Administrative Documents.* London: Oxford University Press, published on behalf of the Griffith Institute, Ashmolean Museum, Oxford.

———. 1948b. *The Wilbour Papyrus.* Vol. 2, *Commentary.* London: Published for the Brooklyn Museum at the Oxford University Press.

Gasse, A. 1988. *Données nouvelles administratives et sacerdotales sur l'organisation du domaine d'Amon, XXe–XXIe dynasties: à la lumière des papyrus Prachov, Reinhardt et Grundbuch (avec édition princeps des papyrus Louvre AF 6345 et 6346-7).* Bibliothèque d'étude, 104. Le Caire: Institut français d'archéologie orientale.

Graham, A. 2010. "Islands in the Nile: A Geoarchaeological Approach to Settlement Locations in the Egyptian Nile Valley and the Case of Karnak." In *Cities and Urbanism in Ancient Egypt. Papers from a workshop in November 2006 at the Austrian Academy of Sciences,* edited by M. Bietak, E. Czerny, and I. Forstner-Müller, 125–143. Denkschriften der Gesamtakadamie LX. Untersuchungen der Zweigstelle Kairo des Österreichischen Archäologischen Instituts XXXV. Vienna: Verlag der Österreichischen Akademie der Wissenschaften.

———. 2020. "The Interconnected Theban Landscape and Waterscape of Amūn–Rēa." In *Environment & Religion in Ancient & Coptic Egypt: Sensing the Cosmos through the Eyes of the Divine. Proceedings of the 1st Egyptological Conference, Organized by the Hellenic Institute of Egyptology & the Calligraphy Centre of the Bibliotheca Alexandrina at the People's University of Athens (Athens 1–3 February 2017),* edited by A. Maravelia and N. Guilhou, 155–167. Oxford: Archaeopress.

Grandet, P. 2001. "Weights and Measures." In *The Oxford Encyclopedia of Ancient Egypt,* edited by D.B. Redford, 493–495. Oxford: Oxford University Press.

Griffith, F.L. 1927. "The Abydos Decree of Seti I at Nauri." *Journal of Egyptian Archaeology* 13: 193–208.

Griffith, F.L., P.E. Newberry, and G.W. Fraser. 1894. *El Bersheh.* Pt. 2. Archaeological Survey of Egypt Memoir 4. London: Egypt Exploration Fund.

Hillier, J.K., J.M. Bunbury, and A. Graham. 2007. "Monuments on a Migrating Nile." *Journal of Archaeological Science* 34(7): 1011–1015.

Hooke, J.M. 1986. "The Significance of Mid-Channel Bars in an Active Meandering River." *Sedimentology* 33(6): 839–850.

Hornung, E., R. Krauss, and D.A. Warburton. 2006. *Ancient Egyptian Chronology.* Pt 1, *The Near and Middle East.* Handbook of Oriental Studies 83. Leiden: Brill.

Hurst, H.E. 1952. *The Nile: A General account of the River and the Utilization of Its Waters.*

London: Constable.

Ibrahim, E.E.E. 1968. *Aspects of the Geomorphological Evolution of the Nile Valley in the Qena Bend Area*. Newcastle upon Tyne: University of Newcastle upon Tyne.

Janssen, J.J. 1961. *Two Ancient Egyptian Ships' Logs: Papyrus Leiden I 350 Verso, and Papyrus Turin 2008 + 2016*. Oudheidkundige Mededelingen uit het Rijksmuseum van Oudheden te Leiden: Supplement op Nieuwe Reeks 52. Leiden: E.J. Brill.

———. 1985. "Two Variant Accounts?" *Varia Aegyptiaca* 1: 109–112.

———. 1988. "Prices and Wages in Ancient Egypt." *Altorientalische Forschungen* 15: 10–23.

———. 2004. *Grain Transport in the Ramesside Period: Papyrus Baldwin (BM EA 10061) and Papyrus Amiens*. Hieratic Papyri in the British Museum 8. London: British Museum Press.

Jeffreys, D.G. 2010. *The Survey of Memphis*. Vol. 7, *The Hekekyan Papers and other sources for the Survey of Memphis*. Egypt Exploration Society Excavation Memoir 95. London: Egypt Exploration Society.

Jeffreys, D.G., and J.M. Bunbury. 2005. "Memphis, 2004." *Journal of Egyptian Archaeology* 91: 8–12.

Katary, S.L.D. 1989. *Land Tenure in the Ramesside Period*. Studies in Egyptology. London: Kegan Paul International.

———. 2014. "The Wilbour Papyrus and the Management of the Nile Riverbanks in Ramesside Egypt: Preliminary Analysis of the Types of Cultivated Land." In *Riparia, un patrimoine culturel: la gestion intégrée des bords de l'eau*, edited by E. Hermon and A Watelet, 199–215. Proceedings of the Sudbury workshop, April 12–14, 2012 / actes de l'atelier Savoirs et pratiques de gestion intégrée des bords de l'eau—Riparia, Sudbury, 12–14 avril 2012. BAR international series 2587. Oxford: Archaeopress.

Kellerhals, R., M. Church, and D.I. Bray. 1976. "Classification and Analysis of River Processes." *Journal of the Hydraulics Division: Proceedings of the American Society of Civil Engineers* 102: 813–829.

Kees, H. 1961. *Ancient Egypt: A Cultural Topography*, edited by T.G.H. James, translated by I.F.D. Morrow. London: Faber and Faber.

Kiss, T., and G. Sipos. 2007. "Braid-Scale Channel Geometry Changes in a Sand-Bedded River: Significance of Low Stages." *Geomorphology* 84(3–4): 209–221.

Lauffray, J. 1971. "Abords occidentaux du premier pylône de Karnak: Le dromos, la tribune et les aménagements portuaires." *Kêmi* 21: 77–144.

Leopold, L.B., and M.G. Wolman. 1957. *River Channel Patterns: Braided, Meandering and Straight*. Physiographic and Hydraulic Studies of rivers. Geological Survey Professional Paper, 282-B. Washington, D.C.: U.S. Government Printing Office.

Lewin, J., and P.J. Ashworth. 2014. "Defining Large River Channel Patterns: Alluvial Exchange and Plurality." *Geomorphology* 215: 83–98.

Lyons, H.G. 1906. *The Physiography of the River Nile and Its Basin*. Survey Department, Egypt. Cairo: National Printing Department.

Macklin, M.G., and J. Lewin. 2015. "The Rivers of Civilization." *Quaternary Science Reviews* 114: 228–244.

Macklin, M.G., W.H.J. Toonen, J.C. Woodward, M.A.J. Williams, C. Flaux, N. Marriner, K. Nicoll, G. Verstraeten, N. Spencer, and D. Welsby. 2015. "A New Model of River Dynamics, Hydroclimatic Change and Human Settlement in the Nile Valley Derived from Meta-Analysis of the Holocene Fluvial Archive." *Quaternary Science Reviews* 130: 109–123.

Moreno García, J.C. 2013. "Les îles 'nouvelles' et le milieu rural en Égypte pharaonique." *Égypte, Afrique & Orient* 70: 27–36.

Murray, M.A. 2000. "Cereal Production and Processing." In *Ancient Egyptian Materials and Technology*, edited by P.T. Nicholson and I. Shaw, 505–536. Cambridge: Cambridge

University Press.

Nanson, G.C. 1980. "Point Bar and Floodplain Formation of the Meandering Beatton River, Northeastern British Columbia, Canada." *Sedimentology* 27: 3–29.

Popper, W. 1951. *The Cairo Nilometer: Studies in Ibn Taghrî's Chronicles of Egypt I*. University of California Publications in Semitic Philology 12. Los Angeles: University of California.

Said, R. 1993. *The River Nile: Geology, Hydrology and Utilization*. Oxford: Pergamon Press.

Schumm, S.A. 2007. "Rivers and Humans—Unintended Consequences." In *Large Rivers: Geomorphology and Management*, edited by a. Gupta, 517–533. Chichester: John Wiley and Sons.

Scorer, R.S. 1997. *Dynamics of Meteorology and Climate*. Wiley-Praxis Series in Atmospheric Physics. Chichester: John Wiley & Sons.

Seidlmayer, S.J. 2001. *Historische und moderne Nilstände: Untersuchungen zu den Pegelablesungen des Nils von der Frühzeit bis in die Gegenwart*. Berlin: Achet Verlag.

Smith, N.D. 1978. "Some Comments on the Terminology for Bars in Shallow Rivers." In *Fluvial Sedimentology*, edited by A.D. Miall, 85–88. Memoir - Canadian Society of Petroleum Geologists 5. Calgary, Alta.: Canadian Society of Petroleum Geologists.

Toonen, W.H.J., A. Graham, B.T. Pennington, K.D. Strutt, M.A. Hunter, V.L. Emery, A. Masson-Berghoff, and D.S. Barker. 2018. "Holocene Fluvial History of the Nile's West Bank at Ancient Thebes (Luxor, Egypt) and Its Relation with Cultural Dynamics and Basin-wide Hydroclimatic Variability." *Geoarchaeology* 33(3): 273–290.

Traunecker, C. 1972. "Les rites de l'eau à Karnak d'après les textes de la rampe de Taharqa." *Bulletin de l'Institut français d'archéologie orientale* 72: 195–236.

Vleeming, S.P. 1993. *Papyrus Reinhardt: An Egyptian Land List from the Tenth Century B.C.* Hieratische Papyri aus den Staatlichen Museen zu Berlin-Preussischer Kulturbesitz 2. Berlin: Akademie Verlag.

Vogelsang-Eastwood, G. 2000. "Textiles." In *Ancient Egyptian Materials and Technology*, edited by P.T. Nicholson and I. Shaw, 268–298. Cambridge: Cambridge University Press.

von Beckerath, J. 1997. *Chronologie des pharaonischen Ägypten: Die Zeitbestimmung der ägyptischen Geschichte von der Vorzeit bis 332 v. Chr.* Münchner Ägyptologische Studien 46. Mainz am Rhein: Philipp von Zabern.

Waters, M.R. 1992. *Principles of Geoarchaeology: A North American Perspective*. Tucson and London: University of Arizona Press.

Wicker, U. 1997. "Flax and Egypt." *Discussions in Egyptology* 39: 95–116.

Willcocks, W. 1889. *Egyptian Irrigation*. London: E. & F.N. Spon.

———. 1904. *The Nile in 1904*. London: E. & F.N. Spon.

Willcocks, W., and J.I. Craig. 1913. *Egyptian Irrigation*. 3rd ed. London: E. & F.N. Spon.

Williams, M., M. Talbot, P. Aharon, Y.A. Salaam, F. Williams, and K.I. Brendeland. 2006. "Abrupt Return of the Summer Monsoon 15,000 Years Ago: New Supporting Evidence from the Lower White Nile Valley and Lake Albert." *Quaternary Science Reviews* 25(19–20): 2651–2665.

Woodward, J.C., M.G. Macklin, M.D. Krom, and M.A.J. Williams. 2007. "The Nile: Evolution, Quaternary River Environments and Material fFuxes." In *Large Rivers: Geomorphology and Management*, edited by A. Gupta, 261–292. Chichester: John Wiley and Sons.

Notes

[1] Bunbury and Jeffreys 2011, 69–71.

[2]   For example Moreno García 2013, this volume; Vleeming 1993.

[3]   Hurst 1952, 243–244, 250.

[4]   Hurst 1952, 243–244, 250; Said 1993, 12, 15–16, 18–20; Williams et al. 2006, 2653.

[5]   Hurst 1952, 241–242.

[6]   Woodward et al. 2007, 277.

[7]   Williams et al. 2006, 2653.

[8]   Hurst 1952, 242; Adamson et al. 1980, 50 Table 1; Butzer 1982, 481; 1999, 570; 2001, 543; Said 1993, 55; Williams et al. 2006, 2653.

[9]   Jeffreys 2010, 109.

[10]   10th July was the beginning of Hekekyan's observations. The minima would most likely have been before then, but it is not recorded (Jeffreys 2010, 109).

[11]   Willcocks and Craig 1913, 150–187. Table 2 table is an alternate version to the table presented in Graham 2020, which uses the divisor of five for all readings to calculate mean daily rises and falls in the river levels (not given by Willocks and Craig 1913). This table accords with Table 1 in the present paper using a divisor of four for the last readings of February and a divisor of six for those months with 31 days.

[12]   Willcocks and Craig (1913, 172–175, Tables 86 and 87) give five-day mean levels for years 1892, 1907, 1908, and 1912, the mean for 1873–1910 for the Rodah gauge, and for 1892, 1907, 1908, 1912 for the Rosetta Branch barrage. See Willcocks and Craig (1913, 632–655) for discussion of the Delta barrages.

[13]   Willcocks and Craig 1913, 168–169, Table 84.

[14]   The readings are only given on the first of the month for January to April, less regularly but more frequently during May and early June to record the minimum level of the river in bold, and the same during September to record the maximum. In July, August, October, and November they give readings on the first, tenth, and twentieth of each month, and the first, fifteenth, and thirty-first of December (Willcocks and Craig 1913, 179, Table 90).

[15]   Willcocks and Craig 1913, 718.

[16]   Willcocks and Craig 1913, 151.

[17]   Note the discrepancy presented in Table 3, where Willcocks and Craig (1913, 179, Table 90) state that the minimum occurred at 84.40 m on 1 June 1892.

[18]   There is an inconsistency in the recording of the minimum in the individual day measurements as the five-day mean cannot be lower than the lowest level (Willcocks and Craig 1913, Tables 84 and 90). This suggests that the individual measurement on 1 June is not the minimum.

[19]   The minimum occurs between 21–25 May with a mean of 85.08 m a.s.l. during the 1873–1902 mean and the maximum mean is 92.82 m occurring between 1–5 September (Willcocks and Craig 1913, 168–169, Table 84).

[20]   The mean maximum for the five years is affected considerably by a relatively low maximum in 1877 of 91.27 m (Willcocks and Craig 1913, Table 90). The mean for the other four years including 1892 is 93.93 m, which is within 0.15m of the 1892 maximum. See Table 3 of this paper.

[21]   For the levels see Lauffray 1971, Fig. 6 bis; Traunecker 1972, 198 n. 4.

[22]   A reduction of 2.93 m from 20 September to the five-day mean of 1–5 November.

[23]   From 16–20 November until 26–31 December the total fall in the river is 1.44 m in 1892 and 1.37 m in the 30-year period from 1873–1902.

[24]   Willcocks and Craig 1913, Table 85. See also Graham 2020, Table 2.

[25]   Willcocks and Craig 1913, 435.

[26]   Willcocks and Craig 1913, 638.

27 The Asyut barrage was not designed until 1895 with driving in of the sheet piling beginning in 1899. The barrage was completed in 1901/2 and first used in 1903 (Willcocks and Craig 1913, 151, 657–662).

28 A 1.26 m rise in the river level from 51.97 m to 53.23 m from 26–31 August to 26–30 September.

29 The maximum is taken at 20 September in Aswan and between 26–30 September at Asyut.

30 Said 1993, 96.

31 Bonneau 1964, 23–24; Said 1993, 96–97.

32 Said 1993, 96.

33 Said 1993, 97.

34 Said 1993, 96–97.

35 Said 1993, 97.

36 Said 1993, 97.

37 The maximum river level in the Fustat area of Cairo therefore occurred within a range of c. 20–25 days in 180 out of 207 years of records.

38 Said 1993, 97.

39 Collinson 1996, 42.

40 Fourtau 1915; Attia 1954; Graham 2010, 126.

41 Attia 1954, 310.

42 Schumm 2007, 521.

43 Brown 1997, 63; Graham 2010, 125.

44 Collinson 1996, 45.

45 Smith 1978; Collinson 1986, 27; Bridge 2003, 141, 145.

46 Ashmore 1982, 327; Church and Jones 1982, 302–303; Hooke 1986, 842.

47 Leopold and Wolman 1957, 44; Carey 1969, 986; Collinson, 1986, 27; 1996, 47; Hooke 1986, 845; Kiss and Sipos 2007, 219.

48 Bridge et al. 1986, 856.

49 Bridge et al. 1986, 856–857.

50 Jeffreys and Bunbury 2005, 10–11.

51 Leopold and Wolman 1957, 60; Bridge 2003, 154–155, 171–172, Fig. 5.9; Graham 2010, 125.

52 Popper 1951; Said 1993; Seidlmayer 2001; Macklin et al. 2015.

53 Schumm 2007, 521.

54 Schumm 2007, 521.

55 Kellerhals et al. 1976, 822; Bridge 2003, 147.

56 Brown 1997, 63, 67.

57 Lewin and Ashworth 2014, 84.

58 I have previously suggested that the Tana River in Norway (Graham 2010, 126), with its numerous sand bars and sand flats, provides a useful visual analogy for the Nile during its lowest flow stages (see Collinson 1970, Figs. 3, 5, 7; 1986, 25 Fig. 3.7). I have discussed elsewhere two distinctive island morphologies in the Egyptian Nile valley: bars with limbs or "horns" and those emergent and stable islands with bodies of water within them (see Graham, 2010, 128–130, Figs. 4–9).

59 Collinson 1986, 36; Waters 1992, 130.

60 Scorer 1997, 83.

61 Scorer 1997, 83.

62 Collinson 1986, 36; Waters 1992, 130.

63 Collinson 1986, 36; Waters 1992, 130–131; Scorer 1997, 83, 85 Fig. 3.4.vii.

64   Collinson 1986, 36; Waters 1992, 131.

65   The augering was conducted by Judith Bunbury and this author as part of the Karnak Land- and Waterscapes Survey in 2005; see Bunbury 2019, 153–154, Fig. A.4.

66   Toonen et al. 2018, 282, 286.

67   Lyons 1906, 312; Ibrahim 1968, 61; Butzer 1976, 16; Hillier et al. 2007.

68   Lyons 1906, 312; Butzer 1976, 15–16; 2001, 546.

69   Butzer 1976, 15–16, 18; Toonen et al. 2018, 282.

70   Toonen et al. 2018, 282.

71   Macklin and Lewin 2015, 235.

72   Nanson 1980, 23.

73   Nanson 1980, 24.

74   Clagett 1995, 28.

75   von Beckerath 1997, Tables B and C.

76   Hornung et al. 2006, 490–495.

77   Gardiner 1941; Janssen 2004.

78   Janssen (2004, 4–5) discusses the possible dating of the papyrus with no pharaoh mentioned. He argues that some can be ruled out—Ramesses III, IV and VI—as their accession dates are clearly attested (see Dorn 2011). The reigns of Ramesses V, VII and VIII remain possible although the proposed accession dates of Ramesses V and VII may rule them out, leaving Ramesses VIII. Janssen (2004, 5) is not able to solve the issue. I have based my translation of dates upon year 1 of Ramesses VIII reign as beginning in 1130 B.C.E. (Hornung et al. 2006, 493).

79   This is not, nor is it meant to be, a comprehensive assessment of all known references to *mryt*, which include discussions of 'the market place', but is restricted to Ramesside texts and specifically ship's logs.

80   Janssen 2004, 8. Khnum (al-Ashmunein / Hermopolis) is given in three columns of the verso (see Table 4 this paper), which is 85–90 km downstream of Asyut.

81   See the discussion of the Asyut 1892 river levels and we need to take into account the range in dates of the maximum and minimum.

82   Janssen (1961, 55–57) based his dating upon the names of the important persons mentioned in the text and the reference to a Ramesside ruler who obviously reigned for 7 or more years.

83   The ship's log records the delivery, distribution and exchange of a wide range of goods including fish, rushes, salt, cloth, and sesame oil, as well as information about the weather and the crew of the vessel including the two search parties sent out to locate the absent party headed by the scribe Pra'emhab (Ezzamel 2012, 183, 185, 187).

84   Janssen 1961, 67, rt. I, 1.

85   Hornung et al. (2006, 493) propose 1145 B.C.E. as the year of accession for Ramesses VI.

86   Hornung et al. (2006, 493) give c. 1106 B.C.E. as the year of accession for Ramesses XI.

87   See "View of the cliffs of Sheikh Abd el-Qurna from across the river, with a dahabeeyah in the foreground," which shows just the very uppermost part of the levee on the west bank of the Nile, photographed c.1890 and held in the Griffith Institute archives, University of Oxford http://www.griffith.ox.ac.uk/gri/mirage/enlargements/gi00225. html. See Graham 2020, Fig. 1.

88   Condon 1984, 58, 63–64, 71. Condon (1984, 58) interprets P. Brooklyn 35.1453 A as possibly relating to the delivery by boat of rations to temple or "harim" workers. However, Janssen (1985, 110; 1988, 20) argues that the word *iw* should be translated as "entered" and not "delivery" and thus interprets the text (A and B) as recording the trade that occurred between a boat and women at various places along the riverbank

over a period of five days with the verso of the text recording the delivery by the women of the exchanged items to the temple institutions.

89   Condon 1984, 57; 1986, 29; Janssen 1985, 112.
90   Demarée 2018, 135–139. The day 14 of the ship's log is the last one currently known to us.
91   Demarée 2018, 137–138; v. ll. 6–7.
92   Demarée 2018, 131–132, 137. Whilst year 9 is recorded on the recto, the year is lost from the published papyrus fragments on the verso. Demarée 2018 proposes year 10.
93   Hornung et al. 2006, 493.
94   von Beckerath 1997, 195–196, Tables B and C.
95   Gardiner 1941, 37–41; Janssen 2004, 8, 18 ns. 20, 31. The Tenth Upper Egyptian Nome is in the region of Qaw el-Kebir, c. 45 km upstream of modern day Asyut with the Ninth U.E. nome being further upstream in the area of Akhmim, a further 40–45 km upstream.
96   Janssen 2004, 8, 28 Table 1.
97   Janssen 2004, 12 n. 4.
98   From the beginning of the New Kingdom a sack ($\underline{h}^{3}r$) of grain was equivalent to 16 $\underline{h}q^{3}t$ or 76.88 litres (Grandet 2001, 493). Baer (1962, 42) argues a khar of emmer weighed 39.3 kg (86.4 lbs) and one of barley about 51.8 kg (103.7 lbs). I use 40 kg per sack for emmer and 50 kg per sack for barley to estimate the loads and thus the sizes of the Ramesside grain carriers.
99   The estimate of a 1.2–1.5 m draught is based upon the dimensions and tonnage of 19th century C.E. cargo boats given in Willcocks (1889, Table XXX) with the weight of an ardeb taken to be 136 kg as given by Willcocks. Willcocks' (1889, Table XXX) records of the dimensions and tonnage of 19th century C.E. dahabiya cargo boats show that a vessel carrying c. 36 tonnes has a draught of 0.60 m and a larger vessel carrying almost 80 tonnes was only drawing 0.70 m of water so it remains a possibility that the Ramesside vessels could have had a draught as low as 0.7 m.
100   Gardiner 1948a, xii, 30 l. 2,1; 1948b, 206.
101   Willcocks (1904, 16, 121) measured the Nile velocity as 1.75 m/s (6.3 km/hr) during the inundation and 0·85 m/s (3.06 km/hr) during low supply.
102   Katary 2014, 200.
103   The cargo would have been c.15–19 tonnes according to the ratio of emmer to barley.
104   Janssen 2004, 22–23, 100–101.
105   Janssen 2004, 33.
106   Erman and Grapow 1926, WB I, 502, 2.
107   Gardiner 1947, 12*–13*; 1948b, 27 n.1.
108   Gardiner 1948b, 26.
109   Katary 1989, 73.
110   Katary 2014, 207.
111   Gasse 1988, 25.
112   Katary 1989, 257.
113   Katary 1989, 257.
114   Katary 1989, 257.
115   Katary 1989, 258.
116   Wicker 1997, 103; Vogelsang-Eastwood 2000, 270.
117   Griffith et al. 1894, 22.
118   Kees, 1961, 77 n. 2; von Beckerath 1997, 198–199.
119   Murray 2000, 520.
120   Katary 1989, 255. Note that Antoine (2011, 14) states that 2.9% of plots are recorded as

pˁt-land in P. Wilbour.
[121] Katary 1989, 256.
[122] Katary 1989, 256.
[123] Antoine 2011, 14.
[124] Antoine 2011, 15.
[125] Katary (2014, Fig. 4) presents a sketch view of the Nile valley with suggested types of land on the floodplain and places *pˁt*-land in the distal parts of the floodplain without an understanding of the land from P. Amiens/Balwin.
[126] *ḫnty* was proposed to refer to "the southern part" (Gardiner 1948b, 26; Antoine 2011, 15). However, the use of a cardinal direction given the changing direction of the river is misleading and should be understood to be 'upstream'.
[127] Janssen 2004, 24, 102.
[128] Janssen 2004, 24, 101.
[129] Gardiner 1948b, 28 and n. 10.
[130] Gardiner 1947, 10*.
[131] Griffith 1927, 199, pl. 40 ll. 24–25.
[132] Katary 1989, 21, 214.
[133] Katary 1989, 21.
[134] Katary (2014, 207) proposes that "*Nḥb*-land could well be basin-irrigated *qꜣyt*-land that had been restored after cultivation with the growing of grasses of leguminous crops and was therefore 'fresh land' when returned to cultivation, its condition being the reason for its double value."
[135] Gardiner 1948b, 29; Eyre 1994, 70.
[136] Eyre 1994, 70.
[137] Janssen 2004, 32 Table III, 80.
[138] Janssen 2004, 32 Table III, 80.
[139] Janssen 2004, 33.
[140] Graham 2010.
[141] Antoine 2011, 13–14.
[142] Janssen 1961, 79.
[143] Eyre 1994, 75.
[144] Eyre 1994, 75.
[145] Eyre 1994, 75–76.
[146] Eyre 1994, 76.
[147] Moreno García 2013, 30.
[148] Gardiner 1947, 12*–13*.
[149] Janssen 2004, 21.
[150] Janssen 2004, 21 n. 20. It is the only place in the text where it is written with its phonetic complement.
[151] Gardiner 1948b, 29.
[152] Gardiner 1948b, 29.
[153] Such as Katary 1989; Antoine 2011, 2017.

Chapter Seven

Landscape, Settlement, and Populations: Production and Regional Dynamics in Middle Egypt in the *Longue Durée*

Juan Carlos Moreno García

One of the most enduring myths about ancient Egypt was elaborated, in fact, in Antiquity. Herodotus claimed that Egypt was a gift of the Nile and, like many other writers of the Greco-Roman period, the Greek historian was astonished about the agricultural abundance of the land of the Pharaohs. Not by chance, Egypt became one of the most crucial breadbaskets of the Roman empire, and the annual fleets loaded down with grain from the Nile Valley were expected with anxiety by the inhabitants of Rome. Later on, tourists, travelers, and scholars visiting the Nile Valley in the 19th and early 20th century CE were amazed by the prosperous agricultural conditions they found, the combined result of the ingenuity and hard work of the *fellahs* and of the hydraulic achievements of engineers and central administrators, able to domesticate the flows of water and to put the Nile to work for the prosperity of all. However, a pernicious consequence of this myth is that historians have frequently regarded ancient Egypt as an undifferentiated landscape, a homogeneous territory in which arable fields followed one another uninterruptedly from the Delta to Aswan (Fig. 1). Another consequence is that agricultural abundance was conceived as a somewhat "natural" outcome of a rich and fertile land blessed by the annual flood of the Nile, not as the arduous outcome of a continuous process of transformation and shaping of the landscape over the centuries. This process involved different productive strategies, agricultural techniques, forms of labor organization and political choices, in which different, competing productive and occupational strategies coexisted and left their mark on the land and on the habitat depending on a fluctuating balance between different factors: cerealiculture versus herding; sedentary versus mobile lifestyles; taxable and market-oriented agricultural productions versus a diversified mix of activities (agriculture, pastoralism, gathering and fishing) aiming basically for subsistence. That such balance was prone to periodic changes is a fact evident from the documentation, thus suggesting that alternative cycles of intensification and abandonment of sedentary lifestyles followed closely the historical cycles of consolidation and collapse of the monarchy, at least in some regions.[1] Finally, aspects still insufficiently studied—deforestation of wadis and

The Gift of the Nile? Ancient Egypt and the Environment
edited by Thomas Scshneider and Christine L. Johnston
Tucson, Arizona: Egyptian Expedition, 2020a

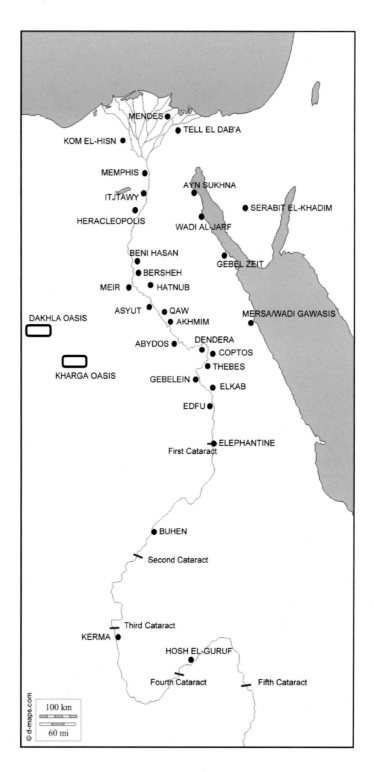

FIGURE 1. Map of Egypt.

FIGURE 2. Island in the Nile. (Image Credit: Shaimaa Ahmed Saleh, CC BY-SA 2.0; commons.wikimedia.org/wiki/File: Flickr_-_shaimaa85_-_palm_tree_island_Nile_river_egypt_ beni_suef.jpg.)

valley areas, emergence of cultivable islands in the Nile (Fig. 2), shifts of the course of the river, local presence of swampy areas, transhumance and herding strategies, etc.— were nevertheless crucial in the organization of the territory and broadened the horizon of economic resources and productive options available for the rural population.[2]

The annual flood had deeper effects on the agriculture, land use, and production systems of Egypt than the mere seasonal rise of the level of the Nile. Minor watercourses and swampy areas—mainly at the bottom of the cliffs bordering the desert—dotted the Egyptian countryside long after the inundation had disappeared. The water, moisture, and fresh vegetation they provided made it possible that occasional herding, fishing, and agricultural activities could be carried out in areas relatively distant from the Nile, or that mounds, settlements, and fields could be found outside the riversides of the Nile.[3] In fact, *phw* "marshland" was a conspicuous element of the countryside, very often mentioned together with the *ww* "districts" in the canonical representations of the landscape of both the Delta and the Valley, in all periods of Egyptian history. The Nile Valley appears thus as a complex landscape of marshes, meadows, and cultivated areas, with shrubs and trees limited to emerged areas close to the river and to the edge of the valley along the cliffs, while other areas—particularly those that separated the villages and their immediate surroundings—consisted of pasture land, bushes, and even woods.[4] It is also possible that such more or less perennial channels and pools attracted the desert fauna as well as pastoral populations living at the margins of the Nile Valley who exploited areas well suited for cattle breeding. In any case, hunting, fishing, and fowling as well as sporadic mentions of the capture of cattle raised by desert nomads appear occasionally in the written record as activities that supported a mobile population important enough as to

147

FIGURE 3. Nilotic landscape at Gebelein. (Image Credit: Rémih, CC BY-SA 3.0; commons.wikimedia.org/wiki/File:Gebelein_Hill_Sheikh_Musa_tomb1.JPG.)

be controlled by officials and check-points.[5] The last remnants of the original vegetation and natural environment of the valley were preserved until recently at Wadi Kubbaniya and provided a glimpse into the rich ecology that once characterized the wadis.[6] In fact, the oldest papyrological archive, the Gebelein Papyri of the 4th Dynasty, shows that hunters, nomads, fowlers, and collectors of honey made up a substantial percentage of the inhabitants of the villages around this locality (Fig. 3).[7] As for irrigation canals and dykes, they are quite rare in both the administrative and archaeological record and they were far from constituting a centralized and coherent large-scale network of hydraulic works aimed at regulating and distributing the annual flood of the Nile. As a consequence, land irrigation would have depended mostly on the arrival of the annual flood, with minimal arrangement of the natural basins in the floodplain, while natural wells and ponds contributed to the cultivation of fields in the immediate surroundings of settlements.[8]

In this perspective, Middle Egypt appears as a privileged field of investigation about the transformations that occurred in a region that often played a crucial political role in Egyptian history. Being crossed both by the Nile and the Bahr Yussef, the canal that connects the river with the Fayyum and which runs parallel to the Nile for about 220 km from Dairut to Fayyum, this region was rich in pasture land and marshes. It was also the point of arrival of desert routes that connected the Nile Valley to the string of oases of the Western Desert that represented, in fact, an alternative way for traders and travellers to the Nile. Not by chance, peoples living in the Western Desert and in Nubia arrived to and travelled through Middle Egypt; they were occasionally represented in the tombs of the elites that ruled this area and, judging from the epigraphic record, they also played an important political role, at least in some periods of the pharaonic past. Finally, this region presents a rather differentiated organization in terms of settlement density and productive activities, with its core situated between Asyut in the south and Beni Hassan in the north. Northwards the density of human occupations seems to fall dramatically, at least up to the Ramesside period. This variability means that Middle Egypt was a microcosm in itself that encompassed some of the most distinctive characteristics of the Nile Valley: abundance of agricultural land but also of pasture areas and marsh zones susceptible to be put under cultivation; a crossroads of river and land routes; easy connections with the neighbouring desert areas; and, finally, an eventful history made of changes in the patterns of occupation of the territory, in the emergence of new types of settlement, in the foundation of "colonies" of foreigners, and in the oscillation between the expansion of agricultural areas (often under the initiative of the crown) and their subsequent contraction and the return to more mobile lifestyles (basically pastoralism). This also means that modern cartography may be rather misleading as it ~~contributes to~~ fixes the image of this portion of the Nile Valley as a homogeneous agricultural territory. In fact, human occupation in this relatively vast area was quite unequal and the presence of the crown and its local collaborators took the form, in many periods of Egyptian history, of a patchy network of urban sites and royal administrative/economic centers, scattered over a large area and separated by bushy and marshy areas. This pattern becomes even more complex when considering that, given the insufficiency of archaeological research on the urban and settlement history of this region, necropoleis and the administrative titles of the officials buried there remain the usual guiding thread to detect the main nodes of power present in this region.[9] These nodes appear then as "islands of authority" subject to periodic shifts from one place to another. In some cases such moves obeyed the fortunes of the local dominant family, as its power declined and it was then replaced by a neighbouring powerful family that was buried elsewhere. In other cases specific necropoleis were designated for particular categories of officials, so that the highest elite (or the dominant family) may have chosen not to share their burial ground with officials of lesser status and decided to build their tombs elsewhere, in separate cemeteries. Finally, there are also instances in which several elite families co-existed in the same area but each one was buried in its own necropolis. In any case, the initiatives took by these families had enduring consequences for settlement organization, the hierarchy of population centers, the management of the territory, and the productive priorities prevalent in Middle Egypt.[10]

A PATCHWORK OF ECOTOPES

The study of the ecotopes and hydrological conditions prevailing in Middle Egypt has received some attention in recent times. From this research emerges a more nuanced picture of the economic and settlement structure of this region. It also reveals several crucial landscape features in the area comprised between the birth of the Bahr Yussef at Dairut, and the Fayyum. Thus, for instance, various additional branches of the Nile and hydrological arteries existed there between the Nile and the Bahr Yussef (in fact, our understanding of the geomorphological history of the Bahr Yussef still remains rather poor). Furthermore,

Figure 4. Agricultural landscape at Beni Hassan (Image Credit: Olaf Tausch, CC BY-SA 3.0; commons.wikimedia.org/wiki/ File:Beni_Hassan_01.jpg.)

due to the form of the floodplain, only a relatively small part of the flood water could drain back into the Nile after the flood season, because it remained trapped between the levees of the Nile and the Bahr Yussef. North of Bersheh and south of the entrance to the Fayyum existed an irregular system of waterways, while large accumulations of water remained in front of the Fayyum entrance long after the end of the flood season. So, the existence of a vast wet zone between the Nile and the Bahr Yussef south of the Fayyum made most of this area unsuitable for the cultivation of cereals as much as for habitation, to the point that even in the 18th century CE it was still thinly populated.[11] Similar conditions prevailed in the zone around Beni Hassan[12] (Fig. 4) as well as at Meir. Here, distinctive crop marks in fields to the south and to the north of El-Qusiya suggest a hydrological origin. They also occurred in high concentrations in a band along the western edge of the valley in the vicinity of Meir. Elongated plots of land sometimes associated with these features can be identified as filled-in canals. As Gillam has noticed, both of these features have also been found on the western edge of the valley near Abydos and have been interpreted as a network of braided channels, representing the waterways and swamps that tended to pool in the low-lying edges of the convex alluvial floodplain.[13] Another feature of the area of Meir is the existence of abandoned levees between 2–4 km from the present location of

150

the Nile bed near El-Qusiya. Other such levees are to be found on the western side of the valley, with a complex undulating profile in between. So, as it happened in the area of Bersheh, in pre-modern times the western bank of the Nile in the Cusite nome appears to have been a complex landscape of waterways, canals, and abandoned levees.[14]

In fact, marshes were a conspicuous landmark of the entire Middle Egypt. The toponymy of this region records many place names built with terms such as *jw* "island," *š3* "basin," *grgt* "flooded area," and *šdyt* "pond." Some inscriptions of Hatnub dating from the very late third millennium BCE mention *Šdyt-š3* "The pond of the marsh," a toponym referring to a basin-like marshy area close to Bersheh.[15] A papyrus of Lahun also mentions some *šdyt* located close to a *grgt* "flooded area" and to a royal foundation.[16] Another significant landscape feature was a third channel of the Nile in Middle Egyt that extended over 125 km from the area of Abusir el-Malek to Gebel et-Teir, 5 km north of Tehna.[17] Finally, the historical move of the Nile eastwards also left its mark on the settlement organization of Middle Egypt. Hermopolis, for instance, was apparently founded on an island, perhaps around 2100 BCE. It was surrounded by irrigable land and basins and when, subsequently, the Nile moved to the east the harbour of the city followed the migration of the river. The inscription in the tomb of Djehutihotep of Bersheh about the transport of a colossal statue from the quarries of Hatnub to Hermopolis by the river mentions the arrival of the ships *r dmj n nwt tn* "to the harbour area of this city."[18] A letter from the Stategus of Hermopolis (around 340 CE) required sailors to be recruited and then escorted by soldiers to the harbour at Antinoopolis, 5 km to the east, thus revealing that a significant harbour existed at Antinoopolis but that the shipping was being managed from Hermopolis, and that Hermopolis was using the Antinoite harbour for its large shipping.[19]

In the end, the apparent abundance of agricultural land in Middle Egypt, as it transpires from modern cartography and from economic conditions going back to the 19th century CE, appears to be quite misleading because it constitutes a relatively recent development in this region. In pharaonic times this was a wetland with abundant marsh and pasturage areas, ideal for herding, while the islands formed by the Nile offered an excellent basis for the foundation of new agricultural domains.

SHAPING THE LANDSCAPE: "NEW ISLANDS"

One of the most common types of land used for agricultural purposes was *(jw) m3w* "(island of) new land," frequently mentioned in the sources of the second millennium in opposition to *q3y* "high" land: "*you walk about in new islands (jww m3w) and endless q3yt fields.*"[20] Judging from the sources, *m3w*-land was reclaimed from the river once the annual flood passed over, when new agricultural areas—highly productive—were formed by the sediments deposited, and by the constant changes of the river bed. It also seems that this type of land was highly prized and object of an active policy of foundation of new royal agricultural domains in such a fertile environment. However, as the centuries passed, it is quite probable that some of these terms finished by evoking general aspects of the landscape and lost their original literal meaning. It has thus been suggested that *q3y* came to refer to the land usually inundated by the Nile while *m3w* indicated the areas of higher elevation of the dams, above the flood level, the *geziras*, and the islands of the Nile.[21]

Land that remained usually inundated was differentiated from good agricultural soil. Fourth and Fifth Dynasty sources mention a category of land—*grgt* "organized, laid out (lit. captured)"—fit for agricultural production but which could revert to a swampy condition.[22] That is why some inscriptions from the late Old Kingdom and from the First

Intermediate Period evoke the motif of the official that finds an area flooded like a *grgt*, only for it to be transformed again into a zone suitable for agricultural production: *gm.n(.j) pr-Ḫww ṯtf(w) mj grgt* "I had found the House of Khuu inundated like a *grgt*"[23]; *[gm.n.j s] w m grgt* "[I had found i]t in the condition of a *grgt*".[24] These inscriptions, as well as that of Henqu discussed *infra*, mark a clear contrast between a territory settled with towns and dedicated to agricultural and herding activities but in which it had prevailed previously more mobile lifestyles based on fishing, fowling, and extensive cattle raising. Later on, the early Middle Kingdom correspondence of Heqanakht evokes the *spȝt* "basined land" in contrast with the *š* "basin-land",[25] while some inscriptions in the area of Asyut, dating from the First Intermediate Period and the Middle Kingdom, state quite precisely that the arrival of the annual flood transformed the high ground into swampy areas: *ḫtm.n(.j) tȝš(w) [...] ḥr sḏȝyt(.j) jr.n(.j) qsȝ[jwt] m jdḥw rdj.n(.j) mḥ ḥˤp(j) ḥr jȝwt.s jr.n(.j) ḥbsw m[ḥw] gswj m jb[...]* "I have sealed the borders [...] thanks to my seal, I have transformed the high fields into marshland, I have made that the inundation reaches her mounds and I have made that the ploughland be cultivated while the neighbours were thirsty";[26] *jn.n.j ḥˤpj m [...] r qȝywt nt jḥwt.ṯ(n) jwḥ(.w) šdw.ṯn* "I have brought the inundation from [...] to the high fields of your ˤḥt-fields so that your plots are (now) irrigated."[27]

Yet it was about the end of the Second Intermediate Period when the sources establish a net distinction between *qȝy* "high" land as well as other categories of riverside land, usually called *ẖrw* "low" in the earlier examples, and *(jw) mȝw* "(island of) new land" (or simply *mȝw(t)* "new (land)") afterwards: *ḥnk.kwj m qȝyt m ẖrw* "I was endowed with high and low land."[28] Many other texts refer to the formation of *mȝw*-land: *ȝḥt stȝt 5 m-ḥnw pȝ šȝw n Tȝ-ˤt-Nḥs[j] m-ḥnw tȝ mȝwt (?) n wˤb* "a field of 5 arouras within the meadow land of The-place-of-the-Nubian within the new land (just) cleared";[29] *...r ḥnk ȝḥt stȝt 10 m-ḥnw pȝw jdbw ȝḥt n(t) wȝḥt Ḥˤpj ntj-jw.w ḏd n.f tȝ mȝy n pr Nt nb(t) Sȝwt* "... in order to donate a field of 10 arouras from within that riverbank field that the inundation has added, which is called the new land of the domain of Neith, lady of Sais."[30] A donation stela from the Second Intermediate Period described the fields (*ȝḥt*) donated as *ḫprww* "appeared"; they were located in an island, surrounded by the river and *sgrw n šˤ* "mounds of sand," thus suggesting that the soil was the result of the accumulation of silt.[31] The report of a land surveyor of the 6th century BCE stated that one of such islands measured 929 arouras and included cultivable land, woods, and sandy areas.[32]

It is important to notice in this respect that the earliest formulae found in the *ushabti*, dating from the end of the 3rd millennium BCE, evoke flooding the riverbanks (*r smḥj wḏbw*), transporting sand (*r jnt šˤ, r ẖnt šˤ, r ẖnt šˤ n jȝbtt r jmntt*), and levelling the ground (*drdrw nw wˤrt*) among the operations involved in country planning (Fig. 5). Several passages from the biography of Khnumhotep II of Beni Hassan refer to the landscape thus resulting, for instance when king Amenemhat I reorganized the Oryx nome in times of Khunmhotep's grandfather: *smnḫ.f gmt.n.f wȝs.t(j) jtt nwt m snwt.s dj.f rḫ nwt tȝš.s r nwt smnḫ(w) wḏw.sn mj pt rḫ(w) mw.sn r ntt m sšw sjp(w) r ntt m jswt* "he (=Amenemhat I) restored what he found ruined (and) what a town had taken away from its neighbour. He caused a town to know its boundary with (another) town, their steles were established like heaven and their waters were known according to what was in writing"; and *psš.n.f jtr ˤȝ ḥr jȝt.f mw.f ȝḥwt.f jsr.f šˤ.f r-mn-m smjwt jmntjwt* "he (=Amenemhat I) divided the great river along its middle, its water, its fields, its tamarisks, and its sand as far as the western deserts."[33] Other mentions evoke erecting stelae to mark the borders of the province. It may be possible that these measures were due to changing environmental conditions resulting in moving waterways as well as sediment deposits. Perhaps not by chance, the father of Khnumhotep II bore the Old Kingdom title of *ḥqȝ nwwt mȝwt* "governor of the new agricultural domains."[34] The

Figure 5. Clearing the land in the tomb of Nakht. (Image Credit: Norman de Garis Davies, public domain; metmuseum. org/art/collection/search/548438.)

new fields thus obtained apparently fell under the control of the crown, as the *Teaching of Amenemope*, the Nauri decree and the papyrus Harris I state: "*(the one) who registers the islands of new land in the great name of His Majesty, who records the markers on the borders of fields, who acts for the king in his listing of taxes, who makes the land-register of Egypt*";[35] "*he made land-charters for him of hundreds of thousands of fresh land (nḥb), islands (jww), high land (qȝyt) and every field (ȝḥwt nb) which is profitable for corn*";[36] "*I made for you ḫȝ-tȝ domains in the new land (mȝwt), with pure barley; I doubled their fields (ȝḥwt) which had been left fallow (fkȝw) in order to double the divine offerings in numerous lists, for your great august and beloved name. I made for you numerous fields (ȝḥwt) in the new islands (jww mȝwt), in the northern and southern districts of the country, by the tens of thousands. There were made for them stelae inscribed with your name, abiding for you, bearing decrees forever.*"[37] Quite often, such new lands were cultivated using forced labor, like criminals, soldiers, or serfs: "*account of the expenses (of) the Nubians belonging to the new land of the tribute (mȝwt n pȝ jnw).*"[38] That is probably why *ḥbs* "ploughland" and *wʿb-ḥt* "cleared (lit. free) of wood" land were listed together in a Middle Kingdom administrative document in which people were assigned to compulsory labour,[39] while other contemporary sources contrasted *ḥbs* and *ḥtyt*, the latter one being sometimes burnt in order to be cultivated, thus suggesting its bushy nature.[40] In any case, clearing land from bush, herbs, etc., in order to prepare it for cultivation was an activity frequently evoked in Egyptian sources, as was burning fields in order to eliminate scrub and weeds and to put them into cultivation.[41] A passage from the Late Ramesside papyrus Leiden I 370 specifies that three *jdb*-plots should be cleared from trees which were on their mounds: "*as the fields (ȝḥwt) which Nesmontu used to cultivate, and you shall prune its trees beginning from the district boundary of Pre to the well (šdt) of the district boundary,*"[42] while papyrus Berlin 8523, from the very late 2nd millennium BCE, states "*as soon as my letter reaches you, you shall attend to this field (ȝḥt) and not be neglectful of it. And you shall remove its weeds and plow it and farm one aroura of land [in] vegetables (wȝḏwt) at this well (šdt).*"[43] Some of the demotic papyri from the archive of Tsenhor reveal that plots of agricultural land also included a wooded area (*šn*) equivalent to 10% of the arable area;[44] not surprisingly, trees were important enough as to be explicitly mentioned in transfers of property together with fields (*ȝḥwt*), meadows (*sḫwt*), and slaves.[45] This was, for instance, the case in a Ptolemaic document: *"they are your island land and your high land above along with the sycamore trees, the date-palms, the dôm-palms and the (other) trees which grow on them."*[46] In general, trees were reckoned by the administration together with hydraulic systems (cf. *"is forbidden to reckon the canals, pools, wells, watering places, and trees in these two pyramid towns"* in the Dashur decree of Pepy I),[47] and they seem to have been a concern for the administration.[48]

In fact, the creation of agricultural fields in riverine areas goes back, at least, to the third millennium BCE, as it appears described in the decrees from the temple of Min at Coptos. The rich epigraphic corpus of royal decrees from this sanctuary provides detailed insight into the foundation of agricultural domains and their impact on neighbouring peasant communities.[49] First of all, the overseer of the sanctuary chose a tract of land in a flooded environment with the assistance of the scribes of the fields, then he marked out the plots of land and named the domain and, finally, an administrative council (*ḏꜣḏꜣt*) was appointed in order to oversee the management of the fields. The labor force (*mrt, nzwtjw*) was provided by the peasants from the neighbouring villages, whose chiefs (*ḥqꜣ nwt*) were part of the council together with the dignitaries of the crown (*srw*). The inscriptions mention that the domains were usually assigned to specialized processing centers whose main concern was the transformation of the agricultural produce into offerings which were later presented to the god. Finally, and quite significantly, the agricultural domain thus created was defined as a *nwt mꜣwt* "new agricultural exploitation." Other sources suggest that such divisions of land and workers, subsequently granted to temples were not exclusive to Coptos, as the titles of several officials at Akhmim and Abydos reveal (e.g., *jmj-r wpt ꜣht mrt m prwj* "overseer of the division of fields and workers in the Double Domain"; *jmj-r wpt ḥtpt-nṯr m mrt ꜣht* "overseer of the division of the divine offerings together with the workers and the fields").[50]

That the foundation of such agricultural domains was particularly important in Middle Egypt may be inferred from many administrative titles from this area. Thus Nikaankh of Tehna (nome 16 Upper Egypt) and his family controlled both the local temple of the goddess Hathor and the royal agricultural centers of the crown in this province at the beginning of the 5th Dynasty (he held, among other duties, those of *jmj-r nwwt mꜣwt* "overseer of the new agricultural domains" and *jmj-r pr n ḥwt-ꜥꜣt* "administrator of a great *ḥwt*"). Later on, the title *jmj-r nwwt mꜣwt* "overseer of the new agricultural domains" appeared in the neighbouring 15th province of Upper Egypt, at Sheikh Said, and at the 9th province, at El-Hawawish, during the 5th–6th Dynasties. The only other provinces where the title was also attested in the third millennium BCE were the Memphite area and Hierakonpolis. Furthermore, there are also several inscriptions in which *nwwt mꜣwt* are related to the funerary complexes of the kings, to temples, and to *ḥwt*-centers of the crown, being thus part of the network of economic and productive institutions spread all over the country, which were more or less dependent on the crown (depending on local particularities, as in the case of temples) and whose production was available for the crown's officials in transit. A passage from the autobiography of Herkhuf of Elephantine describes how this system operated: *"Orders have been brought to the governor(s) of the new agricultural domains (nwwt mꜣwt), the companion(s), and the overseer(s) of priests to command that supplies be furnished from what is under the charge of each from every ḥwt belonging to a processing center and from every temple without any exemption."* The aim of such domains, as it happened at Coptos, was certainly to provide foodstuff and other goods, in this case to expeditions sent to the quarries (Hatnub) and to the oases of the Western Desert. Thus, graffito 1 from Hatnub mentions the delivery of equipment from *ḥwt* to the workforce employed in an expedition to the quarries, and the traces of the sign *mꜣw* following immediately the hieroglyphs of *ḥwt* are reminiscent of the title *jmj-r nwwt mꜣwt ḥwt-ꜥꜣt* borne by Abdu at Giza. Finally, a very fragmentary inscription from the beginning of the 6th Dynasty found at Saqqara mentions the *nwwt m3wt* and *hwt* of the pyramid of Teti in a context of works and supply of grain and textiles in the quarry of Tura. It is thus quite possible that the importance of *nwwt m3wt* in the 15th–16th provinces of Upper Egypt reflect royal initiatives that aimed to create the logistics needed to provide supplies for workers and expeditions alike, mainly sent to the quarries.[51] Later on, during the early Middle Kingdom, Neheri, father of Khnumhotep II of Beni Hassan (16th province of Upper Egypt) still bore the title of *hq3 nwwt m3wt* "governor of the new domains"[52] As for the title of *hq3 hwt*, the recent discovery of the tombs of several Old Kingdom officials at Bersheh has revealed that at least three holders of this function were buried there, together with a *hq3 hwt-'3t*.[53] Having in mind that four *hq3 hwt* were also buried at Sheikh Said, in the same province, these titles confirm the importance of the 15th and 16th provinces of Upper Egypt in the foundation of agricultural domains by the crown.

So, these agricultural domains (*nwt m3wt*) attached to temples, to *hwt*, to *hwt-'3t*, to pyramids, etc., were quite probably the precedent of the later domains *(jw) m3w* "new (islands)" founded in riverside areas in the New Kingdom. Probably not by chance, the increasing interest of the crown in expanding agriculture and cattle raising for fiscal reasons was concomitant with the development of new provincial centers in Middle Egypt, thus continuing a tendency already inaugurated, at least, around the middle of the third millennium BCE and inspired in all probability by the abundance of pasture and potentially agricultural land in this area. In any case, important cemeteries and centers of provincial power are well attested during the 6th Dynasty at Asyut, Zawiyet el-Mayetin, Der el-Gebrawi, Meir, Quseir el-Amarna, Sharuna, Bersheh, and Beni Hassan, among others, while regional officials were appointed specifically to oversee this sector of the Nile valley: Pepiankh "the middle" of Meir was *jmj-r Šm'w m zp3wt hrjwt-jb* "overseer of the middle provinces of Middle Egypt," whereas Niankhpepi of Zawiyet el-Mayetin was *jmj-r wpt m zp3wt 9* "overseer of commissions in the nine provinces." Similar regional responsibilities went back to the 5th Dynasty, as the titles *jmj-r k3(w)t m zp3wt hrjwt-jb Šm'w* "overseer of works in the middle provinces of Upper Egypt" and *jmj-r zp3wt hrjwt-jb Šm'w* "overseer of the middle provinces of Upper Egypt" reveal. The interest and scale of these royal interventions in Middle Egypt—Nekhebu claimed that the king had sent him to Meir to excavate a canal[54]—contrast sharply with the absence of a similar interest (or adequate conditions) in the eight southernmost provinces of the kingdom (with the exception of Elephantine), a traditional focus of royal presence since the beginning of the Old Kingdom but where titles formed with the element *nwwt m3wt* are practically absent.[55]

A Matter of Lifestyles?

Wadi Natrun (*Sht Hm3t*) was a natural gateway from and to the northern Libyan desert, and there is evidence that herds of wild cattle lived and crossed this area. Thus, in year 2 of Amenhotep III, a sighting of 170 wild bulls in the desert near Wadi Natrun prompted a royal hunting party.[56] Wild bulls (aurochs) also figure prominently among the fauna of desert and bordering areas hunted by Khnumhotep II of Beni Hassan, with 400 allegedly captured or killed.[57] Finally, Intef son of Ka was a hunter "for the East, for the West, and for the temples" who chased bulls in their watering places for the Theban kings of the First Intermediate Period.[58] Aurochs constitute in fact an excellent indicator for the existence of a bush and woody environment, a natural milieu characteristic of many zones of the Western Delta, the Fayyum area, and the uppermost regions of Middle Egypt. These zones constituted a "pastoral crescent" crossed by different populations, both Egyptian and foreigner, where cattle raising played an important economic role.[59] And it was during the First Intermediate Period and the early Middle Kingdom that many inscriptions refer, precisely, to a distinctive herding lifestyle in Middle Egypt, as cattle raising seemed more important than the foundation of agricultural domains. What is more, mobile lifestyles were sometimes opposed to those of sedentary populations living in towns and became so crucial in this region that they left their mark even in the organization of settlements.[60]

Several passages from the biography of Henqu of Deir el-Gebrawy, who lived at the very end of the Old Kingdom or the beginning of the First Intermediate Period, provide some hints into these lifestyles:[61]

> *Urk.* I 77, 8–13:
>
> *rdj.n(.j) t ḥnqt n ḥqr nb n J³tf ḥbs n ḥ³y jm.s jw gr(t) mḥ.n(.j) wḏbw.s m mnmnt mḫrw.s m ꜥw.t jw gr(t) ss³.n(.j) wnšw nw ḏwt ḏrwt n(w)t pt m ḫ³w n ꜥwt*
>
> "I gave bread-and-beer to all the hungry of the Mountainviper nome; I clothed the naked one in it. I also filled its shores with cattle, its pastures with small cattle. I also fed the jackals of the mountain and the kites of the sky with hides of small cattle";
>
> *Urk.* I 78, 4–7:
>
> *jw gr(t) grg.n(.j) nwwt b³gb(.w) r(.j) m sp³t tn m s³bwt rmṯ nw k(y.w)t sp³wt wnw jw.sn n mrw jm.sn jr.j jwt.sn m srw*
>
> "I also resettled/reorganized the towns that were enfeebled for me in this nome with spotted cows and *persons of other nomes. Those of them who had been servants, I made their positions into those of official(s)*";
>
> *Urk.* I 78, 13–19, 1:
>
> *ꜥḥꜥ.n(.j) ḥm r ḥq³ m J³tf ḥnꜥ sn(.j) jm³ḫw smr wꜥtj ḫrj-ḥb Ḥm-Rꜥ jm³ḫw gm.n(.j) s(.y) m s³w-prw nw mnmnt grgwt n(w)t wḥꜥww jw grg.n.j j³wt.s nb(w)t jm³ḫw Ḥnqw m rmṯ mnmnt r ꜥwt m bw-m³ꜥ*
>
> "I stood, indeed, as ruler in the Mountainviper nome, together with my brother, the honoured sole companion and lector-priest Hemre, the honoured one. Having found it (=the nome) in the condition of pasture areas for cattle and inundated areas of fishermen/fowlers, I settled/ reorganized all its mounds—me, the honoured Henqu—with people and cattle [as well as] small cattle, in very truth."

The inscription of Henqu evokes a landscape with abundant wetlands and pasturage areas, in which cattle raising and fishing represented the economic basis of non-sedentary lifestyles that should be nevertheless fixed (and controlled) through the creation of towns and stables. Two different logics of production seem then to clash in Henqu's perspective, probably depending on their respective fiscal importance for a local governor like him— one more mobile, the other one more sedentary.[62] Even in the case of small communities, the exploitation of natural resources was far from being a negligible activity and mobile peoples were also present there. This is the case of the papyri from Gebelein from the late 26th century BCE, which shows that hunters, nomads, fowlers, and collectors of honey made up a substantial percentage of the inhabitants of the villages in that area.[63] The importance of such logics is particularly noticeable in Middle Egypt, a region that witnessed crucial changes in its settlement pattern in the late third and early second millennium BCE, when extensive cattle raising, mobile pastoralism, and new types of settlement appear in the epigraphic record there. That is why many biographical inscriptions from the First Intermediate Period mention the abundance of cattle under the care of a local authorities as proof of their capability as leaders and providers of abundance for their people. Khety I, ruler of Asyut, claimed *"I filled the pastures with dappled cattle, the man [...] owning many kinds. Cows gave birth to twins; byres were full of [...] calves. I was favoured by Sekhat-Hor, so that one said, splendid! I am one rich in cattle, whose ox [...] that he lives well."* Similar statements are known in other localities of Upper Egypt. Also in this period, individuals boasted about their acquisition of herds of cattle.[64] Having in mind that the very late third millennium and the very early second millennium BCE was also the period in which the former network of ḥwt disappeared, to be never restored, it is possible that the importance of institutional agriculture decreased and that the rural population preferred instead to turn to a less cereal-dependent and more diversified economy in which cattle raising and the exploitation of pasture land in areas now left uncultivated, even returned to a swampy condition, appeared preferable. This may explain why inscriptions such as that of Ankhtifi of Mo'alla refer to a territory that was reverted to a flooded condition in his time or why the governors of ḥwt at El-Harageh, in the Fayyum area, were involved in the administration of herds.[65] In this vein, the economic reorganization of the area of Dendera included the appointment of governors of ḥwt and the creation of a royal stable. So, according to the Inscription of Rediukhnum, queen Neferukayet *"has resettled/reorganized Upper Egypt, the van of men, from Elephantine to the Aphroditopolite nome, with women together with governors of ḥwt and dignitaries from the whole land,"* *"she placed me at Dendera in her mother's great cattle farm* (mḏȝt)*, rich in records, a foremost enterprise, the greatest estate of Upper Egypt;"* then Redjukhnum said that *"I managed the estate* (pr) *successfully and I enlarged all its departments."* Finally, an inscription from the Coptite nome refers to the reorganization of a locality, including assembling its cattle: *"the Overseer of priests Djefi sent me to the locality of* Jw-šn-šn. *I found it ruined, I refounded/reorganized it, I brought back its cattle and I made an account of absolutely everything (?)."*[66] In the context of armed conflicts between rival powers in Middle Egypt, mobile wealth may have appeared as a more reliable economic option for the populations in the areas affected.

Shortly afterwards, cattle still remained one of the pillars of the tax system restored by the kings that reunified Egypt. Thus the great steward Henenu, for instance, proclaimed that *"I taxed for him* [=the Pharaoh] *Thinis of the Thinite province and the Lower Aphroditopolite province,"* before describing his activities as treasurer of the produce of the (Western) oasis and the assignation of quotas (nḥb) of oxen, goats, asses, and other goods to the provinces of Upper Egypt.[67] As for Imeny of Beni Hassan, a contemporary of Senwsret I, he boasted about the provision of cattle herds with the obligation to return a certain amount as taxes:[68] *"I spent the years as ruler of the Oryx province with all contributions* (bȝkw) *for the king's house being in my charge. I gave gang-overseers* (jmjw-r ṯst) *to the domains of the herdsmen* (gsw-pr nw mnjw) *of the Oryx province and 3000 oxen as their allocation* (nḥbw.sn)*. I was praised for it in the king's house in every year of the cattle tax* (ṯnw rnpt nt jrw)*. I delivered sall their dues* (bȝkw) *to the king's house* (pr-nsw)*, and there was no shortage against me in any bureau of his, for the entire Oryx province laboured for me in steady stride."* In short, cattle feature not only as a valuable possession both before and after the reunification of the country, but also as a correspondingly major source of fiscal income for kings.[69] The Abydos decree at Nauri of Sethi I contains a comparable detailed description of the herding activities carried out in the institutional sphere. On the one hand cattle were penned in stables, on the other hand extensive cattle raising was developed in rich riverine pasture areas:[70]

lines 19–20:

"the stables (mḏwt) are full of oxen, calves, long-horned bulls, goats, oryx, and short-horned cattle therein in (their) hundreds of thousands. There is no limit to the counting of their multitudes, being levied (for) offering at their (due) dates by the regulation of the God's property";

lines 20–22:

"he has multiplied for him all cattle (mnmnt) and all the herds (jȝwt) which are throughout the land. The bulls mount and the herds receive increase. The herbs double in the grass, the reeds come (forth) in season, they double millions, their number being doubled anew, it being given to them outright. The herdsmen (mnjw) cared for their gangs (ṯst.sn) in their charge from son to son forever and ever. Pastures (smw) were given to them in bird-haunts (r-jmyw-ȝpdw), in basins (šȝw), in leaves (ʿḥmyw), and herbs (rnpwt). This land is left to them as forage (wdyw). There are none who can interfere with them upon it, bulls and long-horned cattle are scattered about amongst the basins (šȝw) and the riverbanks (wḏbw).

This circumstance may explain why peoples from the desert were involved in herding activities at the service of the local lords of Middle Egypt. It is not by chance that the development of extensive pastoralism in Egypt since the very late third millennium BCE was concomitant with the emergence of new terms such as *mnmnt* "cattle on the move" and *whyt* "clanic village, tribe," particularly in Middle Egypt, a region frequented by Libyan herders (Fig. 6). In fact, it was around the very end of the third millennium BCE that the term *mnmnt* appeared in Egyptian sources, first at Deir el-Gebrawy, later on in other texts from Middle Egypt. It designates cattle on the move, in contrast to *jȝwt* which referred to penned animals.[71] Mobile herding seems thus to play an important role in the local economy of this region, as a passage in an inscription of Theban king Kamose seems to refer to some kind of cattle transhumance between Middle and Lower Egypt: *"Elephantine is strong and the interior is with us as far as Cusae. Their free land is cultivated for us, and our cattle graze in the Delta fens."*[72] As for the term *whyt* "(clan) village," even "tribe" depending on the context, it appeared at the end of the third millennium in neighbouring Bersheh,[73] further confirming the impression that mobility, transhumance, and new forms of specialized uses of the space, focused on pastoralism and mobile populations, flourished in Middle Egypt at the turn of the third millennium BCE. Additional evidence about the implication of foreign peoples in the cattle economy of Middle Egypt is the mention of "cattle of Retenu" in tombs of Meir and Bersheh, and the recent discovery of a late Old Kingdom burial of a Nubian woman close to Bersheh. Small caravans were depicted in some Middle Kingdom tombs from Beni Hassan. In one case, their protagonists were Asiatics, bringing galena to the owner of the tomb, Khnumhotep II. But in other cases, the caravans represent Libyans arriving with their flocks. Libyans and Asiatics appear thus as notable actors in the local economy of Middle Egypt and their role in cattle raising and in the supply of desert minerals perhaps justify the inclusion of a Libyan section in the execration texts of the Middle Kingdom. As for Nubians, they were represented as soldiers in the wood models and in the scenes of the tombs of Asyut in the First Intermediate Period, evoked in inscriptions related to obscure political troubles in Middle Egypt during the final First Intermediate Period or early Middle Kingdom and, later, they were represented in the company of Libyans as part of the retinue of the governors of Beni Hassan and Bersheh.[74]

FIGURE 6. Caravan of Libyan herders, tomb of Khumhotep I
of Beni Hassan. (Newberry 1893, pl. 47; courtesy of the Egypt
Exploration Society.)

These circumstances explain why control over pasture and mobile populations
appear thus closely connected to desert routes and point to one of the ways followed by
these peoples to penetrate into Middle Egypt and settle there. Shedu of Deshasha, in the
Fayyum area, who lived during the Sixth Dynasty, was *jmj-r sm nb rnpj* "overseer of all
fresh vegetation" and *jmj-r šnṭ* "overseer of police." His case was far from unique, as other
officials monitored the movement of desert populations and controlled access to pasture
areas. Thus, Hagi, from the Thinite nome (tomb SF 5202) was *jmj-r šn-tȝ nb n zpȝt* "overseer
of all vegetation of the nome" as well as *jmy-r wḥʿw nw zpȝt* "overseer of fishers, fowlers
and hunters of the nome" and *jmj-r šnṭ* "overseer of police," among other titles (Fig. 7).
Another Hagi (tomb N 89) was *jmj-r šn-tȝ* "overseer of vegetation" and *jmj-r šnṭ* "overseer
of police." As for Menankhpepy of Dendera, he was *jmj-r šn-tȝ nb n zpȝt* "overseer of all
vegetation of the nome" and *jmj-r wḥʿw nw zpȝt* "overseer of fishers, fowlers and hunters of
the nome."[75] Finally, the epigraphic record reveals that officials in charge of Kom el-Hisn, in
the Western Delta, also controlled pasture land there and, in some cases, the neighbouring
desert areas.[76] In any case, the late third millennium BCE was a period of contacts between
Nubia and Egypt across the deserts, not only because of the Nubian archaeological and
pictorial presence at Elephantine and in other localities in Southern and Middle Egypt, but
also because "Nubians of the desert" were mentioned in late third millennium sources.
An official from Dendera, the overseer of priests Mereri, claimed that he had built a fort
and that he was beloved by the *nḥsyw nw ḫȝst* "Nubians of the desert"[77] and a magic text
mentions *"the Nubian woman who has come from the desert."*[78] And Tjemerery, governor of
Thinis during the First Intermediate Period, said that he was an *"overseer of the army […] in*

Figure 7. Mobile lifestyles included hunters and fowlers. (Image Credit: Rogers Fund and Edward S. Harkness Gift, 1920; public domain. metmuseum.org/art/collection/search/ 544126?img=1.)

repelling foreigners who came down from the southern foreign lands," and it is quite possible that these foreigners presumably came via the oasis route connecting the Thinite province with Nubia.[79] Several centuries earlier an official called Nesutnefer had been in charge, precisely, of fortresses, great-*ḥwt* and missions also in the Thinite and Aphroditopolite provinces,[80] as if such fortresses/forts intended to monitor the movement of desert populations. That "foreigners" penetrated into Egypt following the desert routes is also corroborated by other inscriptions, like that of the steward Mery, who came out to search for the Oasians, or Dediku, who came to *irt rwḏ tꜣ wḥꜣtyw* "secure the land of the Oasians."[81] In fact, exchanges between Egypt and Nubia continued to flourish even after the crisis of the pharaonic monarchy (around 2150 BCE), and this may explain the importance of the desert routes and of the arrival of Libyans and Nubians into Middle Egypt during the First Intermediate Period and the Middle Kingdom.

160

In this light, the case of the term *wḥyt* is intriguing, as it suggests that the foreign populations that established themselves in Middle Egypt and the Fayyum preserved in some cases their distinctive settlements. In fact, the papyri from Ilahun, in the Fayyum area (late 19th–early 18th century BCE), record Asiatics coming from enclosure-like settlements (called *wnt*) situated in its vicinity. Similarly, a Semitic term (*sgr*) served to designate an enclosure or fortification in the area of Wadi Tumilat in the New Kingdom (as it appears in papyrus Anastasi V 19, 7). But the Wilbour papyrus (around 1145 BCE) mentions seven *sgr* in the area between Fayyum and northern Middle Egypt (one of them was situated near Heracleopolis), while inscriptions from Heracleopolis dating from the early first millennium BCE mention the local presence of a "great fortress of the Mashauesh."[82] The epigraphic record of the First Intermediate Period confirms the importance of Asiatic traders and warriors in the Heracleopolitan kingdom, as several officials bore the title of "overseer of the troop of Asiatics (ˁ3mw)."[83] In this vein, the importance of trading activities in the Heracleopolitan kingdom may explain why many late third millennium BCE burials at Kom el-Hisn display Levantine weapons typical of contemporary "warrior tombs" in the Levant[84] (these weapons were in fact markers of adult masculinity, status and wealth, and were associated with traders and mobile populations).[85] Similar weapons have been also discovered in areas under Heracleopolitan control, like Sheikh Farag (in the Fayyum), Helwan and, perhaps, Abydos. To conclude, Libyans and Asiatics settled in Middle Egypt left their mark in the settlement structure of this area, in some cases because they inhabited idiosyncratic types of localities (*wḥyt, wnt, sgr*), different from those used by Egyptians, in others because they were settled in military centers (forts, etc.) related to their occupations at the service of pharaohs.

All this evidence reveals that the particular environmental conditions of Middle Egypt favored cattle raising, the activities of Egyptian and foreign herders and the development of distinctive mobile lifestyles that left their mark in the settlement structure of this region. It is also possible that, as it happened in other regions of the ancient Near East, some regions of Egypt experienced comparable cycles of expansion and retraction of urbanism and sedentary life depending on social and fiscal reasons: agriculture thrived when the state was strong and its tax demands promoted the colonization of formerly uncultivated and little urbanized areas and, on the contrary, *extensive* cattle raising and the exploitation of natural resources appeared as a more attractive, diversified and less uncertain economic choice when the state and its tax system collapsed. It is even possible that the sudden importance in the literature of the early second millennium BCE of peoples and activities linked to pastoralism and mobile lifestyles (*The Eloquent Peasant, The Tale of a Herdsman, The Lament of a Fowler, The Hymn to the Nile Flood*, even the tales in which the king is depicted as a hunter)[86] echoed, in fact, developments that were taking place then in the Nile Valley, such as the frequent references to *sḥtyw* "marsh dwellers" in the epigraphic and literary sources of this period.[87]

LATER DEVELOPMENTS

The New Kingdom was one of those periods in which a solid monarchy promoted a policy of agricultural expansion in Middle Egypt, as it had already happened in previous centuries. However, two new elements contributed now to this policy. On the one hand, the military campaigns in foreign territories meant that a flow of prisoners of war, deportees, people sent in Egypt as tribute, etc., increased the workforce put at the service not of agricultural centers of the crown but of temples instead, now transformed into crucial nodes in the articulation of the economy and the settlement structure of the country. On the other hand, chariotry became an indispensable branch of the army, in need of abundant pasture land to feed the horses it employed. As for cattle raising, its importance continued unquestionable, including the provision of leather for the needs of the army, the export of hides (as recorded in *Wenamun*) and the supply of teams of oxen in order to cultivate the vast tracts of land now administered by the temples and the crown.

The availability of land in Middle Egypt provided the ideal conditions, once more, for the expansion of agriculture and cattle raising in this region. Probably not by chance, the majority of the land registers preserved from the very late second millennium and the very early first millennium BCE record plots of land administered by temples in this area. That is why the Wilbour papyrus, the papyrus Baldwin+Amiens, the Reinhardt papyrus, the Louvre and Griffith fragments, the papyrus Prachov, and perhaps the so-called papyri of El-Hibeh, among others, cover the zone situated between Fayyum in the north and Abydos in the south.[88] As in previous centuries, military colonies and forts were founded mainly in the Fayyum area (as it will happen again in the Hellenistic period). This move probably did not continue much longer after the end of the New Kingdom. The papyrus Reinhardt, for instance, suggests that some kind of shortage of manpower justified the use of compulsory labor again in the cultivation of some tracts of institutional land. Somewhat later, the *Stela of the Apanage* shows that extensive tracts of land controlled by independent tenants included large bushy areas. Of course, the scarce documentation about the agricultural conditions prevailing in the early centuries of the first millennium BCE prevent pushing any conclusion too far, but it may be possible that areas formerly cultivated during the Ramesside era reverted to pasture land and to cattle raising.[89] Thus, for instance, prince Namlot recorded the restoration of daily cattle offerings to Harsaphes, god of Heracleopolis, at the beginning of the first millennium BCE and he provided a detailed inventory of the annual levy, specifying the assessment upon officials and "cities, towns, and settlements of Heracleopolis" responsible for oxen deliveries to the temple. So high-rank officials handed over ten oxen each (but the General of Heracleopolis gave 60), high priests and administrators of the temple between six and ten, two assistants of the general eight each, two administrators of a fortress gave five and six respectively, while 25 localities handed over between one and four oxen. Collectives of specialized workers (coppersmiths, gardeners, warriors, stone masons, potters, builders, etc.) also handed over oxen.[90] Cattle raising was thus economically relevant not only for potentates but also for people of modest condition, capable nevertheless of raising and delivering oxen to a sanctuary at Heracleopolis.

To conclude, the environmental conditions and the abundance of land in Middle Egypt made it a region in which agriculture, herding, and extensive cattle raising could expand and did expand, sometimes as complementary economic activities, in other cases as alternative productive choices, depending on a multitude of elements, perhaps the most important being the existence (or not) of a strong tax-system seeking for taxable wealth (grain, cattle). However, the feeble population density in this region always remained a major obstacle for a sustained expansion of agriculture. Considering the development of the Delta in the first millennium BCE (foundation of cities, agricultural and commercial expansion, etc.), when zones formerly underpopulated (like the Western Delta) thrived and became major political centers (Sais, Alexandria), the fact that Middle Egypt hardly followed a similar path appears as an oddity. A possible cause points to the difficulty to control, manage, and regulate the inundation of the Nile and to drain the water it brought during the millennia preceding the massive hydraulic works of the 19th century CE. This would have represented an immense problem to expand agriculture in a region in which marsh areas and very humid conditions prevailed and in which pastoralism appeared best suited to its ecological conditions. If this was the cause indeed, then Middle Egypt appears as an excellent case study to test the limits of the hydraulic capacities so often ascribed to the pharaonic state.

Works Cited

Allam, S. 1994. "Implications in the Hieratic P. Berlin 8523 (Registration of Land Holdings)." In *Essays in Egyptology in Honour of Hans Goedicke*, edited by B.M. Bryan and D. Lorton, 1–7. San Antonio: Van Siclen Books.

Alleaume, G. 1992. "Les systèmes hydrauliques de l'Égypte pré-moderne: Essai d'histoire du paysage." In *Itinéraires d'Égypte: Mélanges offerts au père Maurice Martin*, edited by Ch. Decobert, 301–322. Cairo: Institut français d'archéologie orientale.

Allen, J.P. 2002. *The Heqanakht Papyri*. New York: Metropolitan Museum of Art.

Antoine, J.-Ch. 2011. "The Wilbour Papyrus Revisited: The Land and Its Localisation: An Analysis of the Places of Measurement." *Studien zur Altägyptischen Kultur* 40: 9–27.

———. 2015. "Landholding and Agriculture in Late Ramesside Theban Documents." *Zeitschrift für Ägyptische Sprache und Altertumskunde* 142: 104–119.

———. 2017a. "The Geographical and Administrative Landscape of Lower Middle Egypt in Text B of the Wilbour Papyrus." *Zeitschrift für Ägyptische Sprache und Altertumskunde* 144: 1–15.

———. 2017b. "Modelling the Nile Agricultural Floodplain in Eleventh and Tenth Century B.C. Middle Egypt." In *The Nile: Natural and Cultural Landscape in Egypt*, edited by H. Willems and J.-M. Dahms, 15–51. Blelefeld: Transcript Verlag.

Baud, M., F. Colin, and P. Tallet. 1999. "Les gouverneurs de l'oasis de Dakhla au Moyen Empire." *Bulletin de l'Institut français d'archéologie orientale* 99: 1–19.

Blouin, K. 2014. *Triangular Landscapes: Environment, Society, and the State in the Nile Delta under Roman Rule*. Oxford: Oxford University Press.

Bowman, A.K., and E. Rogan, eds. 1999. *Agriculture in Egypt: From Pharaonic to Modern Times*. Oxford: Oxford University Press.

Brunner, H. 1937. *Die Texte aus den Gräbern der Herakleopolitenzeit von Siut*. Leipzig: J.C. Hinrichs.

Bunbury, J. 2010. "The Development of the River Nile and the Egyptian Civilization: A water historical perspective with focus on the First Intermediate Period." In *A History of Water. Series II, Vol. 2, Rivers and Society: From Early Civilizations to Modern Times*, edited by T. Tvedt and R. Coopey, 52–71. London: I.B. Tauris & Co.

———. 2013. "Geomorphological Development of the Memphite Floodplain over the Past 6,000 Years." *Studia Quaternaria* 30(2): 61–67.

Bunbury, J., and D. Jeffreys. 2011. "Real and Literary Landscapes in Ancient Egypt." *Cambridge Archaeological Journal* 21: 65–76.

Bunbury, J., and M. Malouta. 2012. "The Geology and Papyrology of Hermopolis and Antinoopolis." *eTopoi: Journal for Ancient Studies* 3: 119–122.

Caminos, R.A. 1954. *Late-Egyptian Miscellanies*. London: Oxford University Press.

Clère, J.J., and J. Vandier. 1948. *Textes de la Première Période Intermédiaire et de la XIème dynastie*. Brussels: Fondation égyptologique Reine Élisabeth.

Collier, M., and S. Quirke. 2006. *The UCL Lahun Papyri: Accounts*. Oxford: Archaeopress.

Darnell, J.C. 2002. *Theban Desert Road Survey in the Egyptian Western Desert*. Vol. 1, *Gebel Tjauti Rock Inscriptions 1–45 and Wadi el-Ḥôl Rock Inscriptions 1–45*. Chicago: The

Oriental Institute of the University of Chicago.

Davies, B.G. 1997. *Egyptian Historical Inscriptions of the Nineteenth Dynasty*. Jonsered: Paul Åströms förlag.

Davies, V.W. 2003. "Kush in Egypt: A New Historical Inscription." *Sudan & Nubia* 7: 52–54.

———. 2009. "La tombe de Sataimaou à Hagar Edfou." *Égypte, Afrique & Orient* 53: 25–40.

De Meyer, M. 2011. "Two Cemeteries for One Provincial Capital? Deir el-Bersha and el-Sheikh Said in the Fifteenth Upper Egyptian Nome during the Old Kingdom." In *Old Kingdom, New Perspectives: Egyptian Art and Archaeology 2750–150 BC*, edited by N. Strudwick and H. Strudwick, 42–49. Oxford: Oxbow Books.

Fischer, H.G. 1964. *Inscriptions from the Coptite Nome, Dynasties VI–XI*. Roma: Pontificium Institutum Biblicum.

———. 1968. *Dendera in the Third Millennium B.C., down to the Theban Domination of Upper Egypt*. Locust Valley: J.J. Augustin.

Gardiner, A.H. 1948a. *The Wilbour Papyrus*. Vol. 2, *Commentary*. Oxford: Oxford University Press.

———. 1948b. *Ramesside Administrative Documents*. Oxford: Oxford University Press.

Gasse, A. 1988. *Données nouvelles administratives et sacerdotales sur l'organisation du domaine d'Amon XXᵉ–XXIᵉ dynasties à la lumière des papyrus Prachov, Reinhardt et Grundbuch*. Cairo: Institut français d'archéologie orientale.

Gernez, G. 2011. "The Exchange of Products and Concepts between the Near East and the Mediterranean: The Example of Weapons during the Early and Middle Bronze Ages." In *Intercultural Contacts in the Ancient Mediterranean*, edited by K. Duistermaat and I. Regulski, 327–341. Louvain-Paris-Walpole: Peeters.

Gillam, R. 2010. "From Meir to Quseir El-Amarna and Back Again: The Cusite Nome in SAT and on the Ground." In *Egyptian Culture and Society: Studies in Honour of Naguib Kanawati*, vol. 1, edited by A. Woods, A. McFarlane, and S. Binder, 131–158. Cairo: Conseil suprême des antiquités de l'Égypte.

Graham, A. 2010. "Islands in the Nile: A Geoarchaeological Approach to Settlement Locations in the Egyptian Nile Valley and the Case of Karnak." In *Cities and Urbanism in Ancient Egypt*, edited by M. Bietak, E. Czerny, and I. Forstner-Müller, 125–143. Vienna: Verlag der Österreichischen Akademie der Wissenschaften.

Grajetzki, W. 2001. "Die Nekropole von El-Haragèh in der 1. Zwischenzeit." *Studien zur Altägyptischen Kultur* 29: 55–60.

Grandet, P. 1994. *Le papyrus Harris I (BM 9999)* (BdE, 109). Cairo: Institut français d'archéologie orientale.

Graves, C. 2013. "The Problem with Neferusi: A Geoarchaeological Approach." In *Current Research in Egyptology 2012*, edited by C. Graves, G. Heffernan, L. McGarrity, E. Millward, and M. Sfakianou Bealby, 70–83. Oxford: Oxbow Books.

Grunert, S. 2009. "Erlebte Geschichte—ein authentischer Bericht." In *Das Ereignis—Geschichtsschreibung zwischen Vorfall und Befund*, edited by M. Fitzenreiter, 125–135. London: Golden House Publications.

Hawkins, S. 2013. "'If only I could accompany him, this excellent marshman!': An Analysis of the Marshman (*s̲ẖty*) in Ancient Egyptian Literature." In *Current Research in Egyptology 2012*, edited by C. Graves, G. Heffernan, L. McGarrity, E. Millward, and M. Sfakianou Bealby, 84–93. Oxford: Oxbow Books.

Hayes, W.C. 1949. "Career of the Great Steward Henenu under Nebhepetrēʿ Mentuhotpe." *Journal of Egyptian Archaeology* 35: 43–49.

———. 1955. *A Papyrus of the Late Middle Kingdom in the Brooklyn Museum (Papyrus Brooklyn 35.1446)*. New York: The Brooklyn Museum.

Helck, W. 1975. *Historische-biographische Texte der 2. Zwischenzeit und neue Texte der 18.*

Dynastie. Wiesbaden: Harrassowitz Verlag.

Janssen, J.J. 2004. *Grain Transport in the Ramesside Period: Papyrus Baldwin (BM EA 10061) and Papyrus Amiens.* London: The British Museum Press.

Kanawati, N. 2005. *Deir el-Gebrawi.* Vol. 1, *The Northern Cliff.* Oxford: Aris and Phillips.

———. 2017. "Ritual Marriage Alliances and Consolidation of Power in Middle Egypt during the Middle Kingdom." *Études et travaux* 30: 267–288.

Kanawati, N., and L. Evans. 2014. *Beni Hassan.* Vol. 1, *The Tomb of Khnumhotep II.* Oxford: Aris and Phillips.

Kitchen, K.A. 1969. *Ramesside Inscriptions: Historical and Biographical I.* Blackwell: Oxford.

Kletter, R., and Y. Levi. 2016. "Middle Bronze Age Burials in the Southern Levant: Spartan Warriors or Ordinary People?" *Oxford Journal of Archaeology* 35: 5–27.

Koenig, Y. 1987. "La Nubie dans les textes magiques. 'L'inquiétante étrangeté.'" *Revue d'égyptologie* 38: 105–110.

Lichtheim, M. 1976. *Ancient Egyptian Literature.* Vol. 2: *The New Kingdom.* Berkeley—Los Angeles: University of California Press.

Luft, U. 2006. *Urkunden zur Chronologie der späten 12. Dynastie: Briefe aus Illahun.* Vienna: Verlag der Österreichischen Akademie der Wissenschaften.

Malinine, M. 1953. *Choix de textes juridiques en hiératique "anormal" et en démotique.* Paris: Honoré Champion.

Manning, J.G. 1994. *The Hauswaldt Papyri: A Third Century B.C. Family Dossier from Edfu.* Sommerhausen: Gisela Zauzich Verlag.

Mathieu, B. 2015. "Chacals et milans, pâturages et marécages, ou le monde selon Henqou." In *Apprivoiser le sauvage / Taming the Wild*, edited by M. Massiera, B. Mathieu, and Fr. Rouffet, 263–273. Montpellier: Université Paul Valéry Montpellier 3 – CNRS, Équipe "Égypte Nilotique et Méditerranéenne" (ENiM).

Meeks, D. 2009. "Une stèle de donation de la Deuxième Période Intermédiaire." *Égypte Nilotique et Méditerranéenne* 2: 129–154.

Montet, P. 1936. "Les tombeaux de Siout et de Deir Rifeh (troisième article)." *Kêmi* 6: 131–163.

Moreno García, J.C. 1996. "Administration territoriale et organisation de l'espace en Egypte au troisième millénaire avant J.-C.: *grgt* et le titre ꜥ(n)ḏ-mr grgt." *Zeitschrift für Ägyptische Sprache und Altertumskunde* 123: 116–138.

———.. 1998a. "La population *mrt*: Uue approche du problème de la servitude en Égypte au IIIᵉ millénaire." *Journal of Egyptian Archaeology* 84: 71–83.

———. 1998b. "Administration territoriale et organisations de l'espace en Egypte au troisième millénaire avant J.-C. (III–IV): nwt mꜣwt et ḥwt-ꜥꜣt." *Zeitschrift für Ägyptische Sprache und Altertumskunde* 125: 38–55.

———. 1999. "J'ai rempli les pâturages avec des vaches tachetées... Bétail, économie royale et idéologie en Egypte, de l'Ancien au Moyen Empire." *Revue d'égyptologie* 50: 241–257.

———. 2006a. "Introduction: nouvelles recherches sur l'agriculture institutionnelle et domestique en Égypte ancienne dans le contexte des sociétés antiques." In *L'agriculture institutionnelle en Égypte ancienne: état de la question et perspectives interdisciplinaires*, edited by J.C. Moreno García, 11–78. Villeneuve d'Ascq: Université Charles-de-Gaulle, Lille 3.

———. 2006b. "Les temples provinciaux et leur rôle dans l'agriculture institutionnelle de l'Ancien et du Moyen Empire." In *L'agriculture institutionnelle en Égypte ancienne: état de la question et perspectives interdisciplinaires*, edited by J.C. Moreno García, 89–124. Villeneuve d'Ascq: Université Charles-de-Gaulle, Lille 3.

———. 2010. "La gestion des aires marginales: pḥw, gs, ṯnw, sḫt au IIIᵉ millénaire." In

Egyptian Culture and Society: Studies in Honour of Naguib Kanawati, vol. 2, edited by A. Woods, A. McFarlane, and S. Binder, 49–69. Cairo: Conseil suprême des antiquités de l'Égypte.

———. 2011. "Les *mnḥw*: société et transformations agraires en Égypte entre la fin du IIe et le début du Ier millénaire." *Revue d'égyptologie* 62: 105–114.

———. 2013a. "The Territorial Administration of the Kingdom in the 3rd Millennium." In *Ancient Egyptian Administration*, edited by J.C. Moreno García, 85–151. Leiden-Boston: Brill.

———. 2013b. "Les îles 'nouvelles' et le milieu rural en Égypte pharaonique." *Égypte, Afrique & Orient* 70: 3–12.

———. 2014. "L'organisation sociale de l'agriculture pharaonique: quelques cas d'étude." *Annales: Histoire, Sciences sociales* 69: 39–74.

———. 2015. "*Ḥwt jḥ(w)t*, the Administration of the Western Delta and the 'Libyan Question' in the 3rd Millennium." *Journal of Egyptian Archaeology* 101: 69–105.

———. 2016. "Temples and Agricultural Labour in Egypt, from the Late New Kingdom to the Saite Period." In *Dynamics of Production in the Ancient Near East, 1300–500 BC*, edited by J.C. Moreno García, 223–256. Oxford: Oxbow Books.

———. 2017. "Trade and Power in Ancient Egypt: Middle Egypt at the Turn of the 3rd Millennium BC." *Journal of Archaeological Research* 25(2): 87–132.

———. 2018a. "Ethnicity in Ancient Egypt: An Introduction to Key Issues." *Journal of Egyptian History* 11: 1–17.

———. 2018b. "Elusive 'Libyans': Identities, Lifestyles and Mobile Populations in NE Africa (Late 4th–Early 2nd millennium BC)." *Journal of Egyptian History* 11: 145–182.

———.. Forthcoming a. "Bronze Age Egypt." In *A Companion to Ancient Agriculture*, edited by T. Howe and D. Hollander. New York-Oxford: Wiley Blackwell.

———. Forthcoming b. "Wells, Small–Scale Private Irrigation and Agricultural Strategies in the 3rd and 2nd Millennium BC." In *Irrigation in Early States: New Directions*, edited by S. Rost. Chicago: Oriental Institute of the University of Chicago.

Newberry, P.E. 1893. *Beni Hasan*. Vol. 1. London: The Egypt Exploration Fund, London.

Obsomer, C. 1995. *Sésostris Ier: Étude chronologique et historique du règne*. Brussels: Connaissance de l'Égypte ancienne.

Pestman, P.W. 1994. *Les papyrus démotiques de Tsenhor (P. Tsenhor): Les archives privées d'une femme égyptienne du temps de Darius Ier*. Leuven: Peeters.

Posener, G. 1940. *Princes et pays d'Asie et de Nubie: Textes hiératiques sur des figurines d'envoûtement du Moyen Empire*. Brussels: Fondation égyptologique Reine Élisabeth.

Posener-Kriéger, P., and S. Demichelis. 2004. *I papiri di Gebelein: Scavi G. Farina 1935*. Turin: Ministero per i Beni e le Attività Culturali-Soprintendenza al Museo delle Antichità Egizie.

Quirke, S. 2004a. *Egyptian Literature 1800 BC: Questions and Readings*. London: Golden House Publications.

———. 2004b. *Titles and Bureaux of Egypt 1850–1700 BC*. London: Golden House Publications.

Redford, D.B. 1997. "Textual Sources for the Hyksos Period." In *The Hyksos: New Historical and Archaeological Perspectives*, edited by E.D. Oren, 1–44. Philadelphia: The University Museum, University of Pennsylvania.

Ritner, R.K. 2009a. *The Libyan Anarchy: Inscriptions from Egypt's Third Intermediate Period*. Atlanta: Society of Biblical Literature.

———. 2009b. "Egypt and the Vanishing Libyan: Institutional Responses to a Nomadic People." In *Nomads, Tribes, and the State in the Ancient Near East: Cross-Disciplinary Perspectives*, edited by J. Szuchman, 43–56. Chicago: Oriental Institute of the University of Chicago.

Sethe, K. 1935. *Urkunden des ägyptischen Altertums*. Vol. 7, *Historisch-biographische Urkunden des Mittleren Reiches*. Leipzig: J.C. Hinrichs.

Spalinger, A. 2008. "A Garland of Determinatives." *Journal of Egyptian Archaeology* 94: 139–164.

Strudwick, N.C. 2005. *Texts from the Pyramid Age*. Atlanta: Society of Biblical Literature.

Théodoridès, A. 1964. "La stèle juridique d'Amarah." *Revue internationale des droits de l'antiquité* 11: 45–80.

Toonen, W.H.J., A. Graham, B.T. Pennington, M.A. Hunter, K.D. Strutt, D.S. Barker, A. Masson-Berghoff, and V.L. Emery. 2017. "Holocene Fluvial History of the Nile's West Bank at Ancient Thebes, Luxor, Egypt, and Its Relation with Cultural Dynamics and Basin-Wide Hydroclimatic Variability." *Geoarchaeology* 2017: 1–18.

Trampier, J. 2005/2006. "Reconstructing the Desert and Sown Landscape of Abydos." *Journal of the American Research Center in Egypt* 42: 73–80.

Ullmann, T., E. Lange-Athinodorou, A. Göbel, C. Büdel, and R. Baumhauer. 2018, 10 January. "Preliminary Results on the Paleo-landscape of Tell Basta /Bubastis (Eastern Nile Delta): An Integrated Approach Combining GIS-Based Spatial Analysis, Geophysical and Archaeological Investigations." *Quaternary International*. https://doi.org/10.1016/j.quaint.2017.12.053.

van den Boorn, G.P.F. 1988. *The Duties of the Vizier: Civil Administration in the Early New Kingdom*. London: Kegan Paul International.

Vandier, J. 1950. *Mo`alla: La tombe d'Anktjfj et la tombe de Sébekhotep*. Cairo: Institut français d'archéologie orientale.

Vittmann, G. 1998. *Der demotische Papyrus Rylands 9*, 2 vols. Wiesbaden: Harrassowitz.

Vleeming, S.P. 1993. *Papyrus Reinhardt: An Egyptian Land List from the Tenth Century B.C.* Berlin: Akademie Verlag.

Wendorf, F., and R. Schild. 1986. *The Prehistory of Wadi Kubbaniya*. Vol. 2, *Stratigraphy, Paleoeconomy and Environment*. Dallas: Department of Anthropology, Southern Methodist University.

Wengrow, D. 2009. "The Voyages of Europa: Ritual and Trade in the Eastern Mediterranean circa 2300–1850 BC." In *Archaic State Interaction: The Eastern Mediterranean in the Bronze Age*, edited by W.A. Parkinson and M.L. Galaty, 141–160. Santa Fe: SAR Press.

Wenke, R.J., R.W. Redding, and A.J. Cagle, eds. 2016. *Kom el-Hisn (ca. 2500–1900 BC): An Ancient Egyptian Settlement in the Nile Delta*. Atlanta: Lockwood Press.

Wente, E. 1990. *Letters from Ancient Egypt*. Atlanta: Scholars Press.

Willems, H. 2007. *Dayr al-Barshā*. Vol. 1, *The Rock Tombs of Djehutinakht (No. 17K74/1), Khnumnakht (No. 17K74/2), and Iha (No. 17K74/3), with an Essay on the History and Nature of Nomarchal Rule in the Early Middle Kingdom*. Leuven-Paris-Walpole (M.A.): Peeters.

Willems, H., and J.-M. Dahms, eds. 2017. *The Nile: Natural and Cultural Landscape in Egypt*. Blelefeld: Transcript Verlag.

Willems, H., H. Creylman, V. De Laet, and G. Verstraeten. 2017. "The Analysis of Historical Maps as an Avenue to the Interpretation of Pre-Industrial Irrigation Practices in Egypt." In *The Nile: Natural and Cultural Landscape in Egypt*, edited by H. Willems and J.-M. Dahms, 255–343. Blelefeld: Transcript Verlag.

Zingarelli, A. 2015. "Comments on the Egyptian Term *whyt*: Family or Quasi-Village?" In *Proceedings of the Tenth International Congress of Egyptologists*, edited by P. Kousoulis and N. Lazaridis, 909–920. Leuven-Paris-Bristol: Peeters.

NOTES

1   Moreno García 2006a, and 2014.
2   Alleaume 1992; Bowman and Rogan 1999; Moreno García 2006a, 2010, forthcoming a and forthcoming b; Graham 2010; Bunbury 2010, 2013; Bunbury and Jeffreys 2011; Blouin 2014; Willems and Dahms 2017; Toonen et al. 2017; Ullmann et al. 2018.
3   Alleaume 1992; Moreno García 2006a; Gillam 2010; Antoine 2011.
4   Moreno García 2010, 2015, and 2018b, with bibliography.
5   Moreno García 2015.
6   Wendorf and Schild 1986.
7   Moreno García 2010.
8   Moreno García 2006a, 45–50; Antoine 2011, 24; 2017; Willems et al. 2017. See also Alleaume 1992; Trampier 2005/2006; Gillam 2010.
9   Antoine 2017a, 2017b; Moreno García 2017; Willems et al. 2017.
10 De Meyer 2011; Moreno García 2013a, 2017; Kanawati 2017.
11 Antoine 2017a, 2017b; Willems et al. 2017.
12 Graves 2013.
13 Gillam 2010.
14 Trampier 2005/2006; Gillam 2010.
15 Willems et al. 2017, 324–325.
16 Luft 2006, 87–90.
17 Antoine 2017a, 6–7.
18 Sethe 1935, 48.
19 Bunbury and Malouta 2012.
20 Caminos 1954, 413.
21 Moreno García 2013b.
22 Moreno García 1996.
23 Vandier 1950, 163.
24 Fischer 1968, 148 n. 650.
25 Allen 2002, 16, 32–33.
26 Asyut V: 7–8 = Brunner, 1937, 65.
27 Der Rifeh VII: 23 = Montet 1936, 159.
28 *Urk.* IV 31: 4, 14. For similar mentions of these types of land cf. Helck 1975, 16; Davies 2009, 34, 36.
29 Ritner 2009a, 433–434 (my own translation differs slightly from Ritner's).
30 Ritner 2009a, 440–441.
31 Meeks 2009, 132–135.
32 Vittmann 1998, 171.
33 Kanawati and Evans 2014, 33.
34 Kanawati and Evans 2014, 34.
35 Lichtheim 1976, 148–149.
36 Nauri decree lines 24–25 = Kitchen 1969, 50; Davies 1997, 286–287.
37 Grandet 1994, 261.
38 Kitchen 1969, 260. Cf. also Kitchen (1969, 324–325) about prisoners put on an island, as well as Janssen (2004) about criminals working on the fields in the islands.
39 Hayes (1955, 29) and, perhaps, also papyrus UC 32186 = Collier and Quirke 2006, 74–75.
40 Moreno García 2006b, 120–121.
41 Caminos 1954, 326; Wente 1990, 127–128, 175–176, 180–181, 209.

42 Wente 1990, 180–181; Antoine 2015, 107.
43 Wente 1990, 209; Allam 1994.
44 Pestman 1994, 36–37, 82–84.
45 Théodoridès 1964, 47; Malinine 1953, 115.
46 Papyrus Hauswaldt 3a, line 4 = Manning 1994, 48–49.
47 Strudwick 2005, 104.
48 Van den Boorn 1988, 234, 236–238.
49 Moreno García 1998a, 71–83; 2006b, 104, 114.
50 Moreno García 1998a.
51 Moreno García 1998b.
52 Kanawati and Evans 2014, 17, 33.
53 De Meyer 2011.
54 Strudwick 2005, 266.
55 Moreno García 2013a, 131–132.
56 Discussion and references in Ritner 2009b, 49 n. 36.
57 Kanawati and Evans 2014, 48 and pl. 130.
58 Stela BM 1203: Clère and Vandier 1948, 19.
59 Moreno García 2015, 83–84.
60 Moreno García 1999.
61 Kanawati 2005, 72–73, pls. 29–30, 56, 66–67; Grunert 2009, 133; Moreno García 2010, 49–50, 61; Mathieu 2015.
62 Moreno García 2010; Mathieu 2015.
63 Posener-Kriéger and Demichelis 2004; Moreno García 2010.
64 Moreno García 1999.
65 Grajetzki 2001.
66 Fischer 1964, 64–65, pl. 16.
67 Hayes 1949.
68 Obsomer 1995, 592.
69 Moreno García 1999.
70 Kitchen 1969, 49; Davies 1997, 284–287.
71 Moreno García 2010, 57; Mathieu 2015.
72 Redford 1997, 13.
73 Willems 2007, 47–48. Willems is rather reluctant to accept "tribe" as one of the possible renderings of the term. However, the Asiatic section of the Middle Kingdom execration texts makes a clear difference between the *ḥqꜣ* "governor, prince" of a country or territory and the *wr n wḥywt* "the chief of the tribes" of other countries or territories (Posener 1940, 88, 89). In some instances, only the *wḥywt* of a territory are mentioned, without any reference to a chief, as in Posener 1940, 93. This is of particular relevance in the case of the *wḥywt Kbn* "the tribes of Byblos" (Posener 1940, 94), as such *wḥywt* are depicted as potential menaces towards an urban centre allied to Egypt and ruled by princes (this explains why it was not considered as a danger in the execration texts). Finally, the inscription of Sobekhotep of Elkab (Second Intermediate Period) refers to a coalition of several Nubian powers and Punt, including Kush and the *wḥywt* of Wawat (Davies 2003), while *wḥywt* are absent in the Nubian section of the execration texts. About the interpretation of *wḥyt*, cf. also Spalinger 2008; Zingarelli 2015.
74 Moreno García 2017, 115–118.
75 Moreno García 2015, 96.
76 Moreno García 2015.

[77] Fischer 1968, 168.
[78] Koenig 1987, 107.
[79] Fischer 1968, 141.
[80] Strudwick 2005, 423.
[81] Baud et al. 1999, 7; Darnell 2002, 73.
[82] Moreno García 2018a, 4–5.
[83] Moreno García 2017, 102–103.
[84] Wenke et al. 2016, 348–350.
[85] Wengrow 2009; Gernez 2011; Kletter and Levi 2016.
[86] Quirke 2004a, 151–165, 180, 197, 199–202, 207–217.
[87] Quirke 2004b, 70–71; Hawkins 2013.
[88] Gardiner 1948a, 1948b; Gasse 1988; Vleeming 1993; Janssen 2004.
[89] Moreno García 2011, 2016.
[90] Ritner 2009a, 180–186.

Chapter Eight

Ceramics as Indicators of Complexity

Leslie Anne Warden

In a volume focused on environmental research in Egyptology, one might expect a ceramics chapter to focus on how ceramics encode environmental data. Perhaps you would turn here thinking to learn more about how ceramic paste reflected the surrounding environment of a site. Maybe you would hope for more about how ceramics help elucidate the relationship of environment to food consumption. While ceramics offer the potential to address those issues, they can only do that if adequate data are thoroughly collected. Instead of dealing with specific case studies here, I will address broad methodological concerns in the belief that methodology informs the questions we can ask and the answers which we may arrive at by determining our data set. In this manner, methodology becomes a huge limiting factor in writing and analyzing history.

Therefore, I would like to take a step back and discuss the role of ceramics and ceramics methodology in establishing complex, multi-scalar research projects. By discussing environment in this volume and in our manifesto, we are obliquely calling for such complexly informed projects and questions. Archaeological evidence itself is created from the fragments of lives and societies that are non-linear and messy; the archaeological record is the end point of humans negotiating and mitigating the forces of family, community, environment, government, life, death, and more. Inquiry into the environment must be tied to more aspects of archaeological inquiry rather treated as a single, reductionist stand-alone question: "What was the environment like?" if our goal is to understand Egyptian society and rewrite Egyptian history rather than just add a metaphorical side-bar to the dialogue. We should aim for an inquiry of complexity and interrelatedness going past simple descriptors into true social analysis. Ceramics, as the most abundant artifact in the Egyptian archaeological record, offer important approaches in this task.

To that end, this chapter will highlight some ways in which ceramics can be studied to yield regional and local data. These complementary data can then be employed in further integrated research questions (including environmental questions, which require local and regional data), forwarding an Egyptological analysis that is collaborative across many

The Gift of the Nile? Ancient Egypt and the Environment
edited by Thomas Schneider and Christine L. Johnston
Tucson, Arizona: Egyptian Expedition, 2020

disciplines and data types. This article is intended not only for ceramicists, but for all those who work with archaeological data. It is but one example of how an artifact type might forward social inquiry and profit research into other areas.

DATASET

The further back into Egyptian history we go, the sparser the textual sources become and the more and more reliant we become upon archaeological data. The data employed in this paper come primarily from the Old through Middle Kingdoms. Especially for the earlier end of this period, there is a dearth of textual records from outside of the royal house. My research has employed ceramics to address society and social continuity across this time, and so it is logical for me to focus on them here. However, the methodologies laid out here are absolutely applicable to other periods.

Additionally, by investigating roughly a thousand-year period that includes two centralized periods and one intermediate period, it becomes obvious that the datasets that scholars lean on to write the (literal) history books differs drastically by period. For the Old and Middle Kingdoms, scholars lean on texts, monumental art, and data from central sites (such as the Memphite necropolis). Though regional archaeology absolutely exists for the Old Kingdom, it seldom makes an impact on the grand arc of Old Kingdom history or Middle Kingdom history. For the First Intermediate Period, scholars look at regional data and regional archaeology, prizing text less simply because that dataset is so sparse. Unsurprisingly, scholarship in general presents a picture of the Old and Middle Kingdoms as centralized, determined by pharaoh, and the First Intermediate Period as regionalized — at the most basic level, the data are biased to this "reading." As we broaden our inquiries to approach the historic narrative of ancient Egypt in a new way, we should include all datasets available to us and cannot chose our data selectively.

REGIONALISM IS LOCALLY AND TEMPORALLY SPECIFIC

In order to work with environment and environmental change and their relationship to society and social change, we must look at environment through the lens of regionalism — meaning, looking at our data with both *local* and *temporal* specificity. Ceramics are typically fundamental to the dating of a site's stratigraphy, so when it comes to determining the *temporal* the work of ceramicists is key. In fact, in some excavations the main (perhaps only) question asked of the ceramics is "what does this strata/feature/site date to?" The chronological capacity of ceramics is common knowledge and I will not dwell on it here. *Local*, though, is more complex and deserves some discussion. The presence of archaeologically attested ceramic workshops at a variety of sites and local variations of ceramic fabric strongly suggest that Egyptian ceramics were locally manufactured, and I will expand upon this point below.[1] However, by saying *local* I push for us not just to accept a point of origin of a vessel and employ it as a piece of culture historic data, but to apply that information to formal, functional, and other statistical analyses which seek to elucidate the social role and meaning of those localisms. In other words, *local* becomes a mode of analysis, requiring synthesis and explanation, rather than simply a data point — regionalism rather than simple location.

Additionally, it is necessary to analyze the data while rejecting imposition of any artificially centralizing narrative upon those data.[2] This point is more difficult than it might seem at first blush, as centralizing narratives are the core of the simplification of Egyptian history and are most often the implicit rather than the explicit narrative. For example: Egypt is the gift of the Nile. Upper and Lower Egypt were unified by pharaoh. The king was the top of a complex administration that controlled the country. Royal control over a unified Egypt created a unit of time, a Kingdom. It is easy to use these truisms as givens, fundamentals that allow for historical analysis. However, these basic assumptions encourage researchers to ignore regionalism in their work rather than engage with it. A regional focus of study naturally complements environmental study at a site, encouraging researchers to think through all their materials in the light of (potential) responses to micro-environments, amongst other things.

APPROACHING REGIONALISM IN THE CERAMIC RECORD

As noted above, the local production of ceramics is commonly recognized. Pottery itself had little intrinsic value and there was little reason for a coarse ware storage vessel or even a fine ware cup to be transported long distances from its point of manufacture. The recent *Handbook of the Pottery of Middle Kingdom Egypt* included a second volume, *The Regional Volume*, precisely detailing what types of vessels were found where.[3] This Handbook is remarkable and an important contribution to Egyptian ceramic studies. However, it does not go past the culture historic approach into a study of regionalism. The listing of types by place includes no synthesis or global analysis, and whether there are differences between sites or what any differences or similarities might mean is lost on the reader. The data are simply bound together and presented, awaiting analysis.

But putting the data from many sites in conversation with each other bears great promise for understanding an Egypt that was regional and small scale rather than national in the outlook of most of its ancient population. We must move past simple lists of what form is at what site and analyze why and how those differences arise. There are many different questions ceramicists may ask of the ceramic data to forward regional analyses. For the sake of brevity I include only three.

First: Analysis of formal variation across sites within one type of vessel. The ceramic corpus for the centrally unified periods—the Kingdoms—is commonly treated as itself centralized, with standardized forms appearing at sites across the country. Morphological variation within the type is therefore assumed to be the same across Egypt, meaning that a vessel type at any site may be dated by comparison to pots from other sites, regardless of distance, though there are certainly counter examples.[4] Certainly one of the most notable aspects of the ceramics of Kingdom periods is that the forms are so immediately recognizable, regardless of where you are in Egypt. We have a limited understanding of how and why this is true or how production was overseen.[5] A Middle Kingdom water jar is immediately identifiable, whether at Memphis or Abydos. An Old Kingdom Meidum bowl can be recognized whether at Giza or Edfu. And certainly, the ceramic corpora of periods of unified rule such as the Old and Middle Kingdoms do show a large amount of consistency in types and forms present across the country, while the First Intermediate Period (for example) includes more site-to-site ceramic variation in types.

The recognizability of a vessel type, however, should not be conflated with standardization of a vessel type. When one closely studies and records the attributes of vessels of the same form at different sites it becomes apparent that a range of variation existed across, and sometimes even within, sites. Take the Meidum Bowl, a common Old Kingdom form, as one example. This fine ware bowl with recurved rim and burnished red slip is regularly used as a chronological marker at Old Kingdom sites.[6] Work by Sarah Sterling focused on length and angles of the rim and its recurve, shows that there is not one trajectory for Meidum bowl evolution, but two—Meidum (the capital region) and a "proto bowl" lineage with unclear origins.[7] This finding suggests the presence of complex social system of regional and national interaction. Study of vessel volume in the ubiquitous Old Kingdom beer jar and bread mould, two utilitarian forms that dominate the Old Kingdom ceramic record, shows that vessel volume varied even within the corpus of one site and ultimately shows no standardization.[8] Such variation within attributes is at the least suggestive of, and in some cases even indicative of, the structure of local potting industries, the relationships between sites forming local and regional power, and situations of individual agency.

Unfortunately, morphological variation within a vessel type, evident both between and within sites, means that dating pottery is tricky and is best done by assemblage and not by individual vessel. With this in mind, the ceramicist alone cannot arrive at a date but must work with the archaeologist, the stratigraphy, and the artifactual assemblage to determine the date and broader chronology of the site. Without doing this complex work, any local variation we have in otherwise recognizable morphology is lost.

Second: Paying attention to the simple presence or absence of a vessel type can help illuminate site functions, locally distinctive traits, or inter-site relationships. For example, Fourth Dynasty Heit el-Ghurob includes a bowl form with a recurved rim and a cream slip inside and outside (form CD 7) that was known at only one other site when it was first published.[9] During the late Twelfth Dynasty, the Senwosret III mortuary temple and the town of *Wah-Sut* at South Abydos both used a small, roughly cylindrical coarse form made of Nile C;[10] it is absent at contemporary sites outside of Abydos. The simple presence of unique forms indicates that an activity unique or uniquely expressed occurred at the site; specific interpretation, of course, is dependent upon greater context.

In order to identify the odd additional form or the oddly absent type, one must be familiar with the corpus of the period as known at different sites. To enable such knowledge, each ceramicist, each excavation, must publish their whole ceramic corpus and not just the forms they find interesting, useful, or exemplary. Common types, exceptional types, and everything in between must appear in a publication of the entire corpus. Publishing a full corpus provides a basic accounting that can build understanding of the site, of course, but also allow for greater understanding of regional difference as other specialists at other sites embark upon comparative work. Extended analyses open the door to uncovering and studying regionally distinct subcultures.

Alternatively, such analyses might uncover temporal consistencies across sites that point to supra-regional culture change. For example, it is well known that ceramic corpora during the First Intermediate Period become regionally distinct.[11] The greater narrative of regionalism and difference has dominated discussion of the ceramic corpora of the period. Within those corpora, however, hides a notable absence—beer jars, so common in the Old Kingdom, disappear from *all* Egyptian sites during the late Old Kingdom/early First Intermediate Period. *Bḏ³* bread moulds are replaced in both Upper and Lower Egypt by different types of moulds, precursers to the conical moulds of the Middle Kingdom. Our knowledge of the specific timing and breadth of these changes is limited at the moment and requires more study of settlement ceramics. However, as beer jars and bread moulds were basic to the Old Kingdom Egyptian economy, their absence during the First Intermediate Period indicates that the economy of Egypt as a whole changed.[12]

We must remember that human cultures are complex and it is unlikely in a state-level society such as ancient Egypt to find total regional identity or total state control.

Remembering complexity challenges ceramicists to look for both presence *and* absence and not accept a facile narrative. To this end, though, an additional note of caution: when highlighting presence or absence, one must be prepared to be proven wrong—and realize that in being so proven a dialogue about site interaction is actually forwarded. Wodzińska's work with Giza form CD 7 highlighted this odd form. Later publication of material from el-Sheikh highlighted the use of the same vessel at another state-sponsored worksite, suggesting that government authorities used this form specifically at centrally controlled site… though for what, exactly (rations?), requires further work.[13] Ceramicists, and archaeologists in general, should not sit on their data until they feel they have incontrovertible evidence. Rather, publish the material, highlight the regularities and the oddities, and start a discussion.

Third: Ceramic analysis should be statistically relevant—meaning, we should understand the above two points through data-rich analyses accounting for frequency and variability, addressing which forms and wares are abundant and which are rare. The abundance of the ceramic record is of course one of the barriers to such an analysis, though the abundance of the record is also what makes it so perfect for statistical analysis. Another barrier, particular to settlement contexts, is that complete vessels are rarely preserved and thus the ceramic record is a sherd record. Most of the sherds will be body sherds; many will be rim or base fragments ("diagnostics"), small and tempting to ignore. Often, archaeologists decide to throw out the body sherds, as they are perceived to carry little value outside of vessel reconstruction. They seem to simply take up valuable magazine space—space that, increasingly, simply does not exist at most Egyptian archaeological sites. So it is tempting to triage the "valuable" diagnostics from the "junk" body sherds.

Yet both sets of data (body sherds, diagnostics regardless of size) require analysis; they must be considered in light of each other to fully understand a context. Body sherds, as the majority of the record, give a snapshot of wares (fabric, technology, surface treatment) that dominate a context; they also allow one to look for evidence of burning suggestive of a relationship between a ware and cooking patterns. Careful accounting of diagnostics allows one to question site formation processes and area function. It is also only by studying all diagnostics that it is possible to understand just *how* prevalent any particular form is—not just the forms that we know or that are instantly recognizable.

How to look at such a vast array of sherds in detail is of course the challenge. There is no way to analyze a mass volume of sherd material without requiring extensive manual work. At Elephantine, in the Realities of Life Project of the German Archaeological Institute (directed by Johanna Sigl), I developed a form to help both standardize the data which is recorded, first in paper and eventually input into the site's database. There are two sheets: one that forces the ceramicist to work through all the body sherds, the other that allows one to work through diagnostic sherds (Tables 1–2). When working through body sherds, I both count and weigh all body sherds by a combination of fabric and surface treatment; technology is not considered, as all vessels under study were wheel made. I also look at charring and blackening with the goal of giving some insight as to cooking traditions. The "fabric" category here is necessarily loose, as it is impossible to give specific fabric identifications without freshly breaking a sherd. It is simply physically impossible to chip every sherd and still process the mass of data. Thus, a general visual and textural division of fabrics by coarse (fabric NSI), medium-fine (fabrics NSII+), bread moulds (fabric NS V) and marls (rare, so accounted for by specific type) serves, with an error rate in identification of 3–5% as compared to the same context when sherds are chipped. The second sheet allows me to count and weigh diagnostic sherds by type as well as ware. Moreover, it requires that the analyst measures the diameter of every rim and base sherd whenever possible.

175

SECONDARY PROCESSING: POTTERY (V3; EDITED 6 NOV 2018)

Note anything interesting in the comment field, such as type of decoration, placement of cream slip, bm lining, etc

BODY SHERDS

Fabric Group	Surface treatment	Normal	Fire in	Fire out	Fire in/out	Rims tstc	Other (decorated, comments, etc)
NS I	Unslipped						
	R slip in						
	R slip out						
	R slip in/out						
	Cream slip						
NS II+	Unslipped						
	R slip in						
	R slip out						
	R slip in/out						
	Cream slip						
NS V	untreated						
MI	See commts						
MII	See commts						
Other marl	See commts						

LOCUS NUMBER:

Processed by: | Date: | Page ____ of ____

TABLE 1.

176

SECONDARY PROCESSING: POTTERY (V3; EDITED 6 NOV 2018)

Note anything interesting in the comment field, such as type of decoration, placement of cream slip, bm lining, etc

Type:	Fabric:	Description:	
	Slip:		1)
			2)
	Black:		3)
			4)
	Addtnl:	Object number concordance (photo'd)	5)
			Diameter/percentage/weight

Addtnl Comments:

Type:	Fabric:	Description:	
	Slip:		1)
			2)
	Black:		3)
			4)
	Addtnl:	Object number concordance (photo'd)	5)
			Diameter/percentage/weight

Addtnl Comments:

Type:	Fabric:	Description:	
	Slip:		1)
			2)
	Black:		3)
			4)
	Addtnl:	Object number concordance (photo'd)	5)
			Diameter/percentage/weight

Addtnl Comments:

Type:	Fabric:	Description:	
	Slip:		1)
			2)
	Black:		3)
			4)
	Addtnl:	Object number concordance (photo'd)	5)
			Diameter/percentage/weight

Addtnl Comments:

LOCUS NUMBER:

Processed by:	Date:	Page ____ of ____

TABLE 2.

While slow and painstaking, these data allow for statistical analyses of local manufacture and variation, contextual analyses of corpora, and analyses of function not by individual form but by context.[14]

Perhaps even more importantly, this type of recording provides an avenue to work through mixed deposits: deposits that were not formed in one specific chronological moment or one single activity. The stratigraphy at most settlement sites is formed of mixed deposits. But when we publish the data, we tend to create period-specific presentations that give the mistaken impression that everything comes from single-phase contexts. By looking at the ceramics from a complete context we might start to discuss local activities and individual depositional patterns. Fine-grained analysis of full contexts has the potential to change our discourse about which vessels are important versus those that were less culturally valuable. Such statistical works allow us to prize function and cultural narratives rather than stopping at cherry-picking forms of interest or that are useful for dating.

Why Should You Care?

Ceramics present a rich, complex dataset that must be recorded in detail to allow for researchers to carry out social analyses. Why, though, does any of this matter in a volume dedicated to the environment?

It is important that Egyptian archaeology seek to model a more complex world than typically embraced by the standard Royal Narrative. By focusing on environment in this volume, we present a new approach to Egyptian history, one where—as the pottery also shows us—at no point is Egyptian culture monolithic, nor can it be reified into simple binaries. The data are evident, but if we look at them, record them, and assemble the numerous small pieces. The challenge is using such fractious data to model the Egyptian world.

The material world is entangled with numerous variables: state and local control over town and craft, the technologies of craft production, the geology and environment, changing cultural mores. Thus, a single narrative cannot explain the full cultural meaning of these sherds. Changing our methodology allows us to see and question difference and distinction in the archaeological record, to move us outside of typology and chronology and suggest that these data themselves might articulate together to form a narrative. These modes of analyses compliment the questions and the local focus of environmental study, breaking us from the traditional timeline and view of Egyptian history and forcing us to look at complex regional narratives by forcing us to put *place* at the forefront of inquiry. Only by seeking to understanding the unique pieces and places of the Nile Valley can we ultimately understand the complex whole of Egyptian history.

Works Cited

Ballet, P. 1987. "Essai de classification des coupes type *Maidum-Bowl* du sondage nord de 'Ayn-Asil (oasis de Dakhla): Typologie et évolution." *Cahiers de la céramique égyptienne* 1: 11–16.

Bourriau, J., P. Nicholson, and P. Rose. 2000. "Pottery." In *Ancient Egyptian Materials and Technology*, edited by P. Nicholson and I. Shaw, 121–147. Cambridge: Cambridge University Press.

Hope, C.A., and A. McFarlane. 2006. *Akhmim in the Old Kingdom. Part II: The Pottery, Decorative Techniques and Colour Conventions*. Oxford: Aris and Phillips Ltd.

Op de Beek, L. 2000 "Restrictions on the Use of Maidum-Bowls as Chronological Indicators." *Chronique d'Égypte* 75: 5–14.

———. 2004. "Possibilities and Restrictions for the Use of Maidum-Bowls as Chronological Indicators." *Cahiers de la céramique égyptienne* 7: 239–280.

Rzeuska, T.I. 2006. *Saqqara*. Vol. 2, *Pottery of the Late Old Kingdom: Funerary Pottery and Burial Customs*. Warsaw: Editions Neriton.

———. 2012. "Elephantine—A Place of an End and a Beginning." In *Handbook of the Pottery of the Egyptian Middle Kingdom*. Vol 1, *The Corpus Volume,* edited by R. Schiestl and A. Seiler, 329—359. Vienna: Austrian Academy of Sciences Press.

Schiestl, R., and A. Seiler, eds. 2012. *Handbook of Pottery of the Egyptian Middle Kingdom*. Vol. 1, *The Corpus Volume*. Vienna: Austrian Academy of Sciences Press.

Seidlmayer, S.J. 1991. *Gräberfelder aus dem Übergang vom Alten zum Mittleren Reich: Studien zur Archäologie der Ersten Zwischenzeit*. Heidelberg: Heidelberger Orientverlag.

Soukiassian, G., M. Wuttmann, and L. Pantalacci. 1990. *Balat*. Vol. 3, *Les ateliers du potiers d'Ayn-Asil*. Cairo: IFAO.

Sterling, S.L. 2004. "Social Complexity in Ancient Egypt: Functional Differentiation as Reflected in the Distribution of Apparently Standardized Ceramics." Ph.D. diss., University of Washington.

———. 2009. "Pottery Attributes and How They Reflect Intentionality in Craft Manufacture/Reproduction." In *Studies on Old Kingdom Pottery*, edited by T.I. Rzeuska and A. Wodzińska, 155–186. Warsaw: Editions Neriton.

Vereecken, S. 2013. "About Bread Moulds and Bread Trays: Evidence for an Old Kingdom Bakery at al-Shaykh Sa'id." In *Functional Aspects of Egyptian Ceramics in their Archaeological Context*, edited by B. Bader and M.F. Ownby, 53–71. Leuven: Uitgeverij Peeters.

Warden, L.A. 2011. "The Organization and Oversight of Potters in the Old Kingdom." In *Abusir and Saqqara in the Year 2010*, edited by M. Bárta, 800–819. Prague: Charles University in Prague.

———. 2014. *Pottery and Economy in Old Kingdom Egypt*. Leiden: Brill.

———. 2019. "Tying Technology to Social, Economic, and Political Change: The Case of Bread Baking at Elephantine." *American Journal of Archaeology* 123(1): 1–17.

Wegner, J.W. 2007. *The Mortuary Temple of Senwosret III at Abydos*. New Haven: The Peabody Museum of Natural History of Yale University.

Wegner, J.W., V. Smith, and S. Rossell. 2000. "The Organization of the Temple Nfr-kꜣ of Senwosret III at Abydos." *Ägypten und Levante* 10: 83–125.

Wodzińska, A. "Preliminary Report on the Ceramics." In *Giza Reports: The Giza Plateau Mapping Project*. Vol. 1, *Project History, Survey, Ceramics, and the Main Street and Gallery III.4 Operations*, edited by M. Lehner and W. Wetterstrom, 283–324. Boston: Ancient Egypt Research Associates, 2007.

NOTES

[1]   For an overview of pottery workshops at select sites, see Bourriau et al. 2000, 137–138; for an example of local variations in fabric at Elephantine see Rzeuska 2012, 331.

[2]   It is, of course, necessary to reject imposition of *any* narrative upon the data during the recording and analysis phase; however, I focus on centralizing narratives as they, rather than localizing narratives, have driven much Egyptological research.

[3]   Schiestl and Seiler 2012.

[4]   For an example of such cross-referencing, see Hope and McFarlane 2006, 36–45. Examples of regional chronology can be found at Balat (Ballet 1987, 7; Soukiassian et al. 1990, 165) and South Saqqara (Rzeuska 2006, 380).

[5]   Bourriau et al. 2000, 138, 141; Sterling 2004; Warden 2011.

[6]   See Op de Beek (2000, 2004) for challenges in dating these bowls.

[7]   Sterling 2004, 2009.

[8]   Warden 2014.

[9]   Wodzińska 2007, 299–300.

[10] Wegner et al. 2000, 106–107, 111–112 (where the type is labeled number 41), fig. 17 (where the type is labeled 33 and 34). Also documented in Wegner 2007, 242 (type 38), where Wegner notes a possible parallel at Lahun.

[11] Seidlmayer 1991.

[12] Warden forthcoming.

[13] Vereecken 2013, 68.

[14] See, for example, Warden 2014, 183–189.

Chapter Nine

Reconstructing Egypt's Paleoecology and Paleoclimate: An Assessment of the Opportunities and Pitfalls

Pearce Paul Creasman

Natural environment is unquestionably one of the most important factors in the development of a civilization, with Egypt being no exception. The term "environment" is used here to encompass climate, topography, and plant and animal life. The complex and dynamic interactions among them form the ecosystem, of which humans are a part, not only because their societies are shaped partly by what surround them, but also because they affect their environment through landscaping, hunting and gathering, plant and animal domestication, and other acts of intervention. The better one understands the ancient environment, therefore, the better one might understand the people who occupied it.

Despite innumerable archaeological excavations conducted during the past two centuries and despite the survival of an extensive written record, the environment of ancient Egypt is still incompletely and imperfectly understood. In addition to historical and archaeological investigations, diverse scientific methodologies can and have been brought to bear on an evaluation of Egypt's ancient environment. This paper reviews the current state of efforts to reconstruct the paleoecology and paleoclimate of Egypt as well as some of the unused or underused but promising methods. Selected opportunities for meaningful gains are identified along with potential pitfalls and challenges. Some topics that might have been included here, or could have been discussed in greater detail, are covered elsewhere in this volume (e.g., landscape changes [see Bunbury], human-environmental interactions [Rowland]).

Due to the breadth of the topic, the scope of the survey will be restricted chronologically to the Holocene, in other words the most recent 11,700 years since the end of the last Ice Age to the present, and with a special focus on the pharaonic era. It should be remembered, however, that many of the same research methods are being applied successfully to the study of prior geological epochs.

According to a synthesis of 500 radiocarbon data from 150 archaeological sites, Egypt and the rest of the Eastern Sahara have witnessed many great climatic changes through

The Gift of the Nile? Ancient Egypt and the Environment
edited by Thomas Schneider and Christine L. Johnston
Tucson, Arizona: Egyptian Expedition, 2020

the Holocene.[1] With the abrupt arrival of monsoon rains around 8500 BCE, the hyper-arid desert was replaced by savannah-like environments, and human settlement became well-established all over the Eastern Sahara by 7000 BCE. Retreating monsoon rains caused the onset of desiccation of the Egyptian Sahara around 5300 BCE, forcing the population to the Nile Valley and the Sudanese Sahara where water was still sufficient.

Another significant climatic shift *may* have occurred in what is today Egypt and the Sudan around 2200 BCE, a time of Mediterranean/Near Eastern megadrought. It coincided at least chronologically with the devolution of many civilizations, including Old Kingdom Egypt.[2] The idea that a major climate change brought about the subsequent First Intermediate Period is not new (see below),[3] but it is only in the last three decades that more scientific evidence for the so-called 4.2 ka BP event is beginning to emerge in Egypt.[4] Incontrovertible evidence is still scarce along the Nile when in comparison to the rest of the Mediterranean and Near Eastern world, leading some to conclude that either the event did not affect Egypt and Sudan as severely as other areas or that the matter has not been investigated sufficiently.[5] As a result, scholars continue to debate whether the 4.2 ka BP event was the primary/direct cause for the end of the Old Kingdom or not.[6]

Textual Analysis

The oldest and still one of the most influential approaches to the investigation of ancient Egyptian environment is the historical interpretation of written records, which vary from royal flood level marks to lengthy non-royal autobiographies. Many of these texts were carved in stone and have been documented epigraphically, while some others were written in cursive hieratic script with ink on papyrus sheets. Since the syntax of the ancient Egyptian language is well-understood, these texts can be translated and interpreted, although some lexicographic questions may remain.

Scholars have long pointed out the notable concentration of texts that discuss famine or large-scale hunger from the First Intermediate Period,[7] and in 1971, Bell synthesized them to argue a case for a catastrophic climate change that resulted in the fall of the Old Kingdom.[8] The texts that Bell analyzed include the autobiography of Ankhtifi from el-Moalla,[9] stela of Iti from Gebelein,[10] stela of Merer,[11] autobiography of Khety from Asyut, three graffiti from Hatnub, and false door of Neferiu from Dendera.[12] Even a literary work, known variably as *The Lament of Ipuwer*, *The Admonitions of an Egyptian Sage*, or *The Dialogue between Ipuwer and the Lord of All* (P. Leiden I 344, recto),[13] has also been cited to support this notion.

These compositions seem like powerful evidence since they represent precisely what ancient Egyptians themselves conceived and decided to write down (or a portion of such that has survived today), but they must be evaluated critically for inherent bias and used with caution before they can be accepted as historical records of environmental changes. Potential problems of the textual analysis have been discussed more extensively by Moreno García[14] and summarized by Moeller.[15] In short, the pious acts, including giving bread for the hungry, are formulaic themes of charity established already in the Old Kingdom, and therefore the famine described in these passages is essentially an ideologically motivated literary motif. The autobiographies were inscribed in tombs so that the deceased will be able to attain their afterlife, and the primary aim of these texts was to emphasize the reputable character of the tomb owners, not to record historical reality. As for *The Lament of Ipuwer*, this poetic dialogue is now thought to be of a late Middle Kingdom composition and has survived in only one Nineteenth Dynasty copy, and therefore it hardly represents an eyewitness description of the First Intermediate Period.

Textual evidence has also been used to reconstruct the changing height of Nile inundations, which in turn might reflect the wider climatic pattern, as the Nile flood levels were determined by the amount of monsoon rains over the river's headwater catchments in East Africa. For example, Bell already argued in 1975 that there was a period of high inundations from the late Twelfth Dynasty to early Thirteenth Dynasty based primarily on the Middle Kingdom flood marks found in the Second Cataract region.[16] One challenge in interpreting the Nile flood markings is comparison of marks from different sites. As the width and depth of the river vary from site to site depending on the local topography and as their diachronic variations are often difficult to reconstruct due to the river's migratory nature, flood markings from different sites and different periods cannot be compared directly. Another pitfall is the motivation behind the marks. High inundations were normally considered more favorable and was thought to reflect the king's fulfillment of his duty as the maintainer of the cosmic order. Such positive occasions are more likely to have been recorded for posterity than less favorable phenomena, and therefore the dataset may be askew from the beginning.

ART HISTORY

Ideological motivations, which influenced the written records, also need to be considered in assessing pictorial representations. For example, the scene depicting a group of emaciated people at the causeway of Unis' pyramid complex cannot reliably be interpreted as evidence for a period of famine at the end of the Fifth Dynasty.[17] Although the exact meaning of the scene is unclear due to lack of descriptive captions, it was probably part of a propagandistic statement that contrasted the deplorable state of the foreigners—probably Bedouins in this case—with the prosperity of the Egyptian population owing to the righteous rule of the divine king.

Images are important sources of information, but they are inherently subjective and need to be interpreted critically, ideally with the support of more objective evidence. One recent study correlated the increase of marsh scenes in late Old Kingdom tomb decoration with a period of prolonged drought.[18] The correlation between increased riverine biomass and aridification may seem counterintuitive, but it makes sense ecologically. A weaker river decreases the rate of soil erosion and thus aids the growth of papyrus plants, which can tolerate high salinity and low pH levels caused by low flood. The clumps of papyrus also slow down the water flow. Papyrus vegetation at the river edges is a valuable food base for small fish, and it serves as a sheltered nesting habitat for birds. Consequently, an environment suited for fishing and fowling activities would be created.

ARCHAEOLOGY

The distribution of human occupation sites has also been used to infer the ancient climate. As already noted above, the middle Holocene site distribution shows that there was a dramatic migration of population around 5300 BCE, when semi-nomadic people abandoned the drying Eastern Sahara in favor of more sedentary subsistence pattern along the Nile Valley with its perennial access to water.[19]

A similar principle has been applied on smaller scales, such as within a region or even a site. For example, the elevations of different settlement phases at Elephantine Island were used as the proxy data for the maximum heights of the Nile in respective periods.[20] The method assumes that the residents would use as much space as available while building at levels high enough to stay safe from the floodwater even at the maximum inundation. This study concluded that the Nile flood level decreased gradually between the First and Sixth Dynasty but actually increased during the First Intermediate Period, contrary to what one might expect from a time of drought and famine. The evidence, therefore, suggests that the 4.2 ka BP event apparently did not affect Elephantine.

If similar studies could be conducted at various points along the Nile, then it would be possible to collect a more holistic data set, evaluate the above conclusion based on the observations made at Elephantine, and formulate larger interpretations about the ancient climate. Unfortunately, settlement sites with as long and well-documented history of occupation as Elephantine are scarce in Egypt, and the selective nature of archaeological sites (both survival and excavation) poses a methodological challenge to such study.

The application of the distribution of human occupation sites to determine ancient environment becomes more problematic when it is based more on the absence of data. For example, one recent study argued that much of the western Delta was uninhabitably wet during the Middle Kingdom and the Second Intermediate Period because very few sites of those periods are known despite extensive surveys conducted in the region.[21] Absence of evidence cannot be taken as evidence of absence, and there are many possible reasons why settlements could have existed in the western Delta but either did not survive or have not been located yet. The study ascribes the extremely wet condition of the western Delta during those periods to the incursion of the sea. According to this theory, the region experienced lower rate of silt deposition and therefore turned into a wetland due to the faster eustatic rise of the sea level.

GEOARCHAEOLOGY

Among the most fundamental aspects of environment is the geography. Egypt's natural topography consists of three main and distinct spheres—the deserts, the river, and the seas— none of which are as static as they might seem at a first glance. A landmass can shift due to tectonic movements, and the surface can be covered by thick layers of aeolian sand after sandstorms. The Nile River is particularly dynamic; it has continuously migrated due to its meandering, and it may have formed oxbow lakes[22] and did form islands while eroding old ones.[23] As mentioned above, the river also carries silt and deposits it downstream, especially at the delta, causing the Mediterranean coastline to extend gradually at the mouths of the branches. Yet, global warming increases the sea level, submerging some of the coastal areas. The dynamic nature of topography has been known since ancient time, but its impact on the Egyptian civilization was first explicitly and systematically studied by Karl Butzer. Since his landmark publication in 1976,[24] there have been an increasing number of geoarchaeological studies along the Nile, and the techniques of data collection and analysis are becoming more sophisticated.[25]

Cartographic survey is still an essential way to document the current topographic features, although measurements are taken more accurately, precisely, and efficiently now with the use of total stations, portable computers, and GPS. A recent advancement in this area is the 3D laser scanning technology (e.g., LiDAR), which can be applied to a wider landscape than ever before.[26] To reconstruct ancient topography and to understand the past geomorphological process, however, scientists must also collect geological data from below ground. One of the more accurate but less efficient methods is the archaeological excavation and stratigraphy. Samples can also be collected without conducting full-scale excavations by drill coring, which can be either simple hand augering or machine-assisted percussion coring.[27] Nowadays, these methods are combined with various types of remote sensing techniques, such as satellite image analysis, magnetometry, electrical resistivity tomography (ERT), and ground-penetrating radar (GPR) to obtain more complete data on the local geomorphology.[28]

The collected sediments can be analyzed geologically for their petrological and lithological properties, and its deposition can be interpreted in terms of ecological history. For example, the about 1.5 m thick layers of culturally sterile sand found at multiple sites near Memphis and Abusir have been understood as aeolian sand that accumulated over a prolonged period of intense aridification.[29] At Dahshur, the correlation with the datable artifacts below and above the sand layer further indicates that it coincided with the temporary abandonment of these sites between the Old and Middle Kingdoms.[30] In western Saqqara, geoarchaeologists noted an undisturbed sequence of natural and anthropogenic layers, which could be marked by distinct facies. Based on the types of sediment (e.g., limestone rubbles, mud, aeolian sand, etc.) in each layer, they could reconstruct the expected rapid aridification and catastrophically low floods as well as more surprising sporadic episodes of heavy rainfalls.[31]

The soil and plants that grow in it can also be analyzed in terms of their chemical compositions. Rare and distinct elements, such as isotopes, have been used to trace certain geological origins, which in turn can serve as proxy data for the environment or climate in those locations. This has demonstrated particularly effective in dendrochronological studies,[32] but no such works have been conducted to date for the ancient periods of Egypt. In soils directly, the ratios of the strontium isotopes (^{87}Sr and ^{86}Sr) in sediments differ between the two main tributaries of the Egyptian Nile (White Nile catchment in Tanzania-Uganda and the Blue Nile-Atbara River catchment in northern Ethiopia), so the changing proportions of these isotopes in Egypt over time might signify the climatic changes along those tributaries. The drill core from northeastern delta shows a steady decrease in the ^{87}Sr/^{86}Sr ratio between 6100–4200 BP (i.e., from the Predynastic Period to the Old Kingdom).[33] The data have been interpreted as a sign for increased soil erosion rate in the Ethiopian highland with low ^{87}Sr/^{86}Sr ratio, which might have been caused by reduced rainfall and consequently decreased vegetation. More recently, such interpretations have been intensively questioned, so such interpretations must be used with caution and cannot be relied upon solely.[34]

Marine sediments can also provide paleoclimatic data for the nearby oceans, because they reflect different levels of salinity and oxygen in the water, which can be proxy data for the ancient environments. Cores taken from the bottom of the Shaban Deep in the northern Red Sea, for example, demonstrates a clearly marked facies around 2200 BCE, between earlier laminated sediments deposited under anoxic conditions and later homogeneous sediments deposited under oxic conditions.[35]

The research into evolving topography, sedimentation history, and changes in geochemical compositions have been used successfully to reconstruct the paleoenvironment around the world. Although their continued application in Egyptian archaeology holds a great potential, these methods are not without pitfalls and challenges. First, one must ensure that the excavated areas and core samples are representative of the wider geological phenomenon if they are to be interpreted as evidence for global or even regional climate changes. The thick sand layer encountered at many Memphite necropolis sites indeed seems to correspond to their abandonment during the First Intermediate Period, but similar strata should be encountered at other contemporaneous sites throughout Egypt if it truly represents the global drought event around 2200 BCE. Similarly, the observable change in the strontium isotopes ratio was based on only one core from northeast delta, basically the farthest point from the sources of sediments carried by the Nile tributaries, and it should be tested for replicability at other locations along the Nile north of Atbara, because it is not impossible that other unknown factors (such as wadi outwash[36]) are affecting the isotope ratios over time. The main challenge so far is the lack of data, and the only way to overcome it is to promote the application of these geoarchaeological methods and to rigorously collect relevant data in the field.

Another possible pitfall is the accuracy and precision of the dating methodologies used in tandem with the geoarchaeological ones. In the abovementioned case of strontium isotopes, for example, the dates of the geological strata were established with radiocarbon dating, which has inherent issues as the authors acknowledge in their article.[37] To calibrate their radiocarbon dates, they adopted a correction factor of 400 years from another study in Israel, which may or may not be appropriate for northern Egypt. Radiocarbon dates are also always expressed in terms of a range and its probability. The methodology may be suited for studying a general long-term climatic trend, but caution must be exercised when identifying short and abrupt historical events that require more precise dates.

One geoarchaeological method that has been rarely used in Egypt is the study of speleothems (cave formations). Stalactites and stalagmites form gradually inside caves, as water dissolves the host limestone and deposits many layers of calcium carbonate. There are at least five such cave formations in Egypt, including Djara in the Western Desert. Speleothems have concentric growth rings in cross sections, and each ring can be subjected to isotope analysis to determine the type of environment in which the mineral was deposited. According to an analysis of uranium and thorium isotopes, the stalagmites at Wadi Sannur Cavern in the Eastern Desert initially formed around 200,000 BP, and this was followed by periods of leaching, which is consistent with the known pluvial stages in the Pleistocene.[38] A speleothem study at Djara Cave in the Western Desert also revealed that none of the secondary carbonates there dated to the Holocene despite archaeological evidence for human occupation during that epoch.[39] For the Holocene, the ratio of stable oxygen isotopes is used to infer environmental factors such as air temperature, humidity, and the amount of precipitation. Greater rainfall is often a response to higher summer radiation and increased monsoonal activity, and to lower winter radiation and a more southerly position for the winter westerlies. Critically, this suggests that Egypt is on a separate environmental system from the rest of the East Mediterranean despite the cultural interconnections among the societies in those regions. It must be remembered, therefore, that climatic trends observed in the Mediterranean did not necessarily impact Egypt.

Archaeobotany

Archaeobotany is another form of archaeological science that aids the understanding of ancient climate and ecology. It focuses on the various plant remains that are found in archaeological contexts, ranging from microscopic pollens to massive ship timbers.

Species identification plays an important role in reconstructing the paleoenvironment, because the abundance or absence of different plants can indicate different climates or, in some cases, human intervention to the ecosystem. One way to identify the variation of plants in an area is palynology, which strictly speaking refers to analysis of pollens, but archaeobotanists also examine other resilient microbotanical remains, such as cuticles and phytoliths, that are found mixed in soil.[40] Samples are collected by drill coring, very much like the geoarchaeological data. The soil from each layer is first mixed with water and then run in a centrifuge to extract the microbotanical remains. Finally, they are examined with an optic microscope or a scanning electron microscope (SEM), and the plant species are identified by comparing the morphology of the pollens with modern samples or known examples of extinct species.

A pollen analysis conducted in the southern Levant found evidence for a short dry event around 2300 BCE and a more prolonged dry period in 2000–1800 BCE, both marked by a significant decrease in trees.[41] The former climate change might be related to the 4.2 ka BP event, although it seems a little early, while the latter climate change was interpreted as a cause for the first major migration of Asiatic population into the northeastern Nile Delta in the early Middle Kingdom. Again, lack of temporal precision complicates such interpretations.

In another study, a core taken near Burullus Lagoon in the northern Delta was studied, and the taxonomical variations of plants in different layers of soil were used to identify four main chronological zones between 7300 BP to the present.[42] This study has found that a family of sedges (Cyperaceae) is an especially sensitive marker of precipitation, not in Egypt itself but in the Sudanese marshes of the White Nile catchment. More Cyperaceae pollen was transported from the headwaters in the time of high Nile, and less was carried by the river in the time of dryness. According to the palynological evidence, dry events occurred around 5000 BP, 4200 BP, and 3000 BP, which roughly correspond to the unification of Upper and Lower Egypt, the end of the Old Kingdom, and the end of the New Kingdom. Another similar study at Alexandria also determined a major change in botanical variation around 3000 BP.[43] As the shift was not always reflected in the lithological properties, this observation demonstrates the importance of analyzing botanical and geological data in conjunction. The same drill core samples were also analyzed for the quantity of microscopic charcoal, which has been correlated elsewhere to fire events, which in turn serve as a good marker for the presence of human activities, when distinguishable from non-anthropogenic fire events.[44]

Charred or uncharred, macro remains such as seeds, fruits, and wood can inform the plant variation, and thus the climatic environment, of the area. For example, many botanical remains were found inside the Djara Cave, where the preservation was notably better than at the occupation sites outside.[45] Botanists identified 21 taxa, including six tree species such as *Acacia nilotica*, and dated them to 6500–5200 BCE. The plant variations indicate that the region, which is hyper-arid today, enjoyed a less dry climate in the early to mid-Holocene.

The generally arid climate of Egypt is ideal for the preservation of wooden artifacts, such as tools, statues, furniture, coffins, and boats. Many types of trees can be identified by looking at the wood macroscopically (e.g., grain colors and patterns) or microscopically (e.g., cellular structures). Some species found in archaeological excavations were native to Egypt, while others were imported. Despite its origin in Sudan and further southward, sycomore fig (*Ficus sycomorus*) became very common in ancient Egypt as well as the rest of North Africa and the Mediterranean world. In the native environment, sycomore fig was pollinated only through the agency of a very specific type of wasp. Since these wasps are not evidenced to have ever existed in Egypt, however, all sycomore figs cultivated in pharaonic Egypt must have been reproduced artificially, ostensibly by hand. If true, it is one of the most intensive acts to shape the ecology in human history. A research project is under way to genetically trace North African and Mediterranean sycomore figs to a common Sudanese ancestor.[46]

Scientific analysis of tree rings not only yield absolute dates with annual resolution (dendrochronology),[47] but also inform about the conditions in which the trees grew (dendroclimatology). Environmental factors, temperature or soil moisture being the most dominant, affect the growth rate of the trees and result in distinct rings that can be correlated to identify certain climatic events.[48] Until recently, there was some skepticism as to whether any taxa native to Egypt produced tree rings that are viable for dendroarchaeological analyses in sufficient volume to address these larger questions. In 2015, however, it was preliminarily found that tamarisk (*Tamarix nilotica*) and perhaps acacia (*Acacia* spp.) and sycamore fig (*Ficus sycomorus*) produce useful annual rings, given the right conditions. One such environment is Nilotic sandbars and small islands where the river flow is limited and therefore responds to the 5 to 7 cm of "annual inundation" that still occur on the river.[49]

Just as archaeobotanical research methods have so much potential for the study of ancient Egyptian environments, they also have many pitfalls and challenges. First, the data collection is still at its early stage. This is especially true for newly applied disciplines like dendrochronology, but more data are needed for other methods like palynology, too. Despite innumerable archaeological excavations that are carried out in Egypt every year, most projects fail to collect relevant samples. For example, an on-site flotation device is a relatively rarer sight in Egypt than elsewhere. Larger botanical remains, such as wooden artifacts, understandably draw more attention, but it is often the smaller remains, such as grass, seeds, and pollens, that are more representative of the wider paleoenvironment, because of their quantity and regionality.

When it comes to certain types of wood, one must consider whether they are native to the land where they were discovered. Dendroclimatic information of imported trees reflects the environment in which the trees grew, not where the wood was last used and deposited. For instance, all cedar wood (*Cedrus libani*) found in Egypt originated from the northern Levant,[50] and therefore, the dendroclimatic information from these woods cannot be used directly to infer the ancient climate of Egypt.

Another challenge to dendroarchaeology in Egypt had been the lack of an appropriate research facility. Since specimens cannot be taken out of Egypt under current regulations, all tree-ring analyses must be done in the country, but there was no centralized repository or laboratory to do so.[51] In part to address this issue, a new research center called Wilkinson House was established recently on the west bank of Luxor. As the only facility in Egypt with the requisite equipment, it can serve as a base for dendroarchaeologists who would go collect tree-ring specimens at various sites and museums, properly preserve the core samples, and analyze them scientifically. Furthermore, a bilingual glossary of relevant terms has also been published to promote the use of dendroarchaeology in Arabic-speaking countries and to facilitate communication between archaeologists and natural scientists.[52]

Zooarchaeology

Like plants, some animals have very specific environmental preferences. Insects, such as beetles, are particularly sensitive and exist only in certain 1–2 °C temperature ranges. The presence of these species, therefore, can be used to infer the local paleoecology at the time of their deposition. An analysis of several ancient faunal specimens recovered at the Old Kingdom site of Abusir presents an innovative application of this methodology.[53] The types of beetles found *in situ* (some stuck in the hot mummification resin) in the early Sixth Dynasty tombs (e.g., *Scarites* spp. and *Poecilus pharao*) commonly inhabit sandy soils near the sea or salt lakes. The presence of these animals, therefore, indicates that Old Kingdom

Abusir was at the intersection of a dry, sandy desert and a stagnant, brackish lake. At the same site, most of the mollusks embedded in the ancient mud bricks and plaster (e.g., *Bellamya unicolor, Bulinus truncatus,* and *Gabbiella senaariensis*) were found to be species that prefer slow-flowing or stagnant waters. Combining this natural science evidence with other historical and archaeological information from other sites, it was concluded that the climatic change that ultimately led to the demise of the Old Kingdom was already starting in the early Sixth Dynasty and that it was a gradual process.

Fishes and other aquatic animals are also sensitive to their environments. For example, some species inhabit deep, saline waters, while others prefer shallow, fresh waters. The proportions of different types of fishes, therefore, are indicative of the nature of the nearby body of water. At the Twenty-Sixth Dynasty site of Tell el-Ghaba in the north Sinai, for example, the majority of recovered fish bones belonged to continental types, such as *Clarias / Heterobranchus.*[54] The two genera of catfish were combined in the study because they cannot be distinguished easily based on isolated bones. The high ratio of freshwater fishes indicates that the site used to be situated by the Pelusiac branch of the Nile, rather than along the Mediterranean coast. The maritime fishes and turtles, which were also found in smaller quantities, probably derived from a lagoon along the coast.

Certain species of animals could be driven to extinction by new climatic or anthropogenic pressures, and subsequently, these animals disappeared from archaeological records and artistic representations. Based primarily on the artistic evidence but also some faunal remains, data were compiled for the presence and absence of various mammal species throughout Egypt's predynastic and pharaonic eras.[55] The data set was more recently used to analyze the impacts of the environmental change on the ecosystems, focusing on the predator-prey interaction among 37 selected large-bodied mammals over the last six millennia.[56] The authors demonstrate that the local extinction of Egyptian mammals was not random. The stability of the predator-prey community changed throughout the Holocene, providing compelling evidence that local dynamic stability is informative of species persistence over time. In short, the composition of animal communities is reflective of the stability of ecosystems.

One of the challenges in zooarchaeology lies in the quality of available data. The pictorial representations, for example, do not necessarily or comprehensively reflect the contemporary natural world. For example, it was concluded from the animals represented in Egyptian art that the predator-prey ratio increased after 4140 BP due to the appearance of the cheetah (*Acinonyx jubatus*), but it might be erroneous to assume that this predator was introduced in the Middle Kingdom simply because its depiction is not known until then. Once again, absence of evidence is not evidence of absence. For example, some motifs could be consciously omitted based on culturally defined appropriateness or the artist's personal training background. Conversely, some extinct species could be portrayed if they were copied from earlier monuments.

It should be noted that large animals are not as reliable of an indicator of the paleoclimate as once thought, because they are more resilient and can adapt to a wider range of environment. Reconstruction of the ancient climate, therefore, should rely more on smaller animals, such as rodents, birds, fish, insects, and mollusks. It must be remembered that some of these creatures can burrow deeply into the ground and thus intrude into older stratigraphic layers. Minute bones and shells do not preserve very well in a wet and acidic condition like the Delta.[57] In a dry and alkaline condition, on the other hand, small faunal remains—even seemingly fragile exoskeletons of insects—survive surprisingly well. Their collection, however, involves fine-sifting and flotation, which are not practiced consistently in Egyptian archaeology due to the lack resources, interest, or both.

189

Since the current Egyptian bureaucratic system does not permit exportation of scientific samples for more thorough lab analysis abroad, all documentation must be done in the fieldwork setting. Zooarchaeologists who examine the excavated faunal remains must be familiar with the whole range of the animal kingdom in that region, including some extinct species, to correctly identify them. This is an extremely difficult task unless they work as a team of mammologists, ornithologists, ichthyologists, entomologists, and other experts.

PHYSICAL ANTHROPOLOGY

Ancient human remains, such as skeletons and mummies, can also yield some information about the environment in which those people lived. Environmental application of paleopathological and environmental osteological research is still in its infancy, but the approach seems to be exceedingly promising.

As with the speleothems and shells, isotopic analyses can be applied to human bones and teeth to infer the paleoenvironment. One might as well call this "environmental osteology." Water is consumed by humans and the elements therein, such as varying ratios of oxygen isotopes, become part of their mineralized tissues. A recent isotopic analysis of bones and teeth from 48 Egyptian mummies of different periods has shown that $\delta^{18}O$ increased progressively from the 5500 BP to 2550 BP, reflecting the decrease of 140 mm in rainfall at the sources of the Nile or an increase of 2 °C in air temperature between the Predynastic Period and the Late Period.[58] It is not yet clear which of the two factors contributed more to the oxygen isotope composition, and it may well have been a combination of both factors.

Paleopathology is the study of ancient diseases. Certain diseases are more prevalent in certain conditions, and therefore their changing rates over time can serve as proxy data for the environment. For example, a study of tuberculosis (TB) from different periods and countries, including predynastic and dynastic Egypt, has shown that this disease is not influenced so much by the macroenvironment, such as climate. Instead, it is associated with settlements, a specific type of human environment, since the infection rate was found to increase significantly among sedentary societies.[59] Tuberculosis can be diagnosed among the ancient human remains in several ways. A long-established method is to identify bone lesions in the vertebrae through visual examination of skeletons (or through X-ray, if mummified). Severe cases of such lesions can cause vertebral collapse and fusion and ultimately result in the curved spine known as "Pott's disease." Anthropologists can also identify TB bacteria in the vertebrae and red blood cells found in trachea and lungs through microscopy. More recently, it has become possible to retrieve a DNA sequence of *Mycobacterium tuberculosis* from the lung tissues or to detect mycolic acids in the bacteria's cells through liquid chromatography.[60]

CONCLUSIONS

This brief survey is not meant to be an exhaustive review of all current researches into Egypt's paleoecology and paleoclimate. It is rather an overview of selected studies that exemplify the wide range of powerful tools that are available and have been applied to reconstruct the environment of ancient Egypt. All methodologies have their advantages and great potentials, but they also have their own problems and field-specific challenges.

To make larger interpretations, therefore, it is essential to collect and consider the available data holistically and synthesize evidence from different disciplines.[61] The research at Abusir, for instance, successfully combines geological, botanical, and zoological data within the archaeological contexts;[62] such an approach should be more widely utilized.

As Egyptologists and archaeologists are joined by their colleagues in geological and biological sciences, the largest challenge that awaits them is perhaps the communication among humanists, social scientists, and natural scientists. Scholars of each group are trained in their areas of expertise, and they publish their research results in academic journals of their own fields. As a result, historians and scientists often do not "speak" the same academic language. Historians might not understand the scientific jargons in chemistry lab reports, while geologists and biologists might misuse the ambiguous translations of ancient texts. Only open-minded curiosity and continued dialogues can lead to successful cross-disciplinary collaborations.

Acknowledgements

The author is grateful for the feedback of Kei Yamamoto, Noreen Doyle and Angus Graham, whose considerations improved this manuscript.

Works Cited

Alexanian, N., and S.J. Seidlmayer. 2002. "Die Residenznekropole von Dahschur: Erster Grabungsbericht." *Mitteilungen des Deutschen Archäologischen Instituts, Abteilung Kairo* 58: 1–28.

Arz, H.W., J. Kaiser, and D. Fleitmann. 2015. "Paleoceanographic and Paleoclimatic Changes around 2200 BC Recorded in Sediment Cores from the Northern Red Sea." In *2200 BC—Ein Klimasturz als Ursache für den Zerfall der Alten Welt? 7. Mitteldeutscher Archäologentag vom 23. bis 26. Oktober 2014 in Halle (Saale)*, edited by H. Meller, H.W. Arz, R. Jung, and R. Risch, 53–60. Halle (Saale): Landesmuseum für Vorgeschichte.

Bárta, M. 2013. "In Mud Forgotten: Old Kingdom Palaeoecological Evidence from Abusir." *Studia Quaternaria* 30(2): 75–82.

Bárta, M., and A. Bezděk. 2008. "Beetles and the Decline of the Old Kingdom: Climate Change in Ancient Egypt." In *Chronology and Archaeology in Ancient Egypt (the Third Millennium B.C.)*, edited by H. Vymazalová and M. Bárta, 214–222. Prague: Czech Institute of Egyptology, Faculty of Arts, Charles University in Prague.

Bell, B. 1971. "The Dark Ages in Ancient History, I: The First Dark Age in Egypt." *American Journal of Archaeology* 75(1): 1–26.

———. 1975. "Climate and the History of Egypt: The Middle Kingdom." *American Journal of Archaeology* 79(3): 223–269.

Bernhardt, C.E., B.P. Horton, and J.-D. Stanley. 2012. "Nile Delta Vegetation Response to Holocene Climate Variability." *Geology* 40(7): 615–618.

Bietak, M. 2017. "Harbours and Coastal Military Bases in Egypt in the Second Millennium B.C.: Avaris, Peru-nefer, Pi-Ramesse." In *The Nile: Natural and Cultural Landscape in Egypt*, edited by H. Willems and J.-M. Dahm, 53–70. Bielefeld: transcript Verlag.

Bronk Ramsey, C., M.W. Dee, J.M. Rowland, T.H.G. Higham, S.A. Harris, F. Brock, A. Quiles, E.M. Wild, E.S. Marcus, and A.J. Shortland. 2010. "Radiocarbon-Based Chronology for Dynastic Egypt." *Science* 328(5985): 1554–1557.

Brook, G.A., N.S. Embabi, M.M. Ashour, R.L. Edwards, H. Cheng, J.B. Cowart, and A.A. Dabous. 2002. "Djara Cave in the Western Desert of Egypt: Morphology and Evidence of Quaternary Climatic Change." *Cave and Karst Science* 29(2): 57–66.

Bryant, V., and J.J. Wrenn. 1998. *New Developments in Palynomorph Sampling, Extraction, and Analysis.* Houston: American Association of Stratigraphic Palynologists Foundation.

Bunbury, J. 2019. *The Nile and Ancient Egypt: Changing Land- and Waterscapes, from the Neolithic to the Roman Era.* Cambridge: Cambridge University Press.

Burn, J. 2014. "Marshlands, Drought and the Great Famine: On the Significance of the Marshlands to Egypt at the End of the Old Kingdom." In *Current Research in Egyptology 2013: Proceedings of the Fourteenth Annual Symposium,* edited by K. Accetta, R. Fellinger, P. Lourenço Gonçalves, S. Musselwhite, and W.P. van Pelt, 34–48. Oxford: Oxbow.

Butzer, K.W. 1976. *Early Hydraulic Civilization in Egypt: A Study in Cultural Ecology.* Chicago and London: University of Chicago Press.

———. 2012. "Collapse, Environment, and Society." *Proceedings of the National Academy of Sciences of the United States of America* 109(10): 3632–3639.

Butzer, K.W., and G.H. Endfield. 2012. "Critical Perspectives on Historical Collapse." *Proceedings of the National Academy of Sciences of the United States of America* 109(10): 3628–3631.

Cílek, V., M. Bárta, L. Lisá, A. Pokorná, L. Juřičková, V. Brůna, A.M.A. Mahmoud, A. Bajer, J. Novák, and J. Beneš. 2012. "Diachronic Development of the Lake of Abusir during the Third Millennium BC, Cairo, Egypt." *Quaternary International* 266: 14–24.

Cione, A.L. 2006. "Fishes from Tell el-Ghaba." In *Tell el-Ghaba.* Vol. 2, *A Saite Settlement in North Sinai, Egypt (Argentine Archaeological Mission, 1995–2004),* edited by P. Fuscaldo, 102–126. Buenos Aires: Consejo Nacional de Investigaciones Cientificas y Técnicas.

Creasman, P.P. 2005. "The Cairo Dahshur Boats." M.A. thesis, Texas A&M University.

———.. 2011. "Basic Principles and Methods of Dendrochronological Specimen Curation." *Tree-Ring Research* 67(2): 103–115.

———. 2013. "Ship Timber and the Reuse of Wood in Ancient Egypt." *Journal of Egyptian History* 6(2): 152–176.

———. 2014. "Tree Rings and the Chronology of Ancient Egypt." *Radiocarbon* 56(4); *Tree-Ring Research* 70(3): S85–S92.

———. 2015a. "The Potential of Dendrochronology in Egypt: Understanding Ancient Human/Environment Interactions." In *Egyptian Bioarchaeology: Humans, Animals, and the Environment,* edited by S. Ikram, J. Kaiser, and R. Walker, 201–210. Leiden: Sidestone Press.

———. 2015b. "Timbers of Time: Revealing International Economics and Environment in Antiquity." In *There and Back Again—The Crossroads.* Vol. 2, *Proceedings of an International Conference Held in Prague, September 15–18, 2014,* edited by J. Mynářová, P. Onderka, and P. Pavúk, 45–58. Prague: Charles University, Faculty of Arts.

———. 2015c. "The Potential for Integrating Precise Chronology, Ancient Egypt, and Its Native Trees." Paper read at the Annual Meeting of the American Schools of Oriental Research, 18–21 November, Atlanta.

———. 2016. "Expanding Methodological Boundaries in Egyptian Archaeology by Land and by Sea (or River!)." Unpublished conference paper. Brown University State of Field: Archaeology of Egypt, Providence, 23–24 September 2016.

Creasman, P.P., and D. Sassen. 2011. "Remote Sensing." In *The Temple of Tausret,* edited by R.H. Wilkinson, 150–159. Tucson: University of Arizona Egyptian Expedition.

Creasman, P.P., D. Sassen, S. Koepnick, and N. Doyle. 2010. "Ground-Penetrating Radar Survey at the Pyramid Complex of Senwosret III at Dahshur, Egypt, 2008: Search for the Lost Boat of a Pharaoh." *Journal of Archaeological Science* 37(3): 516–524.

Creasman, P.P., B. Vining, S. Koepnick, and N. Doyle. 2009. "An Exploratory Geophysical Survey at the Pyramid Complex of Senwosret III at Dahshur, Egypt, in Search of Boats." *The International Journal of Nautical Archaeology* 38(2): 386–399.

Creasman, P.P., H. Touchane, C.H. Baisan, H. Bassir, R. Caroli, N. Doyle, H. Herrick, M.A. Koutkat, and R. Touchan. 2017. "An Illustrated Glossary of Arabic-English Dendrochronology Terms and Names." *PalArch's Journal of Archaeology of Egypt / Egyptology* 14(3): 1–35.

Dabous, A.A., and J.K. Osmond. 2000. "U/Th Isotopic Study of Speleothems from the Wadi Sannur Cavern, Eastern Desert of Egypt." *Carbonates and Evaporites* 15(1). https://doi.org/10.1007/BF03175643.

Dee, M.W. 2017. "Absolute Dating Climatic Evidence and the Decline of Old Kingdom Egypt." In *The Late Third Millennium in the Ancient Near East: Chronology, C14, and Climate Change*, edited by F. Höflmayer, 323–331. Chicago: The Oriental Institute of the University of Chicago.

Enmarch, R. 2005. *The Dialogue of Ipuwer and the Lord of All*. Oxford: Griffith Institute.

———. 2008. *A World Upturned: Commentary on and Analysis of The Dialogue of Ipuwer and the Lord of All*. Oxford: Oxford University Press.

Finkelstein, I., and D. Langgut. 2014. "Dry Climate in the Middle Bronze I and Its Impact on Settlement Patterns in the Levant and Beyond: New Pollen Evidence." *Journal of Near Eastern Studies* 73(2): 219–234.

Finné, M., K. Holmgren, H. Sundqvist, E. Weiberg, and M. Lindblom. 2011. "Climate in the Eastern Mediterranean, and Adjacent Regions, During the Past 6000 Years—A Review." *Journal of Archaeological Science* 38(12): 3153–3173.

Giddy, L.L. and D.G. Jeffreys. 1992. "Memphis, 1991," *Journal of Egyptian Archaeology* 78: 1–11.

Graham, A. 2010. "Islands in the Nile: A Geoarchaeological Approach to Settlement Locations in the Egyptian Nile Valley and the Case of Karnak." In *Cities and Urbanism in Ancient Egypt*, edited by M. Bietak, E. Czerny, and I. Forstner-Müller, 125-143. Vienna: Österreichischen Akademie der Wissenschaften.

Graham, A., and J. Bunbury. 2016. "Migrating Nile: Augering in Egypt." In *Science in the Study of Ancient Egypt*, edited by S. Zakrzewski, A. Shortland, and J. Rowland, 93–97. New York and London: Routledge.

Hassan, F.A. 2007. "Droughts, Famine and the Collapse of the Old Kingdom: Re-Reading Ipuwer." In *The Archaeology and Art of Ancient Egypt: Essays in Honor of David B. O'Connor*, vol. 1, edited by Z. Hawass and J. Richards, 357–377. Annales du Service des Antiquités de l'Égypte Cahier 36. Cairo: Coneil Suprême des Antiquités de l'Égypte.

Hawass, Z., and M. Verner. 1996. "Newly Discovered Blocks from the Causeway of Sahure (Archaeological Report)." *Mitteilungen des Deutschen Archäologischen Instituts, Abteilung Kairo* 52: 177–186.

Hayes, W.C. 1953. *The Scepter of Egypt: A Background for the Study of the Egyptian Antiquities in The Metropolitan Museum of Art*. Pt. 1, *From the Earliest Times to the End of the Middle Kingdom*. New York: The Metropolitan Museum of Art.

Höflmayer, F. 2015. "The Southern Levant, Egypt, and the 4.2 ka BP Event." In *2200 BC— Ein Klimasturz als Ursache für den Zerfall der Alten Welt? 7. Mitteldeutscher Archäologentag vom 23. bis 26. Oktober 2014 in Halle (Saale)*, edited by H. Meller, H.W. Arz, R. Jung, and R. Risch, 113–130. Halle (Saale): Landesmuseum für Vorgeschichte.

———. 2017. "The Late Third Millennium B.C. in the Ancient Near East and Eastern Mediterranean: A Time of Collapse and Transformation." In *The Late Third Millennium in the Ancient Near East: Chronology, C14, and Climate Change,* edited by F. Höflmayer, 1–28. Oriental Institute Seminars 11. Chicago: The Oriental Institute of the University of Chicago.

Jeffreys, D.G., J. Bourriau, and W.R. Johnson. 1997. "Memphis, 1996," *Journal of Egyptian Archaeology* 83: 1–6.

Jeffreys, D.G., L. Giddy, K. Eriksson, and J. Malek. 1995. "Memphis, 1994," *Journal of Egyptian Archaeology* 81: 1–6.

Kuper, R., and S. Kröpelin. 2006. "Climate-Controlled Holocene Occupation in the Sahara: Motor of Africa's Evolution." *Science* 313(5788): 803–807.

Lichtheim, M. 1973. *Ancient Egyptian Literature.* Vol. 1, *The Old and Middle Kingdoms.* Berkley, Los Angeles, and London: University of California Press.

Moeller, N. 2005. "The First Intermediate Period: A Time of Famine and Climate Change?" *Ägypten und Levante* 15: 153–167.

Moreno García, J.C. 1997. *Études sur l'administration, le pouvoir et l'idéologie en Égypte, de l'Ancien au Moyen Empire.* Aegyptiaca Leodiensia 4. Liège: Presses Universitaires de Liège.

Nerlich, A.G., and S. Lösch. 2009. "Paleopathology of Human Tuberculosis and the Potential Role of Climate." *Interdisciplinary Perspectives on Infectious Diseases.* http://dx.doi.org/10.1155/2009/437187.

Nussbaum, S., and F. Darius. 2010. "The Archaeobotanical Evidence of Djara and Its Environmental Interpretation." In *Djara: Zur mittelholzänen Besiedlungsgeschichte zwischen Niltal und Oasen (Abu-Muharik-Plateau, Ägypten),* vol. 2, edited by K. Kindermann, 815–835. Köln: Heinrich-Barth-Institut.

Osborn, D.J., with J. Osbornová. 1998. *The Mammals of Ancient Egypt.* The Natural History of Egypt 4. Warminster: Aris & Phillips.

Parcak, S.H. 2009. *Satellite Remote Sensing for Archaeology.* New York: Routledge.

Rashad, H., and A.M. Abdel-Azeem. 2010. "Lake Manzala, Egypt: A Bibliography." *Assiut University Journal of Botany* 39(1): 253–289.

Sabbahy, L. 2015. "A Decade of Advances in the Paleopathology of the Ancient Egyptians." In *Egyptian Bioarchaeology: Humans, Animals, and the Environment,* edited by S. Ikram, J. Kaiser, and R. Walker, 113–117. Leiden: Sidestone Press.

Seidlmayer, S. 2000. "The First Intermediate Period (c.2686–2125 B.C.)." In *The Oxford History of Ancient Egypt,* edited by I. Shaw, 108–136. Oxford: Oxford University Press.

Sheppard, P.R., R.J. Speakman, G. Ridenour, and M.L. Witten. 2007. "Temporal Variability of Tungsten and Cobalt in Fallon, Nevada." *Environmental Heath Perspectives* 115(5): 715–719.

Shortland, A.J., and C. Bronk Ramsey, eds. 2013. *Radiocarbon and the Chronologies of Ancient Egypt.* Oxford: Oxbow Books.

Stanley, J.-D., and C.E. Bernhardt. 2010. "Alexandria's Eastern Harbor, Egypt: Pollen, Microscopic Charcoal, and the Transition from Natural to Human-Modified Basin." *Journal of Coastal Research* 26(1): 67–79.

Stanley, J.-D., M.D. Krom, R.A. Cliff, and J.C. Woodward. 2003. "Nile Flow Failure at the End of the Old Kingdom, Egypt: Strontium Isotopic and Petrologic Evidence." *Geoarchaeology: An International Journal* 18(3): 395–402.

Touzeau, A., J. Blichert-Toft, R. Amiot, F. Fourel, F. Martineau, J. Cockitt, K. Hall, J.-P. Flandrois, and C. Lécuyer. 2013. "Egyptian Mummies Record Increasing Aridity in the Nile Valley from 5500 to 1500 Yr Before Present." *Earth and Planetary Science Letters* 375: 92–100.

Tronchère, H., F. Salomon, Y. Callot, J.-P. Goiran, L. Schmitt, I. Forstner-Müller, and M.

Bietak. 2008. "Geoarchaeology of Avaris: First Results." Ägypten und Levante 18: 327–339.

Vandier, J. 1936. *La famine dans l'Égypte ancienne*. Recherches d'archéologie, de philologie et d'histoire 7. Cairo: Imprimerie de l'Institut français d'archéologie orientale.

Weiss, H. 1997. "Late Third Millennium Abrupt Climate Change and Social Collapse in West Asia and Egypt." In *Third Millennium BC Climate Change and Old World Collapse*, edited by H. Nüzhet Dalfes, G. Kukla, and H. Weiss, 711–723. NATO ASI series, series I: global environmental change 49. Heidelberg: Springer.

Welc, F., and L. Marks. 2014. "Climate Change at the End of the Old Kingdom in Egypt around 4200 BP: New Geoarchaeological Evidence." *Quarterly International* 324: 124–133.

Williams, M. 2019. *The Nile Basin: Quaternary Geology, Geomorphology, and Prehistoric Environments*. Cambridge: Cambridge University Press.

Woodward, J., M. Macklin, L. Fielding, I. Millar, N. Spencer, D. Welsby, and M. Williams. 2015. "Shifting Sediment Sources in the World's Longest River: A Strontium Isotope Record for the Holocene Nile." *Quaternary Science Reviews* 130: 124–140.

Yeakel, J.D., M.M. Pires, L. Rudolf, N.J. Dominy, P.L. Koch, P.R. Guimarães, and T. Gross. 2014. "Collapse of an Ecological Network in Ancient Egypt." *Proceedings of the National Academy of Sciences of the United States of America* 111(40): 14472–14477.

NOTES

[1]   Kuper and Kröpelin 2006. Unfortunately, none of the sites are from the Nile valley or Egyptian oases.

[2]   Bronk Ramsey et al. 2010, Table S7; Shortland and Bronk Ramsey 2013, Table 5; Höflmayer 2017, 14.

[3]   Bell 1971.

[4]   Weiss 1997, 713, 715–716; Finné et al. 2011; Dee 2017, 323.

[5]   Seidlmayer 2000, 129.

[6]   Moeller 2005; Hassan 2007; Butzer 2012, 3633–3634; Höflmayer 2015.

[7]   Vandier 1936.

[8]   Bell 1971.

[9]   Lichtheim 1973, 1:85–86.

[10]   Egyptian Museum in Cairo JE 29247 = CG 20001; Hayes 1953, 139–140.

[11]   Kraków National Museum; Lichtheim 1973, 1:87–88.

[12]   Metropolitan Museum of Art 12.183.8; Lichtheim 1973, 1:87–88.

[13]   Rijksmuseum van Oudeheden AMS 27; Enmarch 2005, 2008.

[14]   Moreno García 1997.

[15]   Moeller 2005, 165–166.

[16]   Bell 1975, 226–247.

[17]   Hawass and Verner 1996.

[18]   Burn 2014.

[19]   Kuper and Kröpelin 2006, 805–806.

[20]   Moeller 2005, 155–156.

[21]   Bietak 2017, 53–55.

[22]   Rashad and Abdel-Azeem 2010.

[23]   Graham 2010.

[24]   Butzer 1976.

[25]   See Bunbury 2019.

[26]   While valuable, such methods are presently impractical or impossible in Egypt itself,

owing to formal or informal prohibitions on the use of such, and have been since ca. 2015.
27 E.g., Graham and Bunbury 2016.
28 E.g., Parcak 2009; Creasman et al. 2009; Creasman et al. 2010; Creasman and Sassen 2011.
29 Giddy and Jeffreys 1992; Jeffreys et al. 1996; Jeffries et al. 1997.
30 Alexanian and Seidlmayer 2002, 23–25.
31 Welc and Marks 2014, 126–130; although lacking robust temporal controls (as the field lacks for such antiquity at present; Creasman 2014, S85–S87), this may rather reflect weather events than climate.
32 Sheppard et al. 2007.
33 Stanley et al. 2003, 397–401.
34 Woodward et al. 2015.
35 Arz et al. 2015, 54–56.
36 Woodward et al. 2015.
37 Stanley et al. 2003, 398, 401.
38 Dabous and Osmond 2000.
39 Brook et al. 2002, 59–63.
40 Bryant and Wrenn 1998.
41 Finkelstein and Langgut 2014, 222–223, 233.
42 Bernhardt et al. 2012, 615–617.
43 Stanley and Bernhardt 2010, 75–77.
44 Stanley and Bernhardt 2010, 76.
45 Nussbaum and Darius 2010, 817–833.
46 A project, titled "Archeological and Contemporary Perspectives on Climate Change, Urbanization, and their Effects on the Genetic Diversity of an Ecologically and Culturally Significant Tree" is a collaboration of the author, John Nason, Christopher Baisain, Ramzi Touchan, and others.
47 Creasman 2011; 2014, S86.
48 Creasman 2015a, 204; 2015b, 53–54.
49 Creasman 2015c, 2016.
50 E.g., Creasman 2005, 2013.
51 Creasman 2014, S89.
52 Creasman et al. 2017.
53 Bárta and Bezděk 2008, 217–222; Bárta 2013.
54 Cione 2006.
55 Osborn and Osbornová 1998.
56 Yeakel et al. 2014.
57 Tronchère et al. 2008, 330.
58 Touzeau et al. 2013.
59 Nerlich and Lösch 2009, 6.
60 Sabbahy 2015, 113–115.
61 Butzer and Endfield 2012, 3628–3629.
62 Cílek et al. 2012.

196

Chapter Ten

Conclusion: Towards a "Geoegyptology"

CHRISTINE L. JOHNSTON

The importance of the river Nile as a sustaining force in the development of the culture and state of ancient Egypt is rarely unacknowledged.[1] Yet, as noted by the contributors to this volume, the specific cultural and environmental impact of the Nile on the people of Egypt has traditionally been understudied.[2] The problem of insufficient environmental data and analysis is addressed in different ways in each chapter of this volume, while the manifesto prepared by the participants of the 2017 colloquium *Ancient Egypt: The Gifts of the Nile* lays out practical strategies to address and rectify this gap in knowledge. As outlined in the manifesto:

> In order to generate meaningful knowledge about past societies situated along the Nile, it is necessary to pursue holistic research agendas with interdisciplinary frameworks that incorporate a broader range of specialists, including those drawn from the sciences. More robust data must be sought and assessed, including geomorphological and paleoclimatic data, and methodology must be expanded to incorporate ecological models of occupation and land-use and of human responses to environmental change.

The studies presented here reflect the efficacy of incorporating palaeoclimatic and geomorphological data in order to both interrogate traditional paradigms of Egyptian environmental study, and to champion ecologically focused forms of Egyptological inquiry.

The first chapters, Thomas Schneider's overview of the historiography of the Nile and rivers as historical agents and Pearce Paul Creasman's compendium of recent climatic data for the Nile Valley, serve to familiarise the reader with the current status of environmental study within Egyptology, and like the other contributions, highlight opportunities for future research. The remaining contributions in this volume reflect the fruitfulness of

The Gift of the Nile? Ancient Egypt and the Environment
edited by Thomas Schneider and Christine L. Johnston
Tucson, Arizona: Egyptian Expedition, 2020

multi-disciplinary approaches to specific geographical or temporal research questions. This includes an assessment of the evolution of subsistence strategies during the Neolithic period (Rowland), riverine navigation and transportation (Graham and Moreno García), and social and occupational adaptation to environmental changes (Moeller) as well as landscape alterations (see especially Bunbury and Graham). The final chapters by Warden and Creasman discuss practical opportunities for the integration of environmental data from varying sources into future archaeological research in Egypt. The volume concludes with a reiteration of the goals of the project participants, presented in the Manifesto for the Study of the Ancient Egyptian Environment.

The volume Manifesto presents an agenda for the future of Egyptology and outlines the practical steps necessary to increase the data on the environment of Ancient Egypt. Three primary aims are identified for archaeologists working in Egypt: promoting environmental investigation in project development; developing new opportunities for scientific sample analysis; and creating new resources for sharing environmental data and research. These goals collectively encourage the production and dissemination of environmental data among Egyptologists, allowing for the pursuit of increasingly multidisciplinary research questions. Throughout the individual contributions of the volume a number of limitations currently impacting the study of the palaeoenvironment are highlighted, including the relatively limited collection of archaeobotanical samples or sample flotation,[3] as well as a general lack of complete ceramic corpora in published or accessible sources.[4] As addressed in the volume Manifesto, barriers on sample export have limited the analysis possible,[5] however the development of new laboratories, like the dendroarchaeological facilities at the newly established Wilkinson House in Thebes, reflects a positive investment in the infrastructure and research capabilities of Egypt. Recent colloquia—our 2017 meeting in Vancouver and the 2013 meeting on the Nile at the Johannes-Gutenberg-Universität Mainz[6]—as well as the Science and Ancient Egyptian Materials' Technology (SAEMT) conference in Cairo in November 2017, are testament to the awareness of these barriers and the general support among members of the Egyptological community for the development of scientific research in Egypt. As noted by Rowland, this includes the potential identification of existing scientific equipment in Egypt used in other disciplines, with the hope that archaeologists and the broader Egyptian scientific community "can work together to enable the types of analyses on Egyptian material so that Egyptian archaeology can function at the same level of scientific rigour as archaeology in other regions does as a matter of routine."[7]

The relative lack of environmental study in Egyptology, also identified by Willems and Dahms in their recent (2017) edited volume on the environmental history of the Nile Valley, is in part due to the inadequate familiarity of scholars with the specific geomorphology of the river floodplain.[8] In order to address this deficit and to further encourage the incorporation of environmental data into the study of the social and political history of ancient Egypt, a list of relevant Nile citations has been compiled (see Appendix 1). The nearly 750 citations in this bibliography are arranged into six thematic sections: The Geographic and Climatic History of the Nile; Environmental Methodology in the Study of the Nile Valley and Delta; The Environment, Climate Change, and the Political and Social History of Ancient Egypt; Water Management and Navigation, Agriculture, and the Egyptian Economy; The Nile in Religion, Text, and Image; and Studies of the Post-Antique and Contemporary Nile. The entries cover a broad range of themes and methodologies, providing a comprehensive and up-to-date list of major works on the ecological and social history of the Nile Valley. It is important to note that the bibliography is not exhaustive, as it currently omits site reports; the decision to omit site reports, though many present environmental data and research (such as the Tell el-Dab'a and Memphis volumes), was in part a function of necessity, though it is hoped that a thorough survey of excavation reports can be included as part of the ongoing work pledged by the colloquium participants (see the volume Manifesto). Relevant climate data for any Egyptological study should thus be sought in the relevant reports of any projects undertaken in the region of study. The bibliography in Appendix 1, however, provides a compendium of palaeoclimatic, geomorphological, historical, social, and textual data related to Ancient Egypt and the Nile. Hopefully it will serve as a valuable resource for all scholars who study the cultures or environment of the Nile Valley.

REVISING THE NARRATIVE: ENVIRONMENTAL DATA AND HOLISTIC RESEARCH

As noted throughout this volume, Egyptology has developed in relative isolation compared to other culture history fields, in part because the bounty of surviving text has often overshadowed other disciplinary pursuits. The disconnect between culture history and other methodologies was identified nearly half a century ago by Karl Butzer, who recognized that "the almost traditional isolation of Egyptology has not served either archaeology or anthropology well."[9] Egyptological scholarship, particularly up to and throughout the twentieth century, has often operated in a vacuum, isolated methodologically from other studies of the Nile Valley and historiographically from research on other neighbouring cultures of the ancient world.[10] There are notable exceptions, including the work of scholars like Butzer, Barbara Bell, and Fekri Hassan, who—like their contemporaries studying nearby sites in the Near East[11]—began to explore the relationship between the environment and the political history, state development, and demography of Egypt.[12] Yet the pathways of research opened by these pioneering scholars have been less trodden than one may have expected, and their work has rarely been subjected to the critical examination or revision that naturally comes through ongoing research and methodological refinement.

This is particularly true of the pharaonic period, in which textual evidence has predominated.[13] Some topics, which are inherently environmental in their focus—like the 4.2k event and the collapse of the Old Kingdom[14]—have received significant attention (as evidenced by the numerous references on this topic included in the Appendix 1). Yet aside from these events, for which rapid climate change is examined as a potential catalyst,[15] the ecological conditions of the Nile have been treated as relatively static. The Nile river, once seen as the endower of the Pharaonic state (following authors like Herodotus and Pliny[16]), began to be assigned a more despotic role, functionally "caging" the inhabitants of the river valley, and facilitating the growth of the state through institutional monopolization of resources like metals and wood, which were mobilized through riverine networks.[17] Yet the Nile is often still viewed as an environmental backdrop within which human inhabitants operated as "the main agents of history."[18] The overemphasis on sociological, economic, and political factors in the development of the Egyptian state was highlighted by Butzer, and attributed to "the practical exclusion of the highly dynamic variables that condition floodplain ecosystems" in Egyptological scholarship.[19]

Where integration of climatic data and methodologies has been attempted, there has been a tendency towards oversimplification in the characterization and instrumentality of the palaeoenvironment. One of the most prominent of such oversimplifications exists in the application of "hydraulic" theories to the origin of the Egyptian state.[20] The connection between environmental conditions and changes and the emergence of the Egyptian state has been rightly critiqued for being "casual, primitive, and often deterministic,"[21] and for forcibly simplifying the evidence for regional and scalar variability in favour of a monolithic and centralizing state bureaucracy.[22] This model also assumes a fairly homogenous landscape with limited state-sponsored subsistence strategies (cereal production, cattle raising, etc.), distorting the truly variegated ecology of the Nile valley and adjacent areas, which offered assorted resources and economic strategies.[23] For example, as demonstrated by Juan Carlos Moreno García in this volume, the marshy environment and humid conditions prevalent in Middle Egypt (as documented in administrative texts), coupled with the lower population density, encouraged subsistence centered on pastoralism, and limited state-sponsored agricultural expansion.[24] So prominent, however, has the theory been for the hydraulic basis of pharaonic state power that it is only in the last few decades that the multimodal structure of the ancient Egyptian political economy has received general acceptance among economic specialists,[25] though the myth of the highly centralized Egyptian state persists in general literature.

Already in the 1970s the existence of a direct causal link between irrigation management and the development of the Egyptian state was refuted by Butzer.[26] Pointing to iconography like the image of canal building found on the Scorpion Macehead, recovered from the "Main Deposit" in the temple area of Hierakonpolis, Butzer argued that corporate-sponsored irrigation was present already in the Predynastic period, before state formation (Fig. 1a–b).[27] Fifty years on, the placement of corporate irrigation in the predynastic is now known to be premature, as institutional water management in the form of canals or catchment pools dates only to the Old Kingdom or later,[28] long after

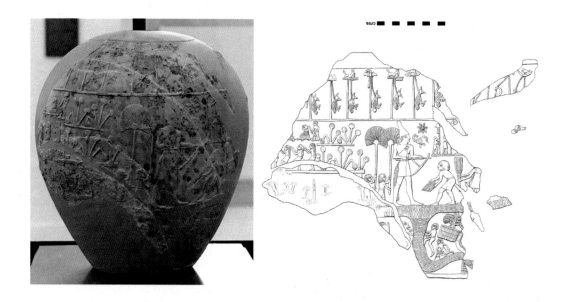

FIGURE 1a–b. Irrigation activity scene on the Mace-head of scorpion king, AN1896-1908.E.3632, Ashmolean Museum, Oxford (fig. 1a: photo modified from image by akhenatenator, CCO 1.0. upload.wikimedia.org/wikipedia/commons/e/eb/Ceremonial_mace-head_of_King_Scorpion.jpg; fig. 1b: line drawing image © Ashmolean Museum, University of Oxford).

state formation. Although irrigation is still seen as an instrument of the state in the Old Kingdom, there is insufficient archaeological evidence in the form of canals and dykes to suggest large-scale state-sponsored irrigation at that time.[29] The surveyed administrative titles of the Old Kingdom show no indication of any comprehensive, centrally administered water management on the national level, either.[30] Although the chronology around water management strategies has changed, there is still no correlation present between the development of state institutions and the emergence of irrigation works, refuting a "hydraulic" origin to the state. Furthermore, historians of the Egyptian economy have recently advocated for a characterization of the pharaonic government, not as a centralized body tasked with administering irrigation and production, but as a "risk consolidating institution" that marshalled labour and resources,[31] mobilized in many cases through a market system,[32] and responded flexibly to fluctuations in the environment.[33]

Fluctuations in the Egyptian environment were caused by changes in the overall North African climate, as well as constant alterations to the landscape of the Nile, as the river migrated across the valley,[34] raising and sinking islands and floodbanks,[35] and modifying the mouth of the delta.[36] The changing river course altered religious landscapes along the Nile and contributed to the rise and fall of proximal settlements. Examples of shifting occupational patterns include the development of the Temple of Karnak on a newly formed island and infilled channels in Thebes,[37] the placement and seasonal use of nautical landing spots,[38] and the abandonment of Piramesses in the 11th century BCE.[39] Ancient Egyptians were aware of the inconstant behaviour of the Nile and its changing course, tying it ideologically to the unpredictability of individual fate and fortune:

> As to him who was rich last year, \ He is a vagabond this year; \ Don't be greedy to fill your belly, \ You don't know your end at all. \ Should you come to be in want, \ Another may do good to you. \ When last year's watercourse is gone, \ Another river is here today; \ Great lakes become dry places, \ Sandbanks turn into depths. \ Man does not have a single way, \ The lord of life confounds him. (Teaching of Any; translation Lichtheim[40])

The seemingly capricious Nile flood, manifesting as the androgynous inundation god Hapi (Fig. 2), was a confounding force to the inhabitants of the Nile valley. While his floodwaters served to "fill the storerooms and enlarge the granaries,"[41] and allowed "the land to prosper to the extent of [his] desire"[42] (see Fig. 3), anomalous flood levels could have catastrophic impacts on cultivation. Extreme weather and fluctuations in the inundation required active intervention, as severe effects could be created by moderate variance from the ideal level.[43] Such anomalous floods could result in either a failure to fully immerse fields, or conversely in a delayed receding of the floodwaters, which could restrict the length of the subsequent growing season.[44]

In order to assuage the anxieties of Egyptian residents by forecasting agricultural yields and heralding the recession of the inundation, Nilometers (in Greek Νειλοσκοπεῖον, "Nile observer"; Figs. 4–5) were established.[45] Inundation levels were recorded with these implements at strategic points, such as the First Cataract, and attended to by designated members of the temple personnel.[46] The awareness of environmental variability evidenced in the Teaching of Any and the attempts to forecast riverine behaviour with Nilometers suggest that Egyptian history can be understood best as "a dialogue between its people and its landscape."[47] Without adequate environmental data, we are only witness to one side of this negotiation.

Figure 2. Unification iconography featuring the inundation god Hapi, statue base of Ramesses II, Luxor (photo by author).

FIGURE 3. Ramesses III plowing and harvesting grain and making offerings to Hapi, Ramesseum (photo by author).

FIGURE 4. Nilometer from Elephantine (Image Credit: Olaf Tausch, CC BY 3.0. commons.wikimedia.org/wiki/ Category:Nilometers_in_Elephantine#/media/File:Assuan_ Elephantine_Nilometer_10.JPG).

203

FIGURE 5. The Nilometer, Island of Rhoda (Image by David Roberts, Library of Congress. hdl.loc.gov/loc.pnp/cph.3g04040).

FIGURE 6. The Flooded Courtyard of Amenhotep III in the
Luxor Temple (Image by Antonio Beato, Getty Collection
Object 84.XM.1382.9). Digital image courtesy of the Getty's
Open Content Program.

The study of the Ancient Egyptian environment itself, like pharaonic state formation
and economics, has traditionally been dominated by the textual evidence. Exceptional
records of irregular rainfall (like the Tempest Stela of Ahmose[48]) and abnormal inundations
(including those that flooded the Karnak Temple[49]; see Fig. 6) have been coupled with
literary references to drought, shortage, and famine in order to write political history. This
is particularly true for the collapse of the Old Kingdom and fragmentation during the First
Intermediate Period.[50] References to drought and famine and ensuing social collapse—
including autobiographies of the First Intermediate Period and prophetic texts from the
subsequent Middle Kingdom, as well as recorded flood levels as preserved in documents
like the Palermo Stone—can now be reassessed in light of climatic data and recorded flood
variation.[51] The conclusions drawn from textual and geoarchaeological and paleoclimatic
data can also be more effectively assessed against broader Mediterranean trends, as
evidenced by the scholarship of the 4.2k event and its impact on the cultures and states of
the Eastern Mediterranean.[52]

An example of the successful integration of textual and paleoclimatic data can be seen
in the positive correlation found between the geoarchaeological evidence for environmental
volatility and the textual attestations of social unrest during the later New Kingdom.
During the Twentieth Dynasty, inundation fluctuations seem to have significantly impacted
agricultural production, causing food shortages,[53] which in turn led to price inflation for
grain (primarily barley, *Hordeum vulgare*, and emmer wheat, *Triticum dicoccum*).[54] Based on

205

administrative records, it appears that prolonged inundation also disrupted the delivery of fish to workers.[55] These delays, to ration payments of both fish and grain, have been tied to episodes of social unrest, most famously seen with the Theban workers' strike recorded during the reign of Ramesses III.[56] In this case, the textual attestations of economic scarcity seem to be supported by the palaeoclimatic and geomorphological evidence for significant fluctuations in the inundation. The Nile's impact on cereal production and fishing, along with its role as a conduit for the mobility of goods and people and as a spreader of disease and mortality,[57] must be approached holistically with the necessary environmental and geoarchaeological data.

TOWARDS A "GEOEGYPTOLOGY"

The growing chorus of Egyptologists and archaeologists advocating for and producing holistic research employing diverse scientific approaches for the history of Ancient Egypt and the Nile is evidenced by the large bibliography provided in Appendix 1. The sources included reflect both general scientific study of the paleoclimate and geomorphology of the Nile floodplain, as well as environmentally centered historical studies of the inhabitants of the river valley. The latter is growing increasingly common, as evidenced by the chronological trajectories of the citations in Appendix 1, here charted according to the thematic sections (Fig. 7). In particular, the studies focused on the relationship between the ancient Egyptian environment and the political, social, and economic histories of the Egyptian state are growing at an exponential rate (see Fig. 7: "Pol & Soc His"; and "Navig & Econ"). This is also true of publications focused on the environmental methodology in the study of the Nile (Fig. 7: "Env Method"). Scholarship on environmental methodology (Env Method) and the political and social history of the Nile (Pol & Soc His) are the two fastest growing fields of interest, with median publication dates of 2007 and 2008 respectively as compared with 1994 for publications on the Nile in Religion, Text, and Image ("Relig & Text"). The increasing publication frequency of these fields reflects the positive steps taken towards producing a more environmentally grounded approach to Egyptian history.

The integration of historical and climatic data and methodologies, once overly simplistic and misleading, is producing increasingly nuanced culture histories. As palaeoclimatic and geomorphological data gradually accumulate and become more widely disseminated, Egyptologists and archaeologists will have the opportunity to ask new questions about the cultures and inhabitants of the Nile basin, and to interrogate previous assumptions about the pharaonic state. The benefits of such inquiry extend beyond the field of Egyptology. Although Egyptological data is often isolated from broader discussions of climate change during the Holocene, Egyptian history, and Egyptian chronology in particular, is often used as a reference point for neighbouring culture histories.[58] The potential peripheral impact of studies on the environmental history of Ancient Egypt and the Nile is evidenced by the tree web of citations of Karl Butzer's seminal study *Early Hydraulic Civilization in Egypt: A Study in Cultural Ecology* (1976; Fig. 8).[59] The citation report included 300 publications found in the Web of Science databases. Although archaeological and anthropological studies predominate, the citation web highlights the impact of Butzer's book across a variety of fields from the sciences, social sciences, and humanities. Of the more comprehensive list of 957 sources was returned by Google Scholar, 649 were found to include references to the Nile, while only 447—about half of the total sources—include references to Ancient Egypt (again highlighting the broad impact of Butzer's book). The value of this work across such multidisciplinary scholarship highlights the potential integration possible between researchers studying the cultures and environment of Egypt and the Nile.

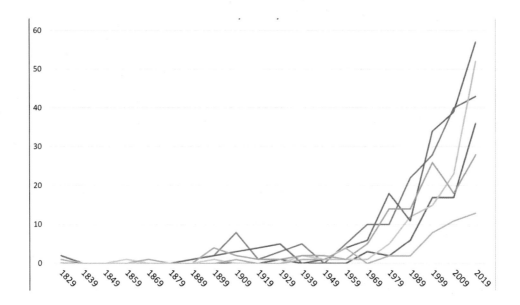

FIGURE 7. Publication trajectory of sources presented in Appendix 1.
Sources are graphed according to thematic grouping: The Geographic
and Climatic History of the Nile (Geo & Clim His); Environmental
Methodology in the Study of the Nile Valley and Delta (Env Method);
The Environment, Climate Change, and the Political and Social
History of Ancient Egypt (Pol & Soc His); Water Management and
Navigation, Agriculture, and the Egyptian Economy (Navig & Econ);
The Nile in Religion, Text, and Image (Relig & Text); and Studies of the
Post-Antique and Contemporary Nile (Post-Ant).

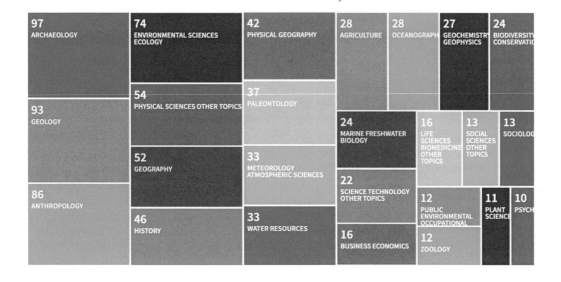

FIGURE 8. Citation web of publications citing Karl Butzer's seminal
study Early Hydraulic Civilization in Egypt: A Study in Cultural
Ecology (1976). Citation Report graphic is derived from Clarivate
Web of Science, Copyright Clarivate 2020. All rights reserved.

The web of scholarship drawing on Butzer's study demonstrates the intersecting and complementary goals of researchers and scientists working in Egypt and the profitability of integrating robust datasets and interdisciplinary frameworks. This will require more collaborative work between historians, archaeologists, and earth scientists—particularly during research design and the preparation of co-authored papers. This is a goal identified, though not achieved, in this volume. In addition to pursuing collaborative research, historians and archaeologists must draw on the vast data sources available and refine our methods and goals in the study of ancient Egypt in order to actualize a new field of "Geoegyptology."

WORKS CITED

Antoine, J.-C. 2006. "Fluctuations of Fish Deliveries at Deir el-Medina in the Twentieth Dynasty: A Statistical Analysis." *Studien zur Altägyptischen Kultur* 35: 25–41.
———. 2009. "The Delay of the Grain Ration and Its Social Consequences at Deir el-Medîna in the Twentieth Dynasty: A Statistical Analysis." *Journal of Egyptian Archaeology* 95: 223–234.
Baines, J. 1974. "The Inundation Stela of Sebekhotpe VIII." *Acta Orientalia* 36: 39–54.
———. 1976. "The Sebekhotpe VIII Inundation Stela: An Additional Fragment." *Acta Orientalia* 37: 11–20.
Bell, B. 1970. "The Oldest Records of the Nile Floods." *The Geographical Journal* 136(4): 569–573.
———. 1975. "Climate and the History of Egypt: The Middle Kingdom." *American Journal of Archaeology* 79(3): 223–269.
Bietak, M. 2017. "Harbours and Coastal Military Bases in Egypt in the Second Millennium B.C.: Avaris, Peru-nefer, Pi-Ramesse." In *The Nile: Natural and Cultural Landscape in Egypt. Proceedings of the International Symposium held at the at the Johannes Gutenberg-Universität Mainz, 22 & 23 February 2013*, edited by H. Willems and J.-M. Dahms, 53–70. Bielefeld: transcript Verlag.
Bini, M., G. Zanchetta, A. Perşoiu, R. Cartier, Al Català, I. Cacho, J.R. Dean, F. Di Rita, R.N. Drysdale, M. Finné, I. Isola, B. Jalali, F. Lirer, D. Magri, A. Masi, L. Marks, A.M. Mercuri, O. Peyron, L. Sadori, M.-A. Sicre, F. Welc, C. Zielhofer, and E. Brisset. 2019. "The 4.2 ka BP Event in the Mediterranean Region: An Overview." *Climate of the Past* 15: 555–577.
Boraik, M., L. Gabolde, and A. Graham. 2017. "Karnak's Quaysides: Evolution of the Embankments from the Eighteenth Dynasty to the Graeco-Roman Period." In *The Nile: Natural and Cultural Landscape in Egypt. Proceedings of the International Symposium held at the at the Johannes Gutenberg-Universität Mainz, 22 & 23 February 2013*, edited by H. Willems and J.-M. Dahms, 97–144. Bielefeld: transcript Verlag.
Boraik, M., M. Ghilardi, S. Bakhit, A. Hafez, M.H. Ali, S. el -Masekh, and A.G. Mahmoud. 2010. "Geomorphological Investigations in the Western Part of the Karnak Temple (Quay and Ancient Harbour). First Results Derived from Stratigraphical Profiles and Manual Auger Boreholes and Perspectives of Research." *Les Cahiers de Karnak* 13: 101–109.
Braidwood, R.J., and B. Howe. 1960. *Prehistoric Investigations in Iraqi Kurdistan*. Studies in Ancient Oriental Civilization 31. Chicago: University of Chicago Press.
Brewer, D. 2007. "Agriculture and Animal Husbandry." In *The Egyptian World*, edited by T. Wilkinson, 131–145. London: Routledge.

Bunbury, J. 2019. *The Nile and Ancient Egypt: Changing Land- and Waterscapes, from the Neolithic to the Roman Era.* Cambridge: Cambridge University Press.

Bunbury, J., A. Tavares, B. Pennington, and P. Gonçalves. 2017. "Development of the Memphite Floodplain: Landscape and Settlement Symbiosis in the Egyptian Capital Zone." In *The Nile: Natural and Cultural Landscape in Egypt*, edited by H. Willems and J.-M. Dahm, 71–96. Bielefeld: transcript Verlag.

Butzer, K.W. 1960. "Archaeology and Geology in Ancient Egypt." *Science* 132 (3440): 1617–1624.

———. 1976. *Early Hydraulic Civilization in Egypt: A Study in Cultural Ecology.* Chicago: University of Chicago Press.

———. 2012. "Collapse, Environment, and Society." *Proceedings of the National Academy of Sciences of the United States of America* 109(10): 3632–3639.

Butzer, K.W., and C.L. Hansen. 1968. *Desert and River in Nubia: Geomorphology and Prehistoric Environments at the Aswan Reservoir.* Madison: University of Wisconsin Press.

Edgerton, W.F. 1951. "The Strikes in Ramses III's Twenty-Ninth Year." *Journal of Near Eastern Studies* 10(1): 137–145.

Eyre, C.J. 2004. "How Relevant Was Personal Status to the Functioning of the Rural Economy in Pharaonic Egypt?" In *La dépendance rurale dans l'Antiquité égyptienne et proche-orientale*, edited by B. Menu, 157–186. Le Caire: Institut francais d'archéologie orientale.

Faulkner, R.O. 1973. *The Ancient Egyptian Coffin Texts.* Oxford: Aris & Phillips.

Finné, M., K. Holmgren, H. Sundqvist, E. Weiberg, and M. Lindblom. 2011. "Climate in the Eastern Mediterranean, and Adjacent Regions, during the Past 6000 Years—A Review." *Journal of Archaeological Science* 38(12): 3153–3173.

Friedman, Z. 2008. "Nilometers." In *Encyclopaedia of the History of Science, Technology, and Medicine*, edited by H. Selin, 1751–1760. New York: Springer.

Gabolde, L. 2013. "L'implantation du temple: Contingences religieuses et contraintes géomorphologiques." *Egypte, Afrique & Orient* 68: 3–12.

———. 2018. *Karnak, Amon-Ré: la genèse d'un temple, la naissance d'un dieu.* Bibliothèque d'étude 167. Cairo: Institut français d'archéologie orientale.

Ginau, A., R. Schiestl, F. Kern, and J. Wunderlich. 2017. "Identification of Historic Landscape Features and Settlement Mounds in the Western Nile Delta by Means of Remote Sensing Time Series Analysis and the Evaluation of Vegetation Characteristics." *Journal of Archaeological Science: Reports* 16: 170–184.

Graham, A. 2010a. "Islands in the Nile: A Geoarchaeological Approach to Settlement Locations in the Egyptian Nile Valley and the Case of Karnak." In *Cities and Urbanism in Ancient Egypt. Papers from a workshop in November 2006 at the Austrian Academy of Sciences*, edited by M. Bietak, E. Czerny, and I. Forstner-Müller, 125–143. Denkschriften der Gesamtakademie LX. Untersuchungen der Zweigstelle Kairo des Österreichischen Archäologischen Instituts XXXV. Vienna: Verlag der Österreichischen Akademie der Wissenschaften.

———. 2010b. "Ancient Landscapes Around the Opet Temple, Karnak." *Egyptian Archaeology* 36: 25–28.

Habachi, L. 1974. "A High Inundation in the Temple of Amenre at Karnak in the Thirteenth Dynasty." *Studien zur Altägyptischen Kultur* 1: 207–214, 296.

Hassan, F.A. 1986. "Holocene Lakes and Prehistoric Settlements of the Western Faiyum, Egypt." *Journal of Archaeological Science* 13: 483–501.

———. 1997a. "The Dynamics of a Riverine Civilization: A Geoarchaeological Perspective on the Nile Valley, Egypt." *World Archaeology* 29(1): 51–74.

209

———. 1997b. "Nile Floods and Political Disorder in Early Egypt." In *Third Millennium BC Climate Change and Old World Collapse*, edited by H.N. Dalfes, G. Kukla, and H. Weiss, 1–23. Berlin: Springer.

———. 1998. "Holocene Climatic Change and Riverine Dynamics in Nile Valley." In *Before Food Production in North Africa: Questions and Tools Dealing with Resource Exploitation and Population Dynamics at 12,000-7000 bp*, edited by S. di Lernia and G. Manzi, 43–51. Forlì: A.B.A.C.O. Edizioni.

Hassan, F.A., and G. Tassie. 2006. "Modelling Environmental and Settlement Change in the Fayum." *Journal of Egyptian Archaeology* 29: 37–40.

Höflmayer, F., ed. 2017. *The Late Third Millennium in the Ancient Near East: Chronology, C14, and Climate Change*. Chicago: The Oriental Institute of the University of Chicago.

Hughes, J.D. 1992. "Sustainable Agriculture in Ancient Egypt." *Agricultural History* 66(2): 12–22.

Jeffreys, D.G., and J.M. Bunbury. 2005. "Memphis, 2004." *Journal of Egyptian Archaeology* 91: 8–12.

Johnston, C.L. 2016. "Networks and Intermediaries: Ceramic Exchange Systems in the Late Bronze Age Mediterranean." Ph.D. diss., University of California, Los Angeles.

Krauss, R. 2006. "Dates Relating to Seasonal Phenomena and Miscellaneous Astronomical Dates." In *Ancient Egyptian Chronology*, edited by E. Hornung, R. Krauss, and D.A. Warburton, 369–379. Leiden: Brill.

Lichtheim, M. 2006. *Ancient Egyptian Literature*. Vol. 2: *The New Kingdom*. Los Angeles: University of California Press.

Lutley, C.J., and J.M. Bunbury. 2008. "The Nile on the Move." *Egyptian Archaeology* 32: 3–5.

Macklin, M.G., W.H.J. Toonen, J.C. Woodward, M.A.J. Williams, C. Flaux, N. Marriner, K. Nicoll, G. Verstraeten, N. Spencer, and D. Welsby. 2015. "A New Model of River Dynamics, Hydroclimatic Change and Human Settlement in the Nile Valley Derived from Meta-analysis of the Holocene Fluvial Archive." *Quaternary Science Reviews* 130: 109–123.

Mann, M. 2012. *The Sources of Social Power*. Vol. 1, *A History of Power from the Beginning to AD 1760*. New ed. Cambridge: Cambridge University Press.

Manning, J. 2012. "Water, Irrigation and their Connection to State Power in Egypt." Paper read at "Resources: Endowment or Curse, Better or Worse?" Yale University, 24 February, New Haven. Accessed 3 April, 2018. http://www.econ.yale.edu/~egcenter/manning2012.pdf.

———. 2018. *The Open Sea. The Economic Life of the Ancient Mediterranean World from the Iron Age to the Rise of Rome*. Princeton: Princeton University Press.

Moeller, N. 2005. "The First Intermediate Period: A Time of Famine and Climate Change?" *Egypt and the Levant* 15: 153–167.

Montserrat, F.R. 2017. "Medamud and the Nile: Some Preliminary Reflections." In *The Nile: Natural and Cultural Landscape in Egypt. Proceedings of the International Symposium held at the Johannes Gutenberg-Universität Mainz, 22 & 23 February 2013*, edited by H. Willems and J.-M. Dahms, 145–170. Bielefeld: transcript Verlag.

Moreno García, J.C. 2010. "La gestion des aires marginales: *pḥw, gs, ṯnw, sḫt* au IIIᵉ millénaire." In *Egyptian Culture and Society: Studies in Honour of Naguib Kanawati*, vol. 2, edited by A. Woods, A. McFarlane, and S. Binder, 49–69. Cairo: Conseil suprême des antiquités de l'Égypte.

———. 2014a. "The Cursed Discipline? The Peculiarities of Egyptology at the Turn of the Twenty-First Century." In *Histories of Egyptology: Interdisciplinary Measures*, edited by William Carruthers, 50–63. New York and London: Routledge.

———. 2014b. "Ancient States and Pharaonic Egypt: An Agenda for Future Research." *Journal of Egyptian History* 7: 203–240.

———. 2014c. "Recent Developments in the Social and Economic History of Ancient Egypt." *Journal of Ancient Near Eastern History* 1(2): 244–252.

———. 2017. "Trade and Power in Ancient Egypt: Middle Egypt in the Late Third/Early Second Millennium BC." *Journal of Archaeological Research* 25(2): 87–132.

———. 2018. "Elusive 'Libyans': Identities, Lifestyles and Mobile Populations in NE Africa (Late 4th–Early 2nd Millennium BC)." *Journal of Egyptian History* 11: 145–182.

———. 2020. *The State in Ancient Egypt: Power, Challenges and Dynamics*. London: Bloomsbury Academic.

Muhs, B. 2016. *The Ancient Egyptian Economy*. Cambridge: Cambridge University Press.

Rashad, H., and A.M. Abdel-Azeem. 2010. "Lake Manzala, Egypt: A Bibliography." *Assiut University Journal of Botany* 39(1): 253–289.

Redding. R.W. 1992. "Old Kingdom Patterns of Animal Use and the Value of Faunal Data in Modeling Socioeconomic Systems." *Paleorient* 18(2): 99–107.

Ritner, R.K., and N. Moeller. 2014. "The Ahmose 'Tempest Stela,' Thera and Comparative Chronology." *Journal of Near Eastern Studies* 37(1): 1–19.

Scheidel, W. 2001. *Death on the Nile: Disease and the Demography of Roman Egypt*. Leiden: Brill.

Schenkel, W. 1978. *Die Bewässerungsrevolution im alten Ägypten*. Deutsches Archäologisches Institut, Sonderschriften 6. Mainz am Rhein: Philipp von Zabern.

Schneider, T. 2017. "'What Is the Past but a Once Material Existence Now Silenced?': The First Intermediate Period from an Epistemological Perspective." In *The Late Third Millennium in the Ancient Near East: Chronology, C14, and Climate Change*, edited by F. Höflmayer, 311–322. Chicago: Oriental Institute.

Seidlmayer, S.J. 2001. *Historische und moderne Nilstände: Untersuchungen zu den Pegelablesungen des Nils von der Frühzeit bis zur Gegenwart*. Berlin: Achet Verlag.

Trigger, B.G., B.J. Kemp, D. O'Connor, and A.B. Lloyd. 1983. *Ancient Egypt: A Social History* Cambridge: Cambridge University Press.

van der Plas, D. 1986. *L'hymne à la crue du Nil*. Leiden: Nederlands Instituut voor het Nabije Oosten.

Warburton, D. 1997. *State and Economy in Ancient Egypt*. Orbis Biblicus et Orientalis 151. Fribourg: Vandenhoeck & Ruprecht.

———. 2007. "Work and Compensation in Ancient Egypt." *Journal of Egyptian Archaeology* 93: 175–194.

———. 2016. *The Fundamentals of Economics: Lessons from the Bronze Age Near East*. Neuchâtel: Recherches et publications.

Wilke, T. 2000. "Ancient Egypt: An Economist's View." *Göttinger Miszellen* 178: 81–96.

Willems, H., and J.-M. Dahms, eds. 2017. *The Nile: Natural and Cultural Landscape in Egypt. Proceedings of the International Symposium held at the Johannes Gutenberg-Universität Mainz, 22 & 23 February 2013*. Bielefeld: transcript Verlag.

Willems, H., H. Creylman, V. De Laet, and G. Vertraeten. 2017. "The Analysis of Historical Maps as an Avenue to the Interpretation of Pre-Industrial Irrigation Practices in Egypt." In *The Nile: Natural and Cultural Landscape in Egypt. Proceedings of the International Symposium held at the Johannes Gutenberg-Universität Mainz, 22 & 23 February 2013*, edited by Willems and Dahms, 255–344. Bielefeld: transcript Verlag.

Wilson, P. 2012. "Waterways, Settlements, and Shifting Power in the North-Western Nile Delta." *Water History* 4(1): 95–118.

———. 2017. "Landscapes of Bashmur: Settlements and Monasteries in the Northern

Egyptian Delta from the Seventh to Ninth Century." In *The Nile: Natural and Cultural Landscape in Egypt. Proceedings of the International Symposium held at the Johannes Gutenberg-Universität Mainz, 22 & 23 February 2013*, edited by H. Willems and J.-M. Dahms, 345–368. Bielefeld: transcript Verlag.

———. 2018. "Human and Deltaic Environments in Northern Egypt in Late Antiquity." *Late Antique Archaeology* 12(1): 42–62.

Wittfogel, K.A. 1957. *Oriental Despotism: A Comparative Study of Total Power*. New Haven: Yale University Press.

Notes

[1] I would like to thank Thomas Schneider and Angus Graham for their generous help in reading and reviewing this contribution.

[2] Notable recent works on the environmental history of the Nile Valley are discussed in Schneider, this volume.

[3] Creasman, this volume, 188.

[4] Warden, this volume, 175–178.

[5] For dendrochronology, see Creasman, this volume, 188. For the need for AMS radiocarbon, stable isotope, and DNA testing facilities, see Rowland, this volume, 76–77.

[6] Willems and Dahms 2017.

[7] Rowland, this volume page 77, n. 104.

[8] Willems and Dahms 2017, 7.

[9] Butzer 1976, 2.

[10] Moreno García 2014a, 51; 2014b, 206–207.

[11] Braidwood and Howe in the 1960s situated human development within the palaeoclimate, arguing that understanding the social and subsistence changes of Neolithic Mesopotamia "demands detailed knowledge of the ancient environment in which the transition took place" (1960, 2).

[12] See for example Butzer 1960, 1976, 2012; Butzer and Hansen 1968; Bell 1970, 1975; Hassan 1986, 1997a, 1997b, 1998; Hassan and Tassie 2006.

[13] Warden, this volume, 172–173. Text has been especially dominant in the study of the ancient economy, which has focused predominantly on surviving administrative records and bureaucratic titles (Warburton 2007, 186–189). Environmental research has been more consistently incorporated into the study of subsistence changes during the Neolithic and Predynastic periods (see discussion by Rowland, this volume, 69–73).

[14] See the discussion by Creasman, this volume, 15–17, 19–27; Macklin et al. 2015. For a recent overview of the 4.2k event in the broader eastern Mediterranean, see Finné et al. 2011; Höflmayer 2017; Bini et al. 2019.

[15] This causal relationship hass been increasingly re-examined as the temporal scale of climate change and its "abrupt" nature have been critiqued (see, for example, Creasman, this volume, 16; Moeller 2005).

[16] Herodotus *Histories*, 2.5.1; Pliny *Naturalis Historia*, 18.47.

[17] Schneider, this volume, 1–2; Mann 2012, 111; Manning 2018, 103.

[18] Schneider, this volume, 4.

[19] Butzer 1976, 111.

[20] This model, first forwarded by Wittfogel (1957), was developed through his study of 'oriental' farming communities that developed "large-scale and government-managed works of irrigation and flood control" (1957, 3). This theory causally connected irrigation intensification to the rise of despotic state institutions and monumental

state-sponsored public works in what he termed "agrobureaucratic" civilizations (1957, 3, 27–45). The concentration of labour in and the enhanced yield generated from irrigated floodplains is also deemed to facilitate economic specialization and redistribution (Mann 2012, 81–82). Mann refutes the role of hydraulic agriculture in the development of the state but maintains that the Nile remained the source of Egypt's state power through its role as a communications network that effectively "caged" the inhabitants of the Nile Valley (2012, 96, 108–115).

21 Butzer 1976, 2.
22 Warden, this volume, 172–173, 178. For an overview of the historiography of the ancient Egyptian economy, see Warburton 1997, 2016; Muhs 2016.
23 See Moreno García, this volume, 145–151; also Moreno García 2010; 2014b, 238–239; 2017; and 2018.
24 Moreno García, this volume, 155–163.
25 Warburton 2007, 180–191; Moreno García 2014b, 208–209; 2014c, 244–245, 249–252; 2020, 3. As an example, see the discussion of palatial and extrapalatial production and sale systems for shabtis (Warburton 2007) and the exchange of Aegean and Cypriot ceramics in the New Kingdom (Johnston 2016, 268–272). Dual concurrent systems of domesticate production for state and local consumption have also been attested archaeologically at sites within Old Kingdom Egypt through faunal remains (Redding 1992, 104–106).
26 Butzer 1976, 110. See also Schenkel 1978; Manning 2012, 23; Schneider, this volume.
27 Butzer 1976, 20–21.
28 See discussion in Willems et al. 2017, 259–261.
29 Moreno García, this volume, 148; Manning 2018, 99–103.
30 Moreno García 2014b, 215–216.
31 Wilke 2000, 81–95; Warburton 1997, 140, 327.
32 Warburton 1997, 140.
33 Butzer 1976, 108; Manning 2012; 2018, 94–103.
34 See contributions by Bunbury and Graham, this volume; Lutley and Bunbury 2008; Graham 2010a; Rashad and Abdel-Azeem 2010. River migration in the region of Thebes is particularly well studied thanks to the program of augering undertaking by the Theban Harbours and Waterscapes Survey (https://www.arkeologi.uu.se/Research/Projects/thaws-en/).
35 See contributions by Bunbury, Graham, Moeller, and Moreno García this volume; also Jeffreys and Bunbury 2005; Wilson 2012, 2017, 2018; Ginau et al. 2017; Bunbury 2019. For the desirability of newly formed islands as cultivatable land, see Moreno García, this volume, 151–155.
36 See contributions by Creasman, Bunbury, and Rowlands, this volume. See also Bunbury et al. 2017; Bunbury 2019.
37 Bunbury 2019, 88–92. See also Schneider, this volume, 7; Graham 2010b. For river migration and the accessibility of the Medamud Temple in Thebes, see Monserrat 2017. See also Gabolde 2013, 2018.
38 See Graham, this volume. Also Boraik et al. 2010; Boraik et al. 2017.
39 Bietak 2017, 63. Pirameses is assumed to have been abandoned after the Pelusiac Branch of the Nile was blocked by sediment.
40 Lichtheim 2006, 142.
41 *Hymn to Hapi*, IV.9; translation after van der Plas 1986, 29.
42 Coffin Texts, Spell 318 (Faulkner 1973, 4:142).
43 Butzer 1976, 51–56. The optimal level or the inundation (1.5 m) was marked on

Nilometers with the *ꜥnḫ* symbol, which signified that the level was sufficient to avoid excess (Eyre 2004, 160).

44 Brewer 2007, 132. Two common causes for variations in inundation heights include the El-Niño Southern Oscillation and temporal non-random fluctuations known as the Hurst Phenomenon (Manning 2012, 6).

45 Diodorus Siculus, *Bibliotheca Historica*, 1.36.11–12; Strabo 17.1.48.

46 It is not clear whether some Nilometers were mobile and set up by attendants during inundation (Bell 1970, 571–572). The potential mobility of the Nilometers has implications for the recorded levels, as the readings from a mobile instrument would not be influenced by the approximately 10 cm of alluvium deposits that accumulated roughly every 100 years (Bell 1970, 571; Butzer 1976, 28). The Nilometer at Elephantine was one of the most significant due to its location at the First Cataract, where the inundation was the highest (Friedman 2008, 1752). Forecasting necessitated the accumulation of long-term data on both flood heights and subsequent harvests—a practice substantiated by Diodorus Siculus, who notes that "accurate records of their observations have been set up by the Egyptians for a long time" (*Bibliotheca Historica*, 1.36.11–12).

47 Bunbury, this volume, 53. See also discussions by Moeller, this volume, 87; Warden, this volume, 172.

48 See for example Ritner and Moeller 2014; Schneider, this volume. For an overview of the geoarchaeological evidence for climate fluctuation, see Creasman, this volume.

49 Textual attestations of anomalous flood levels include records of the flooding of the Temple at Karnak in Year 4 of Sebekhotep VIII (Sixteenth Dynasty), Year 3 of Osorkon III (Twenty-second Dynasty), and Year 3 of Shabitko (Twenty-fifth Dynasty) (Krauss 2006, 372–373). See also Baines 1974, 1976; Habachi 1974.

50 Schneider 2017; Creasman, this volume, 15–16. Creasman (this volume, 16–17) also discusses the interpretive value of art historical depictions of environmental catastrophes.

51 See for example Seidlmayer 2001; Moeller 2005. Barbara Bell recognized early on the environmental potential of the Palermo Stone, analyzing the recorded Nile heights and comparing them to nineteenth and early twentieth century heights recorded by the Roda Nilometer (Bell 1970). Bell was also pioneering in her study of inundation and rainfall evidence and the correlation of this data with social change in the Middle Kingdom (1975).

52 See supra no. 14.

53 Antoine 2009; Butzer 2012, 3634–3635.

54 The clearest instance of this was during the Twentieth Dynasty of the New Kingdom, at which time the price of grain increased 880%, while the price of barley increased 1100% (Trigger et al. 1983, 228 fig. 3.10).

55 Antoine 2006, 33–35.

56 Edgerton 1951. Many scholars have proposed a correlation between anomalous flood levels and periods of political turmoil (see for example Hughes, 1992, 14; Antoine 2009, 232; Butzer 2012, 3634–3635). For a critique of the conflation of inundation instability and the collapse of the Old Kingdom, see Manning 2012, 18–20.

57 See contributions by Schneider and Moreno García in this volume; Scheidel 2001.

58 Creasman, this volume, 16–17.

59 The citation web was produced using Clarivate Analytics' Web of Science Data (https://clarivate.com/webofsciencegroup/solutions/web-of-science/). The citation report was generated on March 25, 2020. © Copyright Clarivate 2020. All rights reserved.

A Manifesto for the Study of the Ancient Egyptian Environment

J. Bunbury, P.P. Creasman, A. Graham, C. Johnston, N. Moeller,
J. Rowland, T. Schneider, L.A. Warden, and W. Wendrich

The study of ancient Egypt lags behind other historical and archaeological disciplines by failing to prioritize the study of the environment. In order to generate meaningful knowledge about past societies situated along the Nile, it is necessary to pursue holistic research agendas with interdisciplinary frameworks that incorporate a broader range of specialists, including those drawn from the sciences. More robust data must be sought and assessed, including geomorphological and paleo-climatic data, and methodology must be expanded to incorporate ecological models of occupation and land-use and of human responses to environmental change. The participants of the 2017 Colloquium on Ancient Egypt and the Environment propose the following three goals for the study of ancient Egypt and, more generally, for historical inquiry.

1. Promoting Environmental Investigation in Project Development

Current study of the Egyptian environment is often haphazard and independent from other excavation and research programs. We endorse consultation and collaboration with diverse specialists at the planning stage of future projects to broaden lines of inquiry and expand the types of data generated in the field.

2. Developing New Opportunities for Scientific Sample Analysis

The primary barrier to developing the study of the Egyptian environment is the restriction on sample exportation. To address this issue we propose three courses of action: support the development of local resources for analysis within Egypt, including increased use of mobile analytical technology in the field and commitment to assist in the development of local laboratories and facilities run by trained staff; broaden our geographic scope to

The Gift of the Nile? Ancient Egypt and the Environment
edited by Thomas Schneider and Christine L. Johnston
Tucson, Arizona: Egyptian Expedition, 2020

include data generated from the Nile basin in neighbouring East African countries; and support institutions and groups that formally advocate with the Ministry of Antiquities to amend restrictions on the exportation of scientific samples.

3. Creating New Resources for Spreading Environmental Data and Research

The study of the Egyptian environment must be integrated into both teaching and research programs. To promote greater literacy of environmental theory and science, we will continue to publish open-access research, data, and guides for the adoption of the study of the environment into Egyptological research. This material will be made available through the UCLA Encyclopedia of Egyptology, and will be supplemented by the organization of additional research, data, and guides for the adoption of the study of the environment into Egyptological research. This online forum will accompany the publication of this volume, and will be supplemented by the organization of additional colloquia and meetings that will include cross-disciplinary participants.

To achieve these goals we advocate for active engagement with related historical disciplines that promote the inclusion of environmental theory and methodology in interdisciplinary research programs. It is critical that we develop collaborative affiliations that enable us to pursue a deeper understanding of the complex relationships between societies and their environments in the past, and to formulate resilient responses to future climate change.

Appendix

Sources for the Study of the Ancient Egyptian Environment

Christine L. Johnston and Leesha Cessna

I. The Geographic and Climatic History of the Nile

Adamson, D., F. Gasse, F. Street, and M. Williams. 1980. "Late Quaternary History of the Nile." *Nature* 288: 50–55.

Allen, R.O., H. Hamroush, and M.A. Hoffman. 1989. "Archaeological Implications of Differences in the Composition of Nile Sediments." In *Archaeological Chemistry IV*, edited by R.O. Allen, 33–56. Advances in Chemistry 220. Washington, D.C.: American Chemical Society.

Amélineau, E. 1893. *La géographie de l'Égypte à l'époque copte.* Paris: Imprimerie nationale.

Andres, W., and J. Wunderlich. 1991. "Late Pleistocene and Holocene Evolution of the Eastern Nile Delta and Comparison with the Western Delta." In *Von der Nordsee bis zum Indischen Ozean. Ergebnisse der 8. Jahrestagung des Arbeitskreises 'Geographie der Meere und Küsten', 12.–15. Juni 1990, Düsseldorf,* edited by H. Brückner and U. Radtke, 121–130. Erdkundliches Wissen 105. Stuttgart: Franz Steiner Verlag.

The Gift of the Nile? Ancient Egypt and the Environment
edited by Thomas Schneider and Christine L. Johnston
Tucson, Arizona: Egyptian Expedition, 2020

Arbouille, D., J.-D. Stanley. 1991. "Late Quaternary Evolution of the Burullus Lagoon Region, North-Central Delta, Egypt." *Marine Geology* 99: 45–66.

Attia, M.I. 1951. "The Nile Basin: A Short Account of its Topography, Geology and Structure." *Bulletin de l'Institut Fouad Ier du Désert* 1: 107–120.

———. 1954. *Deposits in the Nile Valley and the Delta*. Cairo: Geological Survey of Egypt.

Ball, J. 1903. "The Semna Cataract or Rapid of the Nile: A Study in River-Erosion." *Quarterly Journal of the Geological Society* 59: 65–79.

———. 1907. *A Description of the First or Aswan Cataract of the Nile*. Cairo: National Print Deptartment.

———. 1932. "'The 'Description de l'Égypte' and the Course of the Nile between Isna and Girga." *Bulletin de l'Institut d'Égypte* 14: 127–139.

———. 1939. *Contributions to the Geography of Egypt*. Cairo: Government Press, Bulâq.

Bernhardt, C.E., B.P. Horton, and J.-D. Stanley. 2012. "Nile Delta Vegetation Response to Holocene Climate Variability." *Geology* 40: 615–618.

Berry, L., and A.J. Whiteman. 1968. "The Nile in the Sudan." *The Geographical Journal* 134(1): 1–33.

Bietak, M. 1975. *Tell el-Dab'a II. Der Fundort im Rahmen einer archäologisch-geographischen Untersuchung über das ägyptische Ostdelta. Mit einem geodätischen Beitrag von Josef Dorner und Heinz König. Denkschriften der Gesamtakademie, Band: 4. Untersuchungen der Zweigstelle Kairo des Österreichischen Archäologischen Instituts, Band: 1*. Wien: Verlag der Österreichischen Akademie der Wissenschaften.

———. 1983. "Historical Geography in the Eastern Nile Delta." *Bulletin de l'Institut d'Égypte* 60/61: 71–94.

Blue, L.K., and E. Khalil, eds. 2010. *Lake Mareotis: Reconstructing the Past. Proceedings of the International Conference on the Archaeology of the Mareotic Region*. University of Southampton Series in Archaeology 2. Oxford: Archaeopress.

Branton, T. 2008. "Development of the Memphite Floodplain from Borehole Data." Ph.D. diss., Cambridge University.

Bristow, C.S., and N. Drake. 2006. "Shorelines in the Sahara: Geomorphological Evidence for an Enhanced Monsoon from Paleolake Megachad." *The Holocene* 16: 901–911.

Brook, G.A., N.S. Embabi, M.M. Ashour, R.L. Edwards, H. Cheng, J.B. Cowart, and A.A. Dabous. 2002. "Djara Cave in the Western Desert of Egypt: Morphology and Evidence of Quaternary Climatic Change." *Cave and Karst Science* 29(2): 57–66.

Brown, R.H. 1887. "The Bahr Jusuf: Rough Description of its Present State." *Proceedings of the Royal Society of London* 9: 614–617.

Bunbury, J.M. 2012. "The Mobile Nile." *Egyptian Archaeology* 41: 15–17.

————. 2013. "Geomorphological Development of the Memphite Floodplain over the Past 6000 Years." *Studia Quaternaria* 30(2): 61–67.

————. 2016. "Geology of the Valley of the Kings." In *Oxford Handbook of the Valley of the Kings*, edited by R. Wilkinson and K. Weeks, 15–22. Oxford: Oxford University Press.

————. 2019. *The Nile and Ancient Egypt: Changing Land- and Waterscapes, from the Neolithic to the Roman Era.* Cambridge: Cambridge University Press.

Bunbury, J.M., and S. Ikram. 2014. "Kharga Oasis: A Saharan Patchwork of Lakes." *Egyptian Archaeology* 45: 10–12.

Bunbury, J.M., and M. Malouta. 2012. "The Geology and Papyrology of Hermopolis and Antinoopolis." *eTopoi: Journal for Ancient Studies* 3: 119–122.

Bunbury, J.M., E. Hughes, and N. Spencer. 2014. "Ancient Landscape Reconstruction at Kom Firin." In *Kom Firin II: The Urban Fabric and Landscape*, edited by N. Spencer, 11–16. British Museum Research Publication 2(192). London: The British Museum.

Butzer, K.W. 1959. "Contributions to the Pleistocene Geology of the Nile Valley." *Erkunde* 13: 46–67.

————. 1960. "Archaeology and Geology in Ancient Egypt." *Science* 132 (3440): 1617–1624.

————. 1997. "Late Quaternary Problems of the Egyptian Nile: Stratigraphy, Environments, Prehistory." *Paléoenvironment et sociétés humaines au Moyen-Orient de 20 000 BP à 6 000 BP* 23(2): 151–173.

————. 2001. "Nile." In *The Oxford Encyclopedia of Ancient Egypt*, edited by D.B. Redford, 543–551. Oxford: Oxford University Press.

————. 2016. "Landscapes and Environmental History of Ancient Egypt: Review and Prospectus." In *Gedenkschrift für Werner Kaiser*, edited by D. Polz and S.J. Seidlmayer, 59–80. *Mitteilungen des Deutschen Archaologischen Instituts, Abteilung Kairo* 70/71. Berlin and Boston: Walter de Gruyter.

Butzer, K.W., and C.L. Hansen. 1968. *Desert and River in Nubia: Geomorphology and Prehistoric Environments at the Aswan Reservoir.* Madison: University of Wisconsin Press.

Caneva, I. 1988. *El-Geili: The History of a Middle Nile Environment 7000 B.C.–A.D. 1500.* BAR-IS 29. Oxford: Archaeopress.

Caton-Thompson, G. 1952. *Kharga Oasis in Prehistory.* London: Athlone Press.

Caton-Thompson, G., and E. Gardner. 1932. "The Prehistoric Geography of Kharga Oasis." *The Geographical Journal* 80: 369–406.

———. 1934. *The Desert Fayum.* London: Royal Anthropological Institute.

Chen, Z., A. Warne, and J.-D. Stanley. 1992. "Late Quaternary Evolution of the Northwestern Nile Delta between the Rosetta Promontory and Alexandria, Egypt." *Journal of Coastal Research* 8(3): 527–561.

Cílek, V., L. Lisá, and M. Bárta, M. 2011. "The Holocene of the Abusir Area." In *Abusir and Saqqara in the Year 2010*, vol. 1, edited by M. Bárta, F. Coppens, and J. Krečí, 312–326. Prague: Czech Institute of Egyptology, Faculty of Arts, Charles University in Prague.

Cílek, V., M. Bárta, L. Lisá, A. Pokorná, L. Juřičková, V. Brůna, A.M.A. Mahmoud, A. Bajer, J. Novák, and J. Beneš. 2012. "Diachronic Development of the Lake of Abusir during the Third Millennium BC, Cairo, Egypt." *Quaternary International* 266: 14–24.

Conway, D. 2000. "The Climate and Hydrology of the Upper Blue Nile River." *Geographical Journal* 166: 49–62.

Cross, S.W. 2008. "The Hydrology of the Valley of the Kings." *The Journal of Egyptian Archaeology* 94: 303–310.

Dabous, A.A., and J.K. Osmond. 2000. "U/Th Isotopic Study of Speleothems from the Wadi Sannur Cavern, Eastern Desert of Egypt." *Carbonates and Evaporites* 15(1). doi.org/10.1007/BF03175643.

Daressy, G. 1928. "Les branches du Nil sous la XVIIIe dynastie." *Bulletin de la Société Royale de Géographie d'Égypte* 16(3): 225–254.

———. 1929. "Les branches du Nil sous la XVIIIe dynastie." *Bulletin de la Société Royale de Géographie d'Égypte* 16(4): 293–329.

de Heinzelin, J. 1968. "Geological History of the Nile Valley in Nubia." In *The Prehistory of Nubia*, edited by F. Wendorf, 19–55. Dallas: Fort Burgwin Research Center and Southern Methodist University Press.

de Putter, T. 1992. "Le 'problème de Semna' (Nubie) revisité: nouveaux arguments en faveur d'un 'event' climatique au Moyen Empire." In *Sesto Congresso Internazionale di Egittologia: Atti*, vol. 1, edited by the International Congress of Egyptology, 125–127. Torino: Comitato Organizzativo del Congresso.

———. 1996. "Semna-Koumma: un mot encore." *Göttinger Miszellen* 152: 51–54.

De Roller, G.J. 1992. "Archaeobotanical Remains from Tell Ibrahim Awad, Seasons 1988 and 1989." In *The Nile Delta in Transition: 4th–3rd Millennium BC*, edited by E.C.M. van den Brink, 111–115. Tel Aviv: E.C.M. van den Brink.

de Wit, H.E., and L. van Stralen. 1988. *Geo-Archaeology and Ancient Distributaries in the Eastern Nile Delta: Results of the 1987 AUSE Survey in Sharqiya, Egypt.* Reports of the Laboratory of Physical Geography and Soil Science 34. Amsterdam: University of Amsterdam.

de Menocal, P., J. Ortiz, T. Guilderson, J. Adkins, M. Sarnthein, L. Baker, and M. Yarusinsky. 2000. "Abrupt Onset and Termination of the African Humid Period: Rapid Climate Responses to Gradual Insolation Forcing." *Quaternary Science Reviews* 19(1–5): 347–361.

Dorn, A. 2016. "The Hydrology of the Valley of the Kings: Weather, Rainfall, Drainage Patterns and Flood Protection in Antiquity." In *Oxford Handbook of the Valley of the Kings*, edited by R. Wilkinson and K. Weeks, 30–40. Oxford: Oxford University Press.

Dorner, J. 1994. "Die Rekonstruktion einer pharaonischen Flusslandschaft." *Mitteilungen der Anthropologischen Gesellschaft in Wien* 123: 401–406.

Duckworth, T. 2009. "The Development of Islands in the Theban Floodplain." MSc. diss., Cambridge University.

Dufton, D. 2008. "Meander Bends of the Nile in the Abydos Region." MSc. diss., Cambridge University.

Dufton, D., and T. Branton. 2009. "Climate Change in Early Egypt." *Egyptian Archaeology* 36: 2–3.

Earl, E. 2010. "The Lake of Abusir, Northern Egypt." MSc. diss., Cambridge University.

Edelman-Furstenberg, Y., A. Almogi-Labin, and C. Hemleben. 2009. "Palaeoceanographic Evolution of the Central Red Sea During the Holocene." *The Holocene* 19(1): 117–127.

El Shazly, E.M. 1987. "The Ostracinic Branch, a Proposed Old Branch of the River Nile." *Discussions in Egyptology* 7: 69–78.

El-Gamili, M.M., and E.-K. Hassan. 1989. "Geophysical Investigations for Holocene Palaeohydrography in the Northwestern Nile Delta." In *The Archaeology, Geography, and History of the Egyptian Delta in Pharaonic Times*, edited by A. Nibbi, 125–154. Discussions in Egyptology Special Number 1. Eynsham: Cotswold Press.

El-Gamili, M.M., E.H. Ibrahim, A.R.G. Hassaneen, M.A. Abdalla, and A.M. Ismael. 2001. "Defunct Nile Branches Inferred from a Geoelectric Resistivity Survey on Samannud Area, Nile Delta, Egypt." *Journal of Archaeological Science* 28(12): 1339–1348.

Elsheikh, A.S., E.M. Elmiligi, and S.M. Ibraheem. 2008. "Hydrology of Qarun Lake, El Fayoum Depression, Egypt." *Bulletin of the National Research Centre, Egypt* 33: 1–26.

Embabi, N.S., ed. 2004. *The Geomorphology of Egypt: Landforms and Evolution*. Vol. 1, *The Nile Valley and the Western Desert*. The Egyptian Geographical Society, Special Publication. Cairo: The Egyptian Geographical Society.

———. 2018. *Landscapes and Landforms of Egypt: Landforms and Evolution*. World Geomorphological Landscapes. Cham: Springer.

Fairbridge, R.W. 1962. "New Radiocarbon Dates of Nile Sediments." *Nature* 196: 108–110.

————. 1963. "Nile Sedimentation Above Wadi Halfa During the Last 20,000 Years." *Kush* 11: 96–107.

Fanos, A.M. 1986. "Statistical Analysis of Longshore Current Data along the Nile Delta Coast." *Water Science Journal* 1: 45–55.

Faure, H. 1966. "Evolution des grands lacs sahariens à l'Holocène." *Quaternaria* 8: 167–175.

Firhy, O.E., A.M. Fanos, A.A. Khafagy, and P.D. Komar. 1991. "Patterns of Nearshore Sediment Transport along the Nile Delta, Egypt." *Coastal Engineering* 15: 409–429.

Flaux, C., C. Claude, N. Marriner, and C. Morhange. 2013. "A 7500-Year Strontium Isotope Record from the Northwestern Nile Delta (Maryut Lagoon, Egypt)." *Quaternary Science Reviews* 78: 22–33.

Fortau, R. 1915. "Contribution à l'étude des dépôts nilotiques." *Mémoires présentés à l'Institut Egyptien* 8: 57–94.

Frihy, O.E. 1992a. "Sea-Level Rise and Shoreline Retreat of the Nile Delta Promontories, Egypt." *Natural Hazards* 5: 65–81.

————. 1992b. "Holocene Sea Level Changes at the Nile Delta Coastal Zone of Egypt." *Geo Journal* 26(3): 389–394.

Gabriel, B, and P. Wolf. 2007. "River and Landscape at the Fourth Nile Cataract (Sudan) during Late Quaternary." In *Proceedings of the Second International Conference on the Archaeology of the Fourth Nile Cataract*, edited by C. Näser and M. Lange, 28–33. Meroitica 23. Wiesbaden: Harrassowitz Verlag.

Ghilardi, M., Y. Tristant, and M. Boraik. 2012. "Nile River Evolution in Upper Egypt During the Holocene: Palaeoenvironmental Implications for the Pharaonic sites of Karnak and Coptos." *Géomorphologie* 18(1): 7–22.

Gingerich, P.D. 1992. *Marine Mammals (Cetacea and Sirenia) from the Eocene of Gebel Mokattam and Fayum, Egypt: Stratigraphy, Age, and Paleoenvironments*. University of Michigan Papers on Paleontology 30. Ann Arbor: University of Michigan Press.

Goiran, J.-P. 2001. "Recherches géomorphologiques dans la région littorale d'Alexandrie en Egypte." Ph.D. diss., Université de Provence—Aix-Marseille I.

Goncalvez, P.M. 2018. "Landscape and Environmental Changes at Memphis during the Dynastic Period Egypt." Ph.D. diss., University of Cambridge.

Goudie, A., and J. Wilkinson. 1977. *The Warm Desert Environment*. Cambridge: Cambridge University Press.

Graham, A. 2010. "Ancient Landscapes around the Opet Temple, Karnak." *Egyptian Archaeology* 36: 25–28.

Graham, A., and J.M. Bunbury. 2005. "The Ancient Landscapes and Waterscapes of Karnak." *Egyptian Archaeology* 27: 17–19.

Haarland, R., and A. Abdel-Magid. 1995. *Aqualithic Sites along the Rivers Nile and Atbara, Sudan.* Bergen: Alma Mater Forlag.

Hamdan, M.A. 2014. "Sedimentological Characteristics and Geomorphic Evolution of the Holocene Playa of Wadi el Obeiyid." In *From Lake to Sand: The Archaeology of Farafra Oasis, Western Desert, Egypt*, edited by B. Barich, G. Lucarini, M.A. Hamdan, and F.A. Hassan, 81–128. Florence: All'Insegna del Giglio.

Hassan, F.A., R.J. Hamdan, R.A. Flower, N.A. Shallaly, and E. Ebrahem. 2017. "Holocene Alluvial History and Archaeological Significance of the Nile Floodplain in the Saqqara Memphis Region, Egypt." *Quaternary Science Reviews* 176: 51–70.

Haynes, C.V. 1980. "Geochronology of Wadi Tushka: Lost Tributary of the Nile." *Science* 210: 68–71.

Haynes, C.V., P.J Mehringer, and S.A. Zaghloul. 1979. "Pluvial Lakes of North-Western Sudan." *The Geographical Journal* 145: 437–445.

Hillier, J.K. 2007. "Migrations of the course of the River Nile between Luxor and Qift over the Last 4,000 Years." In *Proceedings of the International Conference on Heritage of Naqada and Qus Region, Monastery of the Archangel Michael, Naqada, Egypt, 22–28 January 2007*, edited by H. Hanna, 88–97. Cairo: ICOM.

Hillier, J.K., J.M. Bunbury, and A. Graham. 2007. "Monuments on a Migrating Nile." *Journal of Archaeological Science* 34: 1011–1015.

Holdaway, S., and W. Wendrich. 2017. *The Desert Fayum Reinvestigated.* Monumenta Archaeologica 39. Los Angeles: Cotsen Insitute of Archaeology Press.

Hughes, E. 2007. "In Search of the Wild Western Branch of the Nile." Ph.D. diss., Cambridge University.

Hull, E. 1890. "Sketch of the Geological History of Egypt and the Nile Valley." *Journal of the Transactions of the Victoria Institute* 24: 307–334.

Huss, W. 1990. "Die Quellen des Nils." *Chronique d'Egypte* 65(130): 334–343.

Ibrahim, E.E.E. 1968. *Aspects of the Geomorphological Evolution of the Nile Valley in the Qena Bend Area.* Newcastle upon Tyne: University of Newcastle upon Tyne.

Issawi, B. 1976. "An Introduction to the Physiography of the Nile Valley." In *Prehistory of the Nile Valley*, edited by F. Wendorf and R. Schild, 3–22. New York: Academic Press.

Jeffreys, D., and A. Tavares. 1994. "The Historic Landscape of Early Dynastic Memphis." *Mitteilungen des Deutschen Archaologischen Instituts, Abteilung Kairo* 50: 143–173.

Jones, M. 1997. "Archaeological Discoveries in Doqqi and the Course of the Nile at Cairo during the Roman Period." *Mitteilungen des Deutschen Archäologischen Instituts, Abteilung Kairo* 53: 101–111.

Kater, E.A., T.S. Abd-El-Aal, A.A. Abou-Arab, and A.A. Awadalla. 1997. "Mineralogical and Chemical Composition of the Main Soil Types in Fayoum Area." *Egyptian Journal of Soil Science* 37(2): 153–174.

Kessler, D. 1981. *Historische Topographie der Region zwischen Mallawi und Samalut.* Wiesbaden: Dr. Ludwig Reichert.

Kołodziejczyk, P. 2009. "The Nile Delta During the Predynastic and the Early Dynastic Periods: Recent Discoveries and Perspectives." In *Proceedings of the Fifth Central European Conference of Egyptologists*, edited by J. Popielska-Grzybowska and J. Iwaszczuk, 101–106. Pułtusk: Institute of Anthropology and Archaeology.

Koopman, A., S. Kluiving, S. Holdaway, and W. Wendrich. 2016. "The Effects of Holocene Landscape Changes on the Formation of the Archaeological Record in the Fayum Basin, Egypt." *Geoarchaeology* 31(1): 17–33.

Kröpelin, S., D. Verschuren, A.M. Lézine, H. Eggermont, C. Cocquyt, P. Francus, J.-P. Cazet, M. Fagot, B. Rumes, J.M. Russell, F. Darius, D.J. Conley, M. Schuster, H. von Suchodoletz, and D.R. Engstrom. 2008. "Climate-Driven Ecosystem Succession in the Sahara: The Past 6000 Years." *Science* 320(5877): 765–768.

Kuper, R., and S. Kröpelin. 2006. "Climate-Controlled Holocene Occupation in the Sahara: Motor of Africa's Evolution." *Science* 313(5788): 803–807.

Lario, J., S. Sanches-Moral, V. Fernandez, A. Jimeno, and M. Menendez. 1997. "Palaeoenvironmental Evolution of the Blue Nile (Central Sudan) during the Early and Mid-Holocene (Mesolithic-Neolithic Transition)." *Quaternary Science Reviews* 16(6): 583–588.

Lozach, J. 1935. *Le delta du Nil: Étude de géographie humaine.* Cairo: Société de géographie d'Égypte.

Lutley, K., and J. Bunbury. 2008. "The Nile on the Move." *Egyptian Archaeology* 32: 3–5.

Lyons, H.G. 1905a. "Dimensions of the River Nile and Its Basin." *The Geographical Journal* 26(2): 198–201.

———. 1905b. "On the Nile Flood and Its Variation." *The Geographical Journal* 26(2): 249–271, 395–420.

———. 1906. *The Physiography of the River Nile and Its Basin.* Cairo: National Printing Department.

———. 1908a. "Some Geographical Aspects of the Nile." *The Geographical Journal* 32: 449–480.

————. 1908b. *The Rains of the Nile Basin (1904–1908)*. Cairo: National Printing Department.

Manohar, M. 1981. "Coastal Processes at the Nile Delta Coast." *Shore and Beaches* 49: 8–15.

Marcolongo, B. 1983. "Late Quaternary Nile and Hydrology of the Khartoum-Sabaloka Region (Sudan)." *Origini: preistoria e protostoria delle civiltà antiche* 12: 39–46.

————. 1992. "Évolution du paléo-environnement dans la partie orientale du delta du Nil depuis la transgression flandrienne (8000 B.P.) par rapport aux modèles de peuplement anciens." *Cahiers de recherches de l'Institut de papyrologie et d'égyptologie de Lille* 14: 23–31.

Marks, L., A. Salem, F. Welc, J. Nitychoruk, Z. Chen, M. Blaauw, A. Zalat, A. Majecka, M. Szymanek, M. Chodyka, A. Toloczko-Pasek, Q. Sun, X. Zhao, and J. Jiang. 2017. "Holocene Lake Sediments from the Faiyum Oasis in Egypt: A Record of Environmental and Climate Change." *Boreas* 47(1): 62–79.

Maxwell, T.A., B. Issawi, C.V. Haynes Jr. 2010. "Evidence for Pleistocene Lakes in the Tushka Region, Southern Egypt." *Geoarchaeology* 38(12): 1135–1138.

Mohamed, I.N.L. 2012. "Evolution of the South-Rayan Dune-Field (Central Egypt) and Its Interaction with the Nile Fluvial System." Ph.D. diss., KU Leuven.

Montserrat, F.R. 2017. "Medamud and the Nile: Some Preliminary Reflections." In *The Nile: Natural and Cultural Landscape in Egypt. Proceedings of the International Symposium held at the Johannes Gutenberg-Universität Mainz, 22 & 23 February 2013*, edited by H. Willems and J.-M. Dahms, 145–170. Bielefeld: transcript Verlag.

Murray, G.W. 1951. "The Egyptian Climate: An Historical Outline." *The Geographical Journal* 117(4): 422–434.

Nicholson, P.T., J. Harrison, S. Ikram, E. Earl, and Y. Qin. 2013. "Geoarchaeological and Environmental Work at the Sacred Animal Necropolis, North Saqqara, Egypt." *Studia Quaternaria* 30(2): 83–89.

Nussbaum, S., and F. Darius. 2010. "The Archaeobotanical Evidence of Djara and Its Environmental Interpretation." In *Djara: Zur mittelholozänen Besiedlungsgeschichte zwischen Niltal und Oasen (Abu-Muharik-Plateau, Ägypten)*, vol. 2, edited by K. Kindermann, 815–835. Köln: Heinrich-Barth-Institut.

Osborn, D.J., with J. Osbornová. 1998. *The Mammals of Ancient Egypt*. The Natural History of Egypt 4. Warminster: Aris & Phillips.

Pachur, H.-J., and S. Kröpelin. 1993. "Wadi Howar: Paleoclimatic Evidence from an Extinct River System in the Southeastern Sahara." *Science* 237: 238–300.

Pennington, B.T., F. Sturt, P. Wilson, J. Rowland, and A.G. Brown. 2017. "The Fluvial Evolution of the Holocene Nile Delta." *Quaternary Science Reviews* 170: 212–231.

Pryer, L. 2011. "The Landscape of the Egyptian Middle Kingdom Capital Itj-Tawi." Ph.D. diss., Cambridge University.

Qin, Y. 2009a. "Landscape change in the Saqqara/Memphis area of Egypt from 3000 BC to the present." M.Sci. diss., University of Cambridge.

———. 2009b. "The Development of the Memphite Floodplain, Egypt." Ph.D. diss., Cambridge University.

Raikes, R.L., A. Palmieri. 1972. "Environmental Conditions in the Nile Valley Over the Past 10,000 Years." *Journal of Human Evolution* 1(2): 147–154.

Rashad, H., and A.M. Abdel-Azeem. 2010. "Lake Manzala, Egypt: A Bibliography." *Assiut University Journal of Botany* 39(1): 253–289.

Reid, A. 2003. "Ancient Egypt and the Source of the Nile." In *Ancient Egypt in Africa*, edited by D. O'Connor and A. Reid, 55–76. London: UCL Press.

Revel, M., E. Ducassou, F.E. Grousset, S.M. Bernasconi, S. Migeon, S. Revillon, J. Mascle, A. Murat, S. Saragosi, and D. Bosch. 2010. "100,000 Years of African Monsoon Variability Recorded in Sediments of the Nile Margin." *Quaternary Science Reviews* 29: 1342–1362.

Roubet, C. 1981. "20.000 ans d'environnement préhistorique dans la vallée du Nil et le désert égyptien." *Bulletin de l'Institut français d'archéologie orientale* 81: 445–470.

Rzóska, J., ed. 1976. *The Nile: Biology of an Ancient River*. The Hague: Dr. J. Junk B.V.

Said, R. 1962. *The Geology of Egypt*. Amsterdam: Elsevier.

———. 1975. "The Geological Evolution of the River Nile." In *Problems in Prehistory: North Africa and the Levant*, edited by F. Wendorf and A.E. Marks, 6–44. Dallas: Southern Methodist University Press.

———. 1981. *The Geological Evolution of the River Nile*. New York: Springer.

Said, R., and F. Yousri. 1968. "Origin and Pleistocene History of River Nile near Cairo, Egypt." *Bulletin de l'Institut d'Égypte* 45: 1–30.

Said, R., C.C. Albritton, F. Wendorf, R. Schild, and M. Kobusiewicz. 1972. "A Preliminary Report on the Holocene Geology and Archaeology of the Northern Fayum Desert." *International Center for Arid and Semi-arid Land Studies Publication* 4: 41–61.

Sampsell, B.M. 2014. *The Geology of Egypt: A Traveller's Handbook*. Rev. ed. Cairo: AUC Press.

Schild, R. 1987. "Unchanging Contrast? The Late Pleistocene Nile and Eastern Sahara." In *Prehistory of Arid North Africa: Essays in Honor of Fred Wendorf*, edited by A.E. Close, 13–27. Dallas: Southern University Press.

Sestini, G. 1989. "Nile Delta: A Review of Depositional Environments and Geological History." In *Deltas: Sites and Traps for Fossil Fuels*, edited by M.K.G. Whately and K.T. Pickering, 99–127. Geological Society Special Publications 41. London: Geological Society.

Sewuster, R.J.E., and V.B. Wesemael. 1987. *Tracing Ancient River Courses in the Eastern Nile Delta: A Geo-Archaeological Survey in the Sarqiya Province, Egypt*. Rapporten van net Fysisch Geografisch Bodemkundig Laboratorium. Amsterdam: Universiteit van Amsterdam.

Shahin, M. 1985. *Hydrology of the Nile Basin*. Amsterdam: Elsevier.

Sneh, A., and T. Weissbrod. 1973. "Nile Delta: The Defunct Pelusiac Branch Identified." *Science* 180: 59–61.

Stager, J.C. 1998. "Ancient Analogues for Recent Environmental Changes at Lake Victoria, East Africa." In *Environmental Change and Response in East African Lakes*, edited by J.T. Lehman, 37–46. Monographiae Biologicae 79. Dordrecht: Springer.

Stanley, J.-D. 1988. "Subsidence in the North-Eastern Nile Delta: Rapid Rates, Possible Causes, and Consequences." *Science* 240(4851): 497–500.

———. 1990. "Recent Subsidence and Northeast Tilting of the Nile Delta, Egypt" *Marine Geology* 91(1–2): 147–154.

———. 1997. *Nile Delta: A Geological Excursion*. Washington, D.C.: Deltas-Global Change Program, Smithsonian Institution.

———. 2007. *Geoarchaeology: Underwater Archaeology in the Canopic Region in Egypt*. Oxford Centre for Maritime Archaeology Monograph 2. Oxford: Oxford Centre for Maritime Archaeology.

Stanley, J.-E., J.E. McRea, Jr, and J.C. Wilson. 1996. *Nile Delta Drill Core and Sample Database for 1985–1994: Mediterranean Basin (MEDIBA) Program*. Washington, D.C.: Smithsonian Institution Press.

Stanley, J.-D., A.G. Warne, and G. Schnepp. 2004. "Geoarchaeological Interpretation of the Canopic, Largest of the Relict Nile Delta Distributaries, Egypt." *Journal of Coastal Research* 203: 920–930.

Sutcliffe, J.V., and Y.P. Parks. 1999. *The Hydrology of the Nile*. IAHS Special Publication 5. Wallingford: IAHS.

Swelim, N. 2005. "Layer Monuments and the River." *Supplément aux annals du service des antiquités de l'Égypte* 34(2): 377–381.

Tietze, C. 2011. "Das Geschenk des Nils." In *Ägyptische Gärten*, edited by C. Tietze, F. Naumann-Steckner, and E. Hornung, 28–45. Weimar: Arcus-Verlag.

Toussoun, O. 1925. "Mémoires sur l'histoire du Nil." *Mémoires de l'Institut d'Egypte* 8–10: 1–543.

Trampier, J. 2010. "The Dynamic Landscape of the Western Nile Delta from the New Kingdom to the Late Roman Periods." Ph.D. diss., University of Chicago.

Tronchère, H. 2010. "Approche paléoenvironnementale de deux sites archéologiques dans le delta du Nil. Avaris et la branche Pélusiaque, Taposiris et le lac Mariout." Ph.D. diss., École doctorale Sciences sociales, Lyon.

Tronchère, H., F. Salomon, Y. Callot, J.-P. Goiran, L. Schmitt, I. Forstner-Müller, and M. Bietak. 2008. "Geoarchaeology of Avaris: First Results." *Ägypten und Levante* 18: 327–339.

Trzciński, J., K.O. Kuraszkiewicz, and F. Welc. 2010. "Preliminary Report on Geo-archaeological Research in West Saqqara." *Polish Archaeology in the Mediterranean* 19: 194–206.

Tvedt, T. 2002. *The River Nile and its Economic, Political, Social and Cultural Role: An Annotated Bibliography*. Bergren: University of Bergen.

Vercoutter, J. 1976. "Égyptologie et climatologie: les crues du Nil à Semneh." *Cahiers de Recherches de l'Institut de papyrologie et d'égyptologie de Lille* 4: 139–172.

Verstraeten, G., I. Mohamed, B. Notebaert, and H. Willems. 2017. "The Dynamic Nature of the Transition from the Nile Floodplain to the Desert in Ventral Egypt since the Mid-Holocene." In *The Nile: Natural and Cultural Landscape in Egypt. Proceedings of the International Symposium held at the Johannes Gutenberg-Universität Mainz, 22 & 23 February 2013*, edited by H. Willems and J.-M. Dahms, 239–254. Bielefeld: transcript Verlag.

Wendorf, F., and R. Schild. 1998. "Nabta Playa and its Role in Northeastern African Prehistory." *Journal of Anthropological Archaeology* 17: 97–123.

Wendorf, F., and The Members of the Combined Prehistoric Expedition. 1977. "Late Pleistocene and Recent Climatic Changes in the Egyptian Sahara." *The Geographical Journal* 143(2): 211–234.

Willcocks, W. 1904. *The Nile in 1904*. London: E. & F.N. Spon.

Williams, M.A.J. 2009. "Late Pleistocene and Holocene Environments in the Nile Basin." *Global Planetary Change* 69(1): 1–15.

———. 2019. *The Nile Basin: Quaternary Geology, Geomorphology, and Prehistoric Environments*. Cambridge: Cambridge University Press.

Williams, M.A.J., and D.A. Adamson. 1982. *A Land between Two Niles: Quaternary Geology and Biology of the Central Sudan*. London: Taylor and Francis.

Williams, M.A.J., and H. Faure, eds. 1980. *The Sahara and the Nile: Quaternary Environments and Prehistoric Occupation in Northern Africa.* Rotterdam: A.A. Balkema.

Williams, M.A.J., and M.R. Talbot. 2009. "Late Quaternary Environments in the Nile Basin." In *The Nile: Origins, Environments, Limnology, and Human Use,* edited by H.J. Dumont, 61–72. Monographiae Biologicae 89. Dordrecht: Springer.

Williams, M.A.J., M. Talbot, P. Aharon, Y.A. Salaam, F. Williams, and K.I. Brendeland. 2006. "Abrupt Return of the Summer Monsoon 15,000 Years Ago: New Supporting Evidence from the Lower White Nile Valley and Lake Albert." *Quaternary Science Reviews* 25(19–20): 2651–2665.

Williams, M.A.J., D. Usai, S. Salvatori, F.M. Williams, A. Zerboni, L. Maritan, and V. Linseele. 2015. "Late Quaternary Environments and Prehistoric Occupation in the Lower White Nile Valley, Central Sudan." *Quaternary Science Reviews* 130: 72–88.

Wilson, P., and D. Grigoropoulos. 2009. *The West Nile Delta Regional Survey, Beheira and Kafr el-Sheikh Provinces.* London: Egypt Exploration Society.

Woodward, J.C., and M.G. Macklin. 2001. "Holocene Alluvial History and the Palaeochannels of the River Nile in the Northern Dongola Reach." In *Life on the Desert Edge: Seven Thousand Years of Human Settlement in the Northern Dongola Reach, Sudan,* edited by D.A. Welsby, 6–13. London: British Museum Press.

Woodward, J.C., M.G. Macklin, D. Welsby. 2001. "The Holocene Fluvial Sedimentary Record and Alluvial Geoarchaeology in the Nile Valley of Northern Sudan." In *River Basin Sediment Systems: Archives of Environmental Change,* edited by D. Maddy, M.G. Macklin, and J.C. Woodward, 327–355. Amsterdam: AA Balkema.

Woodward, J.C., M.G. Macklin, M.D. Krom, and A.J. Williams. 2007. "The Nile: Evolution, Quaternary River Environments and Material Fluxes." In *Large Rivers, Geomorphology and Management,* edited by A. Gupta, 261–292. London: Wiley.

Woodward, J.C., M.A.J. Williams, E. Garzanti, M.G. Macklin, N. Marriner. 2015. "From Source to Sink: Exploring the Quaternary History of the Nile." *Quaternary Science Reviews* 130: 3–8.

Wunderlich, J. 1989. *Untersuchungen zur Entwicklung des westlichen Nildeltas im Holozän.* Marburg: Marburger Geographischen Gesellschaft.

Wunderlich, J., and A. Ginau 2016. "Paläoumweltwandel im Raum Tell el Fara'in/Buto: Ergebnisse und Perspektiven geoarchäologischer Forschung." *Mitteilungen des Deutschen Archäologischen Instituts, Abteilung Kairo* 70/71: 485–497.

Zhongyuan, C., and J.-D. Stanley. 1993. "Alluvial Stiff Muds (Late Pleistocene) Underlying the Lower Nile Delta Plain, Egypt: Petrology, Stratigraphy and Origin." *Journal of Coastal Research* 9(2): 539–576.

II. ENVIRONMENTAL METHODOLOGY IN THE STUDY OF THE NILE VALLEY AND DELTA

Abdel-Fattah, S., A. Amin, and L.C. Van Rijn. 2004. "Sand Transport in Nile River." *Journal of Hydraulic Engineering (ASCE)* 130(6): 488–500.

Alawad, S.M. 2015. "Remotely Sensed Data, Cartography, and Geo-Forms as Means for Archaeo-Ecological Information Extraction: Naqa and Musawwarat, Sudan." In *The Kushite World: Proceedings of the 11th International Conference for Meroitic Studies Vienna, 1–4 September 2008*, edited by H. Zach, 23–28. Beiträge Zur Sudanforschung 9. Vienna: Verein der Förderer der Sudanforschung.

Ayyad, S., and P.D. Moore. 1995. "Morphological Studies of the Pollen Grains of the Semiarid Region of Egypt." *Flora* 190: 115–133.

Ayyad, S.M., P.D. Moore, and M.A. Zahran. 1992. "Modern Pollen Rain Studies of the Nile Delta, Egypt." *The New Phytologist* 121(4): 663–675.

Bailey, D.M. 1999. "Sebakh, Sherds and Survey." *Journal of Egyptian Archaeology* 85: 211– 218.

Baioumy, H.M., H. Kayanne, and R. Tada. 2010. "Reconstruction of Lake-Level and Climate Changes in Lake Qarun, Egypt During the Last 7000 Years." *Journal of Great Lakes Research* 36(2): 318–327.

Bernasconi, M.P., J.-D. Stanley, and I. di Geronimo. 1991. "Molluscan Faunas and the Paleobathymetry of Holocene Sequences in the Northeastern Nile Delta, Egypt." *Marine Geology* 9: 29–43.

Bernasconi, M.P., and J.-D. Stanley. 1997. "Molluscan Biofacies, Their Distributions and Current Erosion on the Nile Delta Shelf." *Journal of Coastal Research* 13(4): 1201–1212.

Berry, L. 1960. "Large-Scale Alluvial Islands in the White Nile." *Revue de Géomorphogie Dynamique* 12: 105–108.

Blanchet, C.L., C. Contoux, and G. Leduc. 2015. "Runoff and Precipitation Dynamics in the Blue and White Nile Catchments During the Mid-Holocene: A Data-Model Comparison." *Quaternary Science Reviews* 130: 222–230.

Botros, S.S.S. 1978. "Pollen and Spore Analysis of Samples Taken from Different Borings in the Nile Delta." Ph.D. diss., Alexandria University.

Bottema, S. 1992. "Palynological Investigations of the Ibrahim Awad Deposits (Northeastern Nile Delta): Preliminary Report." In *The Nile Delta in Transition: 4th–3rd Millennium BC*, edited by E.C.M. van den Brink, 123–126. Tel Aviv: E.C.M. van den Brink.

Box, M.R., M.D. Krom, R.A. Cliff, M. Bar-Matthews, A. Almogi-Labin, A. Ayalon, and M. Paterne. 2011. "Response of the Nile and its Catchment to Millennial-Scale Climatic Change Since the LGM from Sr Isotopes and Major Elements of East Mediterranean Sediments." *Quaternary Science Reviews* 30(3–4): 431–442.

Brook, G.A., N.S. Embabi, M.M. Ashour, R.L. Edwards, H. Cheng, J.B. Cowart, and A.A. Dabous. 2003. "Quaternary Environmental Change in the Western Desert of Egypt: Evidence from Cave Speleothems, Spring Tufas and Playa Sediments." *Zeitschrift für Geomorphologie* N.F. Suppl. 131: 59–87.

Bunbury, J.M., A. Graham, and M.A. Hunter. 2008. "Stratigraphic Landscape Analysis: Charting the Holocene Movements of the Nile at Karnak through Ancient Egyptian Time." *Geoarchaeology* 23: 351–373.

Bunbury, J.M., A. Graham, and K.D. Strutt. 2009. "Kom El-Farahy: A New Kingdom Island in an Evolving Edfu Floodplain." *British Museum Studies in Ancient Egypt and the Sudan* 14: 1–23.

Butzer, K.W. 2002. "Geoarchaeological Implications of Recent Research in the Nile Delta." In *Egypt and the Levant: Interrelations from the 4th through the Early 3rd Millennium BCE*, edited by E.C.M. van den Brink and T.E. Levy, 83–97. London: Leicester University Press.

Cione, A.L. 2006. "Fishes from Tell el-Ghaba." In *Tell el-Ghaba*. Vol. 2, *A Saite Settlement in North Sinai, Egypt (Argentine Archaeological Mission, 1995–2004)*, edited by P. Fuscaldo, 102–126. Buenos Aires: Consejo Nacional de Investigaciones Científicas y Técnicas.

Claussen, M. 2003. "Simulation of Holocene Climate Change Using Climate-System Models." In *Global Change in the Holocene*, edited by A. Mackay, R. Battarbee, J. Birks, and F. Oldfield, 422–434. London: Arnold.

Cockerton, H.E., F.A. Street-Perrott, P.A. Barker, M.J. Leng, H.J. Sloane, and K.J. Ficken. 2015. "Orbital Forcing of Glacial/Interglacial Variations in Chemical Weathering and Silicon Cycling Within the Upper White Nile Basin, East Africa: Stable-Isotope and Biomarker Evidence from Lakes Victoria and Edward." *Quaternary Science Reviews* 130: 57–71.

Coleman, J.M., H.H. Roberts, S.P. Murray, and M. Salama. 1980. "Morphology and Dynamic Sedimentology of the Eastern Nile Delta Shelf." *Marine Geology* 41: 325–339.

Creasman, P.P. 2016. "Expanding Methodological Boundaries in Egyptian Archaeology by Land and by Sea (or River!)." Unpublished conference paper. Brown University State of Field: Archaeology of Egypt, Providence, 23–24 September 2016.

De Vartavan, C., and M.V.A. Amorós. 1997. *Codex of Ancient Egyptian Plant Remains/Codex des restes végétaux de l'Egypte ancienne*. London: Triade Exploration.

De Wit, H.E. and V.L. Stralen. 1988. "Preliminary Results of the 1987 Palaeo-Geographical Survey." In *The Archaeology of the Nile* Delta, edited by E.C.M. van den Brink, 135–139. Amsterdam: Wolfkamb.

Di Cosmo, N.. 2018. "The Scientist as Antiquarian: History, Climate, and the New Past. How Could the Constant Interaction between Humans and Nature Not Be Part of History?" Historical Studies. https://www.ias.edu/ideas/di-cosmo-new-past

Edgeworth, M. 2011. *Fluid Pasts: The Archaeology of Flow*. London: Bristol Classical Press.

Evenden, M. 2018, 9 August. "Beyond the Organic Machine? New Approaches in River Historiography." Environmental History. https://doi.org/10.1093/envhis/emy054.

Fahmy, A. 1997. "Evaluation of the Weed Flora from Predynastic to Graeco-Roman Times." *Vegetation History and Archaeobotany* 6: 241–247.

———. 2014. "Plant Food Resources at Hidden Valley, Farafra Oasis." In *From Lake to Sand: The Archaeology of Farafra Oasis, Western Desert, Egypt*, edited by B. Barich, G. Lucarini, M.A. Hamdan, and F.A. Hassan, 333–344. Florence: All'Insegna del Giglio.

Garzanti, E., S. Andò, M. Padoan, G. Vezzoli, A. El Kammar. 2015. "The Modern Nile Sediment System: Processes and Products." *Quaternary Science Reviews* 130: 9–56.

Gatto, M.C., and A. Zerboni. 2015. "Holocene Supra-Regional Environmental Changes as Trigger for Major Socio-Cultural Processes in Northeastern Africa and the Sahara." *African Archaeological Review* 32: 301–333.

Ghilardi, M., and M. Boraik. 2011. "Reconstructing the Holocene Depositional Environments in the Western Part of Ancient Karnak Temples Complex (Egypt): A Geoarchaeological Approach." *Journal of Archaeological Science* 38(12): 3204–3216.

Ginau, A., R. Schiestl, F. Kern, and J. Wunderlich. 2017. "Identification of Historic Landscape Features and Settlement Mounds in the Western Nile Delta by Means of Remote Sensing Time Series Analysis and the Evaluation of Vegetation Characteristics." *Journal of Archaeological Science: Reports* 16: 170–184.

Goodfriend, G.A., and J.-D. Stanley. 1996. "Reworking and Discontinuities in Holocene Sedimentation in the Nile Delta: Documentation from Amino Acid Racemization and Stable Isotopes in Mollusk Shells." *Marine Geology* 129(3–4): 271–283.

Graham, A. 2010. "Islands in the Nile: A Geoarchaeological Approach to Settlement Location in the Egyptian Nile Valley and the Case of Karnak." In *Cities and Urbanism in Ancient Egypt. Papers from a Workshop in November 2006 at the Austrian Academy of Sciences*, edited by M. Bietak, E. Czerny, and I. Forstner-Müller, 125–143. Vienna: Verlag der Österreichischen Akademie der Wissenschaften.

Graham, A., and J. Bunbury. 2016. "Migrating Nile: Augering in Egypt." In *Science in the Study of Ancient Egypt*, edited by S. Zakrzewski, A. Shortland, and J. Rowland, 93–97. New York and London: Routledge.

Hamdan, M.A., and G.A. Brook. 2015. "Timing and Characteristics of Late Pleistocene and Holocene Wetter Periods in the Eastern Desert and Sinai of Egypt, Based on 14C Dating and Stable Isotope Analysis of Spring Tufa Deposits." *Quaternary Science Reviews* 130: 168–188.

Hassan, F.A., M.A. Hamdan, R.J. Flower, and K. Keatings. 2012. "The Oxygen and Carbon Isotopic records in Holocene Freshwater Mollusc Shells from the Faiyum Paleolakes, Egypt: Their Paleoenvironmental and Paleoclimatic Implications." *Quaternary International* 266: 175–187.

Hekkala, E., M.H. Shirley, G. Amato, J.D. Austin, S. Charter, J. Thorbjarnarson, K.A. Vliet, M.L. Houck, R. Desalle, and M.J. Blum. 2011. "An Ancient Icon Reveals New Mysteries: Mummy DNA Resurrects a Cryptic Species within the Nile Crocodile." *Molecular Ecology* 20: 4199–4215.

Hennekam, R., T.H. Donders, K. Zwiep, and G.J. de Lange. 2015. "Integral View of Holocene Precipitation and Vegetation Changes in the Nile Catchment Area as Inferred from its Delta Sediments." *Quaternary Science Reviews* 130: 189–199.

Hoelzmann, P., H.-J. Kruse, and F. Rottinger. 2000. "Precipitation Estimates for the Eastern Saharan Palaeomonsoon Based on a Water Balance Model of the West Nubian Palaeolake Basin." *Global and Planetary Change* 26: 105–120.

Jeffreys, D. 2008. "Archaeological Implications of the Moving Nile." *Egyptian Archaeology* 32: 6–7.

Jolly, D., S.P. Harrison, B. Damnati, and R. Bonnefille. 1998. "Simulated Climate and Biomes of Africa during the Late Quaternary: Comparison with the Pollen and Lake Status Data." *Quaternary Science Reviews* 17: 629–657.

Kassas, M. 2002. "Aridity, Drought and Desertification: Roles of Science." *Bulletin de l'Institut d'Égypte* 78: 1–19.

Keatings, K.W., I. Hawkes, J.A. Holmes, R.J. Flower, M. Leng, R. Abu-Zied, and A. Lord. 2007. "Evaluation of Ostracod-Based Palaeoenvironmental Reconstruction with Instrumental Data from the Arid Faiyum Depression, Egypt." *Journal of Paleolimnology* 38: 261–283.

Kelly, J.M., P. Scarpino, H. Berry, J. Syvitski, and M. Meybeck, eds. 2017. *Rivers of the Anthropocene*. Oakland, C.A.: University of California Press.

Kholief, M.M., E. Hilmy, and A. Shahat. 1969. "Geological and Mineralogical Studies of Some Sand Deposits in the Nile Delta." *Journal of Sedimentary Petrology* 39(4): 1520–1529.

Krom, M.D., J.D. Stanley, R.A. Cliff, and J.C. Woodward. 2002. "Nile River Sediment Fluctuations over the Past 7000 Yr and Their Key Role in Sapropel Development." *Geology* 20(1): 71–74.

Leroy, S.A.G. 1992. "Palynological Evidence of *Azolla nilotica* Dec. in Recent Holocene of the Eastern Nile Delta and Palaeoenvironment." *Vegetation History and Archaeobotany* 1: 43–52.

Macklin, M.G., W.H.J. Toonen, J.C. Woodward, M.A.J. Williams, C. Flaux, N. Marriner, K. Nicoll, G. Verstraeten, N. Spencer, and D. Welsby. 2015. "A New Model of River Dynamics: Hydroclimatic Change and Human Settlement in the Nile Valley Derived from Meta-Analysis of the Holocene Fluvial Archive." *Quaternary Science Reviews* 130: 109–123.

Marcott, S.A., J.D. Shakun, P.U. Clark, and A.C. Mix. 2013. "Supplementary Materials for a Reconstruction of Regional and Global Temperature for the Past 11,300 Years." *Science* 339(6124): 1198–1201.

Marriner, N., C. Flaux, C. Morhange, and J.-D. Stanley. 2013. "Tracking Nile Delta Vulnerability to Holocene Change." *PLoS ONE* 8(7; e69195): 1–9. https://doi.org/10.1371/journal.pone.0069195.

Mehringer, P.J., L. Kenneth, K.L. Petersen, and F.A. Hassan. 1979. "A Pollen Record from Birket Qarun and the Recent History of the Fayum, Egypt." *Quaternary Research* 11: 238–256.

Mohamed, I., and G. Verstraeten. 2012. "Analyzing Dune Dynamics at the Dune-field Scale Based on Multi-Temporal Analysis of Landsat-TM Images." *Remote Sensing of Environment* 119: 105–117.

Nicoll, K. 2004. "Recent Environmental Change and Prehistoric Human Activity in Egypt and Northern Sudan." *Quaternary Science Reviews* 23(5–6): 561–580.

Pennington, B.T., and R.I. Thomas. 2016. "Paleoenvironmental Surveys at Naukratis and the Canopic Branch of the Nile." *Journal of Archaeological Science: Reports* 7: 180–188.

Reille, M. 1992. *Pollen et spores d'Europe et d'Afrique du nord: Laboratoire de botanique historique et palynologie.* Marseilles: CNRS.

Revel, M., E. Ducassou, C. Skonieczny, C. Colin, L. Bastian, D. Bosch, S. Migeon, and J. Mascle. 2015. "20,000 Years of Nile River Dynamics and Environmental Changes in the Nile Catchment Area as Inferred from Nile Upper Continental Slope Sediments." *Quaternary Science Reviews* 130: 200–221.

Ritchie, J.C. 1986. "Modern Pollen Spectra from Dakhleh Oasis, Western Egyptian Desert." *Grana* 25: 177–182.

Ritchie, J.C., C.H. Eyles, and C.V. Haynes. 1985. "Sediment and Pollen Evidence for an Early to Mid-Holocene Humid Period in the Eastern Sahara." *Nature* 314: 352–355.

Robinson, R., F. El- Baz, M. Ozdogan, M. Ledwith, D. Blanco, S. Oakley, and J. Inzana. 2000. "Use of Radar Data to Delineate Palaeodrainage Flow Directions in the Selima Sand Sheet, Eastern Sahara." *Photogrammetric Engineering and Remote Sensing* 66: 745–753.

Rodrigues, D., P.I. Abell, S. Kröpelin. 2000. "Seasonality in the Early Holocene Climate of Northwest Sudan: Interpretation of *Etheria elliptica* Shell Isotopic Data." *Global and Planetary Change* 26: 181–187.

Saad, S.I., and S. Sami. 1967. "Studies of Pollen and Spore Content of Nile Delta Deposits (Berenbal Region)." *Pollen et Spores* 9: 467–503.

Sabbahy, L. 2015. "A Decade of Advances in the Paleopathology of the Ancient Egyptians." In *Egyptian Bioarchaeology: Humans, Animals, and the Environment,* edited by S. Ikram, J. Kaiser, and R. Walker, 113–117. Leiden: Sidestone Press.

Sharaf El Din, S.H., and A.M. Mahar. 1997. "Evaluation of Sediment Transport along the Nile Delta." *Journal of Coastal Research* 13: 23–26.

Sneh, A., T. Weissbord, A. Ehrlich, A. Horowitz, S. Moshkovitz, and A. Rosenfeld. 1986. "Holocene Evolution of the Northeastern Corner of the Nile Delta." *Quaternary Research* 26: 194–206.

Stanley, J.-D., and M.P. Bernasconi. 1998. "Relict and Palimpsest Depositional Patterns on the Nile Shelf Recorded by Molluscan Faunas." *Palaios* 13(1): 79–86.

Stine, R.S. 1991. "Nile Silts and Predynastic Sites: Remote Sensing and Geographic Information Systems Research of Hierakonpolis, Egypt." Ph.D. diss., University of South Carolina.

Toussoun, O. 1922. "Mémoires sur les anciennes branches du Nil: époque ancienne." *Mémoires de l'Institut d'Egypte* 4: 1–212.

Touzeau, A., J. Blichert-Toft, R. Amiot, F. Fourel, F. Martineau, J. Cockitt, K. Hall, J.-P. Flandrois, and C. Lécuyer. 2013. "Egyptian Mummies Record Increasing Aridity in the Nile Valley from 5500 to 1500 yr Before Present." *Earth and Planetary Science Letters* 375: 92–100.

Trampier, J. 2009. "Expanding Archaeology in the Nile Floodplain: A Non-Destructive, Remote Sensing-Assisted Survey in the Western Delta Landscape." *Bulletin of the American Research Center in Egypt* 194: 21–24.

———. 2014. *Landscape Archaeology of the Western Nile Delta.* Atlanta: Lockwood Press.

———. 2017. "In Search of a Future Companion: Digital and Field Survey Methods in the Western Nile Delta." In *The Nile: Natural and Cultural Landscape in Egypt. Proceedings of the International Symposium held at the Johannes Gutenberg-Universität Mainz, 22 & 23 February 2013,* edited by H. Willems and J.-M. Dahms, 215–237. Bielefeld: transcript Verlag.

Trampier, J., W. Toonen, A. Simony, and J. Starbird. 2017. "Missing Koms and Abandoned Channels: The Potential of Regional Survey in the Western Nile Delta Landscape." *Journal of Egyptian Archaeology* 99(1): 217–240.

Tristant, Y., and M. De Dapper. 2009. "Predynastic Man and Landscape in the Samara Area (Eastern Nile Delta, Egypt): A Geo-Archaeological Approach." In *Ol' Man River: Geo-Archaeological Aspects of Rivers and River Plains,* edited by M. De Dapper and F. Vermeulen, 601–615. Ghent: Academia Press.

Ullmann, T., E. Lange-Athinodorou, A. Göbel, C. Büdel, and R. Baumhauer. 2018, 10 January. "Preliminary Results on the Paleo-landscape of Tell Basta/Bubastis (Eastern Nile Delta): An Integrated Approach Combining GIS-Based Spatial Analysis, Geophysical and Archaeological Investigations." *Quaternary International*. https://doi. org/10.1016/j.quaint.2017.12.053.

van den Brink, E.C.M., ed. 1988. *The Archaeology of the Nile Delta: Problems and Priorities*. Amsterdam: NFARE.

van den Brink, E.C.M., ed. 1992. *The Nile Delta in Transition: 4th–3rd Millennium BC (Proceedings Seminar, Cairo 21–24 October 1990)*. Tel Aviv: Netherlands Institute of Archaeology & Arabic Studies.

Williams, M.A.J., F.M. Williams, G.A.T. Duller, R.N. Munro, O.A.M. El Tom, T.T. Barrows, M. Macklin, J. Woodward, M.R. Talbot, D. Haberlah, and J. Fluin. 2010. "Late Quaternary Floods and Droughts in the Nile Valley, Sudan: New Evidence from Optically Stimulated Luminescence and AMS Radiocarbon Dating." *Quaternary Science Reviews* 29: 1116–1137.

Woodward, J., M. Macklin, L. Fielding, I. Miller, N. Spencer, D. Welsby, and M. Williams. 2015. "Shifting Sediment Sources in the World's Longest River: A Strontium Isotope Record for the Holocene Nile." *Quaternary Science Reviews* 130: 124–140.

Yousef, S., and E.M. Raey. 1994. "Major Solar Episodes Reconstructed Using Records of the River Nile, Tree-Ring Indices and Sunspot Number." *Bulletin de l'Institut d'Égypte* 74: 76–108.

III. THE ENVIRONMENT, CLIMATE CHANGE, AND THE POLITICAL AND SOCIAL HISTORY OF ANCIENT EGYPT

Andres, W., and J. Wunderlich. 1992. "Environmental Conditions for Early Settlement at Minshat Abu Omar, Eastern Nile Delta, Egypt." In *The Nile Delta in Transition: 4th–3rd Millennium BC*, edited by E.C.M. van den Brink, 157–166. Tel Aviv: E.C.M. van den Brink.

Arz, H.W., F. Lamy, and J. Pätzold. 2006. "A Pronounced Dry Event Recorded around 4.2 ka in Brine Sediments from the Northern Red Sea." *Quaternary Research* 66: 432–441.

Arz, H.W., J. Kaiser, and D. Fleitmann. 2015. "Paleoceanographic and Paleoclimatic Changes around 2200 BC Recorded in Sediment Cores from the Northern Red Sea." In *2200 BC—Ein Klimasturz als Ursache für den Zerfall der Alten Welt? 7. Mitteldeutscher Archäologentag vom 23. bis 26. Oktober 2014 in Halle (Saale)*, edited by H. Meller, H.W. Arz, R. Jung, and R. Risch, 53–60. Halle (Saale): Landesmuseum für Vorgeschichte.

Atzler, M. 1995. "Some Remarks on Interrelating Environmental Changes and Ecological, Socio-Economic Problems in the Gradual Development of the Early Egyptian Inundation Culture." *Archéo-Nil* 5: 7–65.

Baldi, M. 2015. "Exceptional Rainfall over Thebes in Ancient and Present Times: An Analysis of Possible Driving Mechanisms." In *Egyptian Curses*. Vol. 2, *A [sic] Research on Ancient Catastrophes*, edited by G. Capriotti Vittozzi, 255–264. Rome: CNR Edizioni.

Bar-Oz, G., E. Tsahar, I. Izhaki, and S. Lev-Yadun. 2015. "Mammalian Extinction in Ancient Egypt, Similarities with the Southern Levant." *Proceedings of the National Academy of Sciences of the United States of America* 112(3): E238.

Barich, B. 2019. "Eastern Borders of the Sahara and the Relations with the Nile Valley and Beyond." In *Climate Changes in the Holocene. Impacts and Human Adaptation*, edited by E. Chiotis, 201–220. Boca Raton/London/New York: CRC Press.

Barich, B., and G. Lucarini. 2014. "Social Dynamics in Northern Farafra from the Middle to Late Holocene: Changing Life under Uncertainty." In *From Lake to Sand: The Archaeology of Farafra Oasis, Western Desert, Egypt*, edited by B. Barich, G. Lucarini, M.A. Hamdan, and F.A. Hassan, 467–484. Florence: All'Insegna del Giglio.

Barich, B., G. Lucarini, M.A. Hamdan, and F.A. Hassan. 2014. *From Lake to Sand: The Archaeology of Farafra Oasis, Western Desert, Egypt.* Florence: All'Insegna del Giglio.

Barker, G. 2013. "The Neolithisation of Northeastern Africa: Reflections on Knowns, Unknowns, and Unknown Unknowns." In *Neolithisation of Northeastern Africa*, edited by N. Shirai, 249–256. Berlin: Ex oriente.

Bárta, M. 2013. "In Mud Forgotten: Old Kingdom Palaeoecological Evidence from Abusir." *Studia Quaternaria* 30(2): 75–82.

———. 2015. "Long Term or Short Term? Climate Change and the Demise of the Old Kingdom." In *Climate and Ancient Societies*, edited by S. Kerner, R.J. Dann, and P. Bangsgaard, 177–195. Copenhagen: Museum Tusculanum Press.

Bárta, M., and A. Bezděk. 2008. "Beetles and the Decline of the Old Kingdom: Climate Change in Ancient Egypt." In *Chronology and Archaeology in Ancient Egypt (the Third Millennium B.C.)*, edited by H. Vymazalová and M. Bárta, 214–224. Prague: Czech Institute of Egyptology, Faculty of Arts, Charles University in Prague.

Bell, B. 1975. "Climate and the History of Egypt: The Middle Kingdom." *American Journal of Archaeology* 79(3): 223–269.

Bini, M., G. Zanchetta, A. Perşoiu, R. Cartier, Al Català, I. Cacho, J.R. Dean, F. Di Rita, R.N. Drysdale, M. Finné, I. Isola, B. Jalali, F. Lirer, D. Magri, A. Masi, L. Marks, A.M. Mercuri, O. Peyron, L. Sadori, M.-A. Sicre, F. Welc, C. Zielhofer, and E. Brisset. 2019. "The 4.2 ka BP Event in the Mediterranean Region: An Overview." *Climate of the Past* 15: 555–577.

Blouin, K. 2014. *Triangular Landscapes: Environment, Society, and the State in the Nile Delta under Roman Rule.* Oxford: Oxford University Press.

Boraik, M., M. Ghilardi, and Y. Tristan. 2012. "Nile River Evolution in Upper Egypt during the Holocene: Palaeoenvironmental Implications for the Pharaonic Sites of Karnak and Coptos/Évolution du Nil en Haute Égypte au cours de l'Holocène: implications paléoenvironnementales sur les sites pharaoniques de Karnak et Coptos." *Géomorphologie: relief, processus, environnement* 1: 7–22.

Borsch, S.J. 2004. "Environment and Population: The Collapse of Large Irrigation Systems Reconsidered." *Comparative Studies in Society and History* 46(3): 451–468.

Bubenzer, O., and H. Riemer. 2007. "Holocene Climatic Change and Human Settlement Between the Central Sahara and the Nile Valley: Archaeological and Geomorphological Results." *Geoarchaeology* 22: 607–620.

Buck, P. 2002. "Structure and Content of Old Kingdom Archaeological Deposits in the Western Nile Delta Egypt: A Geoarchaeologica Example from Kom el-Hisn." Ph.D. diss., University of Washington.

Bunbury, J.M. 2010. "The Development of the River Nile and the Egyptian Civilization: A Water Historical Perspective with Focus on the First Intermediate Period." In *A History of Water*. Series II, Vol. 2, *Rivers and Society: From Early Civilizations to Modern Times*, edited by T. Tvedt and R. Coopey, 52–71. London: I.B. Tauris & Co.

Bunbury, J.M., A. Tavares, B. Pennington, and P. Gonçalves. 2017. "Development of the Memphite Floodplain: Landscape and Settlement Symbiosis in the Egyptian Capital Zone." In *The Nile: Natural and Cultural Landscape in Egypt. Proceedings of the International Symposium held at the, 22 & 23 February 2013*, edited by H. Willems and J.-M. Dahms, 71–96. Bielefeld: transcript Verlag.

Burn, J. 2014. "Marshlands, Drought, and the Great Famine: On the Significance of the Marshlands to Egypt at the End of the Old Kingdom." In *Current Research in Egyptology 2013: Proceedings of the Fourteenth Annual Symposium*, edited by K. Accetta, R. Fellinger, P. Lourenço Gonçalves, S. Musselwhite, and W.P. van Pelt, 34–48. Cambridge: Oxbow Books.

Butzer, K.W. 1960. "Remarks on the Geography of Settlement in the Nile Valley during Hellenistic Times." *Bulletin de la Société de Géographie d'Égypte* 33: 5–36.

———. 1983. "Human Response to Environmental Change in the Perspective of Future, Global Climate." *Quaternary Research* 19: 279–292.

———. 1984. "Long-Term Nile Flood Variation and Political Discontinuities in Pharaonic Egypt." In *From Hunters to Farmers: The Causes and Consequences of Food Production in Africa*, edited by J.D. Clark and S.A. Brandt, 102–112. Berkeley/Los Angeles: University of California Press.

———. 1989. "Das Volk des Flusses." In *Ägypten: Schatzkammer der Pharaonen*, 32–71. Berlin: Reise- und Verkehrsverlag.

———. 1997. "Sociopolitical Discontinuity in the Near East C. 2200 B.C.E.: Scenarios from Palestine and Egypt." In *Third Millennium B.C. Climate Change and Old World Collapse*, edited by H.N. Dalfes, G. Kukla, and H. Weiss, 245–296. NATO ASI Series (Series I: Global Environmental Change) 49. Berlin: Springer.

———. 2012. "Collapse, Environment, and Society." *Proceedings of the National Academy of Sciences of the United States of America* 109(10): 3632–3639.

Butzer, K.W., and G.H. Endfield. 2012. "Critical Perspectives on Historical Collapse." *Proceedings of the National Academy of Sciences of the United States of America* 109(10): 3628–3631.

Clarke, J., N. Brooks, E.B. Banning, M. Bar-Matthews, S. Campbell, L. Clare, M. Cremaschi, S. di Lernia, N. Drake, M. Gallinaro, S. Manning, K. Nicoll, G. Philip, S. Rosen, U.-D. Schoop, M.A. Tafuri, B. Weninger, and A. Zerboni. 2016. "Climatic Changes and Social Transformations in the Near East and North Africa During the 'Long' 4th Millennium B.C.: A Comparative study of Environmental and Archaeological Evidence." *Quaternary Science Reviews* 136: 96–121.

Collins, R.O. 2002. *The Nile*. New Haven: Yale University Press.

Church, R.L., and T.L. Bell. 1988. "An Analysis of Ancient Egyptian Settlement Patterns Using Location-Allocation Covering Models." *Annals of the Association of Geographers* 78(4): 701–714.

Dee, M.W. 2017. "Absolute Dating Climatic Evidence and the Decline of Old Kingdom Egypt." In *The Late Third Millennium in the Ancient Near East: Chronology, C14, and Climate Change*, edited by F. Höflmayer, 323–331. Chicago: The Oriental Institute of the University of Chicago.

Dumont, H.J., ed. 2009. *The Nile: Origins, Environments, Limnology, and Human Use.* Monographiae Biologicae 89. Dordrecht: Springer.

El-Baz, F. 2003. "Geoarchaeological Evidence of the Relationships between the Terminal Drought in North Africa and the Rise of Ancient Egypt." In *Egyptology at the Dawn of the Twenty-first Century. Proceedings of the Eighth International Congress of Egyptologists Cairo, 2000*, edited by Z. Hawass, 64–72. Cairo: The American University in Cairo Press.

Evans, L. 2015. "Ancient Egypt's Fluctuating Fauna: Ecological Events or Cultural Constructs?" *Proceedings of the National Academy of Sciences of the United States of America* 112(3): E239.

Ferron, E. 2005. "L'émergence d'une crise régionale au coeur d'un écosystème atypique: le Fayoum." M.A. thesis, Université Laval, Quebec.

Finné, M., K. Holmgren, H. Sundqvist, E. Weiberg, and M. Lindblom. 2011. "Climate in the Eastern Mediterranean, and Adjacent Regions, during the Past 6000 Years—A Review." *Journal of Archaeological Science* 38(12): 3153–3173.

Hamdan, M.A., F.A. Hassan, R.J. Flower, and E.M. Ebrahim. 2016. "Climate and Collapse of Egyptian Old Kingdom: A Geoarchaeological Approach." In *Archaeology and Environment: Understanding the Past to Design the Future: A Multidisciplinary Approach: Proceedings of the International Workshop "Italian Days in Aswan," 15th–18th November 2013*, edited by G. Capriotti Vittozzi and F. Porcelli, 37–48. Rome: Consiglio Nazionale delle Ricerche Istituto di Studi sul Mediterraneo Antico.

Hamroush, H., and H. Abu Zied. 1990. "The Geology and Geoarchaeology of el-Omari: A Neolithic Settlement Utilizing both Desert and River Environments." In *El Omari: A Neolithic Settlement and Other Sites in the Vicinity of Wadi Hof, Helwan*, edited by F. Debono and B. Mortensen, 83–93. Mainz: Philipp von Zabern.

Hassan, F.A. 1981. "Historical Nile Floods and Their Implications for Climatic Change." *Science NS* 212(4499): 1142–1145.

———. 1986. "Holocene Lakes and Prehistoric Settlements of the Western Faiyum, Egypt." *Journal of Archaeological Science* 13: 483–501.

———. 1997a. "The Dynamics of a Riverine Civilization: A Geoarchaeological Perspective on the Nile Valley, Egypt." *World Archaeology* 29(1): 51–74.

———. 1997b. "Nile Floods and Political Disorder in Early Egypt." In *Third Millennium BC Climate Change and Old World Collapse*, edited by H.N. Dalfes, G. Kukla, and H. Weiss, 1–23. Berlin: Springer.

———. 2010. "Climate Change, Nile Floods, and Riparia." In *Riparia dans l'empire romain*, edited by E. Hermon, 131–150. BAR S2066. Oxford: Archaeopress.

Hassan, F.A., and B. Stucki. 1987. "Nile Floods and Climatic Change." In *Climate: History, Periodicity, and Predictability*, edited by M.R. Rampino, J.E. Sanders, W.S. Newman, and L.K. Konigsson, 37–46. New York: Springer Verlag.

Hassan, F.A., and G. Tassie. 2006. "Modelling Environmental and Settlement Change in the Fayum." *Journal of Egyptian Archaeology* 29: 37–40.

Henfling, E. 1994. "Nilflutnotation und Thronwechsel von König Semerchet zu König Qaa der I. Dynastie: Fragment Kairo I 3,9 des Annalensteins." In *Quaerentes scientiam: Festgabe für Wolfhart Westendorf zu seinem 70. Geburtstag überreicht von seinen Schülern*, edited by H. Behlmer, 55–61. Göttingen: Seminar für Ägyptologie und Koptologie.

Hoffman, M.A., H.A. Hamroush, and R.O. Allen. 1987. "The Environmental Evolution of an Early Egyptian Urban Centre: Archaeological and Geochemical Investigations at Hierakonpolis." *Geoarchaeology* 2: 1–13.

Höflmayer, F. 2014. "Dating Catastrophes and Collapses in the Ancient Near East: The End of the First Urbanization in the Southern Levant and the 4.2 ka B.P. Event." In *Overcoming Catastrophes: Essays on Disastrous Agents Characterization and Resilience Strategies in Pre-classical Southern Levant*, edited by L. Nigro, 117–140. La Sapienza Studies on the Archaeology of Palestine and Transjordan 11. Rome: La Sapienza.

————. 2015. "The Southern Levant, Egypt, and the 4.2 ka BP Event." In *2200 BC—Ein Klimasturz als Ursache für den Zerfall der Alten Welt? 7. Mitteldeutscher Archäologentag vom 23. bis 26. Oktober 2014 in Halle (Saale)*, edited by H. Meller, H.W. Arz, R. Jung, and R. Risch, 113–130. Halle (Saale): Landesmuseum für Vorgeschichte.

Höflmayer, F., ed. 2017. *The Late Third Millennium in the Ancient Near East: Chronology, C14, and Climate Change*. Chicago: The Oriental Institute of the University of Chicago.

Honegger, M., and M. Williams. 2015. "Human Occupations and Environmental Changes in the Nile Valley During the Holocene: The Case of Kerma in Upper Nubia (Northern Sudan)." *Quaternary Science Reviews* 130: 141–154.

Hurst, H.E. 1952. *The Nile: A General Account of the River and the Utilization of its Waters*. London: Constable.

Huzayyin, S.A. 1941. *The Place of Egypt in Prehistory: A Correlated Study of the Climates and Cultures of the Old World*. Cairo: L'Institut Francais D'Archéologie Orientale.

Jeffreys, D.G. 2010. "Regionality, Cultural and Cultic Landscapes." In *Egyptian Archaeology*, edited by W. Wendrich, 102–118. Oxford: Wiley-Blackwell.

Jeffreys, D.G., and H.S. Smith. 1988. "Memphis and the Nile in the New Kingdom." In *Memphis et ses nécropoles au Nouvel Empire*, edited by A.P. Zivie, 55–66. Paris: Éd. du Centre national de la recherche scientifique.

Jucha, M.A. 2009. "The North-Eastern Part of the Nile Delta–Research Perspectives. Polish Archeological Survey in the Ash-Sharqiyyah Governorate." In *Proceedings of the Fifth Central European Conference of Egyptologists*, edited by J. Popielska-Grzybowska and J. Iwaszczuk, 83–88, figs. 33–41. Pułtusk: Institute of Anthropology and Archaeology.

Krzyżaniak, L., M. Kobusiewicz, and J. Alexander, eds. 1993. *Environmental Change and Human Culture in the Nile Basin and Northern Africa until the Second Millennium BC*. Studies in African Archaeology 4. Poznan: Poznan Archaeological Museum.

Kuraszkiewicz, K.O. 2016. "Architectural Innovations Influenced by Climatic Phenomena (4.2 Ka Event) in the Late Old Kingdom (Saqqara, Egypt)." *Studia Quaternaria* 33(1): 27–34.

Labeyrie, J. 1979. "Sea Level Variations and the Birth of the Egyptian Civilisation." In *Radiocarbon Dating: Proceedings of the Ninth International Conference, Los Angeles and La Jolla, 1976*, edited by R. Berger and H.E. Suess, 32–36. Berkeley: University of California Press.

Ludlow, F., and J.G. Manning. 2016. "Revolts Under the Ptolemies: A Paleoclimatological Perspective." In *Revolt and Resistance in the Ancient Classical World and the Near East: In the Crucible of Empire*, edited by J.J. Collins and J.G. Manning, 154–174. Leiden: Brill.

Macklin, M.G., and J. Lewin. 2015. "The Rivers of Civilization." *Quaternary Science Reviews* 114: 228–244.

Macklin, M.G., J.C. Woodward, D.A. Welsby, G.A.T. Duller, F.M. Williams, and M.A.J. Williams. 2013. "Reach-Scale River Dynamics Moderate the Impact of Rapid Holocene Climate Change on Floodwater Farming in the Desert Nile." *Geology* 41(6): 695–698.

Manning, J.G., F. Ludlow, A. Stine, W. Boos, M. Sigl, and J. Marlon. 2017. "Volcanic Suppression of Nile Summer Flooding Triggers Revolts and Constrains Interstate Conflict in Ancient Egypt." *Nature Communications* 8: 1–9.

Marshall, M.H., H.F. Lamb, D. Huws, S.J. Davies, R. Bates, J. Bloemendal, J. Boyle, M.J. Leng, M. Umer, and C. Bryant. 2011. "Late Pleistocene and Holocene Drought Events at Lake Tana, the Source of the Blue Nile." *Global and Planetary Change* 78: 147–161.

Moeller, N. 2005. "The First Intermediate Period: A Time of Famine and Climate Change?" *Egypt and the Levant* 15: 153–167.

Moreno García, J.C. 2015. "Climatic Change or Sociopolitical Transformation? Reassessing Late 3rd Millennium B.C. in Egypt." *Tagungen des Landesmuseums für Vorgeschich Te Halle* 13: 1–16.

———. 2014. "Recent Developments in the Social and Economic History of Ancient Egypt." *Journal of Ancient Near Eastern History* 1(2): 244–252.

———. 2020. *The State in Ancient Egypt: Power, Challenges and Dynamics.* London: Bloomsbury Academic.

Morris, E. 2006. "'Lo, Nobles Lament, the Poor Rejoice': State Formation in the Wake of Social Flux." In *After Collapse: The Regeneration of Complex Societies*, edited by G.M. Schwartz and J.J. Nichols, 58–71. Tucson: University of Arizona Press.

Negus, A.L. 1986. "The Fall of the Old Kingdom: A Great African Drought?" Ph.D. diss, University of California, Los Angeles.

O'Connor, D. 1972. "The Geography of Settlement in Ancient Egypt." In *Man, Settlement, and Urbanism*, edited by P.J. Ucko, R. Tringham, and G.W. Dimbleby, 681–698. Gloucester Crescent: Gerald Duckworth and Co. Ltd.

Parcak, S. 2005. "Settlement Pattern Studies in the Nile's Floodplain: Satellite Imagery Analysis and Ground Survey in Middle Egypt and the Delta." Ph.D. diss., Cambridge University.

Pawlikowski, M. 1994. "Climatic Changes During Holocene in the Region of Armant." In *Predynastic Settlements Near Armant*, edited by B. Ginter and J. K. Kozłowski, 125–132. Heidelberg: Heidelberger Orientverlag.

Pennington, B., J.M. Bunbury, and N. Hovius. 2016. "Emergence of Civilisation Changes in Fluvio-Deltaic Styles and Nutrient Redistribution Forced by Holocene Sea-Level Rise." *Geoarchaeology* 130(1): 17–28.

Pérez Largacha, A. 1993. "Condicionantes ecológicos en la formación del estado en Egipto." *Boletín de la Asociación Española de Orientalistas* 29: 189–201.

Phillipps, R., S. Holdaway, W. Wendrich, and R. Cappers. 2012. "Mid-Holocene Occupation of Egypt and Global Climatic Change." *Quaternary International* 251: 64–76.

Rathbone, D. 1997. "Surface Survey and the Settlement History of the Ancient Fayum." In *Archeologia e papyri nel Fayyum: Storia della ricerca, problemi e prospettive. Atti del convegno internazionale, Siracusa, 24–25 Maggio 1996*, edited by A. Di Natale, 7–20. Syracuse: Istituto internazionale del papiro.

Rowland, J.M., and G.J. Tassie. 2014. "Prehistoric Sites along the Edge of the Western Nile Delta: Report on the Results of the Imbaba Prehistoric Survey 2013–2014." *Journal of Egyptian Archaeology* 100: 56–71.

————. 2017. "The Neolithic in the Nile Delta: Topoi Research Project A-2-4." *Edition Topoi*. DOI: 10.17171/1-9.

Sandford, K.S., and W.J. Arkell. 1939. *Paleolithic Man and the Nile Valley in Lower Egypt*. Chicago: University of Chicago Press.

Scheidel, W. 2001. *Death on the Nile: Disease and the Demography of Roman Egypt*. Leiden: Brill.

Sestini, G. 1991. "Implications of Climatic Changes for the Nile Delta." In *Climate Change and the Mediterranean*, edited by L. Leftic, J.D. Milliman, and G. Sestini, 535–601. London: Edward Arnold.

Shaltout, M., and M. Azzazi. 2014. "Climate Change in the Nile Delta from Prehistoric to the Modern Era and their Impact on Soil and Vegetation in Some Archaeological Sites." *Journal of Earth Science and Engineering* 4: 632–642.

Sheffield, J., and E.F. Wood. 2011. *Drought: Past Problems and Future Scenarios*. London: Earthscan.

Spencer, N., M. Macklin, and J. Woodward. 2012. "Re-assessing the Abandonment of Amara West: The Impact of a Changing Nile?" *Sudan and Nubia* 16: 37–43.

Stanley, J.-D., and M.A. Toscano. 2009. "Ancient Archaeological Sites Buried and Submerged along Egypt's Nile Delta Coast: Gauges of Holocene Delta Margin Subsidence." *Journal of Coastal Research* 25(1): 158–170.

Stanley, J.-D., and A.G. Warne. 1993. "Sea Level and Initiation of Predynastic Culture in the Nile Delta." *Nature* 363: 435–438.

Stanley, J.-D., F. Goddio, and G. Schnepp. 2001. "Nile Flooding Sank Two Ancient Cities." *Nature* 412: 293–294.

Stanley, J.-D., F. Goddio, T. Jorstad, and G. Schnepp. 2004. "Submergence of Ancient Greek Cities Off Egypt's Nile Delta—A Cautionary Tale." *GSA Today* 14: 4–10.

Stanley, J.-D., M.D. Krom, R.A. Cliff, and J.C. Woodward. 2003. "Nile Flow Failure at the End of the Old Kingdom, Egypt: Strontium Isotopic and Petrologic Evidence." *Geoarchaeology* 18(3): 395–402.

Subias, E., J.I. Fiz Fernandez, and R. Cuesta. 2013. "The Middle Nile Valley: Elements in an Approach to the Structuring of the Landscape from the Greco-Roman Era to the Nineteenth Century." *Quaternary International* 312: 27–44.

Toonen, W.H.J., A. Graham, A. Masson-Berghoff, J. Peeters, T.G. Winkels, B.T. Pennington, M.A. Hunter, K.D. Strutt, D.S. Barker, V.L. Emery, L. Sollars, and H. Sourouzian. 2019. "Amenhotep III's Mansion of Millions of Years in Thebes (Luxor, Egypt): Submergence of High Grounds by River Floods and Nile Sediments." *Journal of Archaeological Science: Reports* 25: 195–205.

Toonen, W.H.J., A. Graham, B.T. Pennington, M.A. Hunter, K.D. Strutt, D.S. Barker, A. Masson-Berghoff, and V.L. Emery. 2018. "Holocene Fluvial History of the Nile's West Bank at Ancient Thebes, Luxor, Egypt, and its Relation with Cultural Dynamics and Basin-Wide Hydroclimatic Variability." *Geoarchaeology* 33(3): 273–290.

Tristant, Y. 2004. *L'habitat prédynastique de la vallee du Nil: Vivre sur le rives du Nil aux V et IV millénaires.* Oxford: Archaeopress.

Tristant, Y., M. De Dapper, S. Aussel, and B. Midant-Reynes. 2011. "Cultural and Natural Environment in the Eastern Nile Delta: A Geoarchaeological Project at Tell el-Iswid (South)." In *Egypt at Its Origins.* Vol. 3, *Proceedings of the Third International Conference "Origin of the State. Predynastic and Early Dynastic Egypt", London, 27th July–1st August 2008,* edited by R.F. Friedman and P.N. Fiske, 137–153. Leuven: Peeters.

Uphill, E. 2010. "The Significance of Nile Heights Recorded under the Twelfth Dynasty." In *Echoes of Eternity: Studies Presented to Gaballa Aly Gaballa,* edited by O. El-Aguizy and M.S. Ali, 67–76. Wiesbaden: Harrassowitz.

van den Brink, E.C.M. 1987. "A Geo-Archaeological Survey in the North-eastern Nile Delta." *Mitteilungen des Deutschen Archäologischen Instituts, Abteilung Kairo* 43: 7–31.

van den Brink, E.C.N. 1993. "Settlement Patterns in the Northeastern Nile Delta during the Fourth–Second Millennium BC." In *Environmental Change and Human Culture in the Nile Basin and Northern Africa until the Second Millennium BC,* edited by L. Krzyzaniak, M. Kobusiewicz, and J. Alexander, 279–304. Poznan: Poznan Archaeological Museum.

Van Wesemael, B. 1988. "The Relation between Natural Landscape and Distribution of Archaeological Remains in the Northeastern Nile Delta." In *The Archaeology of the Nile Delta: Problems and Priorities*, edited by E.C.M. van den Brink, 125–134. Amsterdam: Netherlands Foundation for Archaeological Research in Egypt.

Vandier, J. 1936. *La famine dans l'Égypte ancienne*. Recherches d'archéologie, de philologie et d'histoire 7. Cairo: Imprimerie de l'Institut français d'archéologie orientale.

Ventre, A.F. 1894. "Les Égyptiens connaissaient-ils la source de leur fleuve? Essai archéologique sur l'origine physique du Nil." *Bulletin de la Société de géographie d'Égypte* 4(3): 163–203.

Vermeersch, P.M., and W. Van Neer. 2015. "Nile Behaviour and Late Palaeolithic Humans in Upper Egypt During the Late Pleistocene." *Quaternary Science Reviews* 130: 155–167.

Verner, M. 1972. "Periodical Water-Volume Fluctuations of the Nile." *Archiv Orientalni* 40: 105–123.

Weiss, H. 1997. "Late Third Millennium Abrupt Climate Change and Social Collapse in West Asia and Egypt." In *Third Millennium BC Climate Change and Old World Collapse*, edited by H. Nüzhet Dalfes, G. Kukla, and H. Weiss, 711–723. NATO ASI series, series I: Global Environmental Change 49. Heidelberg: Springer.

Weiss, H. 2000. "Beyond the Younger Dryas: Collapse as Adaptation to Abrupt Climate Change in Ancient West Asia and the Eastern Mediterranean." In *Environmental Disaster and the Archaeology of Human Response*, edited by G. Bawden and R.M. Reycraft, 75–98. Albuquerque: Maxwell Museum of Anthropology.

Welc, F., and L. Marks. 2014. "Climate Change at the End of the Old Kingdom in Egypt around 4200 BP: New Geoarchaeological Evidence." *Quarterly International* 324: 124–133.

Wendorf, F., and R. Schild. 1976. *Prehistory of the Nile Valley*. New York: Academic Press.

Wilkinson, J.G. 1853. "On the Decrease of the Level of the Nile, and on Egyptian Fortification." *Transactions of the Royal Society of Literature of the United Kingdom* 2(4): 93–108.

Wilson, P. 2006. "Prehistoric Settlement in the Western Delta: A Regional and Local View from Sais (Sa el Hagar)." *Journal of Egyptian Archaeology* 92: 75–126.

———. 2012. "Waterways, Settlements, and Shifting Power in the North-Western Nile Delta." *Water History* 4(1): 95–118.

———. 2018. "Human and Deltaic Environments in Northern Egypt in Late Antiquity." *Late Antique Archaeology* 12(1): 42–62.

Witthuhn, O. 2009. "Stadt—Land—Fluss: zum Verhältnis zwischen Ortschaft und Nil." *Kemet* 18(1): 17–19.

Woodward, J., M. Macklin, N. Spencer, M. Binder, M. Dalton, S. Hay, and A. Hardy. 2017. "Living with a Changing River and Desert Landscape at Amara West." In *Nubia in the New Kingdom: Lived Experience, Pharaonic Control and Indigenous Traditions*, edited by N. Spencer, A. Stevens, and M. Binder, 227–257. Leuven: Peeters.

Yeakel, J.D., M.M. Pires, L. Rudolf, N.J. Dominy, P.L. Koch, P.R. Guimarães, and T. Gross. 2014. "Collapse of an Ecological Network in Ancient Egypt." *Proceedings of the National Academy of Sciences of the United States of America* 111(40): 14472–14477.

IV. Water Management and Navigation, Agriculture, and the Egyptian Economy

Adams, W.Y. 1977. *Nubia: Corridor to Africa*. Princeton: Princeton University Press.

Aït-Kaci, L., A. Boud'Hors, and C. Heurtel. 2010. "Aller au nord, aller au sud, traverser le fleuve: circulation et échanges au VIIIe siécle dans la région thebaine." In *Thèbes aux 101 portes: mélanges à la mémoire de Roland Tefnin*, edited by E. Warmenbol and V. Angenot, 1–9. Turnhout: Brepols.

Alleaume, G. 1992. "Les systèmes hydrauliques de l'Égypte pré-moderne: Essai d'histoire du paysage." In *Itinéraires d'Égypte: Mélanges offerts au père Maurice Martin*, edited by C. Decobert, 301–322. Cairo: Institut français d'archéologie orientale.

Anagnostou-Canas, B. 1994. "Les différends concernant l'eau dans l'Égypte romaine." In *Les problèmes institutionnels de l'eau en Egypte ancienne et dans l'antiquité méditerranéenne*, edited by B. Menu, 15–28. Paris: IFAO.

———. 2001. "Litiges en rapport avec l'eau dans l'Égypte ptolémaïque." In *Atti del XXII Congresso Internazionale di Papirologia, Firenze, 23–29 agosto 1998*, vol. 1, edited by I. Andorlini, G. Bastianini, M. Manfredi, and G. Menci, 41–49. Firenze: Istituto papirologico G. Vitelli.

Antoine, J.-C. 2006. "Fluctuations of Fish Deliveries at Deir el-Medina in the Twentieth Dynasty: A Statistical Analysis." *Studien zur Altägyptischen Kultur* 35: 25–41.

———. 2009a. "Fluctuations of Fish, Wood, and Grain Supplies at Deir el-Medina as a Proxy of the Nile Regimen in the 20th Dynasty (~1187–1070 BC)." *Mitteilungen des Deutschen Archäologischen Instituts, Abteilung Kairo* 65: 1–9.

———. 2009b. "The Delay of the Grain Ration and its Social Consequences at Deir el-Medîna in the Twentieth Dynasty: A Statistical Analysis." *Journal of Egyptian Archaeology* 95: 223–234.

———. 2011. "The Wilbour Papyrus Revisited: The Land and its Localisation. An Analysis of the Places of Measurement." *Studien zur Altägyptischen Kultur* 40: 9–27.

———. 2017. "The Geographical and Administrative Landscape of Lower Middle Egypt in Text B of the Wilbour Papyrus." *Zeitschrift für Ägyptische Sprache und Altertumskunde* 142(2): 104–119.

Arkell, A., and P. Ucko. 1965. "Review of Predynastic Development in the Nile Valley." *Current Anthropology* 6(2): 145–166.

Arnaud, P. 2015. "Navires et navigation commerciale sur la mer et sur le 'Grand fleuve' à l'époque des Ptolémées." In *Entre Nil et mers: la navigation en Égypte ancienne*, edited by B. Argémi and P. Tallet, 105–122. *NeHeT* 3.

Aubert, J.-J. 2015. "Trajan's Canal: River Navigation from the Nile to the Red Sea?" In *Across the Ocean: Nine Essays on Indo-Mediterranean Trade*, edited by F. De Romanis and M. Maiuro, 33–42. Leiden: Brill.

Bagnall, R. 1998. *Egypt in Late Antiquity*. Princeton: Princeton University Press.

Ballais, J.-L. 2000. "Conquests and Land Degradation in the Eastern Maghreb During Classical Antiquity and the Middle Ages." In *The Archaeology of Drylands: Living at the Margin*, edited by G. Barker and D. Gilbertson, 125–136. London: Routledge.

Barois, J. 1904. *Les irrigation en Égypte*. Paris: Librairie Polytechnique Ch. Béranger.

———. 1911. *Les Irrigations en Égypte*. 2nd ed. rev. et augm. Paris: Librairie polytechnique Ch. Béranger.

Bebermeier, W., N. Alexanian, D. Blaschta, A. Ramisch, B. Schütt, and S.J. Seidlmayer. 2011. "Analysis of Past and Present Landscapes Surrounding the Necropolis of Dahshur." *Die Erde* 142: 325–352.

Bergmann, M. 2014. "Schedia — Zollstation und Flusshafen Alexandrias am Kanopischen Nil." In *Häfen und Hafenstädte im östlichen Mittelmeerraum von der Antike bis in byzantinische Zeit. Neue Entdeckungen und aktuelle Forschungsansätze / Harbors and Harbor Cities in the Eastern Mediterranean from Antiquity to the Byzantine Period: Recent Discoveries and Current Approaches*, vol. 1, edited by S. Ladstätter, F. Pirson, and T. Schmidts, 101–112. Istanbul: Ege Yayınları.

Bertini, L. 2016. "How Did the Nile Water System Impact Swine Husbandry Practices in Ancient Egypt." In *A History of Water: Series III. Vol. 3, Water and Food from Hunter-Gatherers to Global Production in Africa*, edited by T. Tvedt and T. Oestigaard, 75–100. London: I.B. Tauris.

Bietak, M. 2009. "Peru-nefer: The Principal New Kingdom Naval Base." *Egyptian Archaeology* 34: 15–17.

———. 2017. "Harbours and Coastal Military Bases in Egypt in the Second Millennium B.C.: Avaris, Peru-nefer, Pi-Ramesse." In *The Nile: Natural and Cultural Landscape in Egypt. Proceedings of the International Symposium held at the, 22 & 23 February 2013*, edited by H. Willems and J.-M. Dahms, 53–70. Bielefeld: transcript Verlag.

Blouin, K. 2007. "Environnement et fisc dans le nome mendésien à l'époque romaine: réalités et enjeux de la diversification." *The Bulletin of the American Society of Papyrologists* 44: 135–166.

———. 2010. "Fleuve mouvant, rives mouvantes: les terres 'transportées par le fleuve' dans l'Égypte hellénistique et romaine d'après la documentation papyrologique." In *Riparia dans l'empire romai—pour la définition du concept*, edited by E. Hermon, 153–164. BAR-IS 2066. Oxford: Archaeopress.

———. 2016. "A Breadbasket, Mais Encore? The Socio-Economics of Food Production in the Nile Delta from Antiquity Onwards." In *A History of Water: Series III*. Vol. 3, *Water and Food from Hunter-Gatherers to Global Production in Africa*, edited by T. Tvedt and T. Oestigaard, 101–120. London: I.B. Tauris.

Blue, L., and K. Emad. 2011. *A Multidisciplinary Approach to Alexandria's Economic Past: The Lake Mareotis Research Project*. Oxford: Oxford University Press.

Boak, A.E.R. 1926a. "Irrigation and Population in the Faiyûm, the Garden of Egypt." *The Geographical Review* 16(3): 353–364.

———. 1926b. "Notes on Canal and Dike Work in Roman Egypt." *Aegyptus* 7(3–4): 215–219.

Bonneau, D. 1970. "L'administration de l'irrigation dans les grands domaines en Égypte au VIe s. de n.è." In *Proceedings of the Twelfth International Congress of Papyrology*, edited by D.H. Samuel, 45–62. Toronto: A.M. Hakkert.

———. 1971. *Le fisc et le Nil: incidences des irrégularités de la crue du Nil sur la fiscalité foncière dans l'Égypte grecque et romaine*. Paris: Éditions Cujas.

———. 1976. "Le nilomètre: aspect architectural" *Archeologia* 27: 1–11.

———. 1979. "Fiscalité et irrigation artificielle en Égypte." In *Points de vue sur la fiscalité antique*, edited by H. van Effenterre, 57–68. Publications de la Sorbonne, Études tome 14. Paris: Centre Gustave Glotz.

———. 1982. "Le souverain d'Égypte, juge de l'usage de l'eau." In *L'homme et l'eau en Méditerranée et au Proche-Orient*. Vol. 2, *aménagements hydrauliques, état et legislation*, edited by F. Métral and J. Métral, 69–80. Lyon: GIS-Maison de l'Orient.

———. 1991. "Le cycle du Nil: aspects administratifs à l'époque gréco-romaine." *Bulletin de la Société française d'égyptologie* 120: 7–24.

———. 1993. *Le régime administratif de l'eau du Nil dans l'Égypte grecque, romaine et byzantine*. Leiden: Brill.

———. 1994. "Usage et usages de l'eau dans l'Égypte ptolémaïque et romaine." In *Les problèmes institutionnels de l'eau en Égypte ancienne et dans l'antiquité méditerranéenne*, edited by B. Menu, 47–71. Cairo: Institut français d'archéologie orientale.

Boraik, M., L. Gabolde, and A. Graham. 2017. "Karnak's Quaysides: Evolution of the Embankments from the Eighteenth Dynasty to the Graeco-Roman Period." In *The Nile: Natural and Cultural Landscape in Egypt. Proceedings of the International Symposium held at the, 22 & 23 February 2013*, edited by H. Willems and J.-M. Dahms, 97–144. Bielefeld: transcript Verlag.

Boraik, M., M. Ghilardi, S. Bakhit, A. Hafez, M.H. Ali, S. el -Masekh, and A.G. Mahmoud. 2010. "Geomorphological Investigations in the Western Part of the Karnak Temple (Quay and Ancient Harbour): First Results Derived from Stratigraphical Profiles and Manual Auger Boreholes and Perspectives of Research." *Les Cahiers de Karnak* 13: 101–109.

Bowman, A.K., and E. Rogan, eds. 1999. *Agriculture in Egypt: From Pharaonic to Modern Times*. Oxford: Oxford University Press.

Brewer, D. 2007. "Agriculture and Animal Husbandry." In *The Egyptian World*, ed. T. Wilkinson, 131–145. London: Routledge.

Brewer, D.J., and R.F. Friedman. 1989. *Fish and Fishing in Ancient Egypt*. The Natura History of Egypt 2. Cairo: The American University in Cairo Press.

Butzer, K.W. 1959. "Environment and Human Ecology in Egypt." *Bulletin de la Societé de géographie d'Égypte* 32: 43–87.

———. 1961. "Archäologische Fundstellen Ober- und Mittelägyptens in ihrer geologischen Landschaft." *Mitteilungen des Deutschen Archäologischen Instituts, Abteilung Kairo* 17: 54–68.

———. 1976. *Early Hydraulic Civilization in Egypt: A Study in Cultural Ecology*. Chicago: University of Chicago Press.

———. 1978. "Perspectives on Irrigation Civilization in Pharaonic Egypt." In *Immortal Egypt*, edited by D. Schmandt Besserat, 13–18. Malibu, C.A.: Undena Publications.

———. 1996. "Irrigation, Raised Fields, State Management: Wittfogel Redux?" *Antiquity* 70: 200–204.

Butzer, K.W., E. Butzer, and S. Love. 2013. "Urban Geoarchaeology and Environmental History at the Lost City of the Pyramids, Giza: Synthesis and Review." *Journal of Archaeological Science* 40: 3340–3366.

Clarke, J.D. 1971. "A Re-Examination of the Evidence for Agricultural Origins in the Nile Valley." *Proceedings of the Prehistoric Society* 37: 34–79.

Cook, R.J. 2011. "Landscapes of Irrigation in the Ptolemaic and Roman Fayum: Interdisciplinary Archaeological Survey and Excavation near Kom Aushim (Ancient Karanis), Egypt." Ph.D. diss., University of Michigan.

Cooper, J.P. 2009. "Egypt's Nile–Red Sea Canals: Chronology, Location, Seasonality and Function." In *Connected Hinterlands: Proceedings of Red Sea Project IV, Held at the University of Southampton, September 2008*, edited by L.K. Blue, J. Cooper, J. Whitewright, and R. Thomas, 195–209. Oxford: Archaeopress.

—————. 2012. "Nile Navigation: 'Towing All Day, Punting for Hours.'" *Egyptian Archaeology* 41: 25–27.

Creasman, P.P. 2005. "The Cairo Dahshur Boats." M.A. thesis, Texas A&M University.

Daressy, G. 1900. "Le nilomètre de Kom El Gizeh." *Annales du Service des antiquités de l'Égypte* 1: 91–96.

de Sainte Marie, C. 1989. "État et paysans dans les systèmes hydrauliques de la vallée du Nil (Egypte)." *Études rurales*: 59–91.

Eck, W. 1986. "Staat und landwirtschaftliches Bewässerungsystem Ägyptens in römischer Zeit." *Leichtweiß-Institut für Wasserbau der Technischen Universität Braunschweig. Mitteilungen* 89: 253–280.

Edgerton, W.F. 1951. "The Strikes in Ramses III's Twenty-Ninth Year." *Journal of Near Eastern Studies* 10(1): 137–145.

El Beialy, S., K. Edwards, and A. El-Mahmoudi. 2001. "Geophysical and Palynological Investigations of the Tell El Dabaa Archaeological Site, Nile Delta, Egypt." *Antiquity* 75(290): 735–744.

El-Fakharani, F. 2003. "The Pharaonic Port on the Mediterranean: Its Shape, Development, and Importance." In *Egyptology at the Dawn of the Twenty-First Century: Proceedings of the Eighth International Congress of Egyptologists, Cairo, 2000*, vol. 2, edited by Z. Hawass, 203–208. Cairo: American University in Cairo Press.

Endesfelder, E. 1979. "Zur Frage der Bewässerung im pharaonischen Ägypten." *Zeitschrift für ägyptische Sprache und Altertumskunde* 106: 37–51.

—————. 1979b. "Zur Frage der Bewässerung im pharaonischen Ägypten." In *Acts: First International Congress of Egyptology—Actes: Premier Congrès International d'Égyptologie—Akten: Erster Internationaler Ägyptologenkongress. Cairo—Le Caire—Kairo, October 2–10, 1976*, edited by W.F. Reineke, 203–208. Schriften zur Geschichte and Kultur des Alten Orients 14. Berlin: Akademie-Verlag.

Estigarribia, J.V. 2015. "The Hafir as a Water Clarification Device." In *The Kushite World: Proceedings of the 11th International Conference for Meroitic Studies Vienna, 1–4 September 2008*, edited by H. Zach, 29–32. Beiträge Zur Sudanforschung 9. Vienna: Verein der Förderer der Sudanforschung.

Eyre, C. 1994. "The Water Regime for Orchards and Plantations in Pharaonic Egypt." *Journal of Egyptian Archaeology* 39: 118–123.

Fleury, P. 2005. "L'hydraulique ancienne de l'Égypte à Rome." In *L'Égypte à Rome: actes du colloque de Caen des 28–30 septembre 2002*, edited by F. Lecocq, 169–186. Caen: Maison de la recherche en sciences humaines.

Forstner-Müller, I. 2014. "Avaris, Its Harbours and the Perunefer Problem." *Egyptian Archaeology* 45: 32–35.

Friedman, Z. 2008. "Nilometers." In *Encyclopaedia of the History of Science, Technology, and Medicine*, ed. H. Selin, 1751–1760. New York: Springer.

Fuller, D.Q. 2015. "The Economic Basis of the Qustul Splinter State: Cash Crops, Subsistence Shifts, and Labour Demands in the Post-Meroitic Transition." In *The Kushite World: Proceedings of the 11th International Conference for Meroitic Studies Vienna, 1–4 September 2008*, edited by H. Zach, 33–60. Beiträge Zur Sudanforschung 9. Vienna: Verein der Förderer der Sudanforschung.

Gabolde, L. 2013. "L'implantation du temple: contingences religieuses et contraintes géomorphologiques." *Egypte, Afrique & Orient* 68: 3–12.

Garbrecht, G. 1986. "Der Nil und Ägypten." *Mitteilungen des Leichtweiß-Institut für Wasserbau der Technischen Universität Braunschweig* 89: 1–21.

———, ed. 1995. *Meisterwerke antiker Hydrotechnik: Einblicke in die Wissenschaft: Technik.* Leipzig: Teubner.

———. 1996. "Historical Water Storage for Irrigation in the Fayum Depression (Egypt)." *Irrigation and Drainage Systems* 10: 47–76.

Garbrecht, G., and H. Jaritz. 1990. *Untersuchung antiker Anlagen zur Wasserspeicherung im Fayum/Ägypten.* Mitteilungen des Leichtweiß-Instituts für Wasserbau 107. Braunschweig: TU Braunschweig.

———. 1992. "Neue Ergebnisse zu altägyptischen Wasserbauten im Fayum." *Antike Welt* 23: 238–254.

Garcea, E.A.A. 2006. "Semi-Permanent Foragers in Semi-Arid Environments of North Africa." *World Archaeology* 38(2): 197–219.

Gardiner, A.H. 1941. "Ramesside Texts Relating to the Taxation and Transport of Corn." *Journal of Egyptian Archaeology* 27: 19–73.

Gasm el Seed, A.A. 2015. "Environment, Ecology and Meroitic Food." In *The Kushite World: Proceedings of the 11th International Conference for Meroitic Studies Vienna, 1–4 September 2008*, edited by H. Zach, 61–68. Beiträge Zur Sudanforschung 9. Vienna: Verein der Förderer der Sudanforschung.

Girard, P.-S. 1824. "L'agriculture, l'industrie et le commerce de l'Egypte." In *Description de l'Égypte.* Vol. 17, *État moderne*, Tome II. Paris: Imprimerie impériale.

251

Goddio, F., D. Robinson, and D. Fabre. 2015. "The Life-Cycle of the Harbour of Thonis-Hercleion: The Interaction of the Environment, Politics, and Trading Networks on the Maritime Space of Egypt's Northwestern Delta." In *Harbours and Maritime Networks as Complex Adaptive Systems*, edited by J. Preiser-Kapeller and F. Daim, 25–38. Mainz: Verlag des Römisch-Germanischen Zentralmuseums.

Graham, A. 2005. "Plying the Nile: Not All Plain Sailing." In *Current Research in Egyptology 2003: Proceedings of the Fourth Annual Symposium, University College London 2993*, edited by K. Piquette and S. Love, 41–56. Oxford: Oxbow Books.

Graham, A., and K.D. Strutt. 2013. "Ancient Theban Temple and Palace Landscapes." *Egyptian Archaeology* 43: 5–7.

Graham, A., K.D. Strutt, M.A. Hunter, S. Jones, A. Masson, M. Millet, and B. T. Pennington. 2012. "Theban Harbours and Waterscapes Survey 2012." *Journal of Egyptian Archaeology* 98: 27–42.

Graham, A., K.D. Strutt, V.L. Emery, S. Jones, and D.B. Barker. 2013. "Theban Harbours and Waterscapes Survey 2013." *Journal of Egyptian Archaeology* 99: 35–52.

Graham, A., K.D. Strutt, M.A. Hunter, B.T. Pennington, W.H.J. Toonen, and D.S. Barker. 2014. "Theban Harbours and Waterscapes Survey, 2014." *Journal of Egyptian Archaeology* 100: 41–53.

Graham, A., K.D. Strutt, W.H.J. Toonen, B.T. Pennington, D. Löwenborg, A. Masson-Berghoff, V.L. Emery, D.S. Barker, M.A. Hunter, K.-J. Lindholm, and C. Johansson. 2016. "Theban Harbours and Waterscapes Survey, 2015." *Journal of Egyptian Archaeology* 101: 37–49.

Graham, A., K.D. Strutt, J. Peeters, W.H.J. Toonen, B.T. Pennington, V.L. Emery, D.S. Barker, and C. Johansson. 2016. "Theban Harbours and Waterscapes Survey, Spring 2016." *Journal of Egyptian Archaeology* 102: 13–21.

Graves, C. 2013. "The Problem with Neferusi: A Geoarchaeological Approach." In *Current Research in Egyptology 2012*, edited by C. Graves, G. Heffernan, L. McGarrity, E. Millward, and M. Sfakianou Bealby, 70–83. Oxford: Oxbow Books.

Hairy, I. 2011. "Les nilomètres, outils de la mesure du Nil." In *Du Nil à Alexandrie. Histoires d'eaux*, 2nd ed., edited by I. Hairy, 98–111. Alexandria: Editions Harpocrate.

Hamdan, G. 1961. "Evolution of Irrigation Agriculture in Egypt." In *A History of Land Use in Arid Regions*, edited by L.D. Stamp, 119–142. Paris: United Nations Educational, Scientific, and Cultural Organization.

Hartmann, F. 1923. *L'agriculture dans l'ancienne Egypte.* Paris: Librairies-imprimeries réunies.

Hartung, F. 1991. "Das Wasser im alten und neuen Ägypten (2 Teile)." *Naturwissenschaftliche Rundschau* 10(9/10): 342–348; 373–378.

Hassan, F.A. 1998. "Holocene Climatic Change and Riverine Dynamics in Nile Valley." In *Before Food Production in North Africa: Questions and Tools Dealing with Resource Exploitation and Population Dynamics at 12,000–7000 bp*, edited by S. di Lernia and G. Manzi, 43–51. Forlì: A.B.A.C.O. Edizioni.

Hassan, F.A., and M. Hamdan. 2008. "The Faiyum Oasis—Climate Change and Water Management in Ancient Egypt." In *Traditional Water Techniques: Cultural Heritage for a Sustainable Future: SHADUF Project*, edited by F.A. Hassan, 117–147. Luxembourg: European Commission, Sixth Framework Programme.

Hassan, F.A., M. Hamdan, R.J. Flower, and G. Tassie. 2011. "Holocene Geoarchaeology and Water History of the Fayoum, Egypt." In *Natural and Cultural Landscapes in the Fayoum: The Safeguarding and Management of Archaeological Sites and Natural Environments*, edited by R. Pirelli, 116–133. Cairo: UNESCO.

Haug, B.J. 2012. "Watering the Desert: Environment, Irrigation, and Society in the Premodern Fayyūm, Egypt." Ph.D. diss., University of California, Berkeley.

———. 2017. "Water and Power: Reintegrating the State into the Study of Egyptian Irrigation." *History Compass* 15(10): e12394.

Hawass, Z., F.A. Hassan, and A. Gautier. 1988. "Chronology, Sediments, and Subsistence at Merimda Beni Salama." *Journal of Egyptian Archaeology* 74: 31–38.

Herbich, T., and I. Forstner-Müller. 2013. "Small Harbours in the Nile Delta: The Case of Tell el-Dab'a." *Études et Travaux* 26: 257–272.

Hobler, P.M., and J.J. Hester. 1969. "Prehistory and Environment in the Libyan Desert." *The South African Archaeological Bulletin* 23(92): 120–130.

Hobson, D. 1984. "Agricultural Land and Economic Life in Soknopaiou Nesos." *The Bulletin of the American Society of Papyrologists* 21(1/4): 89–109.

Hogarth, D., A. Strahan, C. Watson, J. Burgess, and H. Lyons. 1908. "Some Geographical Aspects of the Nile: Discussion." *The Geographical Journal* 32(5): 475–480.

Holz, R.K. 1969. "Man-Made Landforms in the Nile Delta." *American Geographical Society* 59(2): 253–269.

Hughes, J.D. 1992. "Sustainable Agriculture in Ancient Egypt." *Agricultural History* 66(2): 12–22.

Jaillette, P., and F. Reduzzi Merola. 2008. "L'eau à usage agricole dans la legislation romaine de l'époque tardive: du Code théodosien au Code justinien." In *Vers une gestion intégrée de l'eau dans l'empire romain: Actes dul colloque international, Université Laval, Octobre 2006*, edited by E. Hermon, 229–242. Rome: L'Erma di Bretschneider.

Janssen, J.J. 2004. *Grain Transport in the Ramesside Period: Papyrus Baldwin (BM EA 10061) and Papyrus Amiens*. Hieratic Papyri in the British Museum 8. London: British Museum Press.

Jaritz, H., and M. Bietak. 1978. "Zweierlei Pegeleichungen zum Messen der Nilfluthöhen im alten Ägypten: Untersuchung zum neuentdeckten Nilometer des Chnum-Tempels von Elephantine (Strabon, XVII, 1, 48)." *Mitteilungen des Deutschen Archäologischen Instituts. Abteilung Kairo* 33: 47–62.

Jentel, M.-O. 1990. "Euthenia, coudées et nilomètre." *Echos du Monde Classique/Classical Views* 34, n.s. 9: 173–179.

Kalin, M. 2006. "Hidden Pharaos: Egypt, Engineers, and the Modern Hydraulic." M.Phil. thesis, Oxford.

Karberg, T. 2015. "Culture, Crops, and Cattle. Aspects of Environmental Assessment, Seen through an Archaeologist's Eye." In *The Kushite World: Proceedings of the 11th International Conference for Meroitic Studies Vienna, 1–4 September 2008*, edited by H. Zach, 69–76. Beiträge Zur Sudanforschung 9. Vienna: Verein der Förderer der Sudanforschung.

Katary, S.L.D. 1989. *Land Tenure in the Ramesside Period*. Studies in Egyptology. London: Kegan Paul International.

———. 2014. "The Wilbour Papyrus and the Management of the Nile Riverbanks in Ramesside Egypt: Preliminary Analysis of the Types of Cultivated Land." In *Riparia, un patrimoine culturel: la gestion intégrée des bords de l'eau*, edited by E. Hermon and A Watelet, 199–215. Proceedings of the Sudbury workshop, April 12–14, 2012/actes de l'atelier Savoirs et pratiques de gestion intégrée des bords de l'eau—Riparia, Sudbury, 12–14 avril 2012. BAR international series 2587. Oxford: Archaeopress.

Kehoe, D. 2008. "Economics and the Law of Water Rights in the Roman Empire." In *Vers une gestion intégrée de l'eau dans l'empire romain. Actes dul colloque international, Université Laval, Octobre 2006*, edited by E. Hermon, 243–252. Rome: L'Erma di Bretschneider.

Kemp, B., and D. O'Connor. 1974. "An Ancient Nile Harbour: University Museum Excavations at the 'Birket Habu.'" *International Journal of Nautical Archaeology* 3(1): 101–136.

Khalil, E. 2015. "Where Did the Nile Harbours Go?" In *The Management of Egypt's Cultural Heritage*, vol. 2, edited by F.A. Hassan, L.S. Owens, A. de Trafford, G.J. Tassie, O El Daly, and J. Van Wetering, 163–174. London: Golden House Publications.

Kindermann, K., O. Bubenzer, S. Nussbaum, H. Riemer, F. Darius, N. Pöllath, and U. Smettan. 2006. "Palaeoenvironment and Holocene Land Use of Djara, Western Desert of Egypt." *Quaternary Science Reviews* 25: 1619–1637.

Kirwan, L.P. 1957. "Rome Beyond the Southern Egyptian Frontier." *Geographical Journal* 123: 13–19.

Kraemer, B. 2010. "The Meandering Identity of a Fayum Canal: The Henet of Moeris/ Dioryx Kleonos/Bahr Wardan/Abdul Wahbi." In *Proceedings of the Twenty-Fifth International Congress of Papyrology, Ann Arbor 2007*, edited by T. Gagos and A. Hyatt, 365–376. Ann Arbor: Scholarly Publishing Office, The University of Michigan Library.

Krzyżaniak, L. 1977. *Early Farming Cultures on the Lower Nile. The Predynastic Period in Egypt*. Varsovie: Editions scientifiques de Pologne.

Leone, A. 2012. "Water Management in Late Antique North Africa: Agricultural Irrigation." *Water History* 4(1): 119–133.

Linstädter, J., and S. Kropelin. 2004. "Wadi Bakht Revisited: Holocene Climate Change and Prehistoric Occupation in the Gilf Kebir Region of the Eastern Sahara, SW Egypt." *Geoarchaeology* 19(8): 753–778.

Lobban, R. 2004. "Greeks, Nubians and Mapping the Ancient Nile." In *Nubian Studies 1998: Proceedings of the 9th International Conference of the International Society of Nubian Studies, August 21–26, 1998*, edited by T. Kendall, 341–348. Boston: Northeastern University.

Louis, P., ed. 1986. *L'homme et l'eau en Méditerranée et au Proche-Orient.* Vol. 3, *L'eau dans les techniques. Séminaire de recherche 1981–1982.* Travaux de la Maison de l'Orient méditerranéen 11. Lyon: GS Maison de l'Orient.

Manning, J.G. 2002. "Irrigation et état en Égypte antique." *Annales: Histoire, Sciences Sociales* 57(3): 611–623.

———. 2003. *Land and Power in Ptolemaic Egypt*. Cambridge: Cambridge University Press.

———. 2012, 18 February. "Water, Irrigation and their Connection to State Power in Egypt." Paper read at "Resources: Endowment or Curse, Better or Worse?" Yale University, 24 February 2014, econ.yale.edu/~egcenter/manning2012.pdf.

———. 2018. *The Open Sea: The Economic Life of the Ancient Mediterranean World from the Iron Age to the Rise of Rome*. Princeton: Princeton University Press.

Menu, B., ed. 1992. *Les problèmes institutionnels de l'eau en Egypte ancienne et dans l'antiquité méditerranéenne*. Cairo: IFAO.

Michel, N. 2005. "Travaux aux digues dans la vallée du Nil aux époques papyrologique et ottoman: une comparaison." *Cahier de recherches de l'Institut de papyrologie et d'égyptologie de Lille* 25: 253–276.

Miller, N.F., and W. Wetterstrom. 2000. "The Beginnings of Agriculture: The Ancient Near East and North Africa." In *The Cambridge World History of Food*, edited by K.F. Kiple, and K.C. Ornelas, 1123–1139. Cambridge: University of Cambridge Press.

Moreno García, J.C., ed. 2005. *L'agriculture institutionnelle en Égypte ancienne: État de la question et approches interdisciplinaires.* Cahiers de recherches de l'Institute de papyrologie et égyptologie de Lille 25. Villeneuve d'Ascq: Université Charles-de-Gaulle —Lille 3.

————. 2010. "La gestion des aires marginales: *pḥw, gs, ṯnw, sḫt* au IIIᵉ millénaire." In *Egyptian Culture and Society: Studies in Honour of Naguib Kanawati,* vol. 2, edited by A. Woods, A. McFarlane, and S. Binder, 49–69. Cairo: Conseil suprême des antiquités de l'Égypte.

————. 2013. "Les îles 'nouvelles' et le milieu rural en Égypte pharaonique." *Égypte, Afrique & Orient* 70: 3–12.

————. 2017. "Trade and Power in Ancient Egypt: Middle Egypt in the Late Third/Early Second Millennium BC." *Journal of Archaeological Research* 25(2): 87–132.

————. Forthcoming. "Wells, Small–Scale Private Irrigation and Agricultural Strategies in the 3ʳᵈ and 2ⁿᵈ Millennium BC." In *Irrigation in Early States: New Directions,* edited by S. Rost. Chicago: Oriental Institute of the University of Chicago.

Mumford, G. 2013. "A Late Period Riverine and Maritime Port Town and Cult Center at Tell Tebilla (Ro-nefer)." *Journal of Ancient Egyptian Interconnections* 5(1): 38–67.

Murray, G.W. 1955. "Water from the Desert: Some Ancient Egyptian Achievements." *The Geographical Journal* 121(2): 171–181.

Murray, M.A. 2000. "Cereal Production and Processing." In *Ancient Egyptian Materials and Technology,* edited by P.T. Nicholson and I. Shaw, 505–536. Cambridge: Cambridge University Press.

Pérez Largacha, A. 1995. "Chiefs and Protodynastic Egypt: A Hydraulic Relation?" *Archéo-Nil* 5: 79–85.

Pokorný, P., P. Kočár, Z. Sůvová, and A. Bezděk. 2009. "Palaeoecology of Abusir South According to Plant and Animal Remains." In *Abusir South.* Vol. 2, *Tomb Complex of the Vizier Qar, His Sons Qar Junior and Senedjemib, and Iykai,* edited by M. Bárta, 27–48. Abusir 13. Prague: Czech Institute of Egyptology, Faculty of Arts, Charles University in Prague.

Price, D.H. 1993. "The Evolution of Irrigation in Egypt's Fayoum Oasis: State, Village and Conveyance Loss." Ph.D. diss., University of Florida, Gainesville.

Rathbone, D.W. 1991. *Economic Rationalism and Rural Society in Third-Century AD Egypt: The Heroninos Archive and the Appianus Estate.* Cambridge: Cambridge University Press.

————. 2007. "Mēchanai (Waterwheels) in the Roman Fayyum." In *New Archaeological and Papyrological Researches on the Fayyum: Proceedings of the International Meeting of Egyptology and Papyrology, Lecce, June 8–10, 2005,* edited by M. Capasso and P. Davoli, 251–262. Papyrologica Lupiensia 14. Galatina: Congedo Editore.

Redmount, C. 1995. "The Wadi Tumilat and the 'Canal of the Pharaohs.'" *Journal of Near Eastern Studies* 54(2): 127–135.

Römer, C. 2017. "The Nile in the Fayum: Strategies of Dominating and Using the Water Resources of the River in the Oasis in the Middle Kingdom and Graeco-Roman Period." In *The Nile: Natural and Cultural Landscape in Egypt. Proceedings of the International Symposium held at the, 22 & 23 February 2013*, edited by H. Willems and J.-M. Dahms, 171–191. Bielefeld: transcript Verlag.

Ross, J.C. 1893. "Irrigation and Agriculture in Egypt." *Scottish Geographical Magazine* 9(4): 169–193.

Rossi, L. 2016. "La 'garde du fleuve' dans l'Égypte hellénistique et romaine." *Journal of Egyptian History* 9(2): 121–150.

Rowland, J.M., G.J. Tassie, and G. Lucarini. Forthcoming. *Revolutions: The Neolithisation of the Mediterranean Basin: The Transition to Food Producing Economies in North Africa and Southern Europe. Proceedings of the workshop 29th–31st October 2016, TOPOI, Freie Universität, Berlin.* Berlin: Edition Topoi.

Rowlandson, J. 1996. *Landowners and Tenants in Roman Egypt: The Social Relations of Agriculture in the Oxyrhynchite Nome.* London: Oxford University Press.

———. 2005. "The Organization of Public Land in Roman Egypt." *Cahiers de Recherches de l'Institut de Papyrologie et d'Égyptologie de Lille* 25: 173–196.

Ruf, T. 1995. "Histoire hydraulique et agricole et lutte contre la salinisation dans le delta du Nil." *Sécheresse* 6(4): 307–317.

Said, R. 1993. *The River Nile: Geology, Hydrology, and Utilization.* Oxford: Pergamon Press.

Schenkel, W. 1973. "Be- und Entwässerung." *Lexikon der Ägyptologie* 1: 775–782.

———. 1974. "Die Einführung der künstlichen Feldbewässerung im alten Ägypten." *Göttinger Miszellen* 11: 41–46.

———. 1978. *Die Bewässerungsrevolution im alten Ägypten.* Sonderschrift, Deutsches Archäologisches Institut, Abteilung Kairo 6. Mainz: Zabern.

———. 1994. "Les systèmes d'irrigation dans l'Égypte ancienne et leur génèse." *Archéo-Nil* 4: 27–35.

Schnebel, M. 1925. *Die Landwirtschaft im hellenistischen Ägypten.* Munich: Beck.

Seidlmayer, S.J. 1996. "Die staatliche Anlage der 3. Dynastie in der Nordweststadt von Elephantine. Archäologische und historische Probleme." In *Haus und Palast im alten Ägypten*, edited by M. Bietak, 195–214. Wien: Verlag der österreichischen Akademie der Wissenschaften.

————. 2001. *Historische und moderne Nilstände: Untersuchungen zu den Pegelablesungen des Nils von der Frühzeit bis zur Gegenwart.* Berlin: Achet Verlag.

Seyfried, K. 1976. "Nachträge zu Yoyotte: 'Les Sementiou...'" BSFE 73, P. 44–55." *Göttinger Miszellen* 20: 44–47.

Shaw, B.D. 1995. *Environment and Society in Roman North Africa: Studies in History and Archaeology.* Aldershot: Variorum.

Shirai, N. 2010. *The Archaeology of the First Farmer-Herders in Egypt.* Leiden: Leiden University Press.

————. 2013. "Was Neolithisation a Struggle for Existence and the Survival of the Fittest, or Merely the Survival of the Luckiest? A Case Study of Socioeconomic and Cultural Changes in Egypt in the Early–Middle Holocene." In *Neolithisation of Northeastern Africa*, edited by N. Shirai, 213–235. Berlin: ex oriente.

Sijpesteijn, P.J. 1986. "SB V 8392 and the Inundation." *Zeitschrift für Papyrologie und Epigraphik* 65: 151–153.

Smith, S. 2015. "Desert and River: Consumption and Colonial Entanglements in Roman and Late Antique Nubia." In *Inside and Out: Interactions between Rome and the Peoples on the Arabian and Egyptian Frontiers in Late Antiquity*, J.H.F. Dijkstra and G. Fisher, 91–112. Leuven: Peeters.

Solomon, S. 2010. *Water: The Epic Struggle for Wealth, Power, and Civilization.* New York: Harper Collins.

Stanley, J.-D., and C.E. Bernhardt. 2010. "Alexandria's Eastern Harbor, Egypt: Pollen, Microscopic Charcoal, and the Transition from Natural to Human-Modified Basin." *Journal of Coastal Research* 26(1): 67–79.

Szafrański, Z. 2003. "The Impact of Very High Floods on Platform Constructions in the Nile Basin of the Mid-Second Millennium B.C." In *The Synchronisation of Civilisations in the Eastern Mediterranean in the Second Millennium B.C.*, edited by E. Czerny and M. Bietak, 205–218. Vienna: Verlag der Österreichischen Akademie der Wissenschaften.

Tallet, G., R.J. Garcier, and J.-P. Bravard. 2011. "L'eau disparue d'une micro-oasis: Premiers résultats de la prospection archéologique et geo-archéologique du système d'irrigation d'el Deir." In *Les réseaux d'eau courante dans l'antiquité*, edited by C. Abadie-Reynal, S. Provost, and P. Vipard, 173–188. Rennes: Presses universitaires de Rennes.

Tallet, P., G. Marouard, and D. Laisney. 2012. "Un port de la IVe dynastie au Ouadi el-Jarf (Mer Rouge)." *Bulletin de l'Institut français d'archéologie orientale* 112: 399–446.

Tigani el-Mahim A. 1982. *Fauna, Ecology, and Socio-Economic Conditions in the Khartoum Nile Environment.* Bergen: University of Bergen.

————. 1992. "The Nile Crocodile and Prehistoric Groups: An Ancient Ecological Interaction along the Nile (Sudan)." *Beiträge zur Sudanforschung* 5: 151–164.

Trampier, J. 2005/2006. "Reconstructing the Desert and Sown Landscape of Abydos." *Journal of the American Research Center in Egypt* 42: 73–80.

Tvedt, T. 2000. *The River Nile and Its Economic, Political, Social, and Cultural Role.* Bergen, Norway: University of Bergen.

Vercoutter, J. 1966. "Semna South Fort and the Records of Nile Levels at Kumma." *Kush* 14: 125–164.

Vinson, S. 1998. *The Nile Boatman at Work.* Münchner Ägyptologische Studien 48. Mainz: von Zabern.

Vleeming, S.P. 1993. *Papyrus Reinhardt: An Egyptian Land List from the Tenth Century B.C.* Hieratische Papyri aus den Staatlichen Museen zu Berlin-Preussischer Kulturbesitz 2. Berlin: Akademie Verlag.

Warburton, D. 1997. *State and Economy in Ancient Egypt.* Orbis Biblicus et Orientalis 151. Fribourg: Vandenhoeck & Ruprecht.

————. 2007. "Work and Compensation in Ancient Egypt." *Journal of Egyptian Archaeology* 93: 175–194

————. 2016. *The Fundamentals of Economics: Lessons from the Bronze Age Near East.* Neuchatel: Recherches et publications.

Warne, A.G., and J.-D. Stanley. 1993. "Archaeology to Refine Holocene Subsidence Rates along the Nile Delta Margin, Egypt." *Geology* 21: 715–718.

Westermann, W.L. 1917. "Aelius Gallus and the Reorganization of the Irrigation System of Egypt under Augustus." *The Carlsberg Papyri* 12(3): 237–243.

————. 1919. "The Development of the Irrigation System of Egypt." *The Carlsberg Papyri* 14(2): 158–164.

————. 1925. "Dike Corvée in Roman Egypt. On the Meaning of ΑΦΥΛΙΣΜΟΣ." *Aegyptus* 6(2–3): 121–129.

Wicker, U. 1997. "Flax and Egypt." *Discussions in Egyptology* 39: 95–116.

Willcocks, W. 1889. *Egyptian Irrigation.* London: E. & F.N. Spon.

————. 1899. *Egyptian Irrigation.* 2nd ed. London: E. & F.N. Spon.

Willcocks, W., and J.I. Craig. 1913. *Egyptian Irrigation.* 3rd ed. London: E. & F.N. Spon.

Willems, H., H. Creylman, V. De Laet, and G. Verstraeten. 2017. "The Analysis of Historical Maps as an Avenue to the Interpretation of Pre-industrial Irrigation Practices in Egypt." In *The Nile: Natural and Cultural Landscape in Egypt. Proceedings of the International Symposium held at the Johannes Gutenberg-Universität Mainz, 22 & 23 February 2013*, edited by H. Willems and J.-M. Dahms, 255–343. Bielefeld: transcript Verlag.

Wilson, P., and G. Gilbert. 2002. "Pigs, Pots and Postholes." *Egyptian Archaeology* 21: 12–13.

Yoyotte, J. 1975. "Les sementiou et l'exploitation des régions minières à l'ancien empire." *Bulletin de la Société française d'égyptologie* 73: 44–55.
———. 2013. *Histoire, géographie et religion de l'Égypte ancienne*. Orientalia Lovaniensia Analecta 224. Leuven: Peeters.

V. The Nile in Religion, Text, and Image

Adams, P.R. 1988. "And Ever Flows the Nile: Was the Ancient Egyptian Spirit Geographically Determined." In *Aspects of the African Spirit*, 34–41. New York: Swedenborg Foundation.

Aja Sánchez, J.R. 2015. *Aguas mágicas: el Nilo en la memoria y la religiosidad del Mundo Antiguo*. Santader: Universidad de Cantabria.

Amenta, A., M.M. Luiselli, and M.N. Sordi. 2005. *L'acqua nell'antico Egitto: vita, rigenerazione, incantesimo, medicamento. Proceedings of the First International Conference for Young Egyptologists, Italy, Chianciano Terme, October 15–18, 2003*. Egitto antico 3. Rome: "L'Erma" di Bretschneider.

Antoine, J.-C. 2017. "Modelling the Nile Agricultural Floodplain in Eleventh and Tenth Century B.C. Middle Egypt." In *The Nile: Natural and Cultural Landscape in Egypt. Proceedings of the International Symposium held at the Johannes Gutenberg-Universität Mainz, 22 & 23 February 2013*, edited by H. Willems and J.-M. Dahms, 15–51. Bielefeld: transcript Verlag.

Baines, J. 1974. "The Inundation Stela of Sebekhotpe VIII." *Acta Orientalia* 36: 39–54.

———. 1976. "The Sebekhotpe VIII Inundation Stela: An Additional Fragment." *Acta Orientalia* 37: 11–20.

Ball, J. 1942. *Egypt in the Classical Geographers*. Cairo: Government press, Bulâq.

Balty, J. 1984. "Thèmes nilotiques dans la mosaïque tardive du Proche-Orient." In *Alessandria e il mondo ellenistico-romano: Studi in onore di Achille Adriani*, edited by N. Bonacasa and A. di Vita, 827–834. Rome: L'Erma di Bretschneider.

Bar-Deroma, H. 1960. "The River of Egypt (Naḥal Mizraim)." *Palestine Exploration Quarterly* 92(1): 37–56.

Baumann, S. 2012. "Die Beschreibung der Nilflut in der Nilkammer von Edfu." *Zeitschrift für ägyptische Sprache und Altertumskunde* 139: 1–18.

Beinlich, H. 1979. "Die Nilquellen nach Herodot." *Zeitschrift für ägyptische Sprache und Altertumskunde* 106: 11–14.

————. 1991. *Das Buch vom Fayum: Zum religiösen Eigenverständnis einer ägyptischen Landschaft.* Wiesbaden: Otto Harrassowitz Verlag.

————. 2014. "Wiedergeburt aus dem Wasser: kosmologische Vorstellungen der alten Ägypter nach dem 'Buch vom Fayum.'" *Antike Welt* 5: 17–25.

Bell, B. 1970. "The Oldest Records of Nile Floods." *The Geographical Journal* 136(4): 569–573.

Bickel, S. 2005. "Creative and Destructive Waters." In *L'acqua nell'antico Egitto: vita, rigenerazione, incantesimo, medicamento; proceedings of the first International conference for young Egyptologists, Italy, Chianciano Terme, October 15–18, 2003*, edited by A. Amenta, M.M. Luiselli, and M.N. Sordi, 191–200. Rome: "L'Erma" di Bretschneider.

————. 2009. "The Inundation Inscription in Luxor Temple." In *The Libyan Period in Egypt: Historical and Cultural Studies into the 21st–24th Dynasties. Proceedings of a conference at Leiden University, 25–27 October 2007*, edited by G.P.F. Broekman, R.J. Demarée, and O.E. Kaper, 51–55. Leuven: Peeters.

Bonhême, M.-A. 1995. "Les eaux rituelles en Égypte pharaonique." *Archéo-Nil* 5: 129–139.

Bonneau, D. 1964. *La crue du Nil, divinité égyptienne à travers mille ans d'histoire (332 av.–641 ap. J.-C.) d'après les auteurs grecs et latins, et les documents des époques ptolemaïque, romaine et byzantine.* Paris: Klincksieck.

————. 1992. "La terre saline (ἀλμυρίς) en Égypte d'après les documents papyrologiques grecs." In *Proceedings of the XIVth International Congress of Papyrologists*, edited by A.H.S. El-Mosalamy, 61–75. Cairo: Ain Shams University, Center of Papyrological Studies

————. 1991. "Continuité et discontinuité notionale dans la terminologie religieuse du Nil, d'après la documentation grecque." *Collection de l'Institut des sciences et techniques de l'antiquité* 444: 23–36.

————. 1995. "La divinité du Nil sous le principat en Égypte." In *Aufstieg und Niedergang der römischen Welt II, 18, 5*, edited by W. Haase and H. Temporini, 3195–3215. Berlin: De Gruyter.

Broekman, G.P.F. 2002. "The Nile Level Records of the Twenty-Second and Twenty-Third Dynasties in Karnak: A Reconsideration of their Chronological Order." *Journal of Egyptian Archaeology* 88: 163–178.

————. 2005. "The Chronological Position of King Shoshenq Mentioned in Nile Level Record No. 3 on the Quay Wall of the Great Temple of Amun at Karnak." *Studien zur Altägyptischen Kultur* 33: 75–89.

Bruce, A.R. 2000. "Between Hapi and Yu: Comparative Hydraulics and Irrigation in the Nile Valley and China." *ANKH: revue d'égyptologie et des civilisations africaines* 8/9: 102–127.

Bunbury, J.M., and D. Jeffreys. 2011. "Real and Literary Landscapes in Ancient Egypt." *Cambridge Archaeological Journal* 21(1): 65–75.

Burstein, S.M. 1976. "Alexander, Callisthenes, and the Sources of the Nile." *Greek, Roman and Byzantine Studies* 17(2): 135–146.

Cadell, H. 1970. "Le vocabulaire de l'agriculture d'après les papyrus grecs d'Égypte: Problèmes et voies de recherche." *American Studies in Papyrology* 7: 69–76.

Claus, B. 2005. "Osiris et Hapi: crue et régénération en Égypte ancienne." In *L'acqua nell'antico Egitto: vita, rigenerazione, incantesimo, medicamento. Proceedings of the First International Conference for Young Egyptologists, Italy, Chianciano Terme, October 15–18, 2003*, edited by A. Amenta, M.M. Luiselli, and M.N.Sordi, 201–211. Egitto antico 3. Rome: "L'Erma" di Bretschneider.

Contardi, F. 2015. "Disasters Connected with the Rhythm of the Nile in the Textual Sources." In *Egyptian Curses*. Vol. 2, *A Research on Ancient Catastrophes*, edited by G. Capriotti Vittozzi, 11–26. Archaeological Heritage & Multidisciplinary Egyptological Studies 2. Rome: Consiglio nazionale delle ricerche; ISMA, Istituto di studi sul Mediterraneo antico.

Cribiore, R. 1995. "A Hymn to the Nile." *Zeitschrift für Papyrologie und Upigraphik* 106: 97–106.

Daressy, G. 1895. "Une inondation de l'Egypte sous la XXIIe dynastie." *Bulletin de l'Institut Égyptien* 6: 275–281.

————. 1896. "Une inondation à Thèbes sous le règne d'Osorkon II." *Receuil de Traveaux* 18: 181–186.

De Jong, W.J. 1992. "De Nijl en de god Hapi." *De Ibis* 17(3): 83–86.

de Putter, T. 1993. "Les inscriptions de Semna et Koumma (Nubie): niveaux de crues exceptionnelles ou d'un lac de retenue artificiel du Moyen Empire?" *Studien zur Altägyptischen Kultur* 20: 255–288.

Dewachter, M. 1987. "Le grand coude du Nil à Amada et le toponyme *tȝ qꜥḥ(t)*." *Revue d'égyptologie* 38: 190–193.

Driaux, D. 2016. "Water Supply of Ancient Egyptian Settlements: The Role of the State. Overview of a Relatively Equitable Scheme from the Old to New Kingdom (ca. 2543–1077 BC)." *Water History* 8: 43–58.

Edel, E. 1976. "Der Tetrodon Fahaka als Bringer der Überschwemmung und sein Kult im Elephantengau." *Mitteilungen des Deutschen Archäologischen Instituts, Abteilung Kairo* 32: 35–43.

El-Sawi, A. 1983. "The Nile-God. An Unusual Representation in the Temple of Sety I at Abydos." *Egitto E Vicino Oriente* 6: 7–13.

Feinman, P. 2015. "The Tempest in the Tempest: The Natural Historian." *Bulletin of the Egyptological Seminar* 19: 253–262.

Foster, J.L. 1975. "Thought Couplets in Khety's 'Hymn to the Inundation.'" *Journal of Near Eastern Studies* 34(1): 1–29.

Foster, K.P., R.K. Ritner, and B.R. Foster. 1996. "Texts, Storms, and the Thera Eruption." *Journal of Near Eastern Studies* 55(1): 1–14.

Gabolde, L. 1995. "L'inondation sous les pieds d'Amon." *Bulletin de l'Institut français d'archéologie orientale* 95: 235–258.

———. 2018. *Karnak, Amon-Rê: la genèse d'un temple, la naissance d'un dieu.* Bibliothèque d'étude 167. Cairo: Institut français d'archéologie orientale.

Gaillard, C., V. Loret, and C. Kuentz. 1923. *Recherches sur les poissons représentés dans quelques tombeauc égyptiens de l'Ancien Empire.* Cairo: Imprimerie de l'IFAO.

Gardiner, A. 1908. "The Egyptian Name of the Nile." *Zeitschrift für ägyptische Sprache und Altertumskunde* 45: 140–141.

Germond, P. 1979. "Le roi et le retour de l'inondation." *Bulletin de la Société d'égyptologie de Genève* 1: 5–12.

Girouard, C.E. 1996. "Depictions of the Nile River in Roman Art of the Late Republic and Early Empire." M.A. thesis, Vanderbilt University.

Görg, M. 1985. "Neilos und Domitian: Ein Beitrag zur spätantiken Nilgott-Ikonographie." In *Religion im Erbe Ägyptens*, edited by M. Görg, 65–82. Wiesbaden: Harrassowitz Verlag.

Graham, A. 2020. "The Interconnected Theban Landscape and Waterscape of Amūn–Rēa." In *Environment & Religion in Ancient & Coptic Egypt: Sensing the Cosmos through the Eyes of the Divine. Proceedings of the 1st Egyptological Conference, Organized by the Hellenic Institute of Egyptology & the Calligraphy Centre of the Bibliotheca Alexandrina at the People's University of Athens (Athens 1–3 February 2017)*, edited by A. Maravelia and N. Guilhou, 155–167. Oxford: Archaeopress.

Grieshaber, F. 2004. *Lexikographie einer Landschaft: Beiträge zur historischen Topographie Oberägyptens zwischen Theben und Gabal as-Silsila anhand demotischer und griechischer Quellen*. Göttinger Orientforschungen 4(45). Wiesbaden: Harrassowitz Verlag.

Habachi, L. 1974. "A High Inundation Mark in the Temple of Amenre at Karnak in the 13th Dynasty." *Studien Altägyptischer Kultur* 1: 207–214.

Hassan, F.A. 2007. "Droughts, Famine and the Collapse of the Old Kingdom: Re-Reading Ipuwer." In *The Archaeology and Art of Ancient Egypt: Essays in Honor of David B. O'Connor*, vol. 1, edited by Z. Hawass and J. Richards, 357–377. Annales du Service des Antiquités de l'Égypte Cahier 36. Cairo: Conseil Suprême des Antiquités de l'Égypte.

Hawkins, S. 2013. "'If Only I Could Accompany Him, This Excellent Marshman!': An Analysis of the Marshman (*Sḥty*) in Ancient Egyptian Literature." In *Current Research in Egyptology 2012*, edited by C. Graves, G. Heffernan, L. McGarrity, E. Millward, and M. Sfakianou Bealby, 84–93. Oxford: Oxbow Books.

Hermann, A. 1960. "Die Ankunft des Nils." *Zeitschrift für Ägyptische Sprache und Altertumskunde* 85: 35–42.

Hibbs, V.A. 1985. *The Mendes Maze: A Libation Table for the Inundation of the Nile (II–III A.D.)*. New York: Garland.

Huddlestun, J. 1995. "Who Is This That Rises Like the Nile? Some Egyptian Texts on the Inundation and a Prophetic Trope." In *Fortunate the Eyes That See: Essays in Honor of David Noel Freedman in Celebration of His Seventieth Birthday*, edited by A.B Beck, A.H. Bartelt, P.R. Raabe, and C.A. Franke, 338–363. Grand Rapids: Eerdmans.

Ikram, S. 2010. "Crocodiles: Guardians of the Gateways." In *Thebes and Beyond: Studies in Honour of Kent R. Weeks*, edited by Z. Hawass and S. Ikram, 85–98. Cairo: SCA.

Janssen, J.J. 1987. "The Day the Inundation Began." *Journal of Near Eastern Studies* 46(2): 129–136.

Jaritz, H. 1989. "Nilkultstätten auf Elephantine." In *Akten des vierten Internationalen Ägyptologen—Kongresses München 1985*. Vol. 2, *Archäologie, Feldforschung, Prähistorie*, edited by S. Schoske, 199–209. Hamburg: Buske.

Jeffreys, D.G. 1999. "Written and Graphic Sources for an Archaeological Survey of Memphis, Egypt: From 500 BCE to 1900 CE, with Special Reference to the Papers of Joseph Hekekyan." Ph.D. diss., University of London.

Jentel, M.-O. 1987. "La représentation du dieu Nil sur les peintures et les mosaïques et leur contexte architectural." *Echos du Monde Classique/Classical Views* 34, n.s. 6: 209–216.

———. 1992. "Neilos." In *Lexicon iconographicum mythologiae classicae*, vol. 6, edited by L. Kahil, 720–726. Zürich: Artemis and Winkler Verlag.

Kadish, G.E. 1988. "Seasonality and the Name of the Nile." *Journal of the American Research Center in Egypt* 25: 185–194.

Kaplony-Heckel, U. 2009. *Land und Leute am Nil nach demotischen Inschriften: Papyri und Ostraka*, vol. 1. Ägyptologische Abhandlungen 71. Wiesbaden: Otto Harrassowitz.

Knigge, C. 2005. "'He Keeps the River Nile Flowing, the Field is Full of His Richness': Some Remarks on the Hymn to the Nile and the Inundation and Fertility Motifs in Post-New Kingdom Hymns and Related Texts." In *L'acqua nell'antico Egitto: vita, rigenerazione, incantesimo, medicamento. Proceedings of the First International Conference for Young Egyptologists, Italy, Chianciano Terme, October 15–18, 2003*, edited by A. Amenta, M.M. Luiselli, and M.N.Sordi, 59–68. Egitto antico 3. Rome: "L'Erma" di Bretschneider.

Kockelmann, H. 2018. *Der Herr der Seen, Sümpfe und Flussläufe: Untersuchungen zum Gott Sobek und den ägyptischen Krokodilgötter-Kulten von den Anfängen bis zur Römerzeit*. 3 vols. Ägyptologische Abhandlungen. Wiesbaden: Harrassowitz.

Koenig, Y. 1994. "L'eau et la magie." In *Les problèmes institutionnels de l'eau en Égypte ancienne et dans l'antiquité méditerranéenne: colloque AIDEA Vogüé 1992*, edited by B. Menu, 239–248. Cairo: IFAO.

Krüger, J. 1991. "Terminologie der künstlichen Wasserläufe in den Papyri des griechisch-römischen Ägypten." *Münstersche Beiträge zur antiken Handelsgeschichte* 10(2): 18–27.

Leclant, J. 1994. "Avant-propos: l'eau vivifiante dans l'Egypte ancienne." In *L'eau, la santé et la maladie dans le monde grec*, edited by R. Ginouvès, A.-M. Guimier-Sorbets, J. Jouanna, and L. Villard, 7–11. Suppléments au Bulletin de correspondance hellénique 28. Athens: École française d'Athènes.

Lockyer, J.N. 1893. "The Sacred Nile." *Nature* 47: 464–467.

Loprieno, A. 2005. "Water in Egyptian Literature." In *L'acqua nell'antico Egitto: vita, rigenerazione, incantesimo, medicamento. Proceedings of the First International Conference for Young Egyptologists, Italy, Chianciano Terme, October 15–18, 2003*, edited by A. Amenta, M.M. Luiselli, and M.N .Sordi, 25–40. Egitto antico 3. Rome: "L'Erma" di Bretschneider.

Lurson, B. 2007. *Osiris, Ramsès, Thot et le Nil: Les chapelles secondaires des temples de Derr et Ouadi es-Seboua*. Orientalia Lovaniensia Analecta 161. Leuven: Peeters.

MacCoull, L. 1993. "Stud. Pal. XV 250ab: A Monophysite Trishagion for the Nile Flood." *The Journal of Theological Studies* 40(1): 129–135.

Manning, J.G. 1995. "Irrigation Terminology in the Hauswaldt Papyri and Other Texts from Edfu during the Ptolemaic Period." In *Les problems institutionnels de l'eau en Égypte ancienne et dans l'antiquité méditerranéenne*, edited by B. Menu, 261–271. Cairo: IFAO.

Martin, H.G. 1986. "Zwei Reliefs mit Flußgöttern auf Elephantine." *Mitteilungen des Deutschen Archäologischen Instituts in Kairo* 43: 189–194.

Mathieu, B. 2015. "Chacals et milans, pâturages et marécages, ou le monde selon Henqou." In *Apprivoiser le sauvage/Taming the Wild*, edited by M. Massiera, B. Mathieu, and F. Rouffet, 263–273. Montpellier: Université Paul Valéry Montpellier 3–CNRS, Équipe "Égypte Nilotique et Méditerranéenne" (ENiM).

Meyboom, P.G.P. 1995. *The Nile Mosaic of Palestrina*. Leiden/New York/Köln: Brill.

Naville, E. 1904. "A Mention of a Flood in the Book of the Dead." *Proceedings of the Society of Biblical Archaeology* 26: 251–257, 287–294.

Oestigaard, T. 2011. *Horus' Eye and Osiris' Efflux: The Egyptian Civilisation of Inundation c. 3000–2000 BCE*. BAR-IS 2228. Oxford: Archaeopress.

Ogdon, J.R. 1978. "The Old Kingdom Name for the Canopic Branch of the Nile Delta." *Journal of the Society for the Study of Egyptian Antiquities* 9(2): 65–74.

Otto, G. 2009. "Ein Fluss als Inbegriff des Quells allen Lebens und seine Gedächtnisspur: das Nachleben der ägyptischen Nilverehrung in der griechisch-römischen Antike." *Kemet* 1: 49–56.

Pamminger, P. 1991. "Das Trinken von Überschwemmungswasser: eine Form der jährlichen Regeneration des Verstorbenen." *Göttinger Miszellen* 122: 71–75.

Patch, D.C. 2011. "From Land to Landscape." In *Dawn of Egyptian Art*, edited by D.C. Patch, 20–81. New York: Metropolitan Museum of Art.

Pécoil, J.-F. 1993. "Les sources mythiques du Nil et le cycle de la crue." *Bulletin de la Société d'Égyptologie de Genève* 17: 97–110.

Perdriaud, H. 2019. "L'an 6 de Taharqa, l'année des «merveilles»: 'Une chose pareille n'avait pas été vue depuis le temps des anciens […]' (Kawa V, l. 5)." *Égypte Nilotique et Méditerranéenne* 12: 281–298.

Platz-Horster, G. 1992. *Nil und Euthenia: Der Kalzitkameo im Antikenmuseum Berlin*. Berlin: Verlag Walter de Gruyter and Co.

Postl, B. 1970. *Die Bedeutung des Nil in der römischen Literatur: Mit besonderer Berücksichtigung der wichtigsten griechischen Autoren*. Wien: Verlag Notring.

Prell, S. 2009. "Der Nil, seine Überschwemmung und sein Kult in Ägypten." *Studien zur Altägyptischen Kultur* 38: 211–257.

Quack, J.F. 2013. "Gibt es in Ägypten schriftliche Quellen zum Thera-Ausbruch?" In *1600 – Kultureller Umbruch im Schatten des Thera-Ausbruchs? 4th Archaeological Conference of Central Germany, October 14–16, 2011 in Halle (Saale)*, edited by H. Meller, F. Bertemes, H.-R. Bork, and R. Risch, 221–233. Tagungen des Landesmuseums für Vorgeschichte Halle 9. Halle: Landesmuseums für Vorgeschichte Halle.

Renouf, P. 1890. "Nile Mythology." *Proceedings of the Society of Biblical Archaeology* 13: 4–11.

Ritner, R.K., and N. Moeller. 2014. "The Ahmose Tempest Stela: An Ancient Egyptian Account of a Natural Catastrophe." In *Egyptian Curses 1: Proceedings of the Egyptological Day held at the National Research Council of Italy (CNR), Rome, 3rd December 2012, in the International Conference "Reading Catastrophes: Methodological Approaches and Historical Interpretation. Earthquakes, Floods, Famines, Epidemics between Egypt and Palestine, 3rd–1st Millennium BC. Rome, 3rd–4th December 2012, CNR-Sapienza University of Rome,"* edited by G. Capriotti Vittozzi, 63–81. Roma: CNR Edizioni.

Römer, C., and F. Zanella. 2013. "Nil I." *Reallexikon für Antike und Christentum* 199: 898–915.

Sandri, S. 2017. "Nilometers—Or: Can you Measure Wealth." In *The Nile: Natural and Cultural Landscape in Egypt. Proceedings of the International Symposium held at the Johannes Gutenberg-Universität Mainz, 22 & 23 February 2013*, edited by H. Willems and J.-M. Dahms, 193–214. Bielefeld: transcript Verlag.

Schneider, T. 2012. "Wie der Wettergott Ägypten aus der großen Flut errettete: ein "inkulturierter" ägyptischer Sintflut-Mythos und die Gründung der Ramsesstadt." *Journal of the Society for the Study of Egyptian Antiquities* 38: 173–193.

Schubart, W. 1912. *Ein Jahrtausend am Nil: Briefe aus dem Altertum*. Berlin: Weidemannsche.

Shafei, A. 1946. "Historical Notes on the Pelusiac Branch, the Red Sea Canal and the Route of the Exodus." *Bulletin de la Société Royale de Géographie d'Égypte* 21: 233–287.

Sneh, A., T. Weissbrod, and I. Perath. 1975. "Evidence for an Ancient Egyptian Frontier Canal." *American Scientist* 63: 542–548.

Tallet, G. 2011. "Isis, the Crocodiles and the Mysteries of the Nile Floods: Interpreting a Scene from Roman Egypt Exhibited in the Egyptian Museum in Cairo (JE 30001)." In *Demeter, Aphrodite, Isis, and Cybele: Studies in Greek and Roman Religion in Honour of Giulia Sfameni Gasparro*, edited by A. Mastrocinque and C. Giuffrè Scibona, 137–160. Potsdamer Altertumswissenschaftliche Beitrage 36. Stuttgart: Franz Steiner Verlag.

Thompson, D.J. 1999. "New and Old in the Ptolemaic Fayyum." *Proceedings of the British Academy* 96: 123–138.

Tiradritti, F. 1997. "'I Have Not Diverted My Inundation': Legitimacy and the Book of the Dead in a Stela of Ramesses IV from Abydos." In *L'Impero Ramesside: Convegno Internazionale in onore di Sergio Donadoni*, edited by S. Donadoni, 193–203. Rome: Università degli studi di Roma "La Sapienza."

Tóth, P. 2011. "The Demons of the Air and the Water of the Nile: Saint Anthony the Great on the Reason of the Inundation." In *From Illahun to Djeme: Papers Presented in Honour of Ulrich Luft*, edited by E. Bechtold, A. Gulyás, and A. Hasznos, 239–299. BAR-IS 2311. Oxford: Archaeopress.

Traunecker, C. 1972. "Les rites de l'eau à Karnak d'après les textes de la rampe de Taharqa." *Bulletin de l'institut français d'archéologie orientale* 72: 195–236.

van der Plas, D. 1983. "Een hymne aan de overstroming van de Nijl uit het Nieuwe Rijk." In *Schrijvend verleden: documenten uit het Oude Nabije Oosten vertaald en toegelicht*, edited by K.R. Veenhof, 347–354. Leiden: Zutphen.

———. 1986. *L'hymne à la crue du Nil*. Leiden: Nederlands Instituut voor het Nabije Oosten.

Van Minnen, P. 2001. "P. Oxy. LXVI 4527 and the Antonine Plague in Egypt." *Zeitschrift fur Papyrologie und Epigraphik* 135: 175–177.

Vandorpe, K. 2004. "The Henet of Moeris and the Ancient Administrative Division of the Fayum in Two Parts." *Archiv für Papyrusforschung und verwandte Gebiete* 50: 61–78.

Vaux, W.S.W. 1864. "On the Knowledge the Ancients Possessed of the Sources of the Nile." In *Transactions of the Royal Society of Literature*, vol. 2, pt. 8, 35–66. London: Transactions of the Royal Society of Literature.

Versluys, M.J. 2002. *Aegyptiaca Romana: Nilotic Scenes and the Roman Views of Egypt*. Leiden: Brill.

Vittozzi, C. 2013. *La Terra del Nilo sulle sponde del Tevere*. Rome: Aracne editore S.r.l.

von Beckerath, J. 1966. "The Nile Level Records at Karnak and Their Importance for the History of the Libyan Dynasty." *Journal of the American Research Center in Egypt* 5: 43–55.

von Beckerath, J. 1993. "Die Nilstandsinschrift vom 3. Jahr Schebitkus am Kai von Karnak." *Göttinger Miszellen* 136: 7–9.

Waddell, W.G. 1936. "On the Nile Rising: An English Rendering of Anonymus Florentinus: De Nilo.—Proclus: On Egypt and the Nile.—Lydus: On the Nile Rising." *Bulletin of the Faculty of Arts of the University of Egypt, Cairo* 4: 22–38.

Wainwright, G.A. 1953. "Herodotus II, 28 on the Sources of the Nile." *The Journal of Hellenic Studies* 73: 104–107.

Wild, R. 1981. *Water in the Cultic Worship of Isis and Serapis*. Études préliminaires aux religions orientales dans l'Empire romain 87. Leiden: Brill.

Willems, H. 2012. "The Physical and Cultic Landscape of the Northern Nile Delta According to Pyramid Texts Utterance 625." In *"Parcourir l'éternité": Hommages à Jean Yoyotte II*, edited by C. Zivie-Coche and I. Guermeur, 1097–1107. Bibliothèque de l'École des hautes études. Sciences religieuses 156. Turnhout: Brepols Publishers.

————. 2014. "High and Low Niles: A Natural Phenomenon and Its Mythological Interpretation According to Plutarch's *De Iside et Osiride* 38 and Coffin Texts Spell 168." *Journal of Egyptian Archaeology* 100(1): 488–493.

Wortmann, D. 1966. "Kosmogonie und Nilflut: Studien zu einigen Typen magischer Gemmen griechisch-römischer Zeit aus Ägypten." *Bonner Jahrbücher* 166: 62–112.

VI. STUDIES OF THE POST-ANTIQUE AND CONTEMPORARY NILE

Antes, J. 1800. *Observations on the Manners and Customs of the Egyptians, the Overflowing of the Nile and Its Effects; with Remarks on the Plague, and Other Subjects, Written during a Residence of Twelve Years in Cairo and its Vicinity.* London: J. Stockdale.

Arbel, B. 2000. "Renaissance Geographical Literature and the Nile." In *The Nile: Histories, Cultures, Myths*, edited by H. Erlich and I. Gershoni, 105–119. New York: Rienner.

Belal, A., J. Briggs, J. Sharp, and I. Springuel. 2009. *Bedouins by the Lake: Environment, Change, and Sustainability in Southern Egypt.* Cairo: American University in Cairo.

Bonneau, D. 1981. "L'Égypte dans l'histoire de l'irrigation antique de l'époque hellénistique à l'époque arabe." In *Egitto e storia antica dall'ellenismo all'età araba: bilanco di un confronto. Atti del colloquio internazionale. Bologna 31 agosto–2 settembre, 1987*, edited by L. Crisculo and G. Geraci, 301–313. Bologna: CLUEB.

Borsch, S.J. 2000. "Nile Floods and the Irrigation System in the Fifteenth-Century Egypt." *Mamluk Studies Review* 4: 131–146.

Brock, L.P. 1996. "The Theban Flood of 1994: Ancient Antecedents and the Case of KV 55." *Varia Aegyptiaca* 11: 1–16.

Cookson-Hills, C.J. 2013. "Engineering the Nile: Irrigation and the British Empire in Egypt, 1882–1914." Ph.D. diss., Queen's University.

Cooper, J.P. 2011. "No Easy Option: Nile versus Red Sea in Ancient and Medieval North–South Navigation." In *Maritime Technology in the Ancient Economy: Ship Design and Navigation*, edited by W.V. Harris and K. Iara, 189–210. Journal of Roman Archaeology Supplementary Series 84. Portsmouth, R.I.: Journal of Roman Archaeology.

————. 2014. *The Medieval Nile: Route, Navigation, and Landscape in Islamic Egypt.* Cairo: The American University in Cairo Press.

de Putter, T., M.F. Loutre, and G. Wansard. 1998. "Decadal Periodicities of Nile River Historical Discharge (A.D. 622–1470) and Climatic Implications." *Geophysical Research Letters* 25(16): 3193–3196.

De Veer, M., J.A. Wormgoor, R.G. Rizq, and W. Wolters. 1993. "Water Management in Tertiary Units in the Fayoum, Egypt." *Irrigation and Drainage* 7: 69–82.

Drioton, É. 1952. *Les origines pharaoniques du nilomètre de Rodah*. Cairo: Imprimerie de l'Institut français d'archéologie orientale.

Flaux, C., M. El-Assal, N. Marriner, C. Morhangea, J.-M. Rouchy, I. Soulié-Märsche, and M. Torab. 2012. "Environmental Changes in the Maryut Lagoon (Northwestern Nile Delta) During the Last ~ 2000 Years." *Journal of Archaeological Science* 39(12): 3493–3504.

Gascoigne, A.L. 2007. "The Water Supply of Tinnis: Public Amenities and Private Investments." In *Cities in the Pre-Modern Islamic World: The Urban Impact of Religion, State and Society*, edited by A.K. Bennison and A.L. Gascoigne, 161–176. London: Routledge.

Goodfriend, G.A., and J.-D. Stanley. 1998. "Rapid Strand Plain Accretion in the Northeastern Nile Delta in the 9th c. AD and Demise of the Port of Pelusium." *Geology* 27(2): 147–150.

Hachlili, R. 1998. "Iconographic Elements of Nilotic Scenes on Byzantine Mosaic Pavements in Israel." *Palestine Exploration Quarterly* 130: 106–120.

Hassan, F. 2007. "Extreme Nile Floods and Famines in Medieval Egypt (AD 930–1500) and Their Climatic Implications." *Quaternary International* 173–174: 101–112.

Hermann, A. 1959. "Der Nil und die Christen." *Jahrbuch für Antike und Christentum* 2: 30–69.

Ibrahim, F.N., with B. Ibrahim. 2003. *Egypt: An Economic Geography*. London: I.B. Tauris.

Ibrahim, F.N., and B. Ibrahim. 2006. *Ägypten: Geographie, Geschichte, Wirtschaft, Politik*. Darmstadt: Wissenschaftliche Buchgesellschaft.

Inman, D.L., and S.A. Jenkins. 1984. *The Nile Littoral Cell and Man's Impact on the Coastal Zone of the Southeastern Mediterranean*. SIO Reference Series 84-31. La Jolla: University of California, Scripps Institute of Oceanography.

Johnson, C. 1903. *Egyptian Irrigation: A Study of Irrigation Methods and Administration in Egypt*. Washington D.C.: Government Printing Office.

Kerisel, J. 2001. *The Nile and its Masters: Past, Present, Future. Source of Hope and Anger*. Rotterdam: A.A. Balkema.

Levanoni, A. 2008. "Water Supply in Medieval Middle Eastern Cities: The Case of Cairo." *Al-masaq* 20(2): 179–205.

Mikhail, A. 2010. "An Irrigated Empire: The View from Ottoman Fayyum." *International Journal of Middle East Studies* 42: 569–590.

———. 2011a. "From the Bottom Up: The Nile, Silt, and Humans in Ottoman Egypt." In *Environmental Imaginaries of the Middle East and North Africa*, edited by D.K. Davis and E. Burke III, 113–135. Athens: Ohio University Press.

———. 2011b. *Nature and Empire in Ottoman Egypt: An Environmental History.* Cambridge: Cambridge University Press.

———. 2016. "The Nile and Food in the Early Modern Ottoman Empire." In *A History of Water: Series III.* Vol. 3, *Water and Food from Hunter-Gatherers to Global Production in Africa,* edited by T. Tvedt and T. Oestigaard, 163–184. London: I.B. Tauris.

Popper, W. 1951. *The Cairo Nilometer.* Berkeley: University of California Press.

Rapoport, Y., and I. Shahar. 2012. "Irrigation in the Medieval Islamic Fayyum: Local Control in a Large-Scale Hydraulic System." *Journal of the Economic and Social History of the Orient* 55: 1–31.

Sayed, A.M. 2006. "On the Non-Existence of the Nile-Red Sea Canal all over the Pharaonic Times, and Its Existence from the Persian Period Onwards." In *Aegyptus et Pannonia III: acta symposii anno 2004,* edited by H. Győry, B.T. Múzeum, M.-E. Társaság, and Ó.E. Bizottság, 207–226. Budapest: MEBT-ÓEB.

Shafei, A. 1939. "Fayoum Irrigation as Described by Nabulsi in 1245 A.D. with a Description of the Present System of Irrigation and a Note on Lake Moeris." *Bulletin de la Société Royale de Géographie d'Egypte* 20: 283–327.

———. 1952. "Lake Mareotis: Its Past History and Future Development." *Bulletin de l'Institut Fouad du Désert* 2: 71–101.

Stanley, J.-D., and A.G. Warne. 1993. "Nile Delta: Recent Geological Evolution and Human Impact." *Science* 260(5108): 628–634.

———. 1998. "Nile Delta in its Destruction Phase." *Journal of Coastal Research* 14(3): 794–825.

Strudwick, N. 1995. "Flood Damage in Thebes." *The Biblical Archaeologist* 58(2): 116–177.

Summerhayes, C., G. Sestini, R. Misdorp, and N. Marks. 1978. "Nile Delta: Nature and Evolution of Continental Shelf Sediment System." *Marine Geology* 24: 43–65.

Sutcliffe, J., S. Hurst, A.G. Awadallah, E. Brown, and K. Hamed. 2016. "Harold Edwin Hurst: the Nile and Egypt, Past and Future." *Hydrological Sciences Journal* 61(9): 1557–1570.

Tvedt, T. 2004. *The River Nile in the Age of the British: Political Ecology and the Quest for Economic Power.* London: I.B. Taurus.

Wilkinson, T. 2014. *The Nile: Downstream Through Egypt's Past and Present.* London: Bloomsbury.

Wilson, P. 2017. "Landscapes of Bashmur: Settlements and Monasteries in the Northern Egyptian Delta from the Seventh to Ninth Century." In *The Nile: Natural and Cultural Landscape in Egypt. Proceedings of the International Symposium held at the Johannes Gutenberg-Universität Mainz, 22 & 23 February 2013*, edited by H. Willems and J.-M. Dahms, 345–368. Bielefeld: transcript Verlag.

Index

Italicized page numbers indicate illustrations. Page numbers followed by t *indicate tables.*

The Gift of the Nile? Ancient Egypt and the Environment
edited by Thomas Schneider and Christine L. Johnston
Tucson, Arizona: Egyptian Expedition, 2020

pyramids, agricultural domains attached
to, 155

qanat (*manwir*) technology, 56, 62
Qantir. *See* Piramses
Qar (governor), 97
Qarun, Lake, *57*
Qena, 120, *123*, 124
Qin, Ying, 56, 58
quarries, expeditions sent to, 154

radiocarbon dates and dating, 16, 31,
181–182, 186
rainfall
decrease, 190
increase, 55
Ramesses II
irrigation specialists under, 29,
47n303
reign of, 128
statue base of, *202*
Ramesses III
images of, *9, 203*
work strikes during reign of, 206
Ramesses V, 125, 128
Ramesses VI, 125
Ramesses VIII, 126t
Ramesses XI, 125, 127
Ramesseum, pylon of, 122
Ramses X tomb, 3
raw materials, extraction of, 95, 101
Realities of Life Project, 175
recording and analysis phase, narrative
imposition rejected during, 172, 179n2
Rediukhnum, Inscription of, 157
Red Sea, 23–24, 26, 31
regional archaeology, centralized
archaeology *versus*, 172
regionalism
approaching in ceramic record,
173–175, 178
overview of, 172–173
regional officials, 155
Reinhardt papyrus, 162
remote sensing, 122, 185
research questions, multi-disciplinary
approaches to, 197–198
Rhine, The (Cioc), 4
riverbed, emergence of, 119

river floodplain, settlement systems linked
to, 87
rivers
braided pattern, 118
deposition and meandering on,
121
planform, changes in, 119–120
robust data, 197, 208, 215
Roda (island), Nilometer at, 3, 117, *204*,
214n51
Roman Egypt, 7
Roman empire, 145
Roman world, rivers in, 4
Rosetta barrage, 108, 116
Rosetta branch of Nile, 72
Rowland, J. M., 68, 198
royal court, 96–97
royal estate, 97–98
royal foundation, 88, 97–98
Royal Narrative, complex world beyond,
178
royal stable, 157

Sa el-Hagar
Epipaleolithic data not found in, 75
material culture at, 76
Neolithic activity at, 69
Neolithic evidence at, 74
Neolithic layer, potential at, 70
overview of, 67
Sahara
climate belts, *51*
dessication of Egyptian, 182
maps, *52*
migration from, 56, 59, 183
migration to, 182
sand flux from, 58
seasonal rain increase in, 49
Said, Rushdi, 21, 116, 117
salt concentration, determining, 24, 44n194
sand flats, 119, 120
Sandford, K. S., 75, 85n81
sandstone bedrock, *90, 91*
sandy bedload rivers, 119
sandy bed streams, 119
Saqqara, 25–26, 155, 185
satellite images, 77, 91, 103n16
Scheidel, Walter, 7
Schenkel, Wolfgang, 2

Made in United States
Orlando, FL
26 July 2023

35476289R00170